AF608252

SHARING THE PAST

The Reinvention of History in Canadian Poetry since 1960

J.A. WEINGARTEN

Sharing the Past

The Reinvention of History in Canadian Poetry since 1960

UNIVERSITY OF TORONTO PRESS
Toronto Buffalo London

© University of Toronto Press 2019
Toronto Buffalo London
utorontopress.com

ISBN 978-1-4875-0104-4

Library and Archives Canada Cataloguing in Publication

Title: Sharing the past: the reinvention of history in Canadian poetry since 1960 / J.A. Weingarten.
Names: Weingarten, J.A., 1984– author.
Description: Includes bibliographical references and index.
Identifiers: Canadiana 20190087625 | ISBN 9781487501044 (hardcover)
Subjects: LCSH: Canadian poetry – 20th century – History and criticism. | LCSH: Canadian poetry – 21st century – History and criticism. | LCSH: Social history in literature.
Classification: LCC PS8155 .W45 2019 | DDC C811/.5409—dc23

This book has been published with the help of a grant from the Federation for the Humanities and Social Sciences, through the Awards to Scholarly Publications Program, using funds provided by the Social Sciences and Humanities Research Council of Canada.

University of Toronto Press acknowledges the financial assistance to its publishing program of the Canada Council for the Arts and the Ontario Arts Council, an agency of the Government of Ontario.

Canada Council for the Arts Conseil des Arts du Canada

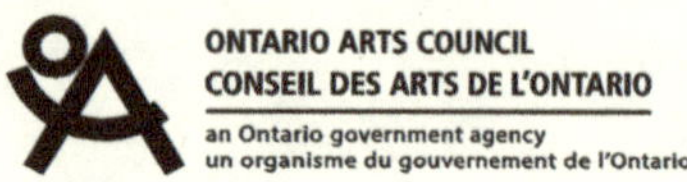

Funded by the Government of Canada Financé par le gouvernement du Canada | Canada

It is with gratitude and respect that I acknowledge that this book was written in various landscapes that represent the traditional territories of the Kanien'kehá:ka, Anishinaabe, Mississauga, Haudenosaunee, Huron-Wendt, Attawandaron, and the Lenape peoples.

This book is dedicated to my parents, Teresa and Murray Weingarten, and my grandparents, Celia and Louis Weingarten, all of whom modestly made many moments of happiness possible for many generations to come.

Contents

Acknowledgments

No one writes a book alone.

First and foremost, Brian Trehearne reviewed the earliest draft of this manuscript and gave me invaluable advice. Without his eye and model of scholarship, this book would have been impossible. Parts of this book were also published in earlier versions in *The Oxford Handbook of Canadian Literature*; *Canadian Literature and Cultural Memory*; *Studies in Canadian Literature*; *Canadian Poetry: Studies, Documents, Reviews*; *Prairie Fire*; and *Open Letter*.

People at several institutions aided me at various points in my research: Shelley Sweeney, Brian Hubner, and their staff at the University of Manitoba; Ramona Rose at the University of Northern British Columbia; Heather Home and the staff of Queen's University's Archives and Special Collections; and Jennifer Toews and Albert Masters of the Thomas Fisher Rare Books Library at the University of Toronto. It was through the generous support of the Social Sciences and Humanities Research Council, the McGill Institute for the Study of Canada, the McGill Department of English, and the McGill Faculty of Arts that I was able to visit these libraries and make use of their archives. During the rewriting process, Ian Rae and Paul Werstine invited me to teach a 2016 seminar at King's College University, which gave me the chance to have valuable conversations with a brilliant group of students whose insights strengthened this book. I am so grateful for their invitation. I am also indebted to Jean Baird and the A-Frame Association, who invited me to spend two weeks at Al Purdy's historic A-Frame cottage while I completed my final edits on this manuscript in 2018.

I owe thanks to those who read sections of this book or with whom I shared enlightening conversations. Michael Sloane, Gregory Betts, Kait Pinder, Eli MacLaren, Allan Hepburn, Ian Kalman, Sam Solecki, Maggie Redekop, Miranda Hickman, Deanna Reder, Emily Sharpe,

Nathalie Cooke, Dale Tracy, Steven High, and others shared their valuable insights with me. I was also blessed to have had the encouragement and editorial support of Siobhan McMenemy and Mark Thompson at University of Toronto Press, as well as to have had two generous experts in the field whose peer reviews greatly improved this book.

Many writers, publishers, and families of writers kindly granted me permission to use interviews, archival material, and copyrighted works in this manuscript. I am grateful to Margaret Atwood and Oxford University Press, the estate of Gwendolyn MacEwen, Nadine McInnis, Stephanie Bolster, Cara-Lyn Morgan, Joan Crate, Louise Halfe, Barry McKinnon, the estate of Florence McNeil, the estate of John Newlove, the estate of Earle Birney, David Dale Zieroth, Eurithe Purdy, Howard White, Lorna Crozier, and Patrick Lane. Every effort was made to contact Mick Burrs, the estate of Peter Stevens, and the estate of Andrew Suknaski to secure permissions, but they could not be reached.

One person, more than any other, deserves my gratitude: as I wrote this book, my wife, Aislinn, listened to me more than anyone should have to listen to another human being. After more than a decade of knowing, loving, and caring for each other, our thoughts are still warm. And now we embark on our next wonderful adventure: bringing our daughter into the world and writing our own family story.

—J.A. Weingarten, August 2018

Abbreviations

Margaret Atwood

JSM – *The Journals of Susanna Moodie* (1970)
TATC – *The Animals in That Country* (1968)
INSOAG – *In Search of Alias Grace* (1997)

Elizabeth Brewster

TWH – *The Way Home* (1982)

Joan Crate

PARL – *Pale as Real Ladies: Poems for Pauline Johnson* (1989)

Emma LaRocque

WTOM – *When the Other Is Me: Native Resistance Discourse, 1850–1990* (2010)

Florence McNeil

GT – *Ghost Towns* (1975)
BA – *A Balancing Act* (1979)

John Newlove

BNW – *Black Night Window* (1968)
MIA – *Moving in Alone* (1965)

Al Purdy

BATE – Birdwatching at the Equator (1982)
BR – Beyond Remembering: The Collected Poems of Al Purdy (2000)
CH – The Cariboo Horses (1965)
EE – The Enchanted Echo (1944)
HOE – A Handful of Earth (1977)
NOS – North of Summer (1967)
NWS – Naked with Summer in Your Mouth (1994)
PAA – Poems for All the Annettes (1962; rev. 1968)
RBS – Reaching for the Beaufort Sea (1993)
S&D – Sex and Death (1973)
SFA – Starting from Ameliasburgh: The Collected Prose of Al Purdy (1998)
WGW – Wild Grape Wine (1968)

Andrew Suknaski

WMP – Wood Mountain Poems (1976)

SHARING THE PAST

The Reinvention of History in Canadian Poetry since 1960

Introduction

> For the generation of writers who came of age during the post-War years Canadian history became an obsession. Their desire was to write it into existence. As they explored their imagined place they created a new image of Canada. This remaking or reimagining transformed the official record, the facts as they were known.
>
> Lane, "The Unyielding Phrase" 59

Since about 1960, Canadian poets have been participating in the reinvention of history. This reinvention has been marked primarily by the declining popularity of "objective" grand narratives that embrace critical distance and stress national unity and, as well, by the growing appeal of social histories attentive to the local and its everydayness. Unlike the sprawling histories of nations and political destinies that once held favour, these social histories are often very finely focused. They survey regional, cultural, and familial pasts, and they encourage readers to see history through the eyes of those who lived it. In Canada, a relatively young and multicultural country, the emergence of these new histories and perspectives has been one response to a predominant interest of historians: national identity as an expression of the cultural past, present, and future of a country. Over the last few decades, Canadian historians and creative writers have opted to explore a wide range of historical issues, but the relationship between history and national identity remains a fundamental and provocative subject of discussion, one that continues to captivate readers. And in debates on the subject, one still encounters compelling questions about Canada's social development and accommodation of individual and cultural difference.

Indeed, those debates have not disappeared; they have, however, become more complex. Out of the protest and political fervour of the 1960s came a pervasive scepticism among activists and writers about the inclusivity, completeness, and objectivity of Canada's grand narratives. Nurtured by anti-colonial nationalisms, federal multicultural policy, and sexual revolutions distinctive of that era, such scepticism had major ramifications for the writing of history. Scepticism cultivated new historical content and new research methods, both of which were intended to establish a more culturally representative and socially responsible set of narratives.

As poets working within a loose web, Margaret Atwood, Joan Crate, Al Purdy, Barry McKinnon, John Newlove, and Andrew Suknaski have been guiding figures for each other and their readers in reinventing Canadian history as an expression of this modern scepticism. Their distrust of conventional history has spurred a new discourse that uses the particularities of region and family, instead of the nation at large, as the basis for historical writing. In so doing, they have reimagined history as a lively and lyrical expression of the "I," rather than as an elite grand narrative told solely by academics. This book is a study of that reinvention, a consideration of the ways in which history has become a shared space and of the poets who, sometimes in direct collaboration with each other, have anticipated and contributed to that process.

The role poets have played in Canadian historiography is part of a much larger story that begins immediately after the Second World War. Canada's wartime contributions reinvigorated national pride and spurred new discussions about the distinctive nature and the future of the country. In response, provincial and federal governments made efforts to move the country away from its identity as a former colony of the British Empire to that of a politically and culturally sovereign nation. Canada shed its Dominion status in 1946, entered Newfoundland into Confederation in 1949 (thus extending geographic unity), and inaugurated the Royal Commission on National Development in the Arts, Letters and Sciences (1949–51), a cross-country investigation into the fabric of the national culture.[1] The figures behind such endeavours believed in a convenient conflation of "nation" (a cultural community) and "state" (a politically governed community with clear geographic borders) by presuming that Canada's national character could be synonymous with its predominating systems of political power.

For a time, Canadian historians played a pivotal role in deepening and explaining the prideful nationalism behind these governmental efforts. Until the 1960s, a relatively small group of historians guided that discourse: Donald Creighton, Harold A. Innis, George F.G. Stanley, Chester Martin, Arthur Lower, and other academics spoke as "national sages" in popular histories that represented an exclusively English-based Canadian identity (Bliss 7). They wrote of a unified country with a common and coherent past, and their emphasis fell on a narrow set of topics. The "Laurentian thesis" was key: it emphasized, in the words of Creighton, "the relations between the commercial system of the St. Lawrence and the political development of Canada during almost a century of its history" (v).[2] That widely deployed thesis was used to illuminate the steps different governments took to secure their economic and political footholds in Upper and Lower Canada, thus catapulting the nation toward the uniting effort of Confederation. It was a thesis that celebrated those in power and imagined Canadian history primarily within frameworks that valorized the contributions of the English-heritage elite.

The second half of the twentieth century, however, was a period of once-unimaginable and widespread social unrest that unsettled those exclusionary frameworks. In the years between 1960 and 1990 – what I'm calling the "centennial era"[3] – the very concept of a united Canadian identity became inconceivable: the creation of the New Democratic Party in 1961 cultivated an increasingly divided political landscape, the Front de libération du Québec protested the dominance of English-Canada, centennial-era feminism became one of numerous reformist movements challenging traditional hierarchies in society, the Red Power movement raised greater awareness of Canada's violent colonialism, and multiple, sometimes conflictual, cultural groups fought for equal recognition in the history and future of the country. In the face of so much social and political change, the conventional frameworks for and methods of writing history seemed out of touch. Where history once reiterated a conservative narrative that upheld romantic nationalist ideals, it was now "a force for remedial action and moral criticism" (Berger, "Writings" 294). History was adapting to its era. Its content and methods had to be reinvented.

This reinvention has not been peaceable; Christopher Dummitt has even gone so far as to call its defining debates the "History Wars" (99). The political turmoil of the 1960s and its aftermath bred strong reactions against the "European," "middle-class," "heterosexual," and "male" academics (Strong-Boag 4) that once dominated the entire field of history. Some were wary of these calls to action. Desmond Morton spoke for the old guard when, in 1979, he expressed concern that the move away from the "grand synthesis" of an English-based Canadian history (7) would mark the "inglorious end of the Confederation dream" (8).

But he was not wholly shocked or perturbed by that "end": the discipline of history had grown exponentially after 1960, and, in Morton's eyes, that "explosi[ve]" growth was inevitably going to "foster new methodologies and insights inappropriate or, more often, overlooked in more traditional" histories (6–7).

Tensions between the old guard and new historians simmered for decades, and the widespread "censure" of "conventional history" (Berger, "Writings" 294) engendered a "massive shift." Centennial-era historians, Michael Bliss argues, began moving away from "political and constitutional" frameworks and toward (at least in some branches of the historical profession) frameworks more invested in the circumstances of individuals, families, and communities. This was to be a new history: a social history invested in capturing and giving voice to "the experiences of people" (6).

This has been a revolutionary shift with ramifications not just for the content of history, but also for the methods historians use to research and write it. In order to get at "the experiences of people," writers of history have had to pay greater attention to personal stories – in other words, to first-hand testimonies. To approach history so personally was unusual in the 1970s and 1980s, but that method has, since the 1990s, gained greater legitimacy in academic circles, especially for historians attentive to the political and cultural groups vocally emergent in Canada since the centennial era. But because such historians value closeness to the past, they have been perceived by some to be too much against the grain of old institutional standards; traditional historians have long insisted on objectivity in academic research and writing, which tends to mean that historians must maintain professional distance from their subject of study in the service of clear, unbiased reporting that captures the past – in Leopold von Ranke's famous words – "as it really was."

Hence, Canadian historians have struggled to affirm the legitimacy of subjective methods while others in the field have openly questioned and devalued such research. The historian Steven High, for instance, remembers that his graduate school training "in the 1990s" still stressed objectivity in order to help historians "find their authority in distance." He recalls a stern lesson from his coursework: "The more distance we put between ourselves [as historians] and our subjects ... the better" (22). Nevertheless, historians like High continue to argue that there is genuine epistemological value in getting closer to the past, if only because interviews and oral testimony can present readers with a version of history – often from the perspectives of silenced or marginalized voices – that productively counters whatever story has reigned "official."

This process entails what Michael Frisch calls a "shared authority." For Frisch, "what is most compelling about oral and public history is a capacity to redefine and redistribute intellectual authority, so that this might be shared more broadly in historical research ... rather than continuing to serve as an instrument of power and hierarchy" (xx). Redefining and redistributing authority in the writing of history can, in Frisch's view, reflect complementary redistributions of power in society. History thus becomes a productive cacophony, told from various centres rather than a single one contested by those writing from arbitrary margins. I take Frisch's concept as a point of departure for this book, and my title, *Sharing the Past*, gestures to one of my central arguments: that the authority to explain and narrate the past can and should be shared in and outside the academy. To do so would achieve a discourse akin to the one that Henry Giroux imagines, in which history "is not an artifact to be merely transmitted, but an ongoing dialogue and struggle over the relationship between representation and agency" (68).

Efforts to reinvent history as such have certainly occurred within a community of historians, but historians have acknowledged that powerful interventions have also happened "outside the historical establishment" (Berger, "Writings" 294). In Margaret Prang's 1977 presidential address to the Canadian Historical Association, she urged historians to pay close attention to Canadian literature. Much like Morton and Bliss, Prang summed up the shift in Canadian history from "old well-worn national themes" to social histories attentive to "limited identities" – a term centennial-era historians used to describe specific communities that work within frameworks more "limited" (i.e., focused) than "Canadian" (i.e., frameworks defined by gender, region, ethnicity, class).[4] And then, near the end of her address, Prang proposed something unexpected. She said that "the sharpest and most convincing portrayals of [limited] identities ... come not from historians but from our poets, novelists and short story writers." Citing John Newlove's "The Pride" (1964) as an example, she added,

> creative writers, *especially the poets*, have a strong sense of community, very often know one another, and frequently enjoy a reading public extending across the country. Both the general reader and the social historian find their sensitivity to the impact of place and history on the Canadian consciousness heightened by [these writers]. (8, emphasis added)

This is an astounding scene to imagine. Prang was speaking to an audience of leading Canadian historians: Ramsay Cook (the academic who coined the term "limited identities"), A.G. Bailey (the celebrated poet and historian), and the cantankerous J.L. Granatstein (a staunch defender of old-guard histories) were all in attendance. And as Prang stood at the podium, rehearsing for them the ground-breaking moves in historical study, she emphasized not the achievements of these scholars, but rather the literary power, historiographic sensitivity, and nationwide popularity of poets. She ended with an inviting plea to historians to understand that they, as much as those poets, "have a part to play in strengthening" the general public's "capacity to comprehend and feel" the diversity of Canadian identities, past and present (9).

I love that phrase: "to comprehend and feel." It asks us to read the past empathetically, to get closer to, rather than further from, the events and lives at which conventional historians have looked too fleetingly or of which they have altogether seemed dismissive. It was Prang's belief that Canadian poets were actively reinventing history for "general reader[s]" and "historian[s]" alike by achieving, even if unintentionally, the goal vital to social history: "to recover the life experiences of 'ordinary' people and reduce the prominence of unrepresentative individuals and elites and past politics" (Berger, "Writings" 316).

Through a study of works by major and minor centennial-era writers, this book traces the development of this recovery and reinvention as it occurred in Canadian poetry. In the process of doing so, I draw an essential distinction between "distance" and "closeness": whereas conservative historians have traditionally advocated for objectivity and distance as essential to the writing of history (an approach that has put limits on what qualifies as permissible evidence and content), poets have explored and embraced the productive dissonance manifest when the past is more intimately rendered. I argue that lyric poetry – an inward meditation on the relationship between the self and the outside world – has been an instrumental testing ground for the future of historical writing. In that future, history is a shared practice in which lyric serves as not just a compelling literary mode, but also as an inventive historiographic method – a method that gives narrative power to diverse voices in and outside of the academy.

Throughout this book, I return to two interrelated concepts in order to argue that point: the philosophy of modern scepticism and the lyric mode. Many poets in my study inherited this philosophy and this mode from earlier writers in and outside of Canada, and that inheritance gave them the means to write progressive histories. The idea of literary inheritance helps explain poets' drive and ability to experiment freely with history in ways academics could not. There was, to put it a different way, little theoretical or conceptual groundwork required of modern poets in order for them to be progressive historians; they were tasked instead with repurposing philosophical concepts and literary modes with which they were already familiar.

Modern Scepticism and the Reinvention of Content

One purpose of this book is to open up broader discussions of Canadian writing since 1960 by moving away from the common assumption that "postmodernism" (and the term Linda Hutcheon ties to its literature, "historiographic metafiction") defines the era and by proposing instead a more inclusive discussion of "scepticism." For Hutcheon and those who came after her, scepticism vis-à-vis historiographic metafiction means self-referential and typically comic literature in which the past seems so impossible to represent faithfully that an author self-reflexively parodies any desire to represent it. Hutcheon's model of scepticism connects to poststructuralist thought, a link endorsed by critics like Herb Wyile, who claims "there is no question that the insights of postmodernism and poststructuralism have profoundly shaken the discipline of history" ("Attack" 193); Robert Kroetsch, too, argues that "scepticism," "hesitation," and "doubt about our ability to know" are defining qualities of postmodernist thinking ("Disunity as Unity" 23).

Such claims are reactions to international discourses on historiography that reached their peak in the 1970s and 1980s, at which point leading scholars reflected on the nature of history writing and the extent to which any historian can claim to be objective or to have incontestable knowledge of the past. Two pivotal works in these debates were Jean-François Lyotard's *The Postmodern Condition* (1979) and Hayden White's *Metahistory* (1973): Lyotard famously defines the postmodern condition as an "incredulity toward metanarratives" such as national history (xxiv), and White argues that history is organized in much the same way as creative fiction (i.e., historians construct and shape characters and events with certain narrative goals in mind). Those positions were reinforced by theorists and philosophers of the era: Edward Said debated the legitimacy of cultural, historiographic, or ethical authority and declared that "authority can, indeed must, be analyzed" (20), while Michel Foucault's philosophically disruptive writings on discourse, archaeology, genealogy, and the archive led some historians to regard his work as "a long-craved, complete, and perfect nourishment" for the modern academic (Goldstein 3). These global discussions, with their celebration of epistemological doubt and critical subversion, markedly affected the philosophies, even the very tone, of historians like Prang and Morton who would advocate for (or at least predict) professional reform. This reform was, like the theory itself, global: the

French historian Michel de Certeau remarked on the biases of "socially marked" histories that are *made* by the historian (*The Writing of History* 67), and the American scholar Natalie Zemon Davis was so fascinated by historiographic verisimilitude that she built on White's work and theorized the fiction (that is, the "forming, shaping, and molding elements") of historical documents (3).

Put simply, these theorists and philosophers, and the historians whom they influenced, were articulating what was on the tip of many tongues; that is not the same, however, as saying (as Wyile or Kroetsch seem to say) that postmodernist theory is inextricable from the concept of philosophical scepticism. To say so puts the proverbial cart before the horse: citing theory and philosophy as the source of critical tensions in historical studies dismisses the social and political contexts that occasioned such theory in the first place. Theory is never born in a vacuum; it elaborates on the distinctive conditions of its era. And those living in the decades immediately preceding major publications by Lyotard, White, and a host of other poststructuralists had witnessed revolutions across the globe (the US civil rights movement, the Algerian War of Independence, Quebec's Quiet Revolution, and so forth) that challenged the integrity of long-standing epistemologies embedded in historical writing.[5]

All of that is to say that the idea of a sceptical history or historian is not strictly an academic one. The fact that, as the chapters of this book cumulatively show, an entire generation of Canadians scrutinized concepts of "national identity" or "national history" indicates that critics have kept the concept of scepticism too closely associated with postmodernist theory and literature, especially in regard to novels.[6] This book therefore expands the definition of scepticism by broadening these associations and arguing that scepticism was, in its various forms, a philosophical and generational condition. Even without ground-breaking texts like those of Lyotard and White, the revolutionary spirit of the 1960s led many to question the history, news, and literature they encountered.

In Canada, the circumstances were especially tempestuous. I will say more later about the massive changes ongoing in the historical profession after 1960, but something much bigger was unfolding: the country was experiencing and emerging from the 1960s sceptically and cautiously, watching as a national identity once understood to be monolithic – premised for too long on an English, Christian, and patriarchal identity – was fractured. That claim is one of Bryan Palmer's basic contentions in his recent work on Canada's 1960s. "The irony of Canadian identity in the 1960s," he says, "was that as the old attachment to British Canada was finally and decisively shed, it was replaced only with uncertainty. The ambivalences of the decade fuelled recognition of the crisis of Canada, admittedly a phenomenon overripe for its recognized emergence." While this was a potentially liberating exercise, it nevertheless meant that "Canadians ... were puzzled by what it meant, exactly, to be Canadian" (5). Palmer's language ("uncertainty," "ambivalences," "puzzled") points to the thinking of the era: Canadians began to contrast monolithic national narratives with pluralized ones, certainty with doubt, conservatism with progressive politics.

The same was true of history. The 1960s is the same decade that Carl Berger describes as one of "destruction" in historical study. "[H]istorians," he writes, "no longer agreed upon what was central to their field of study and what was peripheral" (*Writing* 259). The consequence of these events was what Palmer describes as "a mix of defiant realities" (17), a frictional mosaic that heralded "the destruction of simplified impressions of [minority groups] as homogeneous and the revelation of their internal divisions and complexity" (Berger, *Writing* 310). It was a reality to which many remained resistant, if not outright hostile. For those who were more accepting, this "complexity" was productive and gave way to the pluralization of terms like "nationalism," "nation," "history," and "identity."

These changes had long-term consequences. Reflecting on the field in the 1990s, Veronica Strong-Boag reiterated the need for an inclusive social history: "the old history, like the old politics, or the old literary or philosophical canon ... [exhibits a] ... common failure to interrogate power relations and address the reality of oppression within Canadian society" (5). When those "power relations" became subjects of scrutiny and the content of history began to accommodate new topics of study, the "coherence of Canadian history was lost" (Berger *Writing* 259) and the field became a site of exploration and infinite possibility rather than an exclusive story through which Canada's national identity and past were rigidly defined. Palmer sees the era as one of "irony" in that the search for one national identity yielded many identities. I see it, in complementary ways, as one of scepticism: if conservative historians were lacking in healthy scepticism, then what knowledge can earn one's trust? And if what was once considered to be incontestable knowledge can be openly challenged, then what other knowledge may now be explored or insisted upon?

While I do imagine scepticism as a condition heightened by the events of the centennial era, I also see it as part of a legacy of sceptical thinking in Western philosophy and literature. Most modern Canadian poets likely encountered scepticism as a feature of literary modernism, a literary movement of the twentieth century predicated partly on the questioning, interrogating, and reinventing of social experience and systems of knowledge. That modernist legacy – on which I will comment throughout this book – equipped poets, as modern sceptics, to engage productively with epistemological questions about the writing of history.[7] That is not to say, however, that every writer in this book identified as "modernist." Purdy at times accepted the label, whereas Atwood has been characteristically unwilling to label her poetics anything at all.[8] Labels mean much less to my argument than the shared sense of scepticism expressed in the poems, but the concept of modernism does linger in the background of some of those discussions. In context, that lingering is unsurprising: the fact that, by the end of the 1950s, writers like Jay Macpherson or Irving Layton were winning prestigious prizes like the Governor General's Award offers evidence that modernism had, by then, become an institutionalized literary movement in Canada. There is no question that many of the leading writers that came of age during this period – whether through their apprenticeships under older poets (on or off the page), university education, or both – encountered Anglo-American and Canadian modernism. In suggesting that the writers in this book were influenced by a philosophical modernism, I mean to imply only that the institutional recognition of literary modernism made the impact of that movement on writers more diffuse, acceptable, and likely.

If one is talking about scepticism as a modern and literary concept, then its most immediate foundations might be more appropriately located in the work of a figure like T.S. Eliot than in works by leading philosophers preoccupied with the concept since the Enlightenment such as David Hume, René Descartes, Michel de Montaigne, Stanley Cavell, and Paul Tillich. I stress Eliot specifically because he was transparent in both his creative and critical writing about his philosophical development; other critics have located a similarly "modern" scepticism in the writing of Yeats, Conrad, and Woolf.[9] But Eliot is also important because the veneration with which twentieth-century writers regarded him means that his work, as much if not more than any other, provided a foundation for a modern scepticism on which mid-century poets could build. It is telling that Michael Bell, in an article on the development of modernist thought, notes that Eliot's obituary for Henry James ("[he] had a mind so fine that no idea could violate it" [qtd Bell 420]) "encapsulates a widespread modernist skepticism about ideas" (420). None of these claims about Eliot discount the fact that there are numerous varieties of modern scepticism (some neither Eliotic nor modernist), but modern scepticism as a quality of twentieth-century poetry (Canadian or otherwise) can, within particular literary webs, be traced fruitfully to the avant-garde aesthetics and poetics of Anglo-American modernism as embodied by Eliot and those he influenced.

The various interpretations of scepticism as a concept inevitably mean that it has stood for different things for different people: pyrrhonists revel in unceasing doubt and imagine that condition as itself a way of living, whereas Eliot was as enamoured of belief as he was of doubt. His conception of scepticism was also not strictly historical. Eliot sometimes spoke of it in general terms, and it occasionally – even often and increasingly – took on a religious meaning for him. He refined his philosophy of scepticism over the course of his life – from his return to Harvard in 1911, to his conversion to Christianity in the late 1920s, to his publication of *The Four Quartets* in the early 1940s. His scepticism was predicated on qualifiable conviction. After prolonged exposure to myriad concepts of belief and doubt through the works and teachings of F.H. Bradley, Bertrand Russell, Michel de Montaigne, Mādhyamika Buddhism, and numerous others, Eliot concluded that it is "impossible [...] to be without beliefs" (Perl 111).[10] The return to belief was so vital to Eliot that he refused to take seriously anyone who claimed to be "without beliefs"; this was his major critique of Bertrand Russell, avowedly a sceptic, and one whom Eliot goadingly argued had more religious faith than even St Augustine (Perl 55). Scepticism, as Eliot understood it, only begins with judgment, disbelief, and incredulity; it is as much about the cautious return to belief as it is about doubt. Modern scepticism is, Eliot once said, merely "the preface to conversion" (Eliot qtd Perl 55).

To convert in Eliot's sense simply means that one has beliefs, but resists dogmatism and retains doubt: "the skeptic will keep his views but not aspire to their hegemony" (Perl 111). A modern sceptic needs "views" as much as doubt. In retaining belief, though, sceptics reject positions suggestive of superiority; they refuse, rather than reinforce, hierarchies. In this model, each individual's belief is expressive of a personal search. In a late text, *Notes towards the Definition of Culture* (1948), Eliot insists on this point:

> [O]ne of the features of development, whether we are taking the religious or the cultural point of view, is the appearance of scepticism – by which, of course, I do not mean infidelity or destructiveness (still less the unbelief which is due to mental sloth) but the habit of examining evidence and the capacity for delayed decision. Scepticism is a highly civilized trait[;] though, when it declines into pyrrhonism, it is one of which civilization

> can die. Where scepticism is strength, pyrrhonism is weakness: for we need not only the strength to defer a decision, but the strength to make one. (12)

Eliot's notions of critical "examination" and "delay" are akin to what David Hume, centuries earlier, termed a "mitigated skepticism" (161): the intractable doubt that spawns a belief at once cautious, esoteric, and deeply held by the sceptic. Hume, like Eliot, lamented the inaction of pyrrhonism and its inveterate suspension of belief. Both preferred a doubt that asked the sceptic to do the difficult work of amending the definition of useful knowledge. To do so would lead to a belief that is reasoned, tested, and also itself subject to contest. Scepticism is a process that, for Eliot, provides a greater appreciation for the literary and philosophical power of ambiguity and irresolution as a modern individual works toward a personal system of faith. This scepticism trickled down and predisposed later writers to question not just their beliefs but also the world in which those beliefs were formed.

For the poets discussed in this book, the function of scepticism was twofold: first, to question the histories they inherited and their own ability to relate broad histories of which they wrote at a distance (both culturally and temporally) and, second, to use that questioning to fuel a search for new histories through which the "I" achieves both closeness to the past and, relatedly, narrative authority. This is Eliot's pattern: abandon a weak belief for doubt, and then abandon doubt for a stronger belief. When meditating on cultural and temporal distance, poets often produce brief lyrics focused on their inability to overcome that distance (chapter 1 to chapter 4). The poems end quickly, the poet having encountered an epistemological impasse. These brief poems contrast with the long poems or book-length sequences that, through depictions of family, demonstrate a poet's closeness to the past (chapter 5 to chapter 9). In many poets' corpora, the familial long poem has been a logical solution to an epistemological problem: if national or regional history seen at a distance exposes each poet's limited knowledge of the past, then familial history is a remedy for doubt in so far as it assures individual poets some measure of unmatched authority, since it is their history to write. Indeed, family connects us to a past we possess and by which we are possessed. However narrow that history risks appearing, it is nevertheless implicated in broader stories of more general relevance to readers: in *A Social History of Canada* (1988), George Woodcock implies that personal histories are always somewhat communal because "[w]e carry our social and cultural heritages with us as we carry our genes" (2). Our individual stories tie directly to our family's stories, and our family's stories then intersect with a larger community's stories, and so on. In order to recognize lyrical histories as progressive, my reader must suspend any gut assumption that such writing is inherently exclusionary or isolating. Instead, imagine lyrical histories as self-affirming texts in which the "I" explores its own position as a way of pushing itself outward to other stories with full belief in their equivalent value.

This model of history writing contrasts with the historiographic metafiction that is likely more familiar to readers of Canadian literature. This playful literature was progressive in its time and remains popular today because it signals authors' resistance to and deconstruction of any urge to write a history that overconfidently presents itself as *the* past. These writers thus celebrate an essentially pyrrhonic scepticism – in so far as their scepticism leads them to abandon all possibility of belief. That is the kind of scepticism that George Bowering endorses when he says that writers' "hostility" toward history has inspired them to "deconstruct history and thus invent their own version of the post-colonial postmodern" ("Language Women" 101). These are key words: "hostility," "deconstruct[ion]," and playful "invent[ion]." They show a disregard for factuality or accuracy and an embrace of play and reverie when exploring the past. That project spoke well to the centennial generation, and Hutcheon's theories on it guided literary criticism after the 1980s; her work remains influential today because it offered a valuable entry point into historically conscious literature. Hutcheon's work, however, has led to an overemphasis on postmodernist novels as the preeminent literary sites of historical intervention[11] and on pyrrhonic parody as *the* sophisticated response to scepticism.[12]

The primary way in which the model of "modern skepticism" I am proposing differs from the endless deferral of meaning or the playful nihilism in postmodernist writing is that it signifies a refusal to engage in the hostile abandonment or parody of the search for history. Instead, the poets studied in this book sought sustainable narratives that could offer a personally rewarding point of contact with the past. To tie this back to Eliot, they did not simply revel in their doubts about the writing of history, but instead they desired new histories about which they could write authoritatively, without appearing exclusionary, myopic, or unresponsive to their tumultuous social and political contexts. This was often the philosophical basis for sophisticated historical writing after 1960, and, because of their education in modernist literature, many poets had such ideas ingrained in their thinking in ways that popular Canadian historians did not. Historians were responsible to institutions and departments, to an academic tradition wary of divisive narrative shifts. Creative writers had no such responsibilities and their traditions encouraged them early on to explore unfamiliar territory.

The Lyric Mode and the Reinvention of Method

While it may be true that post-1960 Canadian histories offered relatively more diverse content than earlier texts, they still showed that little had been done to innovate on the way in which academics organized their research and writing. The reinvention of method was of pressing concern to historians. "As history became more diverse," T.A. Crowley wrote of the centennial era, "discussions about methodology arose more frequently" (1). But the achievements of those discussions were modest. "The subject matter changed," Steven High says, "but not the research process or our authorial voice. No one speaks of 'truth' or 'objectivity' any more, but the perspective we take remains essentially unchanged" (22). High points to the issue of intellectual authority, and, in the tradition of academic history, such authority can be achieved only by "obeying the rules" of the profession (Berkhofer 227). And because the "rules" of the profession are determined and taught by the same academics who "obey" them, a logical tautology emerges: throughout the twentieth century, university-trained historians taught university students that "only university-trained historians [have] the right to interpret the past" (High 37). This belief justified the authority of the academic historian, who, Robert Berkhofer argues more generally, "defend[s] their authority as well as the autonomy of their profession" by establishing "boundaries" that keep their "intellectual turf" separate from other academic departments and from the public at large (227). Michel de Certeau elsewhere calls this a process of giving Western academic history "the accreditation of erudition," which thus separates it from "ordinary discourse" such as "genealogical storytelling" (*Heterologies* 200).

While the issues that Berkhofer or de Certeau raise are not specifically Canadian, they have nevertheless been of interest to Canadian historians: these were scholars who, after 1950, underwent rapid professionalization and who were therefore driven to define their place in the field, which also meant defining "legitimate" history and characterizing the "legitimate" historian. The rebellious political climate and social upheaval of the 1960s only further pressured historians to define and defend their professional authority as a way of guarding against outsiders to the profession who may have wanted to rewrite or reshape "official" histories.

A strict line was drawn. Academic history was on one side of it; any historical writing that adopted methods or content unfamiliar or unacceptable to trained historians was on the other. This elitism proved alienating. Donald Wright argues that, during the last half of the twentieth century, Canadian history was more like "a private conversation between professional historians" than "a public conversation" (*Professionalization* 169). Many academics did exactly what Berkhofer describes: they "polic[ed] and preserv[ed]" the writing of history by upholding a "standard, normal paradigm of historical practice" determined by those who traditionally have exercised power over that practice (228), and Canadian historians were taught to believe that their authority "derived from their specialized training and their expertise in speaking to 'the public'" (High 24). The old guard's tenacious defence of those views is understandable: implementing changes in focus or methodology risked shifting professional boundaries, which then risked undermining the authority of historians and compromising their "turf." But therein lies a problem: if the authority of historical writing rests with an elite group of professional historians, then these representatives of the profession, even when engaged with and accepting of new content, were not really instituting foundational change. Truly diverse perspectives struggle to flourish when conventional methods (and, arguably, membership) become sacrament.

Indeed, since 1960, innovative historiographic practices, such as oral history, have been sidelined, and this is something of which oral historians are painfully aware: "Except for a brief flurry of activity in the 1970s, the Canadian Oral History Association (COHA) has been largely inactive, publishing an annual journal that few professional historians have ever read ... Canadian historians rose in defence of their disciplinary authority and set out to draw a line between 'historians' on the one hand and 'oral practitioners' on the other. ... oral history became synonymous with 'amateur' or 'popular' history in Canada" (High 28–9). Conventional methods were, for decades, insufficiently countered.

That is not to say, though, that some historians didn't try. The Multicultural History Society of Ontario, for instance, was established in 1976 by several historians (Robert F. Harvey, Frank Iacobucci, and Milton Israel) with the expressed goal of gathering and preserving thousands of taped interviews, photographs, and personal records from immigrants of various cultural backgrounds as a way of documenting their experiences in Canada and abroad. Those sources were valuable to researchers like Susan Papp-Zubrits, who used the MHSO archives to re-examine the 1950s Hungarian refugee crisis. She compared newspaper articles and official histories of the refugees who immigrated to Canada "to the oral testimony of the Hungarians who came to this country" (Papp-Zubrits 29) and was shocked to discover that these refugees, who were slotted into "menial" jobs because of Canadians' assumptions about their abilities, were actually "highly-skilled and well-educated" (32). This was just one of many revelations about the lives and identities of these people that led her to conclude that "oral testimony serves to enrich and give a more complete picture" of the past (33). Papp-Zubrits had effectively proven that the experiences of people could overturn an "official" history by giving voice to those who lived through the experiences themselves. A comparable case is that of the amateur historian Barry Broadfoot, whose books covered a range of topics that included the Depression (*Ten Lost Years* [1973]) and the Wars (*Six War Years* [1974]) as understood through the eyes of average Canadians. The eminent historian Ramsay Cook said that Broadfoot's interviews were far from serious history; with more fury, J.L. Granatstein and Roger Hall also questioned the legitimacy of Broadfoot's approach and belittled any researcher who valued such methods (High 34). Broadfoot's best-selling books were controversial not just because of their popularity, but because he was contesting the methods, voice, and authority of conventional history as a non-academic. So even if some historians were ready for new content during and after the centennial era, that did not necessarily mean they accepted the accompanying innovations in method, which they regarded as unprofessional and inadmissible.

This is why Margaret Prang could not locate the same power she ascribed to Canadian poetry in the existing body of social history circa 1977. Ordinary people were not a part of the writing or reading of history. In 1961, W.K. Ferguson anticipated that problem when he said – as Donald Wright would say decades later – the "professional academic historian" once reached and wrote for "the general reading public," but now historians were beginning "to write for other historians" (2). As the profession grew and the field shifted its interests from the political to the social, that insularity was barely, if at all, addressed. The more historians wrote for or worked with the general public, the less credible their work seemed to other academics. This was particularly true of oral history, even among archivists: "Paradoxically, although archivists ... led oral history initiatives within their own institutions, they were [in the 1970s and 1980s] far from being representative of the whole archival community. Most archivists worked with paper records and questioned the validity of oral history recordings as archival documents. To many, the role of the archivist was to collect the existing record and not to create a new one" (Lochead 47).

Leaders in the field reinforced this status quo.[13] In T.A. Crowley's "book of first principles" (6), *Clio's Craft: A Primer of Historical Methods* (1988), he spoke of changes to the methodologies of historians, but the "Methodology" section of the book consists of fairly traditional perspectives on who defines and writes history: Bruce G. Trigger begins his contribution to that section by saying, "History begins at the point that written documentation appears" (133), Robert Craig Brown champions the power of political biography, Chad Gaffield argues that social history will be most useful when "demographic patterns" (163) are tied back to "more traditional themes such as politics" (175), and John Fogarty advocates for "economic history" as a way of defining "national boundaries" (179). Not one of these authors outlines a major reinvention of methodology. Even the shifts in content feel slight: they reinforce traditional and exclusionary concepts of "history" as a study of the written word (Trigger), of the politically powerful (Brown), of grand national themes (Gaffield), and of the connection between economy and national development (Fogarty). As historians proposing "new" methodologies for the future of historical study, none questions the concept of nation, none interrogates the authority of the historian to write history, and none considers methodologies that might redistribute that authority.

These examples are, I suspect, some of what fuelled Carl Berger's despondence about the achievements of social historians when he reflected on the field in the early 1990s. In Berger's eyes, historians writing between 1974 and 1990 were not "altogether successful in making the inarticulate articulate; from [their] books we learn more about the conditions of life than about people's thoughts and feelings ... the influence of these works was limited" (320). The "ascendancy of social history," High agrees, "represented only a half-revolution" (22). Authority remained with historians, and the "thoughts and feelings" of Canadians (as well as their readership) were insufficiently acknowledged. It was easy for historians to imagine new content; it was much harder for them to question, and even relinquish, their own authority in pursuit of new methods.

And so it went. From the late 1960s until the late 1990s, methods and writing that ran counter to conventional academic decorum remained in tension with existing standards of practice. The failure of social history to make good on its implied promise to let society speak was the premise of Veronica Strong-Boag's speech to the Canadian Historical Association in 1994, in which she said that "historians must *share* space and, more than occasionally, remove ourselves and those like us from centre stage. We must make room for other voices who have so often been silenced" (6, emphasis added). Change came in the later 1990s, but mostly because "the older professors went out the door" (Dummitt 101) and emerging scholars were inherently liberal enough to think more seriously about "a largely progressive history" (Dummitt 102). "The History Wars," Christopher Dummitt declared in 2008, were over by virtue of "attrition through retirement" (102).[14]

The act of sharing history and authority was not so controversial or so contested in Canadian poetry. Canadian writers were capturing "the life experiences of ordinary people" in ways that centennial-era social historians were not by achieving closeness to the past through lyrical writing. What they accomplished perhaps explains why they earned scorn from conservatives such as Bliss, who clearly resented the fact that by the 1990s Canadian "identity was no longer to be discerned through those dry old history texts but was now to be found in *fiction and poetry*" (8, emphasis added). Arguably, the ease with which Canadian poets achieved a reinvention of method is due largely to the fact that they did not have to create a new method; they merely had to repurpose the lyric mode.

Their adaptation of lyric, like that of scepticism, is an instance of literary inheritance. If social history emboldens individuals with narrative authority, then such history is analogous to lyric poetry. As a literary mode, lyric has roots in classical Greek and Latin poetry (that is, poems accompanying music produced by a lyre). Classical lyrics, Jonathan Culler writes, participate in "ritualized, performative speech, sometimes deemed of divine origin ... oracular speech that produces truth[s]" presented publicly and thus generally serving a civic function (49). Though such poems were part of social discourses, they were nevertheless the expression of an "I" whose purpose was to "unify a series of disparate remarks" (54). In the works of the great Athenian lyricists like Pindar, the "I" was tasked with finding the means to organize social experience; several hundred years later in Rome, poets like Horace would draw directly on this Greek model and regard the lyric poet, still, as a mediator of experience. Horace, in fact, regards the lyric poet as a civic figure that "serves great enterprises" (which I take to mean the political and public sphere) in their own "small" way (*Epistle 2.1* line 126). Although Horace and the other Roman poets like Catullus and Longinus were radically different in tone and vision, each in his own way recognized the relationship between the private and the public, inwardly and sometimes quite passionately encountering and articulating the world in which he lived or wished to live. However each generation of writers after Pindar, Horace, Catullus, and Longinus may have interpreted lyric, some of this interplay remained so that the mode has proven enduringly musical, intellectual, and socially engaged yet still intensely personal.

By the nineteenth century, some critics regarded lyric as "the epitome of poetry" because of its emphasis on "feeling," which was for some romantic critics the very "source" of art (Culler 75). As lyric became a central mode in the literary world, romantic poets were encouraged to deepen its personalism by incorporating into their poetry a "highly developed conception of the individual subject" born out of Enlightenment philosophy (1). Writers like Wordsworth, Whitman, and Coleridge zealously explored experience, communicating what W.R. Johnson calls "immediacy" (26): their poems were meditative reactions to a place and time, a "here and now" – and yet these same poets transcended their inner world to approach some broader, spiritual epiphany of significance to the reader's world. Even as romantic poets intensified their emotional expression, lyric retained the potential to be "the intersection of the self and its social environments" (Zimmerman 27). The sense these nineteenth-century romantics had of their keen social vision and introspection assured them of their intellectual and spiritual acuity.

This was not true for twentieth-century writers. Afflicted by a relatively chaotic experience of the mind and world, modern lyricists are no less introspective or "I"-centred than romantic ones, but the uncertainty of their era provokes their suspicion of their own ability to comprehend and depict scenes, images, events, figures, or even the self in any reliable or coherent way. Marjorie Perloff captures some of this shift in her assessment of D.H. Lawrence: "Lawrence's 'I' is not an ecstatic, rapturous shaman, a prophet who must convey ... his mysterious vision. Rather, the voice that speaks to us is conversational, hectoring, nervous, energetic, funny, sardonic – the same voice we meet in Lawrence's remarkable letters" (102). The shattering experience of two world wars, Freud's exploration of the unconscious, urbanization, and technological innovations like airplanes, cars, and weaponry negated the social relevance of the confident and coherent mind behind the romantic "I." Facing this world, modern lyrics like those of Lawrence and other modernists demonstrated, as Michael H. Whitworth argues, an "awareness of both the complexity and the impotence of the self" (*Modernist Poetry* 161); "the complexity of the self," Whitworth says elsewhere, "can be read as a symptom of uncertainty about grand narratives of human history" (*Modernism* 14). Lyric, in other words, no longer unified experience as it did for earlier poets. Instead, it became the mode through which one evaluates and explores doubt about the meaning and identity of "I" and, relatedly, the state and truth of the world in which that "I" finds itself.

In ways useful to my study, Brian Trehearne has traced the development of this more conflicted lyric by thinking about it as a move away from the impersonal poetics that dominated modernist writing during the early twentieth century. Culler observes that the romantic reverence of lyric engendered a "resistance" against it in the late nineteenth and early twentieth centuries (there were of course exceptions, such as Lawrence). For some mainstream modernist writers, the "resistance to the lyric" was "very much a part of poetic practice" (77); one need only read T.S. Eliot's theory of impersonality to find evidence to support Culler's point. Modernist impersonality was an implicit rejection of lyric's expressive nature, and these Anglo-American doctrines influenced Canadian writers of the 1920s and 1930s like A.J.M. Smith, Dorothy Livesay, and F.R. Scott. Trehearne, though, argues that modernist impersonality was of weakening importance to mid-century Canadian writers who had rediscovered the power of lyric "testimony" as a timely and appropriate response to the postwar era, which demanded more than the emotional distance of early modernist art (311). By the end of the 1950s, in other words, lyric no longer seemed passé or socially irrelevant in the thinking of leading Canadian poets like Irving Layton or P.K. Page; it became the essential mode to engage an era more concerned with an emotional, intimate approach to modern scenes, subjects, and experiences.

The revitalization of lyric in the 1950s naturally influenced the work of centennial-era poets. The more closely one looks at poetic legacies, the easier it is to see some important links between these two generations of writers. Many of the poets who spearheaded this initial renewal served as models for emerging writers of the 1960s and 1970s: Layton mentored Al Purdy and was Barry McKinnon's creative writing teacher at Sir George Williams University in Montreal; John Newlove and Margaret Atwood openly admired Page; Purdy himself had a profound effect on Newlove, Atwood, McKinnon, and Andrew Suknaski; Atwood provided a poetic model that Joan Crate followed. Part of what made lyric intuitive to poets of the centennial era and after was this literary inheritance. There was, in other words, continuity between the modes with which Canadian poets of the 1950s experimented and the modes later poets adopted.

As important as these lines of influence are, they are not the sole explanation for postwar Canadian poets' attraction to lyric; the mode served a conceptual function, too. In historically informed poetry, the lyric mode usefully undermines any potential claim to absolute knowledge. Centennial-era writers may not have consciously used lyric as a tactic per se, but they were naturally drawn to it as a way of expressing both their faith in and scepticism about any recorded history – even their own. It would have been impossible and blatantly hypocritical for them to use the "I" as a central device in their poetry and then make the same kinds of claims to an authoritative objectivity espoused by historians who write impersonally. Their poetry surely seems more self-aware and, consequently, more self-critical. Their chosen mode thus situated centennial-era poets within a particular Canadian literary tradition of lyric and aided in their indulgence of the sceptical tradition lingering in modernist thought.

This positioning has allowed lyric to transcend poetic performance, to be more than a literary mode. For the poets in my study, lyric is a historiographic method. Conventional history aspires toward objectivity and hegemony; it exercises what Walter Benjamin calls "conformis[t]" readings of the past that aspire to be monolithic and canonical (255). Such readings hinder the exchange of different perspectives on the past: "every image of the past that is not recognized by the present as one of its own concerns threatens to disappear irretrievably" (257). While that statement captures the tenor of Canadian history until the "History Wars" waned, lyric poetry shows an alternative. A meditative lyric that is sceptical in the Eliotic sense of the term will be cautious in claiming or accepting claims to narrative authority.

The idea of a history that is philosophically sceptical as I have outlined the concept above parallels the idea of "sceptical history" as explained by the historian Hélène Bowen Raddeker, who proposes six guidelines for such a history:

1. transparent self-reflexivity ("self-criticism and self-doubt" [32]) within a text
2. "an emphasis on leaving arguments open" (33)
3. the avoidance of "essentialist representations of the past" (33)
4. "a recognition of 'difference'" (33)
5. "a rejection" of models of "identity" ("national" or "individual") that valorize uniformity (i.e., identity is unexceptional), certainty (i.e., identities are static and unchanging), or notions of authenticity (i.e., identities can be tested and proven) (33)
6. an attentiveness to "historiography" (an engagement with "the discourse of history" rather than a narrative written in intellectual isolation) (33)

These authorial qualities – about which Raddeker speaks hypothetically[15] and optimistically – have been basic to a particular genre of Canadian literature, a genre that synthesizes, discards, and/or critically evaluates fragmented images (sometimes figurative images, sometimes literally photographic ones) of history. These are the essential qualities of what I call "lyric historiography," a creative study of the past that brings readers away from the distance inspired by an elite, academic history and closer to the historical and cultural experiences of people.[16]

In offering examples of lyric historiography, however, I am aiming to do more than prove the existence of those basic qualities in a cross-section of Canadian poetry. This book studies changes in both form and content within lyric historiography over several decades. In order to do so, I examine two branches of this genre: (1) accumulative lyrics (at their height during the 1960s and early 1970s), and (2) developmental or familial lyrics (gaining popularity since the late 1960s). Both types of poems are examples of lyric historiography in so far as they interrogate the limits of individual knowledge and historical authority, but there are essential differences in form and content.

Accumulative poems emphasize strictly a national or regional history disconnected from the individual writer. Such poems are primarily diagnostic: they emphasize the lyric persona's scepticism about the possibility of an authoritative history and explain or evaluate the difficulty of organizing the past into a coherent narrative. They accumulate fragments of the past, but never achieve a narrative of it. The historical authority to do otherwise is always located elsewhere, removed from the poet-speaker, who feels distanced from events in the past; authority belongs to figures who have lived through the past or who feel culturally or hereditarily connected to it.

Developmental lyrics, alternatively, draw directly on the experiences of the poet through genealogy, where the past becomes what Marianne Hirsch calls "postmemory": a memory inherited and possessed by the descendants of those who lived through a particular past. The apparent ability of the poet to visualize the past authoritatively is facilitated by exploring literal or figurative familial histories, and the persona tends to understand this position through visual metaphors of "seeing" history clearly, as well as through a series of poetic, artistic, or photographic "images." The poet threads images together in order to create the same sense of development one finds in narrative. Not only do these narratives explicate a personal history, but they also serve as inroads into a story bigger than, but still rooted in, the individual, thus connecting the experiences of the "I" to broader experiences and episodes in history. The evolution of poetry about Canadian history has been frequently marked by negotiations of this binary: the accumulative poems that foster a sense of distance from a past to which the individual poet has no claim and the developmental lyrics that imagine history as a personal experience that brings the "I" closer to the past.

The authoritative representation of personal experience in developmental lyrics is analogous to social history as a discourse on the "experiences of people": in both, the temporal, spatial, and often genealogical anchoring of individuals is the source of their authority. In such texts, the "I" – any "I" and not just the university-trained historian – is a legitimate source of knowledge that augments readers' understanding of a past recalled both intellectually and emotionally. In that way, social history has the power, through what I would call a fundamentally "lyrical" method (because of its attention to testimony, oral history, and witness), to share authority and overturn habitualized or conventional narratives. The point I want to underscore is this: whereas historians have struggled to legitimate the democratizing principles of shared authority, poets have not. Their philosophical and literary inheritances have made a subjective and sceptical approach to history seem almost intuitive.

Lyric Historiography and the Reinvention of History

In arguing for the importance of lyric historiography, this book has three primary goals: (1) to show that modern Canadian poets have contributed to the reinvention of history as a social discourse concerned with personal experience and amenable to sharing the authority to write the past, (2) to prove their work has serious implications for conservative models of history, nation/nationalism, and identity (personal or communal), and (3) to demonstrate the ways in which this literary project has been born out of a web of influence that includes both well-known authors and lesser-known ones.

This book attends to these goals by taking several new approaches to historically conscious literature during the centennial era. I noted earlier the thorough attention paid to historiographic novels in Canadian criticism, and so one obvious intervention of this book is its shifting of readers' focus from novels to poetry. Taking that approach, I offer a vaguely chronological evolution of lyric historiography from about 1960 to the contemporary era. The works of my six central poets – Purdy, Newlove, McKinnon, Suknaski, Atwood, and Crate – epitomize shifts in either form or content (sometimes both) within the genre of lyric historiography and illustrate the move from the accumulative lyric to the developmental one.

My selection of these writers was not random. During the earliest stages of my research for this book, I knew that I would be providing a partial history of Canadian poetry by stressing the historical and creative legacy of specific works. It therefore seemed imperative to prove that each poet had a measurable impact on their audience, especially when that audience included other writers. I wanted to know if poets spoke to and guided each other, and to find out if what these poets did was important to their readers. Through interviews, critical research, and archival work, I discovered more connections (personal, philosophical, and aesthetic) than I could ever have imagined, connections that are wide-ranging and remarkably observable. Hence, one of the major criteria for my selection of writers had to do with influence – that is, the "more or less conscious" relationship predicated on "transmission" from one author to another (Clayton and Rothstein 3). That quality of this book is my own embrace of Harold Bloom's claim that literary criticism "is the art of knowing the hidden roads that go from poem to poem" (96). Whenever possible, I use my research[17] to chart direct influence and to establish tangible connections between and among individual writers.

When discussing authors influencing authors, I should be clear that I understand influence as a concept based on relation, not on hierarchy. This is a point that Susan Stanford Friedman argues: "Since writers are infrequently clones of precursors, literary historians of influence have often focused as much on the agency of the receiver as on the agency of the originating 'source' [...] The interesting question for the critic has been how the successor(s) adapted, assimilated, revised, transformed, altered, reshaped, or revised the precursor(s)" (155). Picking up on Friedman's parenthetical additions, I also show, whenever possible, other proven influences (non-Canadian literary figures, literary and non-literary historical events, and so forth); this study is not meant to reduce influence to a unidirectional line or to any one kind of influence. Instead, I want to demonstrate an intricate and multidirectional model of influence that complicates our literary history rather than simplifying it.

In order to achieve that kind of complexity, I also move beyond the familiar canon of Canadian poetry to consider poets who have likely been forgotten or altogether unnoticed. Certainly Crate, McKinnon, and Suknaski are much lesser known than Purdy, Newlove, or Atwood. In addition to these writers, I have also included a host of secondary writers whose place in (and sometimes outside of) this web will be explained as they are introduced throughout my study: Dale Zieroth, (a.k.a. David Zieroth), Florence McNeil, Mick Burrs (a.k.a. Steven Michael Berzensky), Eli Mandel, Lorna Crozier, Elizabeth Brewster, Louise Halfe, and Cara-Lyn Morgan. This book therefore balances the work of recognizable poets with the related and equally noteworthy innovations of many neglected writers. The potential novelty of some names today is not an indicator of their talent. These are poets worthy of more critical attention and whose obscurity can be overturned simply by telling a different story of the era than the one already told.

My other processes of selection are more firmly rooted in historical and aesthetic contexts. First, in order to draw important correlations between the rise of social history and the development of Canadian poetry, it was important for me to locate poets whose primary mode was lyric. I noted earlier my own fascination with Prang's suggestion that poetry has captured more forcefully the emotional experience of the past than academic history has done. That quality of poetry is, as I argue throughout this book, integral to lyric: the mode is predicated on an intellectual, emotional, and spiritual assessment of the world that comes from an "I" whose urge to experience that world brings them closer to it. This poetry runs counter to distanced and dispassionate observation, which explains the absence of documentary poets like E.J. Pratt from this study: his book-length poems move among historical voices to create an impersonal and epic narrative. This impersonality drew the ire of Purdy: "It's the I-me in poems, whether first person poems or not, that is most valuable and valid. It's the lack of a single personal human face behind E.J. Pratt's epics that leaves me indifferent to him and them" (*RBS* 119). Especially in light of what Prang says about the emotional power of poetry, it's interesting to me that Purdy would spurn Pratt on the grounds that his poems ensure the reader's "indifferen[ce]" to the past. Purdy is explicit: the lyric "I" creates the conditions necessary for a personal encounter, which is what one aspires to achieve in social history. His sentiment perfectly captures the kind of poetry I have gathered in this study.

In looking for those poems, I felt it was also essential to focus on poets that work through their scepticism, rather than revelling in it. The latter approach has been taken by some of the most studied poets of the centennial era, and so while the exclusion of names like George Bowering, Robert Kroetsch, and Michael Ondaatje from this study might seem unexpected, it is warranted. If there is one problem with the postmodernist response to history, it is the consistent suggestion in the literature that there can be no future for history, because, to quote George Bowering, "[h]istory is impossible" ("A Great Northward Darkness" 12). Kroetsch makes similar suggestions in claiming that "resolution" has been replaced by "doubt" ("Disunity" 25) or that Canadian poets strive to "honour [their] disbelief in belief" ("For Play" 118). Those statements help to explain why the poems of Bowering and Kroetsch so often rely on parody as a simultaneous enactment of – to return to the terms I quoted earlier from Bowering – a "hostility" toward history expressed through poets' passion for play when writing of or about the past. The same claims could be made for Ondaatje's spectacular *The Collected Works of Billy the Kid*, which parodies the act of historical representation: as a preface to the book, a frame surrounds a blank square, a caption beneath it telling the reader this white space is "a picture of Billy" (n.p.), and the picture at the end of the book is of Ondaatje himself, dressed as a cowboy at the age of seven. The self-reflexivity of that poetry is a strategy to free historical discourse from the restrictive myth of historians' objectivity. Such poems, in other words, fancifully display just how subjective history really is.

Yet, I would also argue that authors such as Bowering, Kroetsch, and Ondaatje, in the process of making those timely statements, invalidate the experiences of the "I" as narrative pollution: in *George, Vancouver* (1970), George Bowering conflates himself with George Vancouver and notes, "this is as far as I, George, / have travelled" (39). Bowering's doubled "I," like Ondaatje's photographic self-portrait, is a comic disruption of the historical narrative. The "I" is never represented as a possible and reliable narrative source. While each author's pyrrhonism makes for exciting poetry, their revelry also suggests that it is impossible to mitigate doubts about truth claims or to imagine a better history rooted in personal experience. Those approaches to poetry make these writers of great relevance to their era, but of little relevance to a study of poets who overcome doubt and return to a belief in history through a genuine validation of the lyric "I."

In order to chart that return, my study centres on poets who prove, even if indirectly, Friedman's point that influence is as much about innovation as it is about inheritance. I approach lyric historiography by examining its internal developments since 1960 by beginning with Purdy. Chapter 1 and chapter 2 note transitions in his literary career during the 1950s and his historiographic turn in the early 1960s. Together, these chapters outline Purdy's major revelations as a poet-historian: first, the subjectivity inherent in all historical writing inevitably compels self-reflexive writers to acknowledge the limits of their knowledge about the past; second, history is therefore ambiguous and thus difficult to write authoritatively; and lastly, that those limits of individual knowledge often lead lyric poets to desire a closeness to the past. Purdy's choice of content, lyric method, and philosophical conception of history writing set guiding examples for younger writers of the 1960s, such as John Newlove. Chapter 3 therefore examines Newlove's poetry partly as an extension of Purdy's work, but also as a meditation on the distinctiveness of regional history. Chapter 4 explores a wider range of regionalist poems centred on the nineteenth-century Métis uprisings. The poets in this chapter (Purdy, Newlove, Elizabeth Brewster, Mick Burrs, and Lorna Crozier) collectively articulate their struggle to write history with nearly identical emphases and concerns: each feels and speaks of their distance from the past, expresses a consequent scepticism about their own authority or the authority of others to write an accurate history, and expresses a desire to be closer to the past from which they feel so estranged. That estrangement is not just temporal; it is also cultural. The historical importance of the Métis uprisings is never lost on these writers, but Crozier aptly sums up the conundrum of writing about it with any sense of historical authority: "these," she admits in "Drifting Towards Batoche," "were not my people" (184).

The remaining chapters in this book go beyond these feelings of distance and trace the development of family writing. Chapter 5 does so by reading the poetry of Florence McNeil and Dale Zieroth and showing how family writing presents a confident historical vision, one suggestive of the writer's authority over the past rather than of their self-doubt about their ability to write history. Chapter 6 continues this line of thought by providing a theory of family writing and the developmental long poem through a reading of Barry McKinnon's *I Wanted to Say Something* (1970). Chapter 7 evaluates Andrew Suknaski's familial poetry as it evolved under the sway of writers like McKinnon and Purdy in order to show the way in which family writing brought Canadian poets closer to other lyrical life stories. Chapter 8 shows the mutability of lyric historiography by studying Margaret Atwood's repurposing of it to suit her own politics and interests. Atwood's *The Journals of Susanna Moodie* (1970) retains the developmental and narrative quality of familial lyrics, but her approach invokes a feminist search for foremothers, and so she thus conceives of the family figuratively, rather than literally. Lastly, Chapter 9 studies the foremother as a tactic in anti-colonial writing by thinking about Joan Crate's (Métis) *Pale as Real Ladies: Poems for Pauline Johnson* (1989), which takes the perspective of the nineteenth-century poet E. Pauline Johnson / Tekahionwake (Mohawk). Together, these chapters show an evolving genre in Canadian poetry that complements the work of many contemporary writers whose major influences have been altogether different. I note these complements in my conclusion, paying attention to Louise Halfe (Cree) and noting the promise of studying her work through the lens of what Neal McLeod (Cree) calls a "body poetic." Read alongside each other, these traditions show that Canadian poetry encourages the shared authority that historians have tried to achieve through social history.

I have come to think of this book as a story about the inarguable and swaying power of the creative mind in critical discourses. These writers' diverse approaches to historical writing and poetic form are partly symptomatic of a generation overwhelmed by a rich variety of literary, national, and familial traditions, sociopolitical movements, and nationalisms. Regardless of how each writer's poetics developed amid such chaos, it is evident that these poets, working through lyric historiography and often influenced by each other, saw lyric as the future of history. The best response to faltering grand narratives, they tell their readers, is to reimagine history as a conversation paradoxically enlarged by the contraction of historical lenses. Reinvigorating lyric expression both formally and philosophically, these writers have given the past a future and invited readers to think of Canadian history as a discourse that has been shaken and sustained by its reinvention.

1 Al Purdy's Modern Scepticism

If there was one poet whose corpus best demonstrated for younger authors of the 1960s the creative possibilities in Canadian history, it was Al Purdy. Between 1962 and 1972, major changes in his poetry and political thought led him to become one of the most read Canadian poets of his era. In the poems Purdy wrote during those years, he developed a persona whose meditations on the difficulty of representing the past illuminate the breadth, profundity, and challenges of writing about Canadian history. In so doing, he established an early model for literary approaches to and philosophies of history that would become commonplace in later Canadian writing.

The persona Purdy conjured up during this period had much to do with his own nationalism. He was an ardent nationalist, but his discovery of modernism led him away from the romantic nationalism – defined generally, a naïve vision of the nation's promise of self-determination and unity – some critics mistakenly attribute to him. Throughout the 1960s, he internalized concepts and aesthetics that he inherited from his modernist "tutors" (Purdy, *Collected* xviii): Irving Layton, D.H. Lawrence, T.S. Eliot, Ezra Pound, William Carlos Williams, and W.B. Yeats. Drawing on those influences, he cultivated a sceptical persona that effectively responded to a period in which Canadian history underwent a prodigious reassessment. His poetry is a starting point for thinking about the basic features of personas in lyric historiography: resistant to closure, fallible, and sceptical about the authority or completeness of any one history.

A modernist genealogy in Purdy's evocation of these features is palpable; the romantic nationalism with which he is often associated is not. And yet this romantic view of Purdy has persisted in Canadian criticism.[1] Sam Solecki, for example, reads Purdy's nationalism as an extension of the nationalism expressed by earlier romantic and modern writers such as Charles G.D. Roberts and E.J. Pratt. Solecki stresses two camps into which it seems all Canadian writers fall: one is either a romantic nationalist speaking for all of Canada (Pratt, Roberts, and Purdy) or postnationalist (the politically minded postmodernists that Solecki chastises for their rejection of nationalism). The consequence of that rigidity is his occasionally simplistic reading of Purdy as, to quote Dennis Lee, "our Whitman" ("Running" 16) – but that label seems like Lee's attempt to fulfil E.K. Brown's 1943 prediction that "our Whitman is in the future" (20). Purdy, though, abhorred any proposed likeness to Whitman. In 1973, he began a fairly crotchety exchange with George Bowering about the comparison: "[Whitman is] monotonous, long-winded and fulla shit. [...] I dislike his repetitions, his philosophy of good fellowship and the common man" (Purdy to Bowering). Purdy's frustration here is palpable, and it suggests that he believed his poetry offered something much more sophisticated than a derivative and Whitmanesque love of country. The more closely readers look at his career and poems, challenging that wish-fulfilling comparison to "Whitman," the more likely they are to find a Purdy who fits into the twentieth century rather than the nineteenth.

A particularly good place to start with a better narrative of Purdy is Mark Silverberg's lamentation that Purdy's entanglement in "nationalistic concerns" is often – and I fully agree – more reflective of critics' politics than of Purdy's. Silverberg contends that critics have "reductively Canadianiz[ed] Purdy" and thus "discouraged" themselves and others "from seeing him in other ways" (228). "[N]ationalist reading strategies," he continues, "often miss qualities at the heart of Purdy's work: irony and productive uncertainty" (245). If scholars were to accept that Purdy's poetry is guided by "productive uncertainty," it would be much more difficult to align the poet with Roberts or Pratt as Solecki and others have done, because the romance of certainty in conservative nationalism would be unsustainable as a basis for critical study of his works. That is to say, in Purdy's poetry, especially his poems about history, I don't find much evidence of a persona uncritically celebrating the coherence (conceptually and historically) of "the Canadian nation."

Instead, I see a sceptic. Purdy's attentiveness to diverse geographies and eras is a constant reminder that he actively questioned any monolithic models of Canadian history or identity. Purdy's nationalism had distinctly modern inflections made clear by his refusal to define too firmly what exactly the nation, understood historically, meant to him. I will say more about what terms like "nation" and "nationalist" meant to Purdy in my next chapter, but here I want to chart Purdy's discovery of modern poetry and philosophy, which defined his modern scepticism. This scepticism nurtured, fruitfully, his doubts about his own ability and the ability of others to write an authoritative history. *Poems for All the Annettes* (1962) was a testing ground for poems born out of that discovery, and this was also the book that became a guiding model for numerous emerging poets during the centennial era. This was the book, in other words, that gave him status.

Reaching those heights, however, took time. Although Purdy began writing poetry around 1931, he was almost entirely ignorant of the existence of modernism until the mid-1950s, when he was nearly forty years old and still ensnared in the traditions and poetics of romanticism. He was wholly unaware of the ways in which poetry had changed since the turn of the century: "Up to [the mid-1950s]," he once said, "my own literary gods were Bliss Carman, G.K. Chesterton, W.J. Turner, etc." Upon discovering "T.S. Eliot, Dylan Thomas, W.B. Yeats, Ezra Pound, and others," he realized that he "simply wasn't saying things that [he] should have been capable of saying" (*RBS* 135). The fact that Purdy's ignorance of modern forms persisted until the mid-1950s explains why even his latest poems of the 1990s retain some obviously romantic tendencies.[2]

Although Purdy would later regret the aesthetic and philosophical blandness of his first four books – he described them to Andrew Suknaski in 1973 as "romantic maunderings," a "mix of reality and romanticism [that] was too lopsided on the cloying nostalgia" (Purdy to Suknaski) – they still provided a seed for his later poetic content. By the 1950s, though, Purdy was experimenting with modernist writing and thus realized that romanticism was long outmoded. Still, he could not break old habits. He did not, that is to say, abandon his romantic tendencies. Instead, he negotiated traditions. Purdy continued to explore romantic topics in which he showed an early interest – namely, history and memory – but, after 1960, he did so in ways that showed his grasp of modernist aesthetics and philosophies.

This fusion was crucial to Purdy's later success, because his early poems are fettered by influence rather than artistically liberated by it. The fundamental shortcoming of *The Enchanted Echo* (1944), *Pressed on Sand* (1955), *Emu, Remember!* (1956), and *The Crafte So Longe to Lerne* (1959) is that they unintentionally caricature romanticism. The poet's lyrical, sentimental, and nostalgic speakers offer little more than derivative imitations of writers like Bliss Carman – one of Purdy's major influences during his early period. Carman's lyrics were Purdy's early models: "writing poems began for me at age thirteen, when I read Bliss Carman

[...] So I wrote my own poems, even worse than Carman's. Blessedly, I didn't know that" (*RBS* 38). To be sure, *The Enchanted Echo* springs straight from Carman:

> I saw the milkweed float away,
> To curtsy, climb and hover
> And seek among the crowded hills
> Another warmer lover. ("The Enchanted Echo" 11)

In several interviews and his autobiography, Purdy deems this passage one of his worst. Solecki goes further and excoriates the entire collection: "If there's a single image or line [in *The Enchanted Echo*] that shows any poetic life, I haven't found it" (52). However harsh those criticisms may seem, Solecki is at least right to note Purdy's unoriginality in those first four books: the humdrum image of "the road" in "Summons to Vagabonds" (*EE* 16) and the repetitive banality of an "unknown road" in "A Remembrance" (*EE* 33) are lifted right from Carman's *Songs from Vagabondia* (1894); Purdy's "rolling valleys" (*EE* 34) are Carman's "rolling valleys" (140); his "sanguine waves" ("Eccentricity" *EE* 20) are Shelley's "sanguine waves" ("Laon and Cythna" 214); and his "sturdy oaken door" ("Eccentricity" 20) is William Wymark Jacobs's "sturdy oaken door" (72).

Imitation and derivativeness persist in Purdy's volumes of the 1950s. The tone and diction of a poem such as "Seasonal Malady" (1955) sound vaguely like Carman-meets-Eliot-who-meets-Layton ("April has been feminine to my masculine mood" [line 1]), and most other poems in *Pressed on Sand* still present Carmanesque personas wandering and loving nature. Carman's presence is the most pronounced in these poems, but most of Purdy's early poems gesture to structures and tropes common to romantic poets: strict metres, inflexible poetic forms (sonnet, ballad, and so on), content relating to pastoralism, nostalgia, avian imagery, and elegiac ruminations on time and death. One could offer almost any individual poem in *The Enchanted Echo* and Purdy's collections from the 1950s as evidence. With few exceptions (only Louis MacKendrick's work on Purdy comes to mind),[3] most critics concur that Purdy's unyielding fidelity to a conventional, even stereotypical, romanticism greatly hindered his early career.

Nevertheless, I agree with D.M.R. Bentley when he argues that "Purdy's [romantic] poetics" was "a vehicle for the themes and characteristics that are writ larger in his more cockily performative later work" ("Unremembered" 42). As early as *The Enchanted Echo*, Purdy was exploring his romantic longing for the past, and that longing is present even in poems Purdy wrote near the end of his life. An early example of such writing is "Declaration of Faith" (*EE* 30):

He is not dead – I call to mind
His image crystal clear:
He is not dead – my eyes are blind,
And I refuse to hear.

Compare the soporific metre, rhyme, and imagery of this ballad from 1944 to one of Purdy's most evocative poems, published exactly fifty years later. In "On Being Human" (*NWS* 90–1), Purdy's persona recalls his mother's last words to him before her death. As she lay in the hospital, his face betrays his resentment at having had to make the long drive to visit her, and his mother sees it: "I thought you'd feel terrible," she says. He recalls that moment years later:

I remember those last words
before the fever took her mind
and the only good thing now
is thinking about those words
and she is instantly
restored to life
in my mind

Even though Purdy's romantic nostalgia is evident, it neither weighs down his poem with clunky sentimentality nor leads him to a voice chained to clichés. "On Being Human" possesses and maintains nuance: the enjambment of "restored to life / in my mind" undermines a brief moment of unequivocal necromancy in the first line with a cautious qualification in the second. His confession of having imagined his mother, rather than truly "restoring" her "to life," conveys more scepticism than the stern, undoubting "He is not dead" in "Declaration of Faith." This interplay between past and present pervades much of Purdy's mature writing. It is basic to his most popular poems (e.g., "The Country North of Belleville") and to his earlier poems, some of which he revised to fit more squarely within a modern poetics.

I therefore hesitate to agree with Solecki's claim that "one can't argue that [romantic poetry] significantly influence[s] Purdy's work after his first collection" (59). Much more survives from these collections than Solecki admits. Critics' frequent discussions of "meditation" (MacKendrick and York), "elegy" (Lalonde), lyricism (Davey, Solecki, and MacKendrick), and "nostalgia" (MacKendrick and Steffler) in

Purdy's poems about history point to strong romantic undercurrents even in his mature writing.

The radical change in Purdy's approach to these modes and topics took place during the six years leading up to *Poems for All the Annettes* (1962), which he regarded as a period of transition in his career: "My style of writing had taken a ninety-degree turn in the direction of – what? – modernism?" (*RBS* 176). Even a cursory glance at Solecki's diligently compiled appendix to *The Last Canadian Poet* (a catalogue of literary allusions in Purdy's poetry) shows just how dramatic this "ninety-degree turn" was: Solecki finds far fewer allusions to Carman and British or American romantics after 1960 and far more to Eliot, Lawrence, Layton, and Yeats. Purdy's intuitive invocation of "modernist" is admittedly hesitant, and yet his changed literary tastes and his increasingly intricate style justify the denomination.

But why would Purdy continue experimenting with lyric after "turning" to modernism, which, under Eliot's sway, was wary of the romanticism and overindulgent emotions associated with that mode? Why, in other words, write personally rather than impersonally? A partial explanation is Purdy's romantic reading, his inability to shrug off that literary influence in its entirety. Another reason, one I offered earlier, is his literary models. Solecki locates Purdy's model for a modern lyric in the poet's reading of D.H. Lawrence during the 1950s. Lawrence's poems taught Purdy to appreciate a more "complex" subjectivity (105), and their impact on Purdy is unquestionable: not only did Purdy co-edit (with Doug Beardsley) the reverent *No One Else Is Lawrence!* (1998), but Purdy's own lyric also often feels like an echo of Lawrence's deictic style. Take Lawrence's "The Wild Common" (1916): "I am here! I am here! screams the peewit; the may-blobs burst out in a laugh as they hear! / Here! flick the rabbits. Here!" (34). Now look for Lawrence's "I am here!" in Purdy's "Still Life in a Tent": "Here I am again / back from the court of the Seal-King / lying in bed with fever / and I'm so glad to be here ... / I'm so glad to be here" (*NOS* 49). The frightened-yet-jocular speaker of Lawrence's "Lui et Elle" (1921) similarly reads like a prototypical Purdy persona: "She has no qualm when she catches my finger in her steel overlapping gums, / But she hangs on, and my shout and my shrinking are nothing to her. / ... / Mistress, reptile mistress, / You are almost too large, I am almost frightened" (359). The lines parallel the visceral physical descriptions in many of Purdy's poems, as well as his tendency toward hyperbole in moments of even the most minor fear, as in "When I Sat Down to Play the Piano" (1967). Purdy's persona compares himself to famed and defeated leaders ("Leonidas," "Montcalm," "Custer") when he experiences what is, I would hope for most people, an unusual challenge: defecating outdoors while "a plague of dogs" threatens him (*NOS* 43). The tonal echo of Laurence is there.

Lawrence's influence is not just a matter of tone. Explicitly or implicitly, Purdy often alludes to Lawrence through poem titles ("Sons and Lovers," "Bestiary," "D.H. Lawrence at Lake Chapala," and "In Etruscan Tombs"), and his memoirs show just how mindful he was of Lawrence's impact on him: "[Lawrence's] *Birds, Beasts, and Flowers,*" he said, "actually changed the way I thought inside a poem" ("Disconnections" 215). Lawrence drove Purdy's creative growth, and the "change" to which Purdy alludes accounts for his internalization of what Marjorie Perloff calls Lawrence's "conversational, hectoring, nervous, energetic, funny, sardonic" lyricism ("Lyric Theater" 102). Such high regard for Lawrence is one of the major reasons Solecki says Purdy was always "[w]riting in Lawrence's shadow" (103).

At the same time, I agree with Frank Davey, if only to a point, when he says that "Solecki is overemphasizing this debt to Lawrence [over Irving Layton]" in order to exaggerate the "originality" of Purdy's contributions to Canadian writing ("Al Purdy" 50–1).[4] In Davey's thinking, Layton came first, and Purdy was the pupillary imitator, but it is unreasonable to assume that adopting lyric after Layton makes Purdy unoriginal. Influence never precludes innovation. Susan Stanford Friedman provides a more useful interpretation of influence: "Writers seldom duplicate their influential precursor(s); rather, they often work within a certain framework established by other writers or generic conventions, but vary aspects of it in significant ways" (155). Friedman's model is important because it allows writers to retain their distinctive beliefs and style in ways that Davey's concept does not. In the context of lyric historiography, this model is important to keep in mind: it proposes that writers of different political or social backgrounds can adopt and repurpose lyric historiography to serve their own ends. Indeed, many examples of lyric historiography in this book deviate dramatically from Purdy's model, even if they show signs of his influence. This will become increasingly evident in my later chapters.

With regard to Purdy specifically, both Davey and Solecki are right: Layton's presence lingers in Purdy's poetry of the late 1950s. At the same time, Davey is in error to assume that what comes after is straight derivation, and Solecki pays too little attention to what Layton gave Purdy beyond much-needed support. Layton participated in the reimagining of lyric voice, and Brian Trehearne's broadest account of his lyric development shows just how crucial was this literary effort: "The new speaking subject of modern poetry would have to stand proof against the complexes of experience that had shattered individuals like [A.M.]

Klein." For Layton, Klein demonstrated that "even the most robust and energetic personae will undergo centripetal social and historical pressures whose force is a continual challenge to identity and rectitude" (175). These qualities that Trehearne observes in Klein, as well as in Layton, offer ways of clearly distinguishing between the optimism and self-celebrating lyric of someone like Carman and the modernist lyric that displays and, in some cases, attempts to counter the anxieties of modern life.

Traces of the latter lyric figure prominently in Purdy's later writing in its references to personal inadequacy: "I'm a fool / of course a fool" ("Archaeology of Snow" *PAA* 16), "I can't think of anything more to say" ("The North West Passage" *NOS* 21), "I do not know very much" ("Over the Pacific" *WGW* 35), "my own Hour of Despond / when I've failed at everything" ("Old Man" *S&D* 34), and so on. Purdy's interpretation of a poet experiencing challenges and "pressures" born out of the "complexes of experience" is not identical to that of Layton or Klein, but his persona (at least in the excerpts above) is most definitely grappling with identity, confidence, and knowledge in ways that suggest the influence of modernism on his lyric.

Once Purdy outgrew the sentimental persona of his first four books and began experimenting with this kind of modernist lyric, his engagements with the past showed greater care in handling history through his "productive uncertainty," to return to Silverberg's term. And that uncertainty is a luxury that, even if intuitive to modernist writers, does not extend to historians: you cannot be an academic historian (not in the 1960s, anyway) and use uncertainty as the organizing principle of your work, because conservative historians, according to Robert Berkhofer, often strive to "justify" their "autonomy and authority" (227). Berkhofer regards this striving as basic to history, in which the seeding of doubt about the historian's authority risks weakening the boundary between expert and audience. In a poem, however, uncertainty is generative and compelling; it draws the reader away from prescriptive interpretations of (among other things) the past. Further, lyrics – in which the inner self is of primary importance to the poem – that *resist* closure also more realistically capture the imprecision of human thought. They demonstrate a process for thinking through an epistemological quandary and thus enact what Rita Felski calls "a 'truer' realism" exemplary of modernist writing, in which poems move "beyond the superficial stability of surface literary conventions" and show an awareness "that reality *is* fluidity, fragmentation, indeterminacy" ("Engendering Genre" 196).

Purdy began exploring this indeterminacy in his poems of the early 1960s, an exploration best exemplified by "Remains of an Indian

Village" (1961; *PAA* 57–8).[5] As a poem that questions the speaker's ability to recover and depict the past, "Remains" is a prototype for Purdy's mature historiographic writing. Solecki rightfully treats the poem as an experiment, an example of Purdy reimagining the ways in which "memory" and "history" might be captured in a modernist poem (162). Certainly, "Remains of an Indian Village" is the first of its kind in Purdy's corpus: a poem that offers an anchor for discussions of his lyric historiography and espouses a modernist aesthetic that makes this poem more complex (formally and epistemologically) than any of his earlier work. The poem gave both Purdy and the poets he influenced a model and language for thinking through the crisis of authority that comes from attempts to organize the past into a coherent narrative.

While the poem epitomizes Purdy's thematic sophistication after the 1950s, there is no question that "Remains of an Indian Village" also demonstrates his vastly improved technical skill. The middle section of the poem is representative and deserves extended quotation:

> Death is certainly absent now
> (death 'takes,' they say –
> implies: theft, cessation, annulments –
> leaves: the mechanical men unwound?) –
> and the birth certificate of cedars
> specifies no memory of a village...
>
> And I have seen myself fade
> from a woman's eyes
> while I was standing there
> and the earth was aware of
> me no longer –
> As I observe the wispy legs of children
> running in this green light from
>   a distant star
> into the near forest –
> wood violets and trilliums of
> a hundred years ago
> blooming and vanishing –

Here Purdy has obviously moved far beyond the conventional metres of *The Enchanted Echo* or the barely loosened half-rhyming ABAB quatrains of his 1950s volumes. Lines 12 to 17 sustain a casual tetrameter; lines 18 to 29, syllabically abbreviated as they are, aurally act out the "fading" he describes. I'm struck, too, by Purdy's ellipses. This technique recurs in his mature writing, and it often denotes contemplation and apprehension. Here, the ellipses signal a speaker who wanders through a hesitant, quasi-romantic meditation that sustains the vitality of the poem. The dashes delay or altogether resist closure, especially in the parentheses about death: Purdy's abrupt end stops enact the "implications" of death (namely, the "cessation" noted in line 14) that the speaker ponders. Form and content are beautifully co-dependent in this poem.

As a poem about history, "Remains" shows Purdy's willingness to accept indeterminacy as a condition of history. Look at his dashes in the above excerpts: like his ellipses, they underscore the fragmentation of both his poem and history. Optically, his dashes disconnect lines from one another. His dashes and ellipses make "Remains of an Indian Village" look like pieces bound together, but with meaningful spaces between them. There is, of course, the literal space created on the page. Implicit in such spaces, however, is a gap in knowledge, time, or narrative – suggestions of things that Purdy does not or cannot know. These aren't self-defeating gestures in the poem; they are merely challenges.

An important quality of "Remains of an Indian Village" is the speaker's acceptance of that challenge, his unrelenting effort to connect the past and present. That struggle is never quite resolved, only accepted and endured. That comes across, more than anywhere else, in the final ten lines of the poem:

> Standing knee-deep in the joined earth
> of their weightless bones,
> in the archaeological sunlight,
> the trembling voltage of summer,
> in the sunken reservoirs of rain,
> standing waist-deep in the criss-cross
> rivers of shadows,
> in the village of nightfall,
> the hunters silent and women
> bending over dark fires,
> I hear their broken consonants –

Perhaps the speaker's redeployment of the dash at the end of the poem intimates that his rumination goes unresolved and continues indefinitely. If this effect was the one Purdy desired, then that explains why he replaced the concluding dash with an ellipsis in the revised 1968 version; the edit is less brusque and takes away the feeling of having been interrupted or cut off from something.[6] The ellipsis at the end thus portrays more effectively an unabated meditation: just as the reader drifts into this meditative poem with ellipses in the earliest published version (the first line is "Underfoot rotten boards, forest rubble, bones ..."), the revised 1968 version keeps the reader drifting amid inconclusive thoughts.

"Remains" also enacts both the absence of a firm conclusion and the speaker's temporal uncertainty; he seems unsure of *when* he is. Purdy's participles are ambiguous: readers might understandably be confused by "standing" in line 40, which appears to modify the long-ago "hunters and silent women," though it actually modifies the contemporary "I." Not only do the present participles tempt the reader to conflate the speaker with his subjects, but they also imply the activeness of the dead, their existence even in the present. Such activity contrasts with the decaying images Purdy uses to begin his poem, scenes that depict "rotten boards," "rubble," and "bones." It is as if the past is reanimated by the poem's end. Yet Purdy's ending is also wrought with contradictions. The persona's powerful "standing," with its impression of authority, seems oddly ambivalent: Purdy juxtaposes images of "standing" with images of sinking or drowning as the reader plunges into the romantic metaphor of fluid time (the "rivers of shadows" mentioned above), which is presumably a descent into history. This psychological immersion conjures up images of *dead* "hunters" and "women" *actively* "bending over dark fires." This is the basic paradox of Purdy's poems about history: the past is alive and speaking to its observer, but it is also absent or at least elusive.

As Purdy negotiates this paradox in his poetry more generally, he tends to imagine the past both visually and aurally. That approach is standard in historiographic poems he wrote after 1960, and he explicitly describes it in "Method for Calling Up Ghosts" (1965). First, he speaks of his method visually: "Imagine [historical figures] as line drawings, / and at once they become visible again [...] this method must be used to think of them / or they disappear" (*CH* 111). Purdy explains the point more clearly in a later interview: "You can feel [...] this so-called transmigration of souls. I thought it was a fascinating concept to imagine everybody living to leave lines behind on the street where they've been in 'Method for Calling up Ghosts.' What it means is you're walking across the paths of the dead at all times. Every time you cross the St. Lawrence River you're crossing Champlain's path" (Purdy and Twigg 229–30). In that interview, Purdy visualizes the past: he *pictures* Champlain, describes an almost physical encounter, a "transmigration of souls" that gives the illusion of having yoked together an apparition of the past and the poet of the present.

But Purdy's idea of the past is more than an image; it is, too, what he calls a "recording" of "word[s]" that "exists in the main deep of sound" ("Method" *CH* 112). Hearing, as much as seeing, is important in Purdy's work, and his aural imagination speaks to the degree of intimacy for which he longs: he wants to hear the past, its irretrievable sounds that predate sound-recording technology. Sounds symbolize the loss to which all history gestures. Jonathan Sterne perfectly articulates this point: "Before the invention of sound-reproduction technologies [...] sound withered away. It existed only as it went out of existence. Once telephones, phonographs, and radios populated our world, sound had lost a little of its ephemeral character. The voice became a little more unmoored from the body, and people's ears could *take them into the past*" (1, emphasis added). Sounds, noises, all the audible waypoints of pre-sound-reproduction history cannot be dug up; they aren't bones or pottery or relics. They are lost and irretrievable vibrations. Even today, if we miss the opportunity to capture a sound, we likely want it back. When my wife's father died, she and I realized almost immediately that we had no record of his voice. No old tapes or videos. The two of us called his work phone that night, so we could hear him on the answering machine; that was the only way we could have him speak to us again in his distinctive, gravelly voice. The absence of a sound is a quiet and powerful reminder of loss. Purdy's desire to get closer to and hear something so absent as the past is a cornerstone of his lyric, and it is also arguably one the most human qualities of his writing.

Purdy hints at these trademarks in "Remains of an Indian Village." As the speaker tries to imagine the past aurally and visually, it moves in and out of visibility, because the "moon's waylaid light," "green light from / a distant star," and "fire" struggle to shine in spite of the "nightfall," "shadows," and the "dark[ness]" that hinder illumination. The speaker is also attempting to *hear* history: with only two full metrical feet (notably shorter than the rest of the poem) spread out across line 36 ("on the weightless bones"), the line itself feels "weightless" and skeletal. The faintly audible line parallels the indistinct echo of the "broken consonants" that he strains to hear at the end of the poem. These sections depict history vacillating between poles of audibility; the past is, as Purdy's speaker says in "Eskimo Graveyard" (1967), "neither wholly among the dead / nor quite gone from the living" (*NOS* 27). These are suggestions of Purdy's limits as an observer of the past, and he often concludes poems with signs of doubt to portray those limits on the page: interruptive dashes ("The Country North of Belleville," "Roblin's Mills," "Prince Edward County"), question marks ("My Grandfather Talking – 30 Years Ago," "Dead Seal"), or meditative ellipses ("Gilgamesh and

Friend," the 1968 version of "Remains of an Indian Village," "Lu Yu"). To conclude poems in these ways is to evoke ambiguity, an effect not unlike the "hesitancy and multiple possibility" that Linda Kinnahan notes in William Carlos Williams's use of dashes (28).

The implicit suggestion of such doubt is interestingly egalitarian. If a writer incorporates this scepticism about narrative finality into their writing, then they would have to concede the possibility of – to borrow Michel de Certeau's phrase – "an *infinite series of 'historical meanings'*" (*The Writing of History* 34). The past cannot be told just one way: it avails itself to other plausible interpretations. This possibility permeates the works of writers central in Purdy's modernist education, especially T.S. Eliot. Speaking on Eliot's work, Jeffrey M. Perl notes the potential for a fusion of historiographic philosophy and modernist aesthetics. Eliot is, Perl argues, *the* modernist sceptic. His consistent resistance to closure and self-questioning pursuit of deeper forms of knowledge generated sagacious, nuanced perceptions on, among other issues, the past: "History was not Eliot's genre, and should have been. For the main difficulty that historical work [...] raises is whether [...] an adequate modern history may be composed" (159). If a history inspires scepticism about its own "adequa[cy]," then how can historians elicit trust from their reader? It's a question Perl loosely proposes, but he decides against pursuing it much further because, as he notes, Eliot was not a historian. Even so, Perl's thought experiment is telling. Critics other than Perl have also noted Eliot's consistent "skeptic[ism] about positive knowledge of the past and of the self" (Riquelme 21) and his intense scrutiny of any belief claimed to be incontestable "knowledge" (Schüller 26), and these readings establish continuities in thought and aesthetics, even if not in content, between high modernists' scepticism and the work of later writers like Purdy, especially with regard to his historiographic poems.

The epistemological doubt underlying that questioning is made more acute in Purdy's poems by the fact that his speakers grapple with a past that is inconceivably long. After Darwin, the human measure of time became geologic – eons rather than millennia. When Clair Patterson determined the exact age of Earth in 1956, it was further proof of a sprawling geologic past. The *size* of the past therefore reminds Purdy of the potential distance between the past and present. Focusing on Purdy's geopoetic writing from the 1980s, Nicholas Bradley makes note of Purdy's occasionally "ludicrous" or "incongru[ous]" pairings of geologic and clock time (58). He tacitly attributes Purdy's complex temporal sense to the poet's interest in evolutionary theory, which his 1979–80 trip to the Galapagos Islands heightened (Purdy, *RBS* 262). But even in Purdy's writing of the early 1960s, there are traces of this grand vision of time. Purdy's opening lines to "Remains of an Indian Village" reveal what Whitworth calls "highly compressed metonymies" (*Modernist Poetry* 170): the brief catalogue of "rotten boards," "bones," and "rubble," and the poet's quick acknowledgment of "smallpox" and genocide compress centuries into just a few lines. His reduction of several generations to three lines seems jarring because it contrasts with the dozens of lines that focus on "here" (line 6) and "now" (line 12). These are Purdy's favourite words: together or separately, "here" and "now" appear throughout his poems as a way of temporally and spatially rooting his speaker in one moment and place.

Although I noted earlier its presence in Lawrence's poems, the "here and now" trope is actually a romantic one, as romantic poets often used locational titles to ground the lyric present, to help the reader see through the eye/I of the poet: Wordsworth's "London, 1802," Coleridge's "Lines Written at the King's Arms," Roberts's *The Tantramar Revisited*, and Carman's "Above the Gaspereau" are all examples of this implied "here and now." This trope is appropriate to Purdy's poems about history, because the present is the only time and place of which he can speak with any kind of authority. Hence the gravity of that moment, which leads Purdy's speaker in "Remains of an Indian Village" to focus so intently on his "here and now." In so doing, he exposes gaps in his knowledge: he may understand the present to one degree or another, but he seems painfully aware of how little he knows about what I assume to be the Gitxsan people.[7]

This points to a Purdyean persona's typical conundrum: he discovers historical fragments that inspire and push him to tell a story about the past, even though this historical narrative either becomes unsustainable or seems incomplete. Understandably, the experience frustrates Purdy's speakers. The concluding image of "Remains of an Indian Village," for example, reveals an overwhelmed speaker, a persona rapidly descending from a "knee-deep" position to a "waist-deep" one. He is figuratively immersed in and, as someone sinking or drowning, *threatened* by history. But even if this meditation is dangerously immersive, a philosophical quicksand, Purdy's speaker never advances beyond a "waist-deep" position. He is stuck in the interstice between the past and the present. It's a taunting image: he cannot experience the full threat of being swallowed by the past.

I imagine some might take that frustrating image as proof that Purdy sees history as a futile effort. And if so, then one could argue there is no purpose in pursuing the past. I wonder if this difficulty is what led writers like George Bowering to regard history as a site groomed for nihilistic play and imaginative fancy. In a poem about Louis Riel, Bowering says, "We need more doubts & fewer questions, no saints" ("Uncle Louis" 125; 1980);[8] in *Allophanes* (1976), he says, "history, its range adds to our being, / not our knowledge" (95). Questions are not worth asking, knowledge is unattainable; there is only doubt. While that attitude toward history may have satisfied Bowering, it was surely unacceptable to Purdy. In poems and essays written after 1960, Purdy never turns to either poststructuralist strategies or pyrrhonic rhetoric. Consider Purdy's edits on rough drafts of "Roblin's Mills [II]" (1968): his concluding line was originally "They had their meaning once / and left a place to stand on" ("Roblin's Mills [II]"), which Purdy later changed to "They had their *being* once / and left a place to stand on" (*WGW* 47, emphasis added). The change hints that he did not want readers to believe that "meaning" was *lost*. Displaced, perhaps – but not lost. There is meaning in the past – and, by implication, in historical writing – but that meaning is always mediated and thus only partially recoverable in the present. The absence of a stable chronicle is not necessarily justifiable grounds for abandoning the entire endeavour of questions and exploration. Purdy works under an assumption that runs counter to that of Bowering, as he believes that there *is* value in the literal and figurative fragments of the past available in such terrific abundance.

These are qualities of "Remains of an Indian Village" that establish it as a prototype for Purdy's later lyrics about the past: his struggles, his imperfect methods, and his destabilized grounding (geographically and temporally) are tethered to a flawed, inquisitive, and doubting "I" enamoured of exploration and sceptical about the integrity of narratives. Like many of Purdy's critics, I read this subjectivity as a vulnerable "I," a characteristic that becomes increasingly obvious as Purdy gets older and this motif becomes habit. More and more, as he fine-tunes a standard persona over the course of his career, he comfortably regards himself, in one form or another, as "a cosmic triviality" ("Bearpaw Sea" [1973] *BR* 187). These are paradoxically authoritative claims for a *lack* of authority, a scepticism about both his own abilities and the coherence of the past, a technique that bears traces of his modernist education.

Although "Remains of an Indian Village" was certainly an important symbol of Purdy's growth, it was not the only poem about history in *Poems for All the Annettes*; "On Canadian Identity" (*PAA* 47–8) is, at the very least, thematically related to "Remains of an Indian Village." If one reads Purdy's later historiographic writing, two tactics are commonplace: the naming of places (his late incantatory poem "Say the Names" is an obvious example) and the recurring use of "ghosts," either as a word or poetic image (one can find dozens of examples across

Purdy's corpus up to and including his preface to *Beyond Remembering*, in which he says he is "left alone to talk with a bunch of ghosts"[21]). In "Remains," however, the "Indian village" is unnamed and historical "ghosts" are absent. "On Canadian Identity" anticipates these changes in his writing. The poem is oddly polemical in its insistent opening:

> Names if you like:
> Illecillewaet and Medicine Hat,
> Winnipeg's prairie sound –
> the whoop and holler of Calgary,
> Gun-a-noot's stammering outlawry,
> the small wooded province Newfoundland –
> But I live in an apt. in Côte des Neiges
> (I like the slur and whisper of that)
> in time and space and a town –
>
> History if you like:
> Verendrye-Moses glimpsing something wonderful,
> mountains in the sky he thought were legendary;
> Riel's pitiful, insular, Métis kingdom;
> the socialist rebellion of '37 [...]

More than "Remains of an Indian Village" – which at least extends *some* motifs common to Purdy's early work – "On Canadian Identity" appears entirely out of place in *Poems for All the Annettes*. Its impetuousness and urgency bear little resemblance to the rest of the book, which features amusing philosophical poems ("Archaeology of Snow" and "Mind Process re a Faucet"), pastoral poems ("Rural Henhouse at Night"), and poems that consider more domestic issues ("The Quarrel" and "Indian Summer"). Unlike many of these poems, "On Canadian Identity" is also rather bland and didactic. The characterizations are reductive – especially the description of Louis Riel. There is little to say about the message of the poem that Solecki doesn't say in *The Last Canadian Poet*: "What the poem hints at on the level of content is the comprehensiveness, at least as far as Canada is concerned, of Purdy's [historical] vision" (43). "On Canadian Identity" signals Purdy's passion for Canadian history, yes; but the content and style are (and with this Solecki agrees) dull.

The greater significance of "On Canadian Identity" is that it foretells important changes in the content of Purdy's post-1960 writing. The poem could have been and quite likely was a late addition to *Poems for All the Annettes*.[9] The diction and message of the poem descend directly from an essay Purdy wrote, but never published, in January or February 1962.[10] Titled "The New Poetry and the Old," the essay criticizes "older poets" for their supposed inattentiveness to history: "Some [of the older Canadian poets] talk of this country as if it were a mean, backward place, empty of heroes and sparsely settled with small inferior citizens. And with these I do not agree. Others speak as if Canada, the land and its people, had some of the invisible elements of greatness [...] they map out the country of the future" (n.p.). His note regarding Canada's ignored "heroes" calls to mind lines from "On Canadian Identity," in which the speaker laments, "all our heroes stayed dead." Moreover, Purdy's compulsive and terse cataloguing of historical events and "names" in the poem certainly expresses a frustration equivalent to that voiced in "The New Poetry and the Old." It seems plausible that Purdy's essay was a mock-up for ideas he would express more cogently, if flatly, in "On Canadian Identity." The link would explain the poem's prosaic style and, in the context of *Poems for All the Annettes*, incongruousness.

I am also tempted to think of Purdy's unpublished essay as a direct response to Earle Birney's final lines in "Canadian Literature" (later titled "Can. Lit."):[11] "It's only by our lack of ghosts we're haunted" (14).[12] Birney's poem first appeared in *Delta*'s January 1962 issue, a journal with which Purdy was involved, and the unpublished essay was written shortly thereafter.[13] The possibility that he read Birney's poem upon publication explains his otherwise baffling whim in that essay to critique older poets' (he specifically names Birney) inattention to history. That critique seems to have made its way into "On Canadian Identity," a poem that includes lines from Birney's "Canada: Case History" (a 1945 poem published in 1948's *The Strait of Anian*, chosen in place of "Canadian Literature," perhaps because it would surely have been better known to a 1962 audience). Purdy's contemptuous nod to Birney's quips about Canada's "high school land" and "dull people" evidently extends his irritation with Birney in "The New Poetry and the Old."

However strong this specific link, there is nevertheless an obvious change in Purdy's poetry after 1962: "poems dealing with naming and with Canadian places," Solecki notices, "are conspicuous by their absence in [Purdy's] first four books" (167). The significance of 1962 therefore rests on more than just the publication of Purdy's breakthrough collection *Poems for All the Annettes*: Purdy's fascination with memory and time is partly rooted in his romantic literary tastes, whereas his more engaged ruminations on Canadian history as of that year appear to stem from evident frustrations that culminated in what he perceived to be, rightly or wrongly, an inattentiveness to history in earlier

Canadian writing. The poems in that book are early evidence in Canadian poetry that modern scepticism and the modern lyric mode could yield a sophisticated engagement with the past.

After 1962, the features of "Remains of an Indian Village" and "On Canadian Identity" discussed above became typical of Purdy's poetry. His writing after *Poems for All the Annettes* obsessively lists historical figures, events, and eras. Place names, too: every single poem in *North of Summer* concludes by naming the location at which Purdy composed it. Also after 1962, Purdy incessantly uses the word "ghost" in poems, essays, prefaces, and book reviews. It would be a remarkable coincidence if the habit had nothing to do with his reading of Birney's "Canadian Literature" in 1962. The word occurs a handful of times in Purdy's first four books (only once, for example, in each of *Pressed on Sand* ["Seasonal Malady"] and *The Enchanted Echo* ["The Sprite"]), but it appears with astonishing regularity after Birney's "Canadian Literature" was published. The regular presence of the word in Purdy's writing – it appears even in poems ("Her Gates Both East and West")[14] and prose ("Preface") he wrote the year of his death – points to the seriousness with which he detested the concept of a Canada that "lacks" "ghosts."

"Remains of an Indian Village" and "On Canadian Identity" are therefore important pivots in Purdy's career. Both speak to aesthetic, historical, and philosophical interests that were, as of 1962, still incipient and spurring new thoughts about what history might mean to the present – thoughts that would become increasingly important to Purdy's generation as debates about Canadian identity entered and disrupted mainstream media during the 1960s and thereafter. Even if mere prototypes, both poems are entry points into a deeper discussion of what I call "lyric historiography": poetry sceptical about the truth and authority of any representation of all history. The poems that came after these prototypes represent Purdy's sustained effort to refine this lyric historiography, to develop it and affirm it as foundational to his mature style, and to share it with a younger generation of writers.

2 Developing a Lyric Historiography

After 1962, Al Purdy continued to modernize his lyric, emphasizing still the historical intrigue and scepticism one finds in *Poems for All the Annettes*. The persona he developed during this period exhibits several consistent traits related to those explored in my last chapter: an introspective scepticism about any essentialist reading of the past (even his own), a resistance to narrative closure, a recognition of his own limits as a "historian" rummaging through historical fragments, and an awareness of the temporal distance between "now" and "then." Purdy's typical persona therefore cannot find the confidence to write a full history; he instead contemplates or demonstrates the difficulty of doing so.

Purdy had ample opportunities to refine this persona: more than half of his entire corpus was published between 1965 and 1979. Many of the poems published during those years foreground historical content. There are few satisfactory explanations for why this might be; Earle Birney's impact on Purdy's poetics, which I discussed in my last chapter, only partially explains his obvious enthralment with historiographic poetry throughout this period of his career. Purdy's developing ideas of nationalism and leftism, his historical reading, and his funding and travel opportunities granted by the Canada Council all nurtured his already strong urge to develop a lyric historiography.

That Purdy's abundance of historiographic poems is due at least in part to his developing nationalism during this era is unquestionable, but it is difficult to argue what "nationalism" specifically meant to him. In his prose, Purdy is as likely to speak romantically of Canada's "invisible greatness" as to sombrely confront the reality of a "broken calm," "the internal contradictions" of the "nations [Canada] contains" ("Cartography" 18). Even his pluralization of "nation" in that 1971 phrase shows that Purdy understood he was living during a period of social and cultural turmoil, an era in which a number of "nationalisms" were established: the Quiet Revolution articulated Quebec nationalism in the 1960s (Purdy, in fact, wrote "The Peaceable Kingdom" to elegize his youthful nationalism after Pierre Laporte's death) and the "Red Power" movement laid a foundation for new dialogues about First Nations in the 1980s. The rise of the New Left most definitely influenced Purdy, too. When the New Democratic Party formed in 1961 (replacing the Co-operative Commonwealth Federation [CCF]), he instantly identified with its political goals. In a 1974 letter to Milton Acorn, he said, "I write in my own way toward a society that will probably not come in my lifetime, perhaps never. I regard myself as being a man of the left, with the NDP in this country as my hoped vehicle toward that end." The "end" to which Purdy refers is "a world community" that acknowledges, accepts, and internalizes an openness to cultural difference (Purdy to Acorn).

Purdy's utopian ideal may have roots in the stated philosophies of the New Left, because the formation of that political movement was partly an effort on behalf of Canadian leftists to move away from the rhetoric of class struggle and toward a broader desire to "equalize life opportunities for all" (McKay 180). The NDP wanted to "rewrite Canadian nationalism" (181): the CCF's early enlistment of the proletariat evolved into the NDP's reaching out to *any* marginalized ethnic, cultural, or economic group. That shift appeased a number of CCF advocates, among them Ukrainians and Jews, who had themselves experienced cultural and historical marginalization. With the formation of the NDP, socialist groups were becoming "less likely to focus primarily on the exploitation of the working class." By then, as Ian MacKay argues, "the left's critical vision ranged from the oppressive world of the family [...] to the power of 'race' as a source of oppression." The "older languages of socialism were still at work," but "they were now functioning in a different way" (183–4). Coming from a working-class background and living in poverty for much of his life, Purdy comfortably leaned left (he attributed his leftism partly to his witnessing of a union drive in 1954 while working at Vancouver Bedding [*RBS* 140]). Even a cursory reading of New Left literature would have shown Purdy the rapidly evolving pluralist ideals of the NDP, which may explain why he hesitated to define his nationalism too concretely. He once told Birney that nationalism "includ[ed] a lot of things for [him]" (Purdy to Birney [1969]), and, around the same time, he described it as a response to history's constant state of "flux" ("Introduction" iii). Several years later, he defined nationalism as "a consciousness of self as the last link in a long line of selves, a knowledge of what those others did in the past before the present self fades and rejoins the past" ("Norma" 95). Purdy was deliberately vague, but he firmly and consistently maintained that nationalism, as he understood it, inspired his personal investment in history as a series of evolving gestures toward a better future.

That nationalism was further sustained by Purdy's voracious and wide reading of Canadian history. Purdy noted that his historiographic poetry put history "in [his] own words instead of using the words of the books [he] read" (Purdy and O'Brien 148). He read widely. In the Queen's University Purdy Fonds, there are dozens of Purdy's requests for histories such as Hubert Howe Bancroft's *History of British Columbia* (1887) and *History of the Northwest Coast* (1884), as well as numerous exploration texts. He also requested more contemporary texts and corresponded with their authors; he purchased Helge Ingstad's *Land Under the Pole Star* (1966) the year that it was published, and then contacted Ingstad with questions about the history of Newfoundland's L'Anse aux Meadows.[1] At least two directly related poems came thereafter: "The Runners" (a poem about Leif Erikson, the eleventh-century Viking explorer) and "Over the Hills in the Rain, My Dear" (a loose meditation on the history of L'Anse aux Meadows), both published in *Wild Grape Wine* (1968). Numerous histories were source texts for Purdy's poetry: he read George Best's *The Three Voyages of Martin Frobisher* (1867), Luke Fox's *North-West Fox: Or, Fox from the North West Passage* (1635, rpt 1965), C.F. Hall's *Life with the Esquimaux* (1864), and Sir John Ross's *Narrative of a Second Voyage in Search of a North-West Passage* (1835) before writing two poems titled "The North West Passage" (published separately in 1967 and 1968); the quick mention of Frobisher's "Buttocke" hit by "an Arrowe" in the 1967 poem is an exact quotation from Best's book (131).[2] His historical reading spurred his historiographic writing.

It is unlikely, though, that Purdy could have ever written about such diverse historical topics without the funding he received from the Canada Council for the Arts (CCA; est. 1957). He was living in an era of unprecedented financial opportunities for writers. In the service of a narrowly conceived concept of "national unity," the government prioritized its encouragement of cultural work through the founding of the CCA. Over the course of his career, Purdy's numerous CCA grants facilitated his physical presence in a wide-ranging geography. Such mobility is integral to every one of his major poems. Of course, Purdy already knew the area around his birthplace – Wooler, Ontario – well enough to write his early historiographic poems, such as "Roblin's Mills." But as he obtained more funding in the 1960s, his historiographic and geographic perspective broadened beyond Ontarian events and figures. Western Canadian poems such as "The Cariboo Horses" appeared after he received CCA funding and travelled west in 1960 (*RBS* 174), as did an unpublished manuscript on Haida culture;[3] Maritime poems such as "The Runners" appeared after he visited Newfoundland in "the late 1960s" (*RBS* 238); and poems about the North appeared after his CCA-funded visit to Baffin Island in 1965. Transience kept him writing. A revealing case is Purdy's writing of "D.H. Lawrence at Lake Chapala" (1981). He visited Lake Chapala roughly two years before he published this poem and wrote to Birney, "You're probably aware that: D.H. Lawrence lived in Chapala for two months in 1923. Went down and took a look at the house, a peeling yellow-stucco two-storey place, with a large section of coloured tiles depicting a plumed serpent, the only trace of Lawrence evident. I wrote a coupla poems, which I'm still working on, one of which might turn out to be something" (Purdy to Birney [1979]). In order for D.H. Lawrence to be "at Lake Chapala," it seems Al Purdy had to have been there, too.

Purdy knew it was important to be mobile. He wrote to Margaret Atwood in 1970, "[I] [e]xpect to get some money from Ont. Arts Council for next summer. Also hope to go to Hiroshima, which may seem unusual to you. Does it? But I can anticipate some of the feelings I'd have there, can half-write some poems now, something of the same way I felt before going to the arctic ... In my mind, I label it the big thing, the place that unites feeling and words etc ..." (Purdy to Atwood [Oct. 1970]). He published an entire volume, *Hiroshima Poems*, in 1972. Purdy was not the only writer who felt compelled to experience the places in which historical events occurred. E.J. Pratt "conceived the idea of writing a verse epic on Sir John Franklin's ill-fated 1845 expedition in search of the Northwest Passage" in 1933, but never wrote it. "[T]here was an insuperable obstacle in the way of this poet," Janice Cavell explains: "he had no direct personal experience of the Arctic" (7). In Cavell's reading, the intimacy of "direct personal experience" informs history, and in the absence of such intimacy, Pratt apparently felt incapable of writing the grand epic of the North that he had imagined.[4] His example invites a larger claim: a writer's geographic context determines their critical perspective on the past. This has been of particular concern to historians, who worked within a pseudo-Ptolemaic model of Canada in which Toronto was the centre for academic training, publishing, and critical perspective. Ramsay Cook wrote disparagingly of this fact: "For the health of Canadian historical writing," he said in 1968, "Toronto's monopoly [as a centre of historiographic training and perspectives] must be broken" ("Good-Bye" 277). However much the content of history was changing in the late 1960s, it was still being read through the lens of a Toronto-centric eye.

A poet like Purdy, however, was not so rooted in the years after the CCA was founded: his life at times seemed one of drifting bohemianism. Mobility made the past seem dynamic and novel to him, as sites of historical significance heightened his curiosity and broadened his perspectives. This is one of many reasons he saw this era of his life as one of creative opportunity: "From 1965 on, life opened up for me. At that time it became entirely feasible for me to go anywhere on earth [because of the Canada Council] and to write about it. I was also confident that I would write 'well'" (*RBS* 190).

The discovery of a newfound confidence, diverse histories, and unique geographies helped Purdy write, but a poet needs a public to make an impact. E.K. Brown put that point rather well in *On Canadian Poetry* (1943), noting that "the stimulus" of "the single man of genius" could only be a "passing stimulus, unless it were assisted by social conditions friendly to creative composition" (26–7). Purdy's writing about Canadian history was most prolific between 1962 and 1974; what occurred in public discourses surely confirmed for him the importance of his project. After the founding of the CCA, cultural workers began paying much greater attention to Canadian history and art outside of Ontario and Quebec. This was an era in which the Atlantic provinces, prairie provinces, and the "North" became, for the first time in mainstream Canadian history, legitimate topics of study. For some commentators, this was also an era in which the country was, as the historian Julian Park would put it in 1957, "emerg[ing] from the old colonialism" and thus discovering itself on its own terms (v). Park was writing in the same year that that the CCA was formed, which shows just how tremendous an impact that institution (and, relatedly, the Massey Commission and its Quebec counterpart, the Tremblay Commission) had on the optimism of Canadian nationalists.[5] The existence of these institutions and reports implied that a thorough exploration of Canadian culture was an expectation and an apparent necessity in postwar Canada.

More than that, that exploration was becoming institutional policy. This was an excitable cultural climate that earned Canadian writers a much broader audience than ever before. The public *wanted* to read Canadian writers: it was "the willingness of Canadians to buy books written in the country that produced [...] commercial success[es]" (Finkel 174). "Bookstores," W.H. New writes, "began to stock Canadian books; people read them" (203). It was more than their books, though: in an era of well-funded arts initiatives, creative writers could publish in almost any popular or independent forum available to them. Until the late 1950s, Purdy published primarily in the *Canadian Forum* and *Canadian Poetry Magazine*, at which point new publications sprung up and he began appearing in a more eclectic selection of periodicals: *Delta, Yes*, the *Globe and Mail Weekend Magazine, Maclean's Magazine*, the *Tamarack Review, Evidence, Prism International*, and the *Wascana Review*. George Woodcock was not exaggerating when he said that the "increasing numbers of magazines and presses" and the "upsurge in poetry readings" across the country were putting an "end to the sense of isolation" that affected "so many Canadian writers in the past" ("Poetry" 293). Purdy – like numerous other poets such as Barry McKinnon, John Newlove, and Margaret Atwood – also gave interviews and read poetry on CBC Television and CBC Radio numerous times throughout his career. Tape recordings of poets were sold commercially; CBC's radio show *Anthology* had poets reading on air. For the first time in Canadian history, poets were, as Margaret Prang said admiringly – maybe even enviously – in her 1977 address to the Canadian Historical Association, "enjoy[ing] a reading audience extending across the country" (8).

Purdy's hold over that audience was publicly confirmed when he won his first Governor General's Award for *The Cariboo Horses* (1965), which is a book that attests to his conscious building on earlier historiographic lyrics. Whereas *Poems for All the Annettes* has only two historically themed poems, *The Cariboo Horses* is filled with them. "Music on a Tombstone" (1965; *CH* 16), for instance, is one of several other poems that contribute to Purdy's "history" of the Roblin family in *The Cariboo Horses*. The poem feels like a logical continuation of the scepticism and historiographic intrigue that Purdy experimented with in *Poems for All the Annettes*. He concludes the poem with a note in prose:

> Note: Owen Roblin was born in 1806, died 1903. He built his gristmill and octagonal house in 1842, and the village of Roblin's Mills (now Ameliasburg) came into being. In 1914 one of old Owen's descendants rented the mill to a man named Taylor from Belleville, and Taylor prospered under this rental agreement. Then Will Roblin demanded a share in the profits. Taylor refused, and walked out. The mill never operated again, and the village declined –

Purdy's tedious collection of names and dates replicates the unfortunate flatness of "On Canadian Identity" that I noted in my last chapter. This poem, however, has superior nuance: "Note," for example, can be read as either a noun or an imperative verb. As a noun that appears to signal an explanatory footnote, the word obscures the lyric speaker and denotes instead the objectivity of an impersonal historical text. As a verb, though, "note" implies the intimate relationship between a lyric writer and his audience; the structure highlights an underlying subjectivity in the poem, as does the mention of a speaker grounded in the "now." And even if this "I" provides an apparently confident historical outline, Purdy's poem still ends with his inconclusive dash, which establishes a fruitful contradiction in the text: the last image of "decline" contrasts with the present-tense "now" (an image of a living township) that appears just a few lines earlier. There are obviously pieces missing from this narrative: the village *was* in decline, but it apparently survived to become "Ameliasburg." Whatever occurred in between these events is left unsaid. Although not a particularly compelling example, the poem is critically useful. It offers brief glimpses of Purdy's further experiments with a modernist style that resists closure and foregrounds his limited historical perspective.

More than "Music on a Tombstone," "Roblin's Mills" (*CH* 70–1) typifies much of Purdy's historiographic writing from and after *The Cariboo Horses*. Most vivid is Purdy's more intricate rendering of the relation of past and present in the poem. His recurring burial images emphasize the past as "dead," but the present-tense verbs suggest it is also paradoxically alive: in "the valley graveyard," "maybe the earliest settlers / some stern Martha or speechless Joseph / perhaps meet and mingle / 1 000 feet down –." Nevertheless, it is the image of death, rather than of life, that persists in the poem. The repetition of "down" continually evokes "burial": "The mill was torn down," "their bodies / a little deeper down," and "1 000 feet down." As the past appears "buried" in "Roblin's Mills," the speaker can only imagine Owen Roblin's era from the vantage point of the present. But he struggles to do so:

> the lighting Alters[6]
> and you can see
> how a bald man [Taylor] stood
> sturdily indignant
> and spat on the floor
> and stamped away so hard the flour
> dust floated out from his clothes
> like a white nimbus round his body
> beneath the red scorn –

The speaker attempts to go back (as several lines themselves move back) to the past, but he is continually pulled forward with other lines, as if pulled forward through time and into the present. Alternatively, the arrangement of the verse could simply suggest distortion: the fractured arrangement of the story, like the fickle light source, makes history difficult "to see" (the broken lines further undermining the speaker's feeling that the past can be clearly apprehended) and to "align." Both interpretations suggest that the persona's position in the present distorts his rendering of the past. Significantly, the image that follows this visual distortion is a rather ghostly one: a "nimbus" encircles Taylor. The subtle example of Purdy's "ghost" motif in his post-1962 writing is made more explicit in his 1972 version, which describes a "*ghostly* nimbus" (*Selected Poems* 35, emphasis added). And once Taylor-the-man becomes Taylor-the-ghost, the scene begins to collapse: time accelerates as the speaker leads the reader to the image of burial that lingers in "beneath," at which point an interruptive dash heralds an impasse in the speaker's historical imagination. Both the awkward temporal structure and aposiopetic impasse suggest that the persona can discern a reasonably coherent picture only of the present, and, stuck in the present as he is, his historical vision is faulty and his scepticism is deepened.

The actual content of the poem makes Purdy's scepticism more explicit, because it emphasizes the distance between past and present. The speaker's reflection on the "old ones" highlights this distance:

> Those old ones
> you can hear them on a rural party line
> sometimes
> when the copper wires
> sing before the number is dialed and
> then your own words stall some distance
> from the house you said them in
> lost in the 4th concession
> or dimension of whatever
> a lump in your throat
> an adam's apple
> half a mile down the road
> permits their voices
> to float by
> on the party line sometimes
> and you hang up then
> so long now –

Feelings of disconnection pervade these lines. Purdy's speaker narrates only the unavailability of the past, instead of an authoritative vision of it. The degree to which history appears unavailable in this poem varies. Like the speaker who hears hunters' and women's "broken consonants" in "Remains of an Indian Village," the persona here imagines history as vaguely audible to whoever listens to its "voices." But he cannot *always* hear those voices; he can only hear them "*sometimes*." His repetition of that word reinforces the tentativeness of these voices and, perhaps, even raises questions about the availability of these sounds: can these voices *really* be heard? Perhaps not, because the juxtaposed line endings, "then" and "now," are significantly set apart, kept on separate lines and out of alignment on the page. The arrangement, like the tentativeness with which the speaker listens to the past, is a symbolic rift between past and present that exposes the persona's folly: he imagines his connection to those voices, to "then," but he is rooted too firmly in the "now" to convince the reader of that connection. The scene thus culminates in the poem's ominous final line: "so long" denotes departure ("goodbye") but it also connotes time ("so long ago"), and both readings indicate that the past is hardly more than a vague echo or impression, something that is paradoxically with us and left behind.

Purdy's abstruse dash concretizes such uncertainty. The dash could signify the click of a caller hanging up, the speaker's hesitation (his hesitation *to* hang up?), or, more broadly, his realization that his negotiation of "now" and "then" is irresolvable and must be left indeterminately interrupted at the exact moment in which the voices "float by." It is a moment of uncertainty, an impasse in the speaker's imagining of history that offers evidence of the fact that "Roblin's Mills," like *The Cariboo Horses* as a whole, illustrates Purdy's conscious effort after 1962 to sharpen the complex aesthetics of "Remains of an Indian Village" and reconcile them with the nomenclatural and ghostly fascinations he first articulated in "On Canadian Identity." "Roblin's Mills" shows a poet honing his sceptical expressions of his historical consciousness and, in the process, foregrounding the poet's struggle to present an authoritative narrative of the Canadian past.

Over the 1960s, Purdy steadily increased his output of historically conscious poems; the sheer abundance of them in *North of Summer* (1967) proves just how important this project was to him by the end of that decade, and these poems of the late 1960s have common threads that distinguish them from poems in Purdy's earlier collections: a more prominently featured lyric "I," an intensified obsession with fragments, and a greater attentiveness to the difficulty of history. In "Tent Rings" (*NOS* 68–9) Purdy's speaker explores "an island in the Kikastan group," upon which Purdy's speaker finds artefacts "placed there long ago / to hold down the skirts / of caribou skin tents." The tent rings can be found "[a]ll over the Arctic" and they reveal the existence of "sparkling ghosts." That the speaker observing these fragments perceives some bygone era is unquestionable: he mingles "with the past," encounters "two places" at once, has the experience of "seeing visions" and "hearing voices" that drive him to "madness." All of these features are consistent with the collapse between past and present, the visual and aural rendering of history, and the present participles common to Purdy's earlier writing. But in this poem, Purdy presents the possibility that this experience never actually occurs. To be sure, the speaker's fear or suspicion that history is his own "mad" hallucination complements the generally apprehensive persona in "Roblin's Mills," who appears uncertain if the dead "voices" really do "float by / on the party line." In "Tent Rings," however, the threat of "madness" heightens the speaker's uncertainty about what he observes and experiences. This uncertainty pervades the poem, as he finds "granite" that was "arranged here fifty years ago / or several thousand." Purdy's enjambed qualification emphasizes the persona's somewhat inept attempts to make definite assessments of history. That moment is a reminder of an intricate balancing act in Purdy's poems: his profound respect for the past and his sincere, sometimes comical, struggle to write reliable history.

For me it is that struggle, more than the humour, that sticks with the reader. Purdy wants his reader to appreciate his difficulty, and one straightforward example of this is his decision to reserve entire lines for temporal markers. In "Tent Rings," for instance, he reserves a line for "fifty years ago" and another for "several thousand" years. He often assigns this special gravity to time, as though he is asking the reader to think deeply and only, in the moment of the line, on the distance between the past and the present: he sets aside entire lines for "5,000 years ago" ("Innuit" *NOS* 32), "a hundred years ago" ("Remains of an Indian Village" *PAA* 57), and "from a distance of at least / fifty years ago" ("Iguana" *BATE* 17). Note the last example: that word, "distance," and the way in which the meaning of that word is reinforced by a brief temporal measurement in the brusque line that follows. Purdy's terse lineation underscores for the reader that the past lives at a distance from us, so far in fact that it can feel dead even to a sensitive and historically conscious poet.

Distance is indeed a preoccupation in Purdy's writing. He is particularly baffled and perturbed by the gulf between past and present. As I remarked in my introduction to this book, twentieth-century historians traditionally valued and taught respect for distance. It may seem counterintuitive to imagine, as Purdy does, that distance *obscures* the past, given that (as I noted in my introduction) conservative historians tend to argue that distance ensures a clarifying, disinterested eye. But that counterintuitive premise is one implication of Purdy's emphasis on time in those separated lines; he stresses how far away he is from what he observes, and thus he counters and questions every historiographic certainty and claim to authority, including his own.

Still, Purdy often imagines what it would be like to be closer to the past. "The North West Passage" (*NOS* 20–1) features a persona who, if more comical than the speaker in "Tent Rings," struggles to overcome temporal distance. The poem – which details the speaker's figurative search for Sir John Franklin's lost nineteenth-century ships, *Terror* and *Erebus* – primarily ruminates on the speaker's inability to engage with the past:

The North West Passage is found
and poor old Lady Franklin well
she doesn't answer the phone
tho once she traded her tears for ships
to scour the Arctic sea for her husband
but the *Terror* and *Erebus* sank long ago
and it's still half an hour before dinner
and there isn't much to do but write letters
and I can't think of anything more to say
about the North West Passage
but I'll think of something
maybe
a break-thru
to strawberries and ice cream for dinner

Roughly fifty lines before this excerpt, it is "two hours until dinner," and in the passage above, the speaker appears to write for an additional "half an hour" until he arrives at dessert. But nothing has happened over that nearly three-hour period. The past, like Franklin's ships, is unreachable. Lady Franklin won't "answer the phone," and the story the persona seeks happened so "long ago" that he speaks lackadaisically about what he will do next as part of his search: "write letters" and "think of something" to say. His decision to mail a letter suggests he has mistaken a temporal distance for a geographic one; phones and letters can alleviate the latter, but time is insurmountable. His compulsion to qualify "I'll think of something" with "maybe" inspires little confidence that any epiphany about the past will arrive; the past is simply too far away, "too close to hell," the speaker says earlier in the poem. He wastes time. He achieves neither history nor even dinner, and instead of a "breakthrough," he *breaks "thru"* dinner to find only a consolatory dessert that serves as an unhealthy substitute for the symbolic meal that would have satiated his hunger. The unresolved meditation that parallels his unfulfilling meal is the kind of impasse one finds in poems such as "Roblin's Mills." His imagination is halted. He cannot "think of anything more to say."

That stymied imagination is not always a feature of Purdy's lyric historiography. "Lament for the Dorsets" (1968; *WGW* 54–5) is a much more creative attempt to transcend an epistemological impasse:

> – they have never imagined us in their future
> how could we imagine them in the past
> squatting among the moving glaciers
> six hundred years ago
> with glowing lamps?

Even in the process of asking *how* such an irretrievable history could ever be conjured up, the speaker "imagines" the Dorsets "squatting" "with glowing lamps." The poem is predicated more than anything else on this imaginative act, which gives way to assumptions and unlikelihoods. For example, the persona imagines a Dorset artist figure (Kudluk) in an apparent act of self-projection; only by finding himself can he conjure up the past. This kind of mirroring isn't uncommon in Purdy's corpus; in "The North West Passage," Martin Frobisher misses "tea," just as the speaker misses dinner. There are also inconsistencies in the poem's logic: the persona imagines near the end of the poem that Kudluk's "lame leg" was "chewed" by a bear, which contradicts the description of the Dorsets as "terrifying old men / so large they *broke the backs of bears* / so small they lurk behind bone rafters" (emphasis added). The perfect alignment of "so large" and "so small" on the page already seems incongruous, and Kudluk's defeat is further evidence that the persona either imagines Kudluk unrealistically (within the logic of the poem, that is) or erroneously estimates the strength of the Dorsets – in fact, both are probably fair conclusions to draw. But however one interprets the specifics of this poem, the narrative missteps are indications that the persona's desire to connect with or authentically represent the past is inevitably accompanied by a painful realization that he cannot fulfil that desire without injecting himself or his assumptions and self-contradictions into the text.

These poems establish more than Purdy's persona; they also establish his aesthetic as one of accumulation. To argue that Purdy adopts a model of "accumulation" seems reasonable, because he was, in the mid-to-late 1950s, discovering poets (such as Ezra Pound) who did so in their imagist writing. In the Anglo-American tradition, accumulation is typically marked by a seemingly random accrual of poetic images that underscore the fragmentary quality of the modernist mind, world, and poem. John T. Gage says that imagist poetry is predicated on this paratactic strategy: the "accumulative effect of the whole [poem]" depends on a lack of expectation, a lack of "proper relation" between individual sequences of images. "Accumulative structure predominates in imagist poetry," Gage writes (109). There are Canadian examples of this aesthetic that Purdy would have encountered; P.K. Page's poetry is an exemplary case of a post-imagist "aesthetics of accumulation" in which the poet "adduces imagistic fragments" and "attempt[s] their integration," even if this attempt leads only to tenuous connections between images (Trehearne 78).

Purdy's "Prince Edward County" (1977; *HOE* 59–60) is a helpful example. His anaphoric conjunctions draw special attention to his condensed timelines that tether together various, sometimes mysteriously connected, images:

and the long-ago pine forests
named [this island] with their bodies
and the masts of sailing ships
around the century's turn
named it to the sea
and a bird one springtime
named it bobolink bobolink

Purdy's anaphora resembles Pound's in "Canto IX":

And the Emperor came down and knighted us,
And they had a wooden castle set up for fiesta,
And one year Basinio went out into the courtyard. (lines 15–17)

Both poets use anaphora to portray a steady accumulation of events and, implicitly, of feelings and thoughts that react to a broad spectrum of time. In both poems, the conjunctions artificially link events together – even though years pass in Pound's canto and centuries pass in Purdy's poem. In "Prince Edward County," the rapid succession of eras culminates with a moment of stasis:

And we – the latecomers
white skins and brown men

no voice told us to stay
but we did for a lifetime
of now and then forever

Purdy's caesura after "we" halts the catalogue at the moment in which his speaker meditates on human presence in Prince Edward County. For the speaker, comprehending the enormity of what came during a series of successive and "long-ago" centuries is difficult. The more immediate "now," however, earns roughly as many lines: he can picture the contemporary era more readily because he is *closer* to it. Purdy's distortions of time in a poem such as "Prince Edward County" imply that the lyric present is epistemologically reassuring: several lines might represent a single moment, centuries, or millions of years, but the "here" and "now" always figure more prominently in the poet's mind because, as the speaker in "Iguana" (1982) says, he can "understand nothing but now" (*BATE* 19).

By the end of the 1960s, Purdy had pretty well pinned down the essential features of this historically conscious lyric: sceptical, self-doubting, deeply aware of the time between his "now" and the past with which he desires contact, and contemplative of the difficulty inherent in achieving more than an accumulation of historical fragments. That lyric became so basic to his writing that he actually revised earlier poems to fit his newer mould. He did so with "Remains of an Indian Village" (rev. 1968; *WGW* 119–21), which I discussed in my last chapter as a lynchpin poem in Purdy's career. Notice the differences between the revised "Remains" (left) and the original 1962 version (right):

(And I have seen myself fade
from a woman's eyes
while I was standing there,
and the earth was aware of
me no longer –)
But I come here as part of the process
in the pale morning light,
thinking what has been thought by no one
for years of their absence
in some way continuing them –
And I observe the children's shadows
running in this green light from
                    a distant star
into the near forest –

And I have seen myself fade
from a woman's eyes
while I was standing there
and the earth was aware of
me no longer –
As I observe the wispy legs of children
running in this green light from
                    a distant star
into the near forest –

The revised poem centres on a substantially reconfigured "I" whose authority over history is tenuous. Although the speaker somewhat arrogantly declares that he "continu[es]" history and the stories of marginalized peoples, an abrupt dash suddenly halts the line. The thought may appear complete, but the dash more likely suggests its interruption and thus undermines his claim: both the line and its thought of continuance cease to "continue." What can one achieve through a continuance that is discontinued? The conundrum points to the persona's lack of confidence, which explains the rather delicate historical vision he describes thereafter: the vague "shadows" cast by a telescopically "distant" "light." The persona's history is on shaky ground, especially because he continues history not in the "right" way or the "only way" or in an "objective way," rather in "*some* way" of his own.

The revised "Remains of an Indian Village" also includes qualifications to greater effect than in the original. The 1962 "Remains," as an example, simply states that "Death is certainly absent now." In the revised version, the line is richer: "Death is *certainly* absent now / *at least in the overwhelming sense*" (emphasis added). Here again is proof that Purdy's speakers can rarely just *say* something without undermining it almost immediately (or, as in "Lament for the Dorsets," contradicting it later in the poem). The persona speaks to his intellectual limits, knowing how little he knows, though always on the cusp – or at least he hopes – of knowing more. Whether in ways that are logically anticipatory or foolishly expectant, Purdy often adopts speakers in positions of reception, ready to amass the knowledge that they presume to be available to them, which explains the variously recurring image of Purdy's speakers as unknowing children who possess an unfailing sense of wonder: the speaker in "The Battlefield at Batoche" (1972)[7] claims to be a "child" both now and in the past (*S&D* 43), just as the persona in "Winter Walking" (1960; rev. 1968) is a "breathless small boy" (*PAA* [1968] 96),[8] and another in "Ten Thousand Pianos" (1976) is "an elderly boy" (*S&D* 96). There is always some sense that Purdy's speakers have not obtained the kind of mature knowledge they expect of those who have "grown up" – though, those statements might actually capture a *truly* "adult" epiphany: true intelligence is knowing how little you know, especially about a distant past.

Purdy's revision of "Remains" to better represent this epiphany is not an isolated case, but rather a symbol of his broader effort to keep his persona consistent while he matured as poet. Consider his revised "Roblin's Mills" (1972), which contains telling alterations:

lost in the 4th concession
or dimension of wherever
what happened still happens
a lump in your throat
an adam's apple half
a mile down the road
permits their voices
to join living voices
and float by
on the party line sometimes
and you hang up then
so long now –
(*SP* 35; 1972)

lost in the 4th concession
or dimension of whatever
a lump in your throat
an adam's apple
half a mile down the road
permits their voices
to float by
on the party line sometimes
and you hang up then
so long now –
(*CH* 71; 1965)

Both versions of the poem suggest that history can be heard. The added line in the 1972 version, "what happened still happens," enacts that suggestion: Purdy's polyptotonic echo lets readers literally *hear* the past (symbolized by the past-tense "happened") in the present (because the present-tense "happens" uses the same root word as "happened"). The revised version also highlights the distance between the contemporary and the historical through its juxtaposed line endings, "then" and "now." In the later version, Purdy sets "living voices" and "their voices" on different lines to intensify this sense of disconnection – and though the speaker twice claims that these voices share "the party *line*," the divisive lineation certainly weakens the speaker's suggestion that this connection actually occurs. The revision is another example of Purdy's attempt to consolidate his early and later poetics, to be consistent in his authoritative representation of speakers who actually lack authority.

What Purdy developed in the 1960s, then, was a lyric historiography that thoughtfully reflected on the poet's authority to narrate history, a reflection that arose partly out of his romanticism, nationalism, and modern scepticism. Part of this project entailed the steadily increasing prominence of Purdy's fallible "I" in his poetry. Given his urge to revise "Remains of an Indian Village" and "Roblin's Mills" so that they would reflect his lyrics of the late 1960s, it seems reasonable to conclude that Purdy's historiographic interests (and, relatedly, apprehensions) intensified between 1962 and 1972. With so much critical attention to Purdy's "romantic nationalism" and allegedly Whitmanesque aspirations, it has been difficult to perceive his technical and philosophical innovations as a writer of history. I find it almost impossible to accept Solecki's reading of Purdy's poetry as the earnest continuation of nineteenth-century "odes, Romanticism, and [...] nationalism" (170) when the poems themselves show a poet, informed by modernism, grappling with his own inscrutable vision of history and nation.

It isn't necessary to abandon nationalist frameworks when discussing Purdy; they're unquestionably integral to his poetics. But when I comb Purdy's memoirs, essays, and poems, I question that long-running image of him as an uncomplicated Whitman, the sentimental nationalist reinforcing romantic philosophies. That portrayal of Purdy borders on caricature. Conscious as he was of his era, its generational condition of scepticism, and its shifting political landscape, Purdy is better regarded as a modern sceptic engaged with questions about the evolution of those terms within the Canadian state. From that critical perspective, his poetry no longer appears to serve Solecki's argument that Purdy concludes a romantic nationalist "phase" in Canada (10). In fact, reading Purdy as a sceptic makes his work seem more inaugural than conclusive, in so far as his poetry lays the groundwork for one branch of lyric historiography that would prove widely influential in Canadian literature.

Purdy didn't know, of course, that he was laying this foundation. He knew only that his writing had drastically improved and that his vision of history and nation was becoming increasingly unsettled; he would, in fact, say in a later poem about the FLQ crisis in Quebec that he realized he was living "in a different country" than the one he had imagined as a child ("The Peaceable Kingdom" *S&D* 106). Though he could never fully shed those early romantic leanings that drove him to write his first poems at the age of thirteen or to publish his first book in his mid-twenties, he had by the end of the 1960s come to understand that the past, as much as the nation, is always *imagined* to one degree or another. He grew, in other words, to appreciate a healthy scepticism and to recognize the limits of individual perception.

There is an underlying critical concern in this discussion of Purdy's scepticism, though, because, in Eliot's thinking, the only scepticism of value is that which returns the sceptic to a reasoned and cautious belief. The poems I have discussed thus far don't offer that: they centre on the struggle to believe in history and, in some cases, on the explicit failures or shortcomings of the poet seeking the past. In that vein, my discussion of Purdy's poetry is incomplete. It shows Eliot's "habit of examining evidence," but not "the capacity for delayed decision" that yields something concrete *after* a period of doubt (*Notes* 12). In order to speak on that aspect of Purdy's poetry – via a discussion of his family history in *In Search of Owen Roblin* (1974) – much more needs to be said about the influence he had on the younger writers for whom he was a guiding contemporary.

Purdy's influence on those writers was enormous. After 1960, he earned formal recognition: he received numerous honours and awards after 1965, including being inducted into the Order of Canada in 1982. He had public exposure: Purdy was a regular contributor to the *Canadian Forum* and *Canadian Literature,* and he did numerous reading tours and writer-in-residence stints. He seemed ever-present in scholarship, reviews, literary gatherings, and the media. His steady place in the spotlight led scholars like Laurie Ricou to argue that Purdy "had more influence on contemporary Canadian poetry than [...] any other Canadian writer" ("Poetry" 8) on the level of both "subject-matter" and "form" ("Poetry" 11–12). Ricou is hardly alone here. George Woodcock, too, says that "Purdy's melding the sense of history in a new country suddenly grown old in its feelings with the awareness of place as a visual reality has perhaps enlightened rather than inspired many younger poets, so that a genuine poetry of place and time now exists in Canada" ("Canadian Poetry" 193). I generally hope to avoid such absolute or grand statements in my scholarship, because they have much more to do with the perspective of the critic than the reality of the literary scene; Purdy was not all things to all writers, and many important writers of the era did not read him at all. That fact notwithstanding, there were leading English-language poets who, at the outset of their careers, learned from him: Margaret Atwood, Barry McKinnon, John Newlove, Andrew Suknaski, and many more. It was not Purdy's work on various histories during his later career (of China, Hiroshima, and ancient Etruria) that captivated these younger poets. It was his early lyric historiography about Canadian history that left a place for them to stand on.

3 Lyric and Regionalism: Challenging Histories, Part 1[1]

Given the enthusiastic public reception of Al Purdy's lyric historiography during the 1960s and 1970s, the veritable explosion of historically conscious poetry after 1962 is unsurprising, but it is a curious fact that such writing was, for a time, eccentrically focused on prairie history. Despite being an Ontarian, Purdy's greatest influence was arguably on prairie writers. When asked by Robert Enright about the roots of prairie poetry and its interest in local history and daily life, the Albertan poet Robert Kroetsch remarked, "People doing it in the east, like Al Purdy, I'm sure were pretty important in the development of Prairie poetry [...] Purdy was central" (28). Purdy's poetics is resonant in the work of numerous prairie poets, many of whom were well acquainted with Purdy himself, his writing, or both. He became a self-described "father-figure" to younger writers (qtd Bradley, *We Go Far Back* 212). That description isn't vanity – or at least it's not *just* vanity. Purdy's poetry of the 1960s showed emerging centennial-era writers that it was possible to write about Canadian history without replicating the impersonal style of E.J. Pratt's epics and to adopt the lyric mode without appearing unfashionably romantic. His example helps explain the method prairie poets used to write about the past, but his influence is only part of a very complex series of connected events that allowed prairie poetry (that is, poetry *about* the prairies, not just writing by prairie-born authors) to flourish during the 1960s and 1970s. Still, his example was vital to prairie poets at a time when prairie-centric literary communities were just beginning to form: new presses were founded, new magazines and periodicals were published, the first widely read prairie-based histories were published, and new creative writers emerged and found success in a growing and excitable literary community. In that climate, lyric historiography was a sensible genre in which to work. It provided a generation of prairie poets with the means to give fuller expression to western Canada and to undo long-standing caricatures of the west as a barren wasteland without a history or culture of its own.

For that generation, John Newlove was a guiding figure. He deepened young writers' respect for regionalist poetry and was the first modern prairie poet to demonstrate the rich cultural heritage of the prairies through lyric historiography.[2] Newlove's well-known and controversial poem "The Pride" is an effective starting place to map what D.M.R. Bentley calls the prairie "renaissance" (*Gay]Grey* 66) and to imagine, too, lyric historiography as a regionalist's genre. I think of regionalism as landscape understood through the individual exploration of histories, social structures, and cultures associated with a physical geography.[3] This definition accommodates the projects of Newlove and other regionalist poets, whose approaches to region subtend a model of lyric historiography that is, as Lorna Crozier has said of regionalist writing, "rooted in place" (Crozier and Philips 50), but still attentive to a multiplicity of traditional and alternative historical narratives. This attentiveness yields what Purdy finds in his poetry: fragmented and unresolved pasts that remind the poet of the difficulty inherent in the writing of history.

Whereas modern regionalist poetry thrived after 1960, prairie poets had few frames of reference for such writing before that time. George Melnyk's sombre note that "[f]rom 1946–1969, only three [Albertan] poets published in volume form" exemplifies the limited production of prairie writing during this period (63); the poetry scene on the prairies was even more dismal before the Second World War. Literary studies of prairie poetry are therefore quite few because, for the most part, the prairies had been meaningfully represented only in fiction for the first half of the twentieth century.[4] George Woodcock noted this trend in an article he published in the *Globe and Mail* in 1981:

> I was astonished when I began to read Canadian books in the fifties to find that there was virtually no poetry evoking this strange and haunting country, though the Prairies had already given rise to a special kind of realist novel that was one of the most interesting strains of Canadian fiction. [...] But until the sixties, not a single prairie poet of any significance appeared. ("Strong New Voices" BL7)

There were, of course, prairie poets who made names for themselves before 1960, namely Dorothy Livesay and Eli Mandel. It was not until after 1960, however, that either writer earned a reputation as a poet writing *about* personal or historical experiences on the prairies.

Prose fiction held sway over prairie writers for several reasons, and Dennis Cooley has helpfully outlined reasons for this trend. First, there was, until the mid-twentieth century, "limited cultural and intellectual contact with what was happening in the rest of the world; a serious lack of support in universities and literary societies." If those living on the prairies were lucky enough to acquire an education, such institutions "operated primarily as agricultural and theological institutions [...] Whole waves of teachers, who knew nothing about Modern or Canadian poetry, spilled into the schools, where in turn their students didn't learn about such writing either" ("RePlacing" 13). The comparably low literacy rates in prairie provinces did little to encourage individuals to explore difficult poetry (Heinemann 4). Nor did the fact that this region "reeled from one crisis to another" between 1914 and 1960 help cultivate a literary community: as Cooley notes, "the loss of proportionately more young men than any other part of Canada" during the First World War, the devastating economic conditions of the Dirty Thirties and the Depression, and a general impulse to leave the prairies to "mak[e] a living" in Toronto or Montreal prevented would-be poets from gaining "intimacy" with prairie geography and culture ("RePlacing" 14). Cooley also observes that there was little interest among prairie readers in modern poetry: "mimetic literature" was "more accessible" and less demanding than complex poetry that didn't offer "a world [readers] could immediately recognize." His point offers an explanation for why the relatively readable prose of modern fiction writers like Frederick Philip Grove, W.O. Mitchell, and Sinclair Ross "had, with few exceptions, no formal counterparts in poetry" until the 1960s (15).

After the creation of the Canada Council for the Arts in 1957, the cultural conditions for these counterparts were more favourable. Reflecting in 1991 on the tremendous pride and energy of individual provinces and regions, Carl Berger noted that "provincial governments became more prominent and the depths of regional discontent more apparent" during the centennial era. There was, he argued, an increasingly "strong identification with, and an admiration for, the integrity of local cultures" (Berger, "Writings" 304). One sign of such identification and admiration was the formation of numerous poetry communities that were complemented by the genesis of prairie literary magazines. After 1957, a plethora of prairie magazines emerged; *The Wascana Review* (est. 1966), *Salt* (est. 1969), *Grain* (est. 1973), and *Prairie Fire* (est. 1983) received funding from organizations such as the CCA, the Manitoba Writers' Guild (est. 1981), and the Saskatchewan Writers' Guild (est. 1969). These magazines allowed poets to begin their writing careers on the prairies, whereas earlier prairie writers typically absconded to

Montreal, Toronto, or Vancouver. That constant urge to go and publish elsewhere is why Lorna Crozier admired *Grain*, which, she said, provided a necessary "outlet for so many poets" (Crozier and Philips 140) who had no prairie-based alternatives.

As magazines became decentralized, so did presses. If you were a modern Canadian poet trying to publish your first book in 1950, your choices were few; leading publishers were unlikely to publish modern verse for fear it would not sell or that it might offend public sensibilities. Lorne Pierce's Ryerson Chap-Book series was a likely outlet for such young writers (it was, in fact, where Purdy found a home for two of his early books from the 1950s), but the tenor of the series, with some exceptions, was imitatively romantic and the chapbooks generally sold poorly. The other option for young poets was to self-publish, an expensive option without some sort of financial backing. When, after Pierce's death in 1962, the Ryerson Chap-Book series ceased production, there existed a publishing vacuum in the Canadian poetry community. In major cities such as Toronto, this vacuum was filled by established presses (such as McClelland and Stewart) that became increasingly willing to publish poetry once they had better funding after 1957, as well as by newer presses like Contact (1952–67) and Coach House (est. 1965). Although these Toronto-based venues remained appealing to young poets, a slew of independent prairie presses emerged that helped decentralize publishing in Canada. Aided by the Saskatchewan Arts Board (est. 1948) and its "assistance program," Thistledown Press and Coteau Books were launched in 1975 (Crozier and Hyland 247). Young bohemian poets like Andrew Suknaski began their careers by starting avant-garde presses that were portable: Elfin Plot (est. 1969), Anak (est. c. 1970), and Deodar Shadow (est. c. 1970) published the earliest work from new talents of the late 1960s and early 1970s like Sid Marty, Barry McKinnon, and Glen Sorestad.

Writing groups further stimulated literary production. In 1952, W.O. Mitchell helped organize creative workshops in Saskatchewan, but his initiative was uncommon until the 1970s. The "Moose Jaw Group" (which included Robert Currie, Lorna Crozier, E.F. Dyck, Barbara Sapergia, Gary Hyland, Byrna Barclay, Elizabeth Allen, and others) was one of the more notable groups of serious prairie poets to emerge after 1960.[5] Other groups established themselves in Edmonton: Mick Burrs, an American ex-pat turned Canadian poet, moved there in 1969 and, at the behest of Dorothy Livesay, joined a collective that included Elizabeth Brewster, Douglas Barbour, Stephen Scobie, and Sid Stephen. These magazines, presses, and groups were emblems of a flourishing prairie literary culture during the postwar era that took newfound pride in its sense of place.

The lively literary climate was a complement to the work of prairie-based historians. In his foreword to James A. Jackson's *The Centennial History of Manitoba* (1970), W.L. Morton asked, "What is it that makes Manitoba history so interesting? One thing [...] is that it has so much history" (n.p.). Morton's jokey note might fall flat today – *every* region has "so much history" – but to claim in 1970 that the prairies had over 10,000 years of history would surely have surprised many readers. It was not until the last quarter of the twentieth century that historians recognized and respected the geographical space of the prairies; complimentary portraits of the region were not often found in criticism contemporary with Morton's. Take Dick Harrison's work: he said in 1977 that the prairies initially "had no [historical] association, no ghosts, none of the significance imagination gives to the expressionless face of the earth after men have lived and died there" (ix). Harrison's statement is a gross reduction of prairie history that discounts the diversity and extensive cultural history of the region, and these statements motivated creative writers and historians to dispel such baseless arguments.

Revisionist projects mushroomed after Morton published *Manitoba: A History* (1957), which was "immediately recognized as Canada's first provincial history" and "guided a generation of students" (Friesen, "Historical Society" 102). Morton had long felt frustration with the conventions of Canadian history, specifically the continued pull of the so-called "Laurentian thesis." In 1946, Morton famously contested the Laurentian thesis, lamenting that "narrowly political [and] essentially colonial" histories of Canada adopt "the Laurentian theme: the metropolitan destiny of the St. Lawrence River" ("Clio" 106). "No more than French Canada," he wrote, "can the West accept a common interpretation of Canadian history." He hoped that the West would eventually make a place for itself in Canadian history – or, in his words, "free itself, and find itself" (109).

Morton's unabashed study of prairie history was therefore an act of protest against academic convention, and that resonated with young prairie writers. Margaret Laurence said as much: "When I first read Morton's *Manitoba: A History*, it was with a tremendous sense of excitement, combined with an angry sense of having been deprived, when young, of my own heritage. I have since done a great deal of reading of prairie history, but it was Morton who first gave me the sense of my place's long and dramatic past" ("Books" 245). Laurence's statement nicely captures Morton's impact, as well as the general need authors felt to explore prairie history during the centennial era. Her pride and enthusiasm in that statement are reflected in her "Manawaka" series, in so far as those books explore connections and disconnections among prairie communities and cultures whose fates intersect and collide in the past and present. Such regional pride captures something integral to the prairie writing boom of the 1960s and after: a pride of place, an intuitive turn to the local that is, in many ways, a personal connection to the past.

The publication of Morton's *Manitoba* was one of many signs of a regionalist turn in Canadian thinking, both in history and creative writing. Attacks launched by both historians Ramsay Cook and J.M.S. Careless against the hopeful "plot of nation-building" in history catalysed an outpouring of "regional" histories in the early 1970s (Careless, "Limited Identities" 1). Speaking in 1954 to the Canadian Historical Association, Careless was the first to argue that historians "must think beyond nationalism," which he said was an "antiquated nineteenth-century" framework for historical study that had resulted in the neglect of "regional divisions" in Canada ("Canadian Nationalism" 12–13). Careless valued such divisions as metonyms of "the world at large" (15): if Canadians were to acknowledge the "constantly adjusting strains between divergent groups" (14) within the country, he hoped that would then give citizens of the country a unique advantage in a global future more in touch with "world variety" (15). That is a remarkably prescient thing to say several decades before Pierre Trudeau would announce a formal policy of multiculturalism, and it caused controversy at the conference. In the question period that followed, Arthur Lower told Careless that there are "no grounds for apology" in "examining Canadian nationalism" (qtd 18),[6] and a choir of historians supported his position. To all of them, Careless seemed like something of a radical, contesting convention and declaring that "Canadian nationalism is anything but monolithic, uniform, or clearly defined" (16).

These statements sowed seeds for Careless's work of the late 1960s, which built on Ramsay Cook's model of "limited identities": identities read within frameworks that are productively (if only relatively) more focused than those used to read the amorphous "Canadian identity." Cook hoped the term would help historians "understand and explain the regional, ethnic, and class identities" that constitute the Canadian mosaic ("Canadian Centennial" 663). Two years later, Careless reiterated Cook's comments: "Canadian historiography has often dealt too wishfully with nationalism – and *ergo* with unification – thus producing both expectations and discouragements out of keeping with realities" ("Limited Identities" 1). It was not so much that specific Canadian regions were excluded from conventional histories – though northern communities often were. It was much more an issue of the Toronto-centric perspective out of which historians wrote, a perspective that failed to grasp the intricacies of local environments. That quality of conventional history is likely why Morton described *Manitoba* as "a general history of Manitoba *for Manitobans*" (vii, emphasis added). He wanted Manitobans to know they, too, had a voice in the writing of history.

In the academy, the related ideas of "limited identities" and regionalism had far-reaching effects on the thinking of historians, but changes in content came slowly. One problem in the advancement of historical writing was, again, the limitations put on the historian by their standards of professionalization. Historians may have recognized, in Cook's words, the "unfortunate sameness [of] Canadian historical writing" ("Good-Bye" 277) – the insistence on the Laurentian thesis, the nineteenth-century concepts of nationalism, the Toronto-based perspective – but their ability to change the narrative was sometimes limited by the expectations of their profession. Writing as the editor of the *Canadian Historical Review*, Cook regretted that "if a submission [to the *Canadian Historical Review*] deals with a 'national' question, it has an immediate advantage over a local or provincial subject." A regional piece, Cook felt, would have too little appeal to a broader readership. It was, to put it simply, against a historian's best interests to publish on regional issues. Cook spoke somewhat despondently of the situation: "This is the force of habit and tradition – but it is a harmful tradition" (276). Though many historians may have sympathized with Cook and Careless, there were very few incentives or opportunities for them to professionalize as "regional" historians.

Working outside the traditions and standards of academia, however, many young authors saw regionalist writing as an opportunity to break new ground and build on the lyric historiography of Purdy. What those writers needed was a model. Historians like Morton could seed an interest in history and regionalism (as he did for Laurence), but they could offer little in the way of a literary aesthetic on which to base regionalist poetry. This is what John Newlove offered poets working within settler literary traditions. To those writers, he was for prairie poetry what Morton was for prairie history.

Newlove had no literary equivalent before 1960. His breakthrough collection, *Moving in Alone* (1965), has been regarded as the first modern book of poetry published by a prairie-born poet and about the prairies (at least, from a settler perspective). Granted, there was Anne Marriott's *The Wind Our Enemy* (1939) – a leftist long poem set on the prairies during the Depression – but prairie-born poets regarded the British Columbian poet's work, perhaps unfairly, as the work of an outsider: "competent," but not genuine or guiding (Cooley, "RePlacing" 16–17). The Regina-born Newlove was an insider – prairie through and through. For some emerging prairie poets, Newlove was therefore as significant an influence as Purdy. There were even comparisons in the media: reviewers read both poets favourably and some (specifically Robert Weaver and Louis Dudek) portrayed them as writers on the cusp of a meteoric and parallel rise.[7] Newlove also had formal recognition through awards and institutions; he won the Governor General's Award in 1972, held writer-in-residence posts at Loyola College, the University of Western Ontario, the Regina Public Library, and the University of Toronto, and was mandatory reading for courses in Canadian literature at the University of Saskatchewan and the University of Regina (Crozier and Hyland 243–5).

By the early 1970s, Newlove became a mentor to emerging writers. This status was apparent in letters Newlove received from young poets: in a letter dated 17 September 1971, Dale Zieroth wrote to Newlove after the older poet offered to write a letter of recommendation for Zieroth's Canada Council grant: "Thanks for saying you'll write the letter to the Council for me. You said you didn't think it would do any good. Well, I don't know what the ins and outs of the Council are all about, but I do know the poets whom I consider my peers (people like Bill [Howell], for example), we consider you to be one of the top poets in Canada. And one of the best and most imaginative of craftsmen" (Zieroth to Newlove). There are dozens of letters like this one in Newlove's archives at the University of Manitoba, and they show just how sought-after Newlove was in his time. Other comments came in interviews: speaking on his own urge to write about the regional past, Andrew Suknaski remarked, "I think the really resonant voices that influenced me, and many of us in the West, were the voices of Al Purdy and John Newlove" (Suknaski and Hillis 124), and Fred Wah felt that "Newlove's presence" and influence were "still considerable" even in 1986 (217).

Whereas the poetry of Newlove and Purdy gave many younger prairie poets the confidence to approach history in their own writing, the prairie past gave them an abundance of material to explore in verse. Historians had yet to appreciate that wealth. In fact, one major critique of Morton's text has been his focus on agrarian history and the "sea-farers who had begun the history of Manitoba" (Morton, *Manitoba* 9), a lens that some historians have argued proved Morton's inability "to say anything of consequence about the era of native dominance [on the prairies]. Research [from Morton's era] had not yet established the richness and variety of these native societies" (Friesen, *Canadian Prairies* 10). Yet the range of topics that centennial-era poets addressed is astounding: the personal struggles of individual figures such as Big

Bear and Sitting Bull, the transnational plains experience, urban histories, turn-of-the-century Ukrainian immigration, the Riel uprisings, and Chinese-Canadian contributions to the construction of the Canadian Pacific Railway are just a few examples. I'm interested, however, in histories that were, in multiple meanings of the word, "challenging": in the first place, the poems of interest to me challenge conventional readings of Indigenous groups, and yet they were, simultaneously, challenging for the poets to write.

Newlove's poetry exemplifies that doubleness. While his poetry contests dehumanizing or reductive readings of Indigenous peoples, he also adopts conventions used by the historians he detests: he employs the "vanishing race" myth, indulges in various stereotypes, and adopts diction that is today inappropriate (e.g., "Indian"). His poems – and specifically, "The Pride" – show that he understands the inadequacy of conventional histories, and yet he also demonstrates (sometimes intentionally and sometimes unintentionally) his own inability to treat the past fully and respectfully. Newlove's poetry is, in that way, an extension of Purdy's accumulative lyrics. His personas often articulate both his temporal *and* cultural distance from the past, positioning the lyric "I" as a sceptic who accumulates fragments of stories, aware that they have been excluded from or inadequately portrayed in conventional history. "The Pride" meditates on the narrative potential inherent in these stories.

That positioning of the poet captures the lyric sophistication of Newlove's "The Pride," a poem he drafted in July 1964. "The Pride" was something of an epiphany for the struggling twenty-six-year-old writer. He realized through writing it that history could foster compelling poetry. Newlove's impulse to write about history was rooted first in his own reading. Much later in his life, he wrote to a young student, "You also ask what brought on 'The Pride.' Looking back, it seems quite simple to me. I had been reading masses of materials, anthropological and cultural history, about North American Indians; and I think that I was so stuffed with information and excitement about the things I was learning, that it had to sort itself into some sort of coherent-to-me-form and then burst out" (Newlove to James English).

At the same time, Purdy validated Newlove's impulse to write his first poem about history; Douglas Barbour believes that even if Newlove never "sound[s] like Purdy," his poems "definitely acknowledge [Purdy's] presence as a new master of Canadian poetry" ("Newlove" 285). Barbour's intuition is actually well supported, and the connection he theorizes goes beyond the content of the poems: Newlove's poetry career was, in fact, launched with the help of Purdy, who introduced

Newlove to Peter Miller of Contact Press and helped orchestrate the publication of *Moving in Alone*. Purdy wrote to Newlove in 1963, "I've mentioned you to Peter Miller before, and will do all I can to help you with a book if you're interested" (Purdy to Newlove). Purdy sent Miller Newlove's poems in October 1963, which led to a book deal in spring 1964 and the release of *Moving in Alone* in 1965. "Purdy was incredible," Newlove later said. "He just kept pushing me to write" (Newlove and Bartley 142). Newlove was in regular contact with Purdy after their first meeting in 1963,[8] and in the same letter quoted above, he acknowledges, "when [...] *Poems for All the Annettes* was first published [in 1962], I was astonished and admiring: it seemed to show me greater areas for the subject-matter of poetry than I had considered" (Newlove to James English). Purdy had also been sending Newlove new poems throughout 1963 and 1964, sharing and exchanging philosophies about the function of and possibilities for poetry. This kind of evidence is more in line with Barbour's claim in that it speaks to more than just Purdy's editorial assistance. Purdy actively showed Newlove what could happen inside a poem. The "subject-matter" to which Newlove refers may be ambiguous, but Purdy's historiographic writing in *Poems for All the Annettes* surely would have appealed to the younger poet, a voracious and "violen[t]" reader of history (Newlove and Pearce 115).

Whatever inspired "The Pride," it erupted from Newlove's pen: he wrote several hundred lines of poetry in less than four days and almost immediately sent it off to the *Tamarack Review*. It was published the following year.[9] The poem caught the attention of critics and anthologists, and, until the 1980s, it was considered by many to be a breakthrough poem in Canadian literature.[10]

Yet, today, Newlove's poem holds precarious footing in Canadian literary history. It is controversial to champion "The Pride" in an era when literary criticism has been dramatically affected by decolonization theory and when critics are distrustful of early representations of Indigenous cultures by non-Indigenous writers. I think of postcolonialism as Judith Leggatt does, as "an ongoing attempt to find means of cross-cultural communication that escape the repressive hierarchies of colonial encounters" (111), and from that perspective, I want to consider the ways in which Newlove's poem is both a part of that "ongoing attempt" and, in some ways, an impediment to it. "The Pride" has many shortcomings, which I discuss in this chapter, even though the poem also, as Patrick Lane once put it, "shock[ed] a whole generation of readers" into feeling a "new pride of place" ("Unyielding Phrase" 60). More to the point: "The Pride" proved that a poetic treatment of the prairies and its history could be both aesthetically and thematically sophisticated without resorting to the "wasteland" motifs of earlier writers that stressed the bleakness of the land. The popularity of Newlove's poem has rested mainly on the judgments of writers who, like Lane, were eager to articulate their own geo-historical visions: Douglas Barbour, Dennis Cooley, Gary Geddes, Patrick Lane, and many others.[11]

While Newlove's contemporaries found much about "The Pride" to praise, some scholars have more recently denounced his poem as a careless appropriation or romantic dismissal of Indigenous history and culture. Margery Fee argues that Newlove's poem is one of many from his era that bears traces of "Romantic theory, which sees the poet as the mouthpiece of the inarticulate and illiterate people" ("Romantic" 20–1). Diana Brydon describes "The Pride" as a "classical colonial literary move [...] the prior history of native peoples is assimilated into the white Canadian present so that the descendants of white settlers may be freed to claim Indians as their ancestors" (39). Frank Davey denigrates Newlove's "resonances of European romantic primitivism" (*Post-National* 53) and "Euro-Canadian appropriation of Indian culture" (55). Patrick Sheeran implies, through a blatant misreading, that Newlove's "pride" refers to the pride of white Canadians (287). E.F. Dyck says that Newlove's poem "is flawed by naïveté (at best) or racism (at worst)." "It is," Dyck concludes, "Newlove's personal ride [...] to a dubious affirmation of 'this land is my land'" ("Place" 79). I don't fundamentally disagree with the core issue in these assessments, because Newlove's "The Pride" *is* ambiguous, even self-contradictory: his persona criticizes colonial history even as he adopts a fundamentally colonial perspective on the past. While that quality of his text hardly proves the arguments of critics like Sheeran or Dyck – that "The Pride" is a *celebration* of colonialism, which it assuredly is not – it does raise questions about the contemporary relevance and the lasting reputation of a poem that, in its time, challenged long-standing stereotypes of the prairies as a blank wasteland without a history.

In putting some pressure on the singularity of these critics' assessments, I'm not questioning the value of discourses and methodologies that critically evaluate Canada's colonial history; the vast body of theory and criticism that has documented and critiqued the impact of colonialism on Indigenous societies, in Canada or elsewhere, has shaken the foundations of the humanities for the better. At the same time, the importing of various concepts of "postcolonial" or "decolonization" theory into literary studies has occasionally provoked the exclusion of writers who lend themselves less obviously to such methodologies. To react in that way to authors without attention to the historical, social, or literary context of a given work often results in caricatures or erroneous, if still well-intentioned, suppressions of literatures with complex legacies. None of what made Newlove's poem important to many of his contemporaries puts it or him above criticism for his representation of Indigenous stories and communities – and in chapter 9 and my conclusion, the writing of Indigenous poets such as Joan Crate and Louise Halfe will give a different perspective on such issues. In this chapter, though, I want to think historically about Newlove's poem by articulating both its positive impact on the poet's contemporaries and its flaws when read retrospectively.

The primary reason why Newlove's "The Pride" had a major impact on his readers was, as I've said, because it worked against the motif of the prairies as a "wasteland" (he would, in fact, play on Eliot's *The Waste Land* with his title *The Green Plain* in 1979).[12] Newlove instead portrays the prairies as a fertile space that nurtures the creative and historical imagination and achieves this depiction by layering voices from the past and present. The effect of that technique is the speaker's (and the reader's) entanglement in a dynamic and conflicted past. Eliot's own intrusive voice is one example of multi-vocality in "The Pride," but Newlove also draws on others. Two of the central voices here are G.E. Hyde – a twentieth-century historian whose writings were largely unsympathetic to Indigenous cultures negatively affected by colonialism – and David Thompson – an eighteenth-century explorer whom Newlove depicts as a more sympathetic observer of such cultures. The clash of these perspectives points to a complex prairie past, and Newlove connects that vision to Eliot's own use of "fragments" in *The Waste Land*. Eliot sorts through an Anglo-American literary history; Newlove sorts through prairie histories. As he does so, he comes to regard the prairie past as a "half-understood massiveness" (107) in need of more diverse historical and literary perspectives.

These were the elements of Newlove's poem that secured its popularity amongst his contemporaries. His cautious exploration of history in "The Pride" epitomized, as Patrick Lane argues, some writers' need to "revise" conventional Canadian histories (59). Even if "The Pride" has seemed unsatisfying to later critics, it invigorated new discourses on prairie literature and history. My focus on literary and historical allusions in this poem – namely to Eliot, Hyde, and Thompson – brings those efforts to the fore, as these allusions aid in unpacking the intricate historical vision Newlove intended to construct: a vision modernist in its literary aims and sceptical in its representation of history.

These qualities of "The Pride" have much to do with Newlove's reading of Eliot's *The Waste Land*. His allusion to Eliot illuminates both the multi-vocality of "The Pride" (as Eliot's voice infiltrates the text) and his speaker's productive anxiety as he imagines a fragmented vision of the prairie past. Thinking on the history of prairie cultures and events, the persona finds the past too difficult to contain or control:

> III
> But what image, bewildered
> son of all men
> under the hot sun,
> do you worship,
> what completeness
> do you hope to have
> from these tales,
> a half-understood massiveness, mirage,
> in men's minds – what
> is your purpose;
> with what force
> will you proceed
> along a line
> neither straight nor short,
> whose future
> you cannot know
> or result foretell,
> whose meaning is still
> obscured as the incidents
> occur and accumulate? (*BNW* 107–8)

The speaker's diction and tone in Newlove's poem obviously derive from *The Waste Land*:

> What are the roots that clutch, what branches
> Grow? Son of man,
> You cannot say, or guess, for you know only
> A heap of broken images, where the sun beats,
> And the dead tree gives no shelter, the cricket no relief; (lines 19–23)

Whereas Eliot's speaker chiefly grapples with fragments of literary history, Newlove's persona centres on a fragmented regional one. In their representation of such grapples, both poets pose multiple rhetorical questions, tethered to a single question mark, though Newlove's syntax is far more labyrinthine than Eliot's. As a result, the reader and the speakers experience – to borrow Newlove's term – an intimidating "accumulation" of questions and histories that for me echoes the imagistic accumulation of much modernist writing. And this is what Newlove is doing by invoking Eliot: he amplifies the modernist struggle to shore up fragments in order to illuminate the ambiguous and incomplete images of prairie cultures. Exploring accumulation and ambiguity threatens the coherence of the past in the persona's mind; certainly Newlove's dash, which paradoxically interrupts and continues his speaker's catalogue of questions, shows the persona's distractive state of anxiety, the zigzagging of his mind as he confronts an overwhelming history. Eliot's vision of a "heap of broken images" thus complements Newlove's own effort to portray the anxiety of the poet who tries to make such an elaborate and fragmented past more intelligible to his reader. The accumulative tendencies of the writing bespeak another subtle modernist legacy, what Barbara Herrnstein Smith calls a faith in art that finds "resolution [...] in the affirmation of irresolution" (241).

Newlove writes about this same anxiety in an unpublished poem, appropriately titled "History" (n.d.; n.p.), which he described (in a handwritten note on the draft itself) as "not a poem. yet." The piece complements the unease the speaker in "The Pride" experiences:

> The accumulation makes fools of us: too hard
> to fight time filled with facts,
> or even to listen to it.
> The only fact available for use
> is found in the Now, and that is not graspable.

Newlove's model of "accumulation" here exemplifies my own use of the term in describing his and Purdy's aesthetic: readers randomly accumulate stories, perspectives, and information as they sift through the past. Narrative is historians' resistance to such an incoherent accumulation, their "fight" to control a mass of knowledge. As historians shape narratives, however, they inevitably misrepresent and even fail to "listen" to the past. Newlove's last two lines echo one of the fundamental claims of much historiographic theory: that, as Michel de Certeau puts it, "historians begin from present determinations" (*The Writing of History* 11). The speaker in Newlove's poem says that the "Now" is available, but the idea that all history is written in and for the "Now" is an idea that "is not graspable." In other words, the presentism of all historical writing is unacknowledged; alternatively, the speaker may simply be saying that even *the present* is ungraspable, and so all knowledge, past and present, is elusive. In the first case, those who presume to write objectively about a massive history without grasping their subjectivity seem "fool[ish]"; in the second, those who presume to understand the past when even the present is elusive and ungraspable are, as well, "fool[ish]." Both interpretations caution readers against overconfidence when it comes to asserting knowledge.

These sentiments are likewise manifest in "The Pride," a poem that illuminates the difficulty of organizing bygone voices. Newlove's allusion to Eliot is one example of this difficulty, because readers contend with the vast, fragmented collection of voices associated with Eliot's poem. Some of these associations manifest in the sinuous set of images associated with the line quoted above, "[s]on of all men." It rings of both Eliot's "Son of man" and Ezekiel 2:1: "He said to me, 'Son of man, stand up on your feet and I will speak to you.'" Voices and texts converge, even at the level of a single line. This layering extends to other sections of the poem and is a way of thinking about the many historical voices and images that enter Newlove's poem: the prairie past is, like Eliot's own wasteland of allusions, a "handful / of fragments" (*BNW* 111). Newlove's other sections do more to identify these fragments in a specific way, but I have begun my discussion with section III in order to identify the general vision of prairie history that Newlove espouses: multi-vocal, massive, and anxiety-inducing for the poet who, aware of his contemporary location, cannot organize the past.

Newlove may have found Eliot's modernist multi-vocality and fragmentation useful for describing the accumulating history of the prairies, but he disburdens himself of the arid "wasteland" imagery that other writers like Anne Marriott and Sinclair Ross used to describe the physical (and often, by extension, metaphysical) condition of the region. Both D.M.R. Bentley and Anne Geddes Bailey remark on Marriott's literalization of the "wasteland" image: Bentley describes the "barren field" of the prairies that inspired the poet to "apply techniques learned from the high Modernists" (*Gay]Grey* 71), and Bailey studies Marriott's rendering of an "infertile environment" (56) that is "dry, dusty and barren" (58). Likewise, Sinclair Ross felt that Eliot's "wasteland" represented "an appropriately grim and lonely landscape to 'take [a personal sense of isolation] out on'" (*Collecting Stamps* 138); his comment readily applies to his best-known novel, *As for Me and My House* (1941), in which a literal drought parallels the artistic and sexual drought that Philip and Mrs Bentley experience.

For much of the twentieth century, there were few alternatives in Canadian literature to this "barren" prairie motif. When Laurie Ricou edited *Twelve Prairie Poets* (1976), he appears to have used the book to substantiate his argument in *Vertical Man/Horizontal Horizon* (1973) that the prairie landscape provided a useful metaphor for the barren and sterile Depression-era life; indeed, Susan Gingell notes that *Twelve Prairie Poets* "bear[s] out" Ricou's earlier arguments ("Prairie Harvest" 184). The motif of the "barren wasteland" was equally prominent in poetry published after Ricou's anthology, and titles alone often suffice as evidence of either an invocation of the motif or of Ricou's impact on younger prairie writers (or both): Garry Raddysh's "The Land Is Flat" (1978), Peter Christensen's "Flatness Communion" (1977), and Lorna Crozier's "Vertical Man" (1976). Ricou imagined prairie literature as a collective nod to Eliot's poetic evocation of "sterility," "bewilderment," "alienation," and "universal meaninglessness" in *The Waste Land*, all of which "the prairie landscape" effectively mirrors (*Vertical Man* 120). Not an especially cheery reading of someone's home.

Of course, Newlove did not endorse this motif. He still drew parallels between Eliot's wasteland and the prairies, but not because of barrenness or alienation. For Newlove, the parallel was something more profound. Eliot portrayed history as a heap of images, fragments, and voices, and this chaotic vision of a rich and diverse past appealed to Newlove. That is why his persona insists that "the plains are bare, / not barren" (*BNW* 108). The distinction is essential: "bare" suggests a blankness, like an unwritten, unspoken, or unacknowledged story waiting for recognition, whereas "barren" would suggest that there is nothing *to* recognize. I imagine this would have been an important statement for prairie writers with whom Newlove was contemporary. Imagine being one of the many writers who contributed to the intense poetic activity on the prairies after 1965 and finding no positive images of your local world, no reason to explore it, no engaging history on which to draw. Newlove reframed the prairie experience.

"The Pride" thus represents Newlove's early effort to invigorate prairie history by reflecting on pasts that, in the 1960s, remained largely unexplored or, at best, ignorantly represented by mainstream voices in history and literature. But the poem is not narrative. It is, to be sure, an accumulation. W.H. New's proposal that Newlove's poem is "whole" and "unfragmented" is misleading (155) because Newlove's speaker only conjures up fragments or remnants of a past that survives in the present: he names "the haida and tsimshian tribes," the "thunderbird hilunga," "nootka tootooch," "kwunusela" who was named "by the kwakiutl," "d'sonoqua," and other mythical or historical figures and peoples (*BNW* 106). The section concludes, "they are all ready / to be found, / the legends / and the people, or / all their ghosts and memories, / whatever is strong enough to be remembered" (*BNW* 107). That statement surely seemed progressive in 1964, though it is ideologically tangled. On the one hand, Newlove's catalogue of names shatters the misleading image of a pan-Indian identity used often in non-Indigenous film and literature. Newlove instead appreciates the distinctiveness of nations and hopes that the stories of Indigenous peoples – their cultures a "mirage, / in men's minds" – might now be "found." On the other hand: found *by whom*? I want to believe that Newlove was imagining explorations undertaken by Indigenous researchers, historians, artists, and storytellers, but the language of his poem is too vague to argue that interpretation convincingly, especially because the poem comes back to the "ghostliness" of Indigenous communities – Newlove doesn't produce one satisfying image of a living, breathing Indigenous figure who can tell the stories he knows exist.

Yet Newlove is also highly critical of "romantic" histories written within Western frameworks. His persona grapples for an extended period with G.E. Hyde's *Red Cloud's Folk: A History of the Oglala Sioux Indians* (1937), a historical text that documents the westward movement of the Sioux during the nineteenth century. Because Newlove appended notes about Hyde's text to his diary entry from 10 July 1964, it appears that he was reading *Red Cloud's Folk* the day he began to write "The Pride." Hyde's presence in the text is unmistakable. Newlove borrows directly from him, as in the instance of Newlove's "crazy dogs, men / tethered with leather dog-thongs to a stake, fighting until dead" (*BNW* 105), an image that comes directly from Hyde: "it would appear that the Sioux warriors who were killed about 1801 were Crazy Dogs who staked themselves out with dog-ropes and remained where they were until killed" (32n8). These are not reverential allusions to Hyde; they are condemnatory renderings of historians writing in the colonialist grain.

Newlove is clearly critical of Hyde's colonial vision. Consider the excerpt below, on which Newlove drew in "The Pride":

> [J.B.]Truteau found the [Teton Sioux] coming on friendly visits to the Arikaras and even warning that tribe that some other Sioux bands were planning to attack their villages. We may therefore picture the little Teton camps about the year 1760 coming in on foot, with their little tipi poles tied in bundles to the sides of their big dogs [...] But these Tetons, being the wild, fickle folk that they were also raided the villages [...] (18)

Hyde's prejudices are obvious: his condescending "picture" of the "little" camps and the peoples' "little" tools is as objectionable as his animalistic description of the "wild, fickle" Teton Sioux. Compare

Hyde's passage with Newlove's opening lines, which I've drawn from two versions of the poem:

<table>
<tr><td>The image: the pawnees
in their earth-lodge villages,
the image
of teton sioux, wild
fickle people the chronicler says
(Tamarack 37; 1965)</td><td>I
The image/   the pawnees
in their earth-lodge villages,
the clear image
of teton sioux, wild
fickle people the chronicler says
(BNW 105; 1968)</td></tr>
</table>

The introductions to the 1965 and 1968 versions share the implied exhortation, directed at the reader, to conjure up an "image," which is not unlike Hyde's self-effacing line: "*we* may therefore *picture*" (emphasis added). Even if Hyde's visual language lingers in these lines, Newlove's endorsement of them seems unlikely. If, for example, Newlove's intention in the above excerpts from "The Pride" was to describe a "clear image" as Hyde attempts to do, then his decision to replace (in line 1) his grammatically sound colon from the 1965 version with an interruptive backslash in the 1968 version and to add a distracting gap preceding "the pawnees" is mystifying. Newlove's revisions, in fact, highlight his initial distrust of Hyde's historical vision: the "clear image" is symbolically distorted or obscured by the backslash. And the physical gap on the page between Hyde's narrated image and the "pawnees" is an equally symbolic distance between the observer and the observed, as though one bears little relation to the other – a gap, in other words, in understanding. Likewise, his addition of "clear" seems ironic (or at least deeply conflicted), because the speaker later says that "mirage[s]" are embedded in these "clear image[s]" (*BNW* 105; "mirage" repeats in section III [107]).

The irony of a "clear" image is made more explicit when Newlove reflects on the consequences of colonialism in an allusion to Hyde's *Red Cloud's Folk*. The relevant passage from Hyde needs extended quotation:

> The Arikaras were no longer the timid folk, without horses or metal weapons [...] They now were mounted; they had Spanish sabre-blades with which to point their long, heavy buffalo-lances, and in the open plains they could ride down and destroy any small body of Sioux, that people still being afoot. [...] We may therefore accept without hesitation the statement made by the Arikaras to Lewis and Clark in 1804; namely, that they had not formerly feared the Sioux, that it was the smallpox that destroyed

their power, and that it was only after this disease had carried off most of their people that the Sioux began to annoy them seriously. (17)

For the most part, Hyde's tone implies that he believes colonial contact helped the Arikaras: it permitted trade and thus these peoples' obtainment of horses and "metal weapons" to defeat their enemies. He celebrates the strength of the Arikaras, who use "long, heavy" weapons to destroy their weaker, "small[er]" enemy. Hyde's romantic reading of the Arikaras blinds him to the negative effect of colonialism, and he appears utterly indifferent to the consequences of smallpox. My reading of Hyde complements Newlove's in the first section of "The Pride":

image, arikaras
with spanish sabre-blades
mounted on the long
heavy buffalo lances,
riding the sioux
down, the horsemen
scouring the level plains
in war or hunt
until smallpox got them,
4,000 warriors
(*Tamarack* 37; 1965)

image: arikaras
with traded spanish sabre blades
mounted on the long
heavy buffalo lances,
riding the sioux
down, the centaurs, the horsemen
scouring the level plains
in war or hunt
until smallpox got them,
4,000 warriors
(*BNW* 105; 1968)

In 1980, Susan Wood correctly hypothesized that Newlove drew on a source text by an author inattentive to the fact that "the lives of these post-contact tribes are being disturbed, even destroyed, by the white presence" (233). There is evidence of that disturbance even in Newlove's earlier version of "The Pride": his terse lineation and emphasis on death tolls weightily stresses the post-contact trauma brought on by "spanish" weapons and "smallpox." In his revised version, he further underlines the negative colonial influence with additions such as "*traded* spanish sabre blades." The anti-colonial sentiments are as genuine here as in Newlove's later poem, "Ride Off Any Horizon" (1965): "at times to be born / is enough, to be / in the way is too much – // some colonel otter, some / major-general middleton will / get you, you – // indian" (*BNW* 36–7).

Narrative violence concerns Newlove as much as this physical violence; his speaker is troubled by the fragments that others like Hyde have carelessly crafted into historical narratives. "[T]he indians,"

Newlove insists, "are not composed of / the romantic stories / about them" (*BNW* 111). The historian's (that is, Hyde's) image is a distorted vision of the past, one tainted by romanticism and cultural prejudices. Picking up on this suggestion, Wood recognizes that Newlove's "images [...] are incomplete. Not only are they fragments without context, but they are drawn from potentially *unreliable sources*: the white 'chronicler'" (233, emphasis added). It's an important point: readers are expected to attribute this section and its romantic resonances to Hyde and historians like him, not to Newlove.

There are, however, histories toward which Newlove seems more inclined. Section V of "The Pride" starkly contrasts David Thompson's voice with that of Hyde. Newlove invokes the explorer's description of Saukamappee, an "old Man of at least 75 or 80 years of age" (*The Writings of David Thompson* 289): "In 1787, the old cree saukamappee, / aged 75 or thereabout, speaking then / of things that had happened when he was 16, / just a man, told david thompson, / of the raids the shoshonis" (*BNW* 108).[13] The fact that Thompson mediates Saukamappee's story makes his distortion of it inevitable, but that is not something Newlove disguises; Thompson's role as an intermediary is made clear to the reader. But even still, Thompson's text brings Newlove closer to Saukamappee's own voice than the disengaged histories written by figures like Hyde. That idea fascinates me, and it speaks to something on which I remarked in Purdy's poetry: both Purdy and Newlove seem immediately aware that the "I" is fallible when temporally and culturally removed from historical events, and so they both attempt to overcome that sense of removal. Purdy does so through imagination, whereas Newlove combs through testimonials and travel journals. This is a poetic voice drawn to historical ones. Newlove's speaker knows what he cannot know, and thus seeks out a testimonial source, rather than an "objectively" distant academic one, to satiate his curiosity. That is, I suspect, one of the reasons why Newlove never ventures far into broad cultural pasts even as he ponders them.

Newlove's persona, however, is not focused entirely on the past. He desires to populate the "bare" prairies with more diverse "stories" that cumulatively offer "the grand poem / of our land" (*BNW* 109). The "grand poem" should be regarded as a distant ideal, rather than as an impending or realized event. The poet, as Jan Bartley points out, "wants to believe in history regardless of the difficulty" (23):

we seize on
what has happened before,
one line only

will be enough,
a single line and
then the sunlit brilliant image suddenly floods us
with knowledge, shocks our
attentions, and all desire
stops, stands alone (*BNW* 109–10)

The "sunlit brilliant image" contrasts with the distorted "image" that begins Newlove's poem, as well as with the "image" that is tellingly paired with the word "bewildered" at the outset of section III. "The grand poem" is perfectly illuminated knowledge (hence Newlove's pun on "brilliant"), which significantly comes as a "flood"; the allusion to the story of Noah implies that knowledge, like God's flood, will cleanse the world. There is, in other words, a spiritual and ethical benefit to "flood[ing]" the country with new histories. Clément Moisan argues that "The Pride" *is* the "grand poem" (116) – and this claim seems implicit in many antagonistic readings of Newlove's poem – but the speaker's forward-looking language ("one line only / *will* be enough") proves he is *awaiting* this poem, the moment in which "all desire / stops," a seemingly impossible utopian moment in which the world no longer waits for any knowledge.

This leaves the speaker hovering between the histories he challenges and the ones he desires, observing the world through the aperture between the fraudulent, crumbling "romantic stories" of the Anglocentric past and present and the desired "grand poem" of the future. Like Purdy's poems, there is a narrative imagined and desired, but not crafted; the persona's estrangement, culturally and temporally, prevents that final process. This interstitial position may not lead to the fulfilment of anyone's desire for a "clear image" of history, but it allows his speaker to voice the historical crisis he observes, his hope for the future, and his faith in the stories of the prairies, as well as his evident, if subtle, desire to hear unheard voices who can speak personally of events and stories from the past. These features gesture to the poetic model Newlove established: a sceptical lyric attentive to regionalism and historical ambiguity but resistant to romantic representations of the past.

Although my reading of "The Pride" in the context of its composition, modernism, and allusions clarifies Newlove's project and proposes reasons for its importance to his contemporaries, the shortcomings of his poem should not be ignored. Newlove was sceptical of what he read; it seems only fitting that readers should be sceptical of him, too. Certainly, Newlove's description of "d'sonoqua" as "the wild woman of the woods" (*BNW* 107; he also uses the phrase in "The Big Bend" [*BNW* 102]) reinforces stereotypes of the romanticized "Indian" who is "closely associated with the wilderness" (Francis 162). There are, too, his damning final lines.[14] Indigenous peoples, the persona says,

still ride the soil
in us, dry bones a part
of the dust in our eyes,
needed and troubling
in the glare, in
our breath, in our
ears, in our mouths,

in our bodies entire, in our minds, until at
last we become them
in our desires, our desires,
mirages, mirrors, that are theirs, hard-
riding desires, and they
become our true forbears, moulded
by the same wind or rain,
and in this land we
are their people, come
back to life. (*BNW* 111)

This is a difficult passage. Newlove's suggestion that "their people" survive only through "us" is a blatant invocation of the vanishing race motif, and neither the fact that the motif was commonplace in 1964 nor the poet's sympathetic rendering of it makes the experience of encountering it any less disconcerting. And here is yet another tension in Newlove's poem: as he replicates colonial tropes here, he is also lamenting settlers' obliviousness to the antecedent peoples who first "r[ode] the soil" and first experienced the "same wind or rain." Paul Denham reads "The Pride" by focusing on that aspect of it and regarding these lines as a reminder "that the history of the prairies antedates the history of white settlement" (27). To put it another way: "we" (i.e., settlers) are like "their" (i.e., Indigenous) ancestors and descendants by virtue of a shared regional experience, and so "we" ignorantly breathe the dust "*they've*" made. The lines may not be a paean to imperialism, but they are profoundly flawed if only because Newlove replicates a divisive colonial binary ("us" and "them") and invokes the proverbial "vanishing race" myth.

This is a moment in the poem that unmistakably shows Newlove, regardless of his evident intentions to do otherwise, failing to step outside his own position. The poem speaks to and from within a settler tradition, which means that it also potentially disrupts or altogether sabotages readers' ability to see Indigenous history from a different perspective, one less indulgent in stereotypes of cultural atrophy or vanishing. These aspects of Newlove's poem are obvious challenges to any suggestion of his general progressiveness – including my own.

While "The Pride" was influential in its time, it now seems much less relevant and there is understandably much less likelihood for it to influence a contemporary audience. To some extent, Newlove sensed the poem's shortcomings, even if he couldn't quite identify what they were; he confessed to Robert Bringhurst that the poem was and always would be "somehow [...] unfinished" (Newlove to Bringhurst). Readers can and should approach the poem from the perspective of the present, but it is also important to appreciate that the poem once ignited writers' excitement about prairie history. "The Pride," Susan Gingell notes, obliged writers to "credit" Newlove with "helping to create a voice in which Saskatchewan and other prairie poets could speak" ("Ways" 124). Denham similarly concludes that "[p]erhaps no single person can be assigned the credit for making the prairies available at last for poetic treatment, but John Newlove has excellent claim. [...] Newlove's first three books [...] broke ground, pointed the way" (26).

Newlove's poem was also a sign to historians that Canadian poetry was beginning to articulate a social history, however rudimentary, of the country. When Margaret Prang gave her 1977 address to the Canadian Historical Association, she singled out Newlove as one of the poets who "heightened" the "sensitivity" of "the general reader and the social historian ... to the impact of place and history on the Canadian consciousness" (8), and went on to quote "The Pride" as a poem exemplary of "diverse, limited identities" in Canada (9). As Canadian historical narratives moved in the direction of "regional and local history," they were, according to Prang, becoming better equipped to deal with "the contemporary realities of this country" by abandoning "the old well-worn" and "unifying" narratives for a more inclusive history. Prang thus invokes Cook's term "limited identities" in order to stress the importance of regionalist history as a set of stories that evidence the great diversity of Canadian experiences, both past and present: "Our capacity to comprehend and feel these regional identities," Prang said as she quoted excerpts from "The Pride" to her audience, "provides firm ground for the hope that we are creating a nation which can continue to be a home for all of us" (9).

Today, Prang would surely look to a more culturally diverse set of writers than she had in 1977 in order to make her point. Still, her preoccupation with Newlove's "The Pride" at that time is understandable: widely read and well known, the poem posed provocative questions about habitualized and narrow colonial narratives familiar to her generation. Newlove was urging readers and writers to explore and create new literatures to serve as a foundation for new discourses on prairie literature and history. In that respect, the poem would surely have seemed progressive to a settler historian like Prang, who said that historians must learn to "illuminate the tensions and compromises [of a] pluralist society" and "abandon [their] apologetic stance toward regional and local history" (9). Perhaps that is what compelled Prang to use Newlove as an example in her talk, because "The Pride" is one of many preliminary, if deeply problematic and inconsistent, engagements with fundamental questions about "limited identities" and the impact of colonialism on people living in Canada. In the years after 1964, poets would take part in a more ubiquitous effort to pay even closer attention to such topics.

4 The Métis Uprisings: Challenging Histories, Part 2

As historians and creative writers began to show more interest in the regional past and "limited identities" after 1960, they evidently learned that scepticism was not just intuitive but also critically necessary when challenging conventional histories and experiencing the challenge of writing better ones. Centennial-era prairie poetry exemplifies this epistemological bind, especially in poems where writers confront the limits of their perception and knowledge. A case in point is centennial-era poetry about the two uprisings that Louis Riel and the Métis led against the Canadian government – the first in 1869–70 and the second in 1885.[1]

My purpose in exploring these poems is not just to provide deeper insight into a progressive regional history as a feature of much lyric historiography, but also to probe more thoroughly the difficulty that poets faced as they studied the past, even when adopting a local perspective. In the specific case of poems about the Métis, distance is a recurring concern, especially for non-Indigenous poets for whom distance has as much to do with each poet's cultural position as with their temporal distance from earlier eras. With that observation in mind, I have opted for the moment to focus on non-Indigenous poets in this chapter for two primary reasons: first, to keep continuity with previous chapters by writing about those who were directly tied to the projects Purdy and Newlove began in the 1960s; and second, to maintain my attention to the relationship between historical distance (temporal, genealogical, and cultural) and narrative ambiguity, which is less at issue in poems about the Métis uprisings written by later Indigenous writers like Beth Cuthand ("Seven Songs for Uncle Louis") and Gregory Scofield (*Louis: The Heretic Poems*), both of whom emphasize connections between, rather than distances between, the author and their subject. Distance indeed remains key in this chapter, as each poem I present proves a point essential to understanding the literary endeavours I will explore in later chapters: for a mindful poet, the confidence to narrate history with a genuine feeling of authority depends in large part on the strength of that writer's personal connection to the past they represent.

In many cases, non-Indigenous representations of the Métis uprisings do not offer such authority, and one often finds a very divided portrayal of events, both in history and literature. Before 1980, histories about the Métis uprisings tended to focus on Riel to the exclusion of most other historical figures, and so the picture of the period is often incomplete and distorted. Writers also indulged in polarized readings of Riel. Before 1967, historians typically regarded him as Canada's stock antagonist, a villain who, as the historian Carl Wittke described him in 1928, "stalked across the stage of Canadian history" (202). That view reigned until "the Riel boom," which Pierre Trudeau helped inaugurate by declaring Riel "a national hero" in 1967 (Dales 12).[2] To some historians and writers, Riel was an ideal historical figure: he was malleable enough to serve any purpose historians and creative writers needed because he had far-reaching political, religious, and ethnic associations that allowed numerous groups to champion him. He became a Canadian underdog in various cultural discourses: for some he symbolized French-Canadian resistance, to others he embodied the resilience of the Métis people and other Indigenous communities, and some even regarded him as "a Father of Confederation" (Braz 3). The diversity and incompatibility of such readings epitomize the challenge of historical consensus.

While it would seem impossible to argue credibly for an incontestable narrative about Riel or the Métis uprisings, some writers have tried to do so. Most post-1967 histories that were sympathetic to Riel may have seemed "new" relative to the villainizing histories written during the first half of the century. And yet those new narratives were no less polarized and no less biased than the Anglocentric anti-Riel narratives that preceded them; the political turmoil of Canada's 1960s did much to steer this "new" history and its more favourable interpretation of the Métis uprisings. Readers may find these later histories preferable to the colonially minded and antagonistic ones, but the pro-Riel narratives are still exclusionary to one degree or another: many centennial-era academics excluded the Métis at large from their histories (except, of course, Riel), while others frequently sidestepped questions about Riel's personal struggles as a leader. This vacillation between one polarized reading and another perfectly exemplifies the instability of historical representation.

In Canadian poetry, there were similar developments. Some poets remained willing to be absolute in villainizing or heroizing Riel. Raymond

Souster, over a period of years, did both. In "Riel, 16 novembre, 1885" (1962), his speaker attacks Riel as a selfish madman who "talks with God" and refuses to do the "dirty work" of revolutions (*Collected II* 239). When Riel became the proverbial underdog of Canadian history during the 1970s, however, Souster celebrated him as a poet and as an overlooked historical figure (Dales 9).[3] Dorothy Livesay's documentary poem *Prophet of the New World: A Poem for Voices* (1972) is an exasperatingly approving and mawkish reading of Riel, the gentle "boy" who, affirmed and spoken to by God Himself, grew wisely to be "a hunter, yet a dreamer" (148). Don Gutteridge's *Riel: A Poem for Voices* (1968) is equally one-sided. His Riel speaks in perfect English, even when he questions his own fluency: "You will excuse me, you know my difficulty in speaking English" (62). Riel's elided Métis accent is, I suspect, meant to make him more "reader-friendly" for English audiences than Gutteridge's barbarous Thomas Scott, whose self-incriminating lines are spoken in an alienating and slang-ridden dialect; there may be a variety of speakers in Gutteridge's poem, but it seems clear that he has pre-decided with whom he wants his readers to connect.

Other poets inveighed against indeterminate histories as an alternative to definitive ones. In "Louis Riel" (1965), William Hawkins appears to recognize and, at times, even appreciate the inherent difficulty of historical study, but by the end of his poem, the speaker unexpectedly does an about-face: he draws on Souster's impetuous concluding lines from "Riel, 16, novembre, 1885" and bitterly condemns Riel's "fucked up visions" (65). Jennifer Reid is right to read Hawkins's conclusion as evidence that the poet has become "exasperated by the gulf in understanding" and indifferent to the fact that Riel's "ambiguity [...] has sustained the interest of Canadians for more than a century" (47). For Hawkins, ambiguity is undesirable, even when it is logical. But by resisting ambiguity, many such portrayals of the Métis uprisings offer colourless treatments of history that date themselves. That is why I find Patrick Holland's argument that such poetry is characteristically "ironic" (213) a bit too charitable: Livesay's poem is hardly "Eliot[ic]" (215) in tone, and I have sincere reservations about Gutteridge's *Riel* as "a deep phenomenological probing" (220) that "cannot gather to one voice" (221). Hawkins, Souster, Livesay, and Gutteridge adopt fair approaches to poetry, but the history each poem conveys is oversimplified.

There are, however, poems about the Métis uprisings that better capture the ambiguous legacy of these events. Like the work of Newlove and Purdy generally, this poetry does not purport to offer "better" versions of history. The poets emphasize a series of epistemological quandaries, rather than an urge to accept a totalized or new historical narrative. These are the qualities of various poems by Newlove ("Crazy Riel"), Purdy ("The Battlefield at Batoche"), Lorna Crozier ("Drifting Towards Batoche"), Elizabeth Brewster ("At Batoche"), and Mick Burrs ("Under the White Hood"), all of which were written and published between 1965 and 1985. During this twenty-year period, these writers were well acquainted with each other. I've already demonstrated Newlove's connection to Purdy in chapter 3. Crozier has spoken candidly about Purdy and Newlove as influences: while describing herself as a poet "rooted in place," she noted Purdy's paradigmatic role as a "poet of place" (Crozier and Philips 150), and Crozier's fifth book of poetry, *The Weather* (1983), drew its title and epigraph from Newlove's poem of the same name. Brewster titled one of the poems in *In Search of Eros* (1974) "Poem for Al Purdy," and she and Purdy presented together at the University of Ottawa's 1989 conference on Bliss Carman. A friend to Brewster during the late 1960s and early 1970s when she lived in Edmonton, Mick Burrs recalls that it was reading the poems of Purdy and Newlove, especially those "with an historical base to them" that "influenc[ed]" his own urge to write about the past (Burrs and Weingarten).[4] These tangible connections are useful in establishing some sense of a loose-knit group of writers drawn together as leading figures in a growing community of Canadian poets. At the same time, an equally important connection among them is their shared expression of scepticism in their writing. Reading these five poets side by side shows a range of poems, written by poets familiar with each other's work, that exemplify lyric historiography in so far as they continue to explore the concept of "limited identities" in regional history while also contemplating the limits and potential of history as an expression of the "I."

Newlove's "Crazy Riel" (1965; *BNW* 18–19) is an early example.[5] Like "The Pride," "Crazy Riel" balances the speaker's ambiguous faith in the value of history with his frustrated meditation on fragments of the past. The speaker's undertaking may seem Sisyphean, but his desire to know allows him to endure history's chaos. The desire here, of course, is for the recovery of a lucid history. From the beginning of the poem, though, the speaker's faith in the coherence of history and even of poetry appears threatened: "Time to write a poem / or something. / Fill up a page." Immediately, the reader is disoriented: the poet-persona's distrust of his own skill as a poet (as he can only produce "something" and not necessarily a poem), of the "page" (as something mindlessly "filled up"), and, in later lines, of "young men['s]" knowledge signals a distrust of identity, epistemology, history, and even the possibilities of poetry. This dense opening seeds various doubts that persist throughout the poem, all of which relate back to the poet-speaker's immediate struggle to apprehend the past.

Newlove's sudden slips between time periods and generally vague distinctions between the past and present feed his doubt. There are the "young men" who "keep quiet, / contemporaneously," a passage paired with the persona's memory of his "boyhood home" where children "catch [frogs] for bait or sale / Or caught them." Not only does the abrupt change in tense signal the persona's confused sense of time, but it also echoes Purdy's compulsion to qualify statements and declarations in his lyric historiography. In moments such as these, Newlove's speaker appears temporally disoriented, even if spatially grounded. This experience compounds as the speaker continues: the poem seems to adopt Riel's point of view when the speaker sees "[h]uge massed forces of men / hating each other" on the battlefield. Temporally unstable as they are, these lines mark the confluence of the speaker's present, his boyhood, and Riel's memories. The confusion thus denotes a chronological collapse: as in Newlove's other poems (e.g., "The Pride") the persona experiences history and time spatially. He simultaneously regards multiple fragments of history from a physical point in his present: the oscillation between, even conflation of, past and present denotes a problematic relationship between the speaker's personal memories of his boyhood home and broader cultural ones such as the Riel rebellions. The speaker's memories determine his entry point into a broader history.

A coherent and objective image of the past therefore is difficult to retrieve. What emerges instead is a synesthetic image, one made up of "noise":

> To fill up a page.
> To fill up a hole.
> To make things feel better. Noise.
> The noise of the images
> that are people I will never understand.
> Admire them though I may.
> Poundmaker. Big Bear. Wandering Spirit,
> those miserable men.
> Riel. Crazy Riel. Riel hanged.

Here is a more complex example of the "history-as-image" motif than appears in "The Pride." Accumulation and an appeal to the "image" of history appear codependent, which further highlights the imagist quality of Newlove's writing. "[A]ccumulative structure," John Gage notes, "predominates in imagist poetry" (109). Such structure relies heavily on catalogues, which offer "a principle of continuation, but no principle of closure" (119). The catalogic properties of Newlove's passage are obvious: at the end of this excerpt, he explicitly names several historical figures and thinly alludes to Kittimakegin (also known as "Miserable Man"), who was hanged alongside Wandering Spirit on 27 November 1885. The consequence of a structure predicated on this dense accumulation of images is an inevitable disorientation that the speaker shares with the reader. Newlove's passage, that is to say, is laden with paradox: historical figures are both admirable and unknowable. Such self-contradictory claims cast aspersions on the persona's authority over historical narrative. So, too, does his allusion to Miserable Man, which can be interpreted variously: the persona may have made a joke (though the sombre tone makes this possibility seem unlikely to me), has mistaken part of the Cree name for an adjective, or is simply ignorant of how closely he treads to the name of another Cree; his appallingly abridged history of Riel certainly reveals his limitations as a historian or storyteller. The indeterminable function of the reference is the point. Confusion is integral to Newlove's perspective on history.

The poet-speaker therefore contends with a synesthetic "noise" of "images" that impedes his desire to "understand" the men he "admires." The visuality/aurality of these historical figures, in effect each one's historical identity, appears inchoate: "Politics must have its way. / The way of noise. To fill up. / The definitions bullets make." Newlove's familiar description of a heedless "filling up" reappears in these lines, but he fragments the syntax more noticeably than in earlier lines: "to fill up a page" versus "To fill up. / The definitions." Syntax, like historical meaning, feels less and less coherent at such moments. The lines also feel enjambed, as though politicians want to "fill up the definitions bullets make." The line implies concealment, as though politicians (and, presumably, historians) hide unsavoury aspects of history. Narratives can only be "noise," as opposed to knowledge. Newlove's word choice, then, is ironic: the eager "filling of definitions" actually impedes a "definitive" Canadian history: dominant models of history are predicated on the politics of the present.

Similarly troubling is the fact that history might be interpreted variously, which the speaker's shifts between the lyric "I" and the second-person pronoun highlight. The early articulation of "people [the speaker] will never understand" returns at the end of the poem in the second person:

The images of death hang upside-down.
Grey music.
It is only the listening for death,
fingering the paraphernalia,
the noise of the men you admire.
And cannot understand.
Knowing little enough about them.

Although the pronoun "you" might be a self-reflexive or general referent, the suggestion that the men Newlove's "I" admires may differ from those "you" admire remains implicit. What is common to both "I" and "you," though, is the inability to "understand" or to "know" these historical figures, which is rooted in Newlove's returned auditory image; the inverted "image" and "grey music" are paired. But this returned noisy image feels even more difficult to comprehend: the image is inverted, synesthetic, and, one infers, coloured a neutral "grey." The image of "grey music" is baffling. What was audible is now (or is also) visual, yet it appears in grey scale. The sheer difficulty of the image is surely Newlove's point: it is indefinable and lends itself to a "grey" significance, rather than to a "black" and "white" meaning. Coupled with the audible image is death's silence, for which the speaker waits. He pauses, "listening for death," perhaps for the deaths "of the men [he] admire[s]." Yet, the speaker has already said that "you are the only listener" for the "noise your dying makes," in which case listening for another's death would be futile. The passage is a superb example of Newlove's complex vision of history: an upside-down, grey, inaudible music.

If Newlove's preoccupation with the idea of "images" does in fact stem from the imagist movement of the 1910s, then he has radically reinterpreted the imagists' faith in "direct treatment of the thing." For Anglo-American imagists, Gage maintains, the image was "a means of discovering" the "true nature of things" (12). But even if Newlove is drawn to the idea of such an image, his lyric historiography often confronts an elusive historical truth. A sceptic reading history cannot expect a true past to reveal itself, but the interrogation of truth itself can lend greater value to whatever faith the poet retains in what can only be partially comprehended. His faith is understandably minimal, but still felt in the poem: history is difficult, but still inhabits the poet's memory and thoughts. The ongoing desire for the direct image, more than the achievement or comprehension of it, is more palpable. This desire is the crux of Newlove's lyric.

Newlove's lyric historiography, then, finds the reader's experience of the confusion and paradox ingrained in historical study more profitable than a specious claim for historical truth or a forced and flawed sense of closure. The past is necessarily but also productively fragmented. It engenders an ongoing and sceptical negotiation of subjectivity, perspectivism, politics, noise, and the "now/then" binary collapse. His conclusion to "Crazy Riel" epitomizes such experiences:

> The knowledge waxing.
> The wax that paves hell's road,
> slippery as the road to heaven.
> So that as a man slips
> he might as easily slide
> into being a saint as destroyer.
> In his ears the noise magnifies.
> He forgets men.

In three short lines, Newlove offers three images of "slipping," an image one finds enacted throughout "Crazy Riel": temporal slippages or the slips between first- and second-person pronouns. In this passage, the persona refers primarily to semantic or characterological "slips," as one might label Riel a saint (as Livesay does in *Prophet of the New World*) or a destroyer (as Souster did, before changing his opinion years later). Yet Newlove's use of "as" offers another reading, where "as" functions as a preposition: the saint, paradoxically, as a destroyer. In light of so many interpretive possibilities, "knowledge" appears "slippery" and the historical record dissonant: there are multiple incompatible perspectives from which one can view the past.

This dissonance is the ominous and magnifying "noise" in Newlove's piece. Noise here might refer back to "noise" that politicians make, but as the poem has accumulated images, names, sounds, ambiguous audible colours, and temporal fragments, the poem might itself now be regarded as noise. If the poem has become noise, then Newlove implicates himself as a participant in history's troubling dissonance. Like Purdy, he asserts his authority through a persuasive argument of his own failure to overcome subjective history. Whatever its source, this noise "magnifies" until an ambiguous male figure becomes a negligent narrator who "forgets men." The pronoun in the final line might refer to Riel or to a more contemporary, even self-reflexive, voice. Whoever "he" is, his insular reception of historical noise reveals that the narrative act is solipsistic and unreliable in its egotism. Deafened by the noise of history, individuals hear only themselves and forget others and their points of view. The speaker's general doubt about his own ability to represent Riel marks history's instability, but so too do the generally indeterminate referents at the end of the poem, which undermine any sense of closure.

"Crazy Riel" evidences Newlove's tremendous strides toward a fuller realization of content and themes that he first experimented with in "The Pride," particularly with regard to his complex meditation on subjectivity and its relationship to historical narrative. He explores a major fault line in historical study: the subjective apprehension of an inscrutable history. Difficulty becomes a necessary feature of his poetry because a precise, objective history is impossible; the subjectivism of lyric poetry is all that is left to him. Hence Newlove adopts the lyric mode so that he may sombrely explore whether and how history can exist independently of the historian's or the poet's present – but, of course, it cannot exist as such. Authority thus seems suspended, whether that be the authority of politicians, historians, or poets who attempt to "fill up" spaces with noise. As Purdy does in his lyric historiography, Newlove underscores his limitations as an observer of a potentially unresolvable and distant history. The poem also brilliantly captures the aura of imagistic accumulation, which is – as I argued in my last chapter – integral to Newlove's poetics. In the absence of stable historical images, he uses accumulation to structure his poems, and in this "Crazy Riel" is an archetype. Newlove catalogues disconnected and fragmented images of the past (the images of frogs, men fighting, Riel hanging, et cetera) and also provocatively juxtaposes audible and visual experiences in order to entangle the reader in a synesthetic picture: the "noisy" "image" of history.

The reaching for a clear, audible past in Newlove's "Crazy Riel" is a defining quality of Purdy's "The Battlefield at Batoche" (1972; *S&D* 41–3). Sightseeing with his wife, Purdy's persona hears one particular sound, which appears to be history itself. The poem revolves around this vague sound, but Purdy's speaker is unable to identify it unequivocally:

> I hear a different kind of murmur
> – no more than that at least not definitely
> the sort of thing you do hear
> every now and then in a city never
> questioning because it's so ordinary
> but not so ordinary here

The sound is the primary event in "The Battlefield at Batoche." Its source is uncertain, but Purdy offers some clues as to its origin or nature. The poet's significantly homophonic pairing of "hear" and "here" roots this sound of the past in the present, which implies that history has paradoxically become contemporaneous. The familiar pairing of "now and then" is equally revealing. Most obviously, it is an idiomatic suggestion of something cyclical (things happen now and then, over and over). Also the pairing reminds the reader of a temporal distinction (now is not then). Yet it also hints at commonality (the sound is here now and was there in the past), which fits well with Purdy's assessment of his poetry in his essay, "The Cartography of Myself" (1971): "then and now merge somewhat in my mind" (*SFA* 16). History is both "now and then": a fragment of some vague cultural memory lingers in the present, but Purdy's speaker remains too far removed from its source to determine its meaning. He thus resists narrating the past. Objective distance becomes meaningless, because distance here means that the poet is simply too far from history to observe or represent it faithfully.

Central to this struggle is the persona's hope that history is audible. Although the idea of an "audible" history lingers throughout Purdy's oeuvre (in chapter 1 and chapter 2, I noted examples in "Method for Calling Up Ghosts," "Remains of an Indian Village," and "Roblin's Mills"), the motif features more prominently in "The Battlefield at Batoche." Purdy can only "wonder" about the "the day of May 12 in 1885" and how that day may have sounded in the ears of those who were there.

Purdy's poetic construction actually mimics his speaker's feeling of distance: "The Battlefield at Batoche" is composed of erratic and partial rhymes that parallel the faint aurality of history. The rhymes are utterly unpredictable. He begins the poem with brief ABCA rhyme patterns: "trees" (line 1) and "groceries" (line 4), "murmur" (line 9) and "never" (line 12). The scheme vanishes, but returns in the final pseudo-quatrain: "me" (line 102) and "eternity" (line 105). Sprinkled throughout the rest of the poem are perfect couplets ("force" [line 49] and "force" [line 50]) and sparsely placed end rhymes: "definitely" (line 10), "ordinary" (line 13), "Company" (line 55), "eternity" (line 105), "anyway" (line 41), "Desjarlais" (line 68), "say" (line 78), and "away" (line 89). Other examples of repetition, such as "demonstrator" and "demonstrating" (lines 55, 56) or "distant" and "distance" (lines 24, 36; a key word for Purdy to repeat, in light of my reading), are further examples of the poem's various echoes. These rhymes and polyptotonic structures leave sounds lingering throughout the poem, just as the past lingers aurally in the speaker's mind. Yet neither the poem nor history takes a readily discernible form. The past is an accumulation of "whispers," barely heard by the listener. The poem, like Newlove's "Crazy Riel," portrays the poet's yearning to hear more than a whisper, to overcome temporal and cultural distance so that the past will speak for itself. That yearning, of course, is never fulfilled.

As a poet who came into contact with the lyric historiography of both Purdy and Newlove, Lorna Crozier likewise emphasizes her temporal and, in ways much more overt than Purdy or Newlove, cultural distance from the past. While I wouldn't argue that Crozier's poetry is best known for its historical dimension (she writes much more often about gender and sexuality), she has occasionally written lyrics that exhibit her sceptical reading of the past. That aspect of her historically themed poems complements Susan Gingell's broader reading of Crozier's lyric in a poem such as "Myth," which, according to Gingell, is a paradigm of Crozier's "I": the deeply introspective speaker who prefers "a plurality of possible ways of understanding human beginnings" to any "single" or "sacred" interpretation ("Let Us Revise" 67). Arguing for that confidently sceptical lyric is an echo of the existing criticism on Crozier, which is consistently attentive to her "I" as a speaker who Marilyn Rose says offers "provisional" interpretations of the world that are "rooted in longing" and only "partial" with regard to their sense of resolution or coherence (56). So while Crozier may not be the most prolific writer of historiographic poems, her broader poetics is a continual gesture to the kind of persona typical of lyric historiography: introspective and sceptical.

When Crozier is writing about history, these qualities of her poetics shape her encounters and near-misses with the past, as in "Drifting Towards Batoche" (1985; Amabile and Dales 184). Canoeing to Batoche and observing herons flying overhead, her persona tries to piece together a specific image of the past. Crozier wrote the poem after a "canoe trip down the Saskatchewan River," during which she passed Batoche, the location of Riel's last battle in May 1885: "There's a strong sense of mystery to the old townsite where the battle [of Batoche] took place [...] I struggled with finding words for that place as I saw it that one afternoon. I wanted to be sure that I captured something of the feelings it evoked but I was wary of making any false claims" (Email from Crozier). I admire the caution in Crozier's poetic vision: she is respectful of "mystery," creatively driven by "struggle," and "wary" of misleading her reader to some overarching, and inevitably insincere, truth about the past. Because she explores these tensions in "Drifting Towards Batoche," the poem rises above superficial feelings of closure and reaches instead for genuine exploration. The title of the poem is itself suggestive of such things: the image of a speaker drifting invokes a journey that is more a meditative wandering than a guided exercise, and so there is, by implication, some doubt as to whether or not she will reach her destination. That is a curious point of contrast with romantic poets, whose lyric speakers are often geographically grounded by the title of their poems (think Carman's "Low Tide at Grand Pré" or Whitman's "Manhattan"). Here, Crozier's lyric persona is actually at a distance from Batoche, hoping to move toward it, which reinforces my earlier assertions that lyric historiography values and understands the effort involved in getting "closer" to a past that is, in the poet's mind, tentative and amorphous. That is likely why Crozier places so much emphasis on images of water (and thus fluidity) rather than on (literally or figuratively) firmer ground.

Indeed, the image of fluidity captures the difficulty of grasping and holding onto the past. Crozier's speaker sometimes seems on the brink of a historical connection, but she also continually, and I would say more emphatically, acknowledges her disconnection:

> The river we travel is the one
> Gabriel crossed. The same
> feeling rises in my breast
> each time I see the heron,
> hear the word Batoche. A sense of loss
> and grief. A distant pride,
> though these were not my people.

Striking here is Crozier's interpretation of Purdy's "transmigration of souls," the metaphysical trace people leave behind them. In Crozier's poem, her speaker appears to transcend time through this method: she feels a trace of Gabriel Dumont's historical self in the water that they have, in different eras, shared. But the passage simultaneously posits a Heraclitean dilemma; one cannot step twice in the same river – that is, one can neither experience the river as Dumont did nor meet him there. The logic unfolds slowly and brilliantly here, with Crozier masterfully manipulating our reading experience with her enjambment and caesurae. She first tempts the reader to believe this river is the "same" river that Dumont rode, and she emphasizes that connection with her mid-line pause. Then, in line 13, she completes the thought. She appears to mean now that it is not (or maybe not just) the river she shares with Dumont, but a feeling instead. In that moment, read in isolation from the lines that follow, the speaker suggests that travelling the same route as Dumont makes his emotional response immanent in her. That connection weakens as the reader moves further into the poem: the speaker completely dissociates the feeling from Dumont. It is not that she feels the "same" things Dumont did; rather, she feels the "same" things she has felt before. At this point, the poem becomes less about the Purdyean "transmigration of souls" and more about the persona's "sense of loss" and her "distant pride" as she reflects on a distant past. That word, "distant," obviously has some connotations pertinent to lyric historiography: it is, on the one hand, suggestive of temporal distance, but, on the other hand, it is also a cultural distance (because Dumont and his followers "were not [her] people"). It's an interesting trajectory: the stanza begins with diction that optimistically suggests history can be "one" and "the same" with the present, but the speaker drifts away from that premise. Although Crozier's title describes her drift closer to the geographical space of Batoche, her drifting lines actually make it feel as if she is moving further from the past.

As the past becomes unavailable to Crozier's persona, so does Batoche itself. The title does have the positive connotation I note above: a sense of progress, some encouraging note that even if the persona cannot find the past, she can find a relevant geographical space in the present. Given the intense historical consciousness of the speaker, though, I wonder whether or not finding present-day Batoche would satisfy a speaker who seems to want to visit a time more than just a place. The Batoche about which she fantasizes is not the one she will encounter if she proceeds down the river: she wants a geography alive with the history she imagines, which, of course, present-day Batoche is not. She is much more likely to discover what Charles G.D. Roberts once called "the hands of chance and change" ("Tantramar Revisited" line 64), evidence only of her removal from the past. And so I come back to the act of "drifting" as both physical and metaphysical aimlessness. That is exactly what Crozier's open ending further suggests: her persona moves ominously "[p]ast" "the graveyard" and into her own "century," and then, in a moment reminiscent of Joseph Conrad's *Heart of Darkness*, she sees only the "darkness" of Batoche ahead; neither the speaker nor the reader actually reaches the destination. And Crozier introduces a terrific paradox: she knows Batoche is there, she can sense its imminence, only because she cannot see it. She is, to put it a different way, nearest to understanding the past from which she feels estranged once she acknowledges how difficult it is to observe and articulate that past.

Crozier's poem unsurprisingly ends inconclusively, stuck between the place of departure and the place of arrival; never arriving at her destination, the closing lines suggest a purgatorial image that complements Purdy's ending to "Remains of an Indian Village" (which ends with his speaker descended only halfway into history) and Newlove's "The Pride" (which concludes with Newlove's speaker awaiting the arrival of the "grand poem"). Crozier's purgatorial image is as memorable. Most obviously, her trek down the waterway recalls Charon, the underworld ferryman who moves between the worlds of the living and the dead. Crozier's speaker performs that role: her thoughts hover between the living present and dead past. She is stuck in transit (a beautifully conceived paradox). Moving, but never arriving, doomed like the damned Sisyphus to repeat a futile task for all eternity. Crozier's final lines convey this insufferable repetition, as the speaker ruminates on "the heron repeating itself / over and over and over in our eyes." That conclusion is made more compelling by an earlier point of confusion in the poem, when the speaker is unsure whether she sees "the same [heron]" flying overhead or "many herons" in her field of vision. That field is enormously broad: the past, the present, the river, the sky, Batoche now, and Batoche then. Crozier meditates on the limits of lyric sight: how much can the "I" / "eye" see, and how accurately? The massive scope in Crozier's poem is a hindrance to her persona's ability to see anything clearly, and so the reader ends the poem with the feeling of irresolution familiar in lyric historiography.

Unlike Crozier's "Drifting Towards Batoche," Elizabeth Brewster's "At Batoche" (1982; *TWH* 50–2) concerns a speaker who has reached her geographical destination, and yet a better or more resolved vision of history still seems out of reach for Brewster's persona. Partly, this is because Brewster, like Crozier, is often transfixed by what she cannot render, see, or know. Crozier imagines an intangible and fluid history; the river image helps her persona make sense of her own difficulty in grasping a chaotically flowing timeline. Although Brewster does not use water imagery in "At Batoche," literally or abstractly "fluid" movement is a frequent motif in her writing. In "The Moving Image" (1990), Brewster, contemplating Ezra Pound's poetry, says that "marble" can easily "seem liquid" when the only "natural image is a moving image" (16). That line sums up Brewster's personal philosophy as an intellectual, and when her poems pursue lines of inquiry, they tread carefully. Her lyric foregrounds a doubtful "I" forced to question her powers of observation: "So small an insect crosses my page / I almost fail to see it. / Would a bird see it?" (16). The potential "fail[ure] to see" is common in Brewster's writing, even when her persona is looking at herself: in "Seeing My Picture as a Young Girl" (1982), her speaker notes, "I realize now I was pretty / though I always thought I was plain" (*TWH* 19). Even Brewster's earliest chapbooks grapple with these moments of self-doubt, if somewhat more playfully: "My mind," the persona in *Lilloet* (1952) says, "can never find / It possible to make objective analysis, / But remains in a sort of emotional paralysis, / Unable to proceed beyond the personal" (*Collected* I.79). These lines are neither the most modern (Brewster is working in heroic couplets) nor the most skilled in Brewster's oeuvre, but they do capture her profound awareness of her epistemological limits. It's an aspect of her poetics that she reiterated forty years after *Lilloet* in her autobiography: "what is autobiography? Is everything any author writes autobiographical, since (even if she wishes) she cannot go totally beyond the boundaries of her experience and observation?" (*Invention* 5).

Brewster's lifelong awareness of her limits as an observer of anything, including history, has meant that her poems continuously convey what Tom Marshall appropriately calls a "healthy skepticism" ("Introduction" 5). Marshall's summation of Brewster's poetics as inclined to scepticism naturally points to some philosophical overlap among the works of writers I've already discussed, and it is a summation that Bina Freiwald has recently upheld by arguing that Brewster is generally drawn to personas who "can question familiar notions of space, time, and identity (personal, collective, or national)" (103).

This sceptical impulse is what one finds in Brewster's "At Batoche." The poem centres on her persona's wonder as she drifts through historical names and events in her mind. Her persona feels like an outsider, not just because Brewster herself was Maritime-born, but also because her speaker clearly struggles to get close enough to the past to understand. Everything she imagines seems far away:

> Batoche ...
> a strange wild name
> (a trader's nickname, really
> but sounding like a battle-cry)
> a fierce trumpet name
> like Hastings or Culloden.
> Battleground once, now peaceful
> as the sound of summer wind in wild grasses.

The distance here is between the past that "once" was and the "now" that is. The intervening time has obscured even the meaning of names. Naming, though, can be epistemologically affirming. It gives character and identity to an object, time, place, or person. That is definitely one of Purdy's strategies in his poetry ("Say the Names" or "The Country North of Belleville," for instance). Brewster does something slightly different, though. The act of naming assures her speaker of nothing, and the poem becomes something like an endless act of free association. It is no surprise that she finds "wildness" in the names, because she cannot tame them. Some wildly move among different definitions: Batoche is of course the name of the town, but it is also the name of Riel's last battle, the nickname of Xavier Letendre,[6] a "trumpet name" the speaker hears, and a "battle-cry." There are contradictions here, too: the name "Batoche" may seem "fierce," but the battle of Batoche was "no great battle anyway." Whatever Batoche has been in the past or is in the present, its meaning and character seem obscure to Brewster's modern persona.

The slipperiness of "Batoche" as a signifier is only one of many instances in Brewster's poetry that proves knowledge is not something easily obtained, especially knowledge about historical figures. Albert Braz overlooks this aspect of Brewster's poem when he claims that her speaker "finds it surprisingly easy to identify with Gunner Phillips merely upon spotting the young Canadian soldier's grave" (64). His claim misrepresents Brewster's poem, because her speaker flat-out confesses that she "know[s] nothing about" Gunner Phillips. She casually thinks up a catalogue of details about him, all of which she scrutinizes and questions: she presumes Phillips "just turned nineteen," only to claim later that he could have been "forty" when he enlisted. It is noteworthy that, as the persona juggles different possibilities for the past, she notices that tourists take two paths to see Phillips's grave ("under the trees / or down a flight of stone steps"); Brewster's persona metaphorically approaches him, and the past generally, in different ways. Her obvious doubts echo the hesitations of Newlove's speaker in "Crazy Riel," who struggles to comprehend men he "admires" but does not "understand."

Doubt is typical of Brewster's lyric historiography more broadly. In "The Hero as Escape Artist" (1982; *TWH* 53–5), Brewster's persona meditates on the invention of heroes and the ways in which subjectivity affects our reading of the past: for someone on the prairie, "the folk hero is Louis Riel," but "[i]n Ontario, I suppose it's his arch-enemy / the victorious Scot old John A." As her attention shifts toward New Brunswick (her birthplace), Brewster's speaker decides that "the Escape Artist, the Convict Houdini, / Henry More Smith / (alias Frederick Henry More) / tailor, pedlar, burglar, horse-thief / and theatrical showman" is the provincial hero. It's a noteworthy choice: Brewster picks the nefarious Smith, a nineteenth-century conman who lived part of his life in New Brunswick, as the hero of her province, celebrating an "escape artist" who escapes definition. His wiliness is evident in the description above, because the speaker associates Smith with so many names and characteristics that he becomes increasingly mystical to her: he is a "magician, / maybe the Devil himself." Historical identities in "At Batoche" are equally ambiguous: Brewster's speaker wonders if Gunner Phillips was "[p]atriotic" or if Gabriel Dumont and Riel were "[f]olk heroes maybe? / or a parcel of rebels / as my grandfather thought them / and half crazy at that?" None of the historical figures Brewster names in "At Batoche" is less of an "escape artist" than Henry More Smith: if each person can be interpreted so variously (Riel the hero of the prairies and the "half crazy" villain of Ontario, Macdonald the other way around), then each is impossible to capture in any objective sense. There is an implicit quandary here that justifies the scepticism that writers like Brewster exhibit in their poems.

Even in the case of poets like Mick Burrs, who worked closely with a range of historical sources, such scepticism is acute. Through the connections he made in Edmonton, Burrs encountered "more than a few poets writing individuals poems [...] steeped in Canadian history," but it was when Burrs relocated to Regina in 1973 that his "historical consciousness [...] blossomed" (Burrs and Weingarten). He was hired to "annotat[e] the oral history tapes of the Métis people who had been interviewed by Carol Pearlstone for the Saskatchewan Department of Culture and Youth" (Burrs and Weingarten). During the time he spent with these tapes, Burrs found himself enthralled not just by the history to which they testified but also by the dynamic variety of perspectives they documented. In the tapes, Burrs recalls, he "kept hearing over and over stuff about Louis Riel":

> I knew so little about [Riel], but found myself intrigued: for one man to have so much historical significance! I decided to read some books about him, namely George F.G. Stanley's *Louis Riel* and Joseph Howard's *Strange Empire*. Then I had thought of putting together a book of found poems based on the actual transcribed words of the Métis people on the tapes. My boss, Don Graham, thought this was a terrific idea. That is how *Going to War: Found Poems of the Métis People* was born. By the time I finished that project, I found myself writing many poems about Louis Riel. (Burrs and Weingarten)

It would be impossible to encounter Riel from so many perspectives and not feel confusion about the identity and meaning of this historical character. On the one hand, Burrs had George Stanley's depiction of Riel as an agitator, a portrayal that Stanley defended more vigorously in a slimmer text – *Louis Riel: Patriot or Rebel?* (1954) – that he published with the Canadian Historical Association. In that text, Stanley frames Riel's uprisings as a clash between an advanced society and a "primitive" people; he is cavalier and says quite plainly of Riel's role in the uprisings, "Louis Riel was not a great man; he was not even what Carlyle would call a near great" (24). He crudely sums Riel up as "the voice of an inarticulate race" (24). Then, on the other hand, Burrs had the American journalist Joseph Howard's *Strange Empire* (1952), which sympathetically portrays Riel as a revolutionary who, despite having "no precedents to guide him," "did astonishingly well" as a leader (149). Burrs's other influences were the found poems he compiled for *Going to War*, in which interviewees talk about the almost familial relationship the community had with "Old Gabriel [Dumont]" ("Mrs. Nicolas" *Going to War* 31).[7] When Burrs's curiosity about Riel finally had him writing historically conscious poetry, the poems enacted something these books and tapes taught Burrs about people generally: "Human beings are naturally ambiguous." He knew then that a good poem – a good history – had to be "open-ended" (Burrs and Weingarten).

This resistance to closure is an obvious feature of Burrs's "Under the White Hood" (1976), in which there is a balancing of various, sometimes irreconcilable, perspectives and judgments. The poem can sometimes seem sympathetic to Riel: a deep ambivalence regarding Riel's supposed villainy (a remorseful Riel is "torture[d]" by "dreams" [line 72] of a murdered Thomas Scott) underlies Burrs's poem. That occasional sympathy is not so pronounced in the poem as Burrs's troubled efforts to make the dead speak. One of the central figures in the poem is Riel's hangman, Jack Henderson, who had been a prisoner at Fort Garry after Riel had taken control of it during the 1869–70 Red River uprising. Henderson seized the opportunity to hang Riel; it was his act of revenge for his imprisonment and for the execution of the Orangeman Thomas Scott at Fort Garry. The hinge of "Under the White Hood" is Burrs's repetition of Henderson's infamous and chilling final words to Riel: "Louis Riel, do you know me? You cannot escape from me today." Each time Burrs presents Henderson's words on the page, he rearranges or otherwise alters them:

> Louis Riel,
> do you know me?
> You cannot escape from me today. (lines 25–7)
>
> Louis Riel, do you
> know me? You cannot
> escape from me today. (85–7)
>
> Louis Riel,
> do you know me? You
> cannot escape from me today. (112–14)

Louis Riel, don't you know
me? You
cannot escape from me today. (159–61)

Burrs's reconfiguration of Henderson's phrase spurs divergent readings. In the second instance, the dramatic enjambment ominously pairs "know me? You cannot"; the latter half of that particular line sounds almost declarative – one cannot know these individuals. In one sense, that inability is literal, because, to Riel, Henderson's anonymity is total: "under the white hood," he cannot see Henderson or know his identity. I can't help but extrapolate on Burrs's lineated phrase, because it points to a basic quandary in historical writing: every reading of a historical figure begins with the reader in a position of ignorance about the past, which means the figure (if only at first) seems anonymous – maybe even wholly unknowable. The line is, in other words, of much broader importance: can we know those whom we study? Burrs's conclusion to the line would suggest we "cannot." That disconnection between observer and observed takes different forms in every iteration of Henderson's phrase. In the third case, "do you know me? You" sounds almost like an imperative, a teacher's classroom demand that "you" must answer the question. Alternatively, the next iteration of Henderson's phrase contains the odd juxtaposition of "me? You," which could be read to suggest that these identities are interchangeable: "is it me? No, it's *you*." More possibilities still: the me/you pairing could imply something more competitive, where "me" is pitted against "you." There are other curiosities in the fourth iteration: Burrs's contraction ("don't") makes the construction informal, and the negative phrasing alters Henderson's tone. In other instances, Henderson's question sounds like a chilling reminder, but here it sounds almost passive or surprised – how could Riel *not* know his hangman? That slight change makes Henderson sound more egotistical, though one could also suggest that Riel's forgetfulness pains the hangman – "how could he forget *me*?" Every minor modification in the text is a major modification of Henderson's historical self.

Burrs's lines also imply some fascinating possibilities with regard to the authority of the speaker. Each instance of the phrase is evidence that he cannot bring order to the transcribed lines, and he therefore cannot convince his readers that he has accurately captured their meaning. I wonder, though, what the compulsive tweaking of these lines really signifies: the persona may be attempting to piece the past together like a puzzle and, as part of that attempt, may be deliberately adjusting or even playing with the phrase. At the same time, the more compelling reading might be that Henderson's phrase is entirely out of his control: it forms and reforms itself in the poet's mind, without any conscious will, and each time that it does, the meaning changes. Burrs can retrieve a written phrase from history, but he has difficulty imagining that phrase as it may have been spoken. The tone, the connotations, the sentiment elude him. Burrs is left with a transcription that, at best, only resembles Henderson's meaning. The poem is a spectacular demonstration of history's fragility: a single and slight error, any imperfection in or alteration of the record – move a word, change a phrase, shift the emphasis – and the past reads very differently.

The distance Burrs feels from these figures is made more obvious by his frequent representations of anonymity. Hearing Henderson's words, Riel "cannot recall that face. / And that voice is faceless now. / His eyes have been blanked out" (lines 28–30). It's unclear whose eyes have been blanked out: either Burrs reminds the reader of Riel's blindness "under the white hood" or Henderson's eyes are unrecognizable. Interestingly, Henderson, according to some accounts of the hanging, was also masked (Robertson 43). And Riel is "under the white hood" just as Thomas Scott has a "white cotton bandage / covering his eyes" (lines 47–8). Here is another instance of anonymity: that condition blinds each figure from seeing another, just as Burrs is blind to their historical identities even when he reads and imagines their words. Perhaps this anonymity also represents conflation, because Riel, Henderson, and Scott are all masked: if everyone is hidden, then one hooded face could be confused for another. Distinctiveness fades: the villain can be the hero, the lawless can be the lawful. And if there is, as Burrs's poem implies, no convincing way to distinguish clearly among these figures and voices, then the past is, to one degree or another, unavailable to the present.

I connect that reading to early lines in Burrs's poem, a vague meditation on the nature of memory: "All voices have become whispers / in your final, muted storm" ("White Hood" lines 34–5). While a literal reading of the lines contemplates the oddly quiet composure the "you" (presumably Riel) experiences at the moment of death, I like to think of Burrs's "muted storm" as an appropriate metaphor for history: an audible past out of listening range, reduced to "whispers," a fading aurality. The idea of history as a "muted storm" captures the chaotic enormity of everything that precedes our present, while acknowledging, too, that this massive storm, enveloping and violently fragmenting all that has ever transpired, is unnervingly muted because it is so removed from us. That sequence beautifully captures something paradoxical about our relationship to the past: we cannot look away from something so mammoth as our individual or our collective pasts (they are foundational to our present), but we cannot fully reclaim or hear them, either.

A survey of these various incarnations of lyric historiography points to some common threads. Distance is a continual concern in each poet's writing: temporal, cultural, and often aural. The past is plural, distorted, or ambiguous in the writing, too: Newlove's upside-down music, Purdy's potentially imagined sounds, Crozier's fluid history, Brewster's shifting identities, and Burrs's anonymous faces. Each poet appreciates these impediments to reliable history, even as they demonstrate their own knowledge of historical places, people, and events. And yet, despite their evident knowledge, the poems stop short of becoming narratives. Each poet instead offers brief, meditative lyrics that wonder what the past looked or sounded like, and they resolve themselves to that wonder and their scepticism. No matter how much they appear to have read, heard, or learned, they are too attentive to the range of potential interpretations to be firm in their conclusions. In these relatively short lyrics, this impasse most often occurs when the historical lens is broad (focused on events that are part of a national or regional heritage) and outward-looking (that is, removed from the poet's own temporal and personal experience). Each poet gestures to the writing of history, but a reader won't find in their work an organized, structured narrative.

Thus far, my chapters have explained a trajectory in mainstream poetry communities of the 1960s and 1970s. There is Purdy: the rough-edged and working-class poet whose romantic leanings drew him to the lyric mode and whose tutelage under modernist poets had him modernizing that mode during an era in which a romantic revival was taking place in and outside of Canada. He continued to write in that mode when he channelled his critical energies, nationalistically inflected, into poems about Canada's past. Internalizing the meditative quality of lyric, as well as the scepticism inherent in modernism, and then writing self-consciously from the perspective of his "I," Purdy was producing poems throughout the 1960s and early 1970s that pondered the limits of historical knowledge. When Newlove read Purdy and Anglo-American modernists such as T.S. Eliot, he was encountering that same sceptical philosophy and poetic mode, and using both in poems like "The Pride" or "Crazy Riel," which were articulations – surely, ethnocentric ones – of his own long-held interest in history. It is no coincidence that a number of prairie poems bear noteworthy resemblance to the historiographic projects Purdy and Newlove began in the early 1960s or that their names invariably recur in interviews, articles, reviews, and book dedications. They validated a historiographic (and regional) impulse in Canadian writing after 1960. In the specific context of prairie writing, Newlove was key in demonstrating the dynamic past of the prairies and the potential for that past in poetry. These were new possibilities for emerging poets.

But those possibilities came with limitations. Two major Canadian poets demonstrate to centennial-era writers that a sophisticated history obliges their admission of epistemological limits. And so those admissions become commonplace in the writing of other poets, too, whereby writers such as Burrs, Brewster, and Crozier acknowledge, if in different ways, their disconnection from the past. That acknowledgment would surely have made it difficult, if not impossible, for these poets to give their readers an authoritative history. Instead, they use comparable formal techniques (a resistance to closure, fragmented poetic constructions, an emphasis on distance and eccentrically large timelines, enigmatic images of or sounds from the past, unanswered questions) to portray their scepticism.

Even if the history that results from these poems is obviously incomplete or purposefully undermined by each poet's self-reflexivity, the poets I've studied, in their time, shed new light on old historical narratives or, alternatively, brought to light fragments of stories unfamiliar to conventional history. Regionalist poetry presented opportunities for reconsidering what constituted purposeful Canadian history and acknowledged, sometimes unwittingly, the conundrums of position and perception inherent in historical writing. Regional writing thus liberated settler poets from broad national stories; it provided an opportunity to focus their historical lens. The unexpected irony here is that as that historical lens became more focused, it became harder for writers to imagine a broader "national" experience that was all-encompassing.[8] For these poets, history ceased to be an expression of a unifying impulse. Consequently, creative writers and their readers become more attentive to diverse historical circumstances that offer a more dynamic, even if inconclusive, image of the past. In both history and creative literature, regionalist writing was another sign of a gradual move away from reductive and conventional historical frameworks that privilege unity and a move toward more inclusive histories that accept and explore social or cultural difference at the local level. Indeterminacy is the consequence of that attention. William Carlos Williams's philosophy of writing was that the more "inclusive" any piece of writing was, the more "inconclusive" it became (Zamora 197). In the process of drawing attention to limited identities, Canadian poets showed the ways in which lyric historiography could be an inconclusive offering of narrative possibilities, even if narrative itself continued to elude them.

Within such frameworks, the experiences of individuals feature centrally. Remember that what drew Mick Burrs to Riel were the audio recordings of the Métis testimonies he transcribed, which led him to question the villainization of Riel in, for instance, George Stanley's work. Or there is Newlove, who was stirred more in "The Pride" by David Thompson's first-hand accounts of Saukamappee than he was by G.E. Hyde's insensitive, "objective" study of Red Cloud. As often as regionalist poets were getting readers away from broad national narratives, they were also subtly, maybe even unintentionally, demonstrating the ways in which the lens could be focused even further by getting closer to people's first-hand experiences. Collectively, they were beginning to see that history does not thrive as a distanced study. History, they understood, requires intimacy.

5 Inheriting the Past

When thinking about what Canadian poets achieved as they looked broadly at national and regional pasts, I imagine W.B. Yeats's poet "sing[ing] amid [...] uncertainty" ("*Per Amica Silentia Lunae*" 8). At the same time, what a conundrum that uncertainty must have presented for those writers: doubt yielded sophisticated poems about history, but it did little to alleviate each poet's struggle to find or write a reliable history. Compelling poetry, but an incomplete story. Sophisticated expressions of doubt, but no return to belief. Perhaps the epistemological impasse these poets encountered in strictly national or regional histories is what led so many of them to innovate on lyric historiography by building a tradition of family writing in the early 1970s.

Margaret Atwood once implied the inevitability of that attraction: "I don't think you transcend region, anymore than a plant transcends earth" (Atwood and Brans 82). Atwood's regionalism might risk sounding like some kind of snare in which the writer is trapped, but there is also great potential in poetry that pays attention to the immediacy of individual experience, an immediacy that is natural to a literary mode predicated on the lyric I's rooting in the "here" and "now." Leading critics of the 1970s noted that poets who felt so rooted were "usually express[ing] a very personal sense of history" (Ricou, "Introduction" 6). This personal connection to the past was a logical outcome of regionalist poetry, which encouraged writers to think locally. Many wrote about their birthplaces, which easily gave way to poetry about their family.

Before I can say more about the importance of familial poems in the context of history writing, it is necessary to elaborate on the conceptual appeal of this historical content in relation to "poetic images." The appeal of familial lyrics is best understood with reference to evolving concepts of the "poetic image" as something both aesthetic and historical. Images – variously conceived – appear in the poems I have discussed in earlier chapters: Purdy's highly visual, almost impressionistic, imagining of Indigenous figures in "Remains of an Indian Village," Newlove's "image" of "the pawnees" in "The Pride" and his noisy "images" in "Crazy Riel," and Brewster's "moving image." The prevalence of the image in Canadian poetry during this time is another legacy of Anglo-American imagism. The imagists' adoption of precise and brief poetic forms, revolt against Victorian "ornament" (Gage 34), and masking of the self in the service of an ideally objective poetry (21–2) has certainly lingered in the work of Canadian writers. Brian Trehearne has demonstrated the continued influence of imagism on poets such as P.K. Page and Louis Dudek in *The Montreal Forties*: "Clearly each of [Page, Klein, Layton, and Dudek] thought the experimental tension and difficulty of modernist structures delightful; each of them, even Klein, found the goals, if not the methods, of Imagism exemplary" (317). These writers passed this poetics on to the next generation of poets. Layton, for instance, was a mentor figure for Al Purdy, Leonard Cohen, Eli Mandel, and Barry McKinnon.[1] Newlove thought Page to be one of the finest Canadian writers of the postwar era, so much so that he originally planned to title his last collection *The Permanent Tourist Comes Home*, until he realized he'd accidentally stolen the title from Page's "The Permanent Tourists."[2]

Literary influences thus ensured aesthetic and philosophical inheritances, whereby later Canadian writers and their contemporaries continued to identify with "the goals, if not the methods," of Anglo-American imagism: Louis Dudek says that imagism "poured into the poetry of each generation that has followed the beginning of modernism" ("Theory" 265), D.G. Jones references "the continuing vitality of imagism" of the 1960s (168), Laurie Ricou deems the "compact structure of images" a "near-imagism," typical of postwar poetry ("Poetry" 9–10), and Tom Marshall observes that "imagism in some form has been important everywhere in Canada" (*Harsh* 173). This is what Trehearne calls "the paradox of Imagist history": "its quick death as a coherent doctrine [by 1917], its striking power over future innovation" (55).

The sustained influence of imagism during the latter half of the twentieth century shows that poets' fascination with the image did not attenuate as time went on. In fact, it intensified. If it seems to be so, that is because the "poetic image" during the centennial era was no longer strictly linked to modernism. Its associations became more varied. This was especially true on the West Coast, where there was a well-developed visual arts culture that deepened the appeal of image-based writing to poets living in Vancouver during the early 1960s.

The "cross-fertilization between poetry and painting" has its immediate roots in modernist art between 1930 and 1960 (Rackham 449), but this cross-fertilization continued well into the 1960s on the West Coast. The Vancouver-based artist Takao Tanabe was one of the figures who spearheaded this collaborative arts culture after 1960. He helped design and publish early collections by Gerry Gilbert (*White Lunch*), Roy Kiyooka (*Kyoto Airs*; Kiyooka also did artwork for Newlove's *Grave Sirs*), Florence McNeil (*A Silent Green Sky*), Newlove (*Grave Sirs* and *Elephants, Mothers & Others*), and Phyllis Webb (*Naked Poems*). The extent of this 1960s visual culture tempts one to think that Dennis Lee's assertion that the image was "the fundamental imaginative unit" in poetry written between 1970 and 1985 is if anything an understatement ("Introduction" xxxvii). The influence of such writing had been palpable since the beginning of Canadian modernism in the 1920s.

While the visual culture of such literary communities likely reinvigorated and evolved poets' imagistic sensibilities, the basic conceptual principle of imagism ("direct treatment of things") had many applications, because that principle is fundamentally epistemological; imagism is, like historical knowledge, about accuracy and *precision*. It is a happy coincidence that the idiom of imagistic precision was built into historical writing. Twentieth-century historians were not working within the literary framework of imagism, but they did naturally gravitate toward image-based language. Frank Ankersmit remarks on "a strong inclination towards the use of visual metaphor [in historical study]: we like to speak of 'images of the past,' of the 'point of view' from which the historian 'looks' at the past, of the 'distortions' of historical reality which an incorrect 'viewpoint' is liable to create" (212–13). For poets who read history, those visual metaphors guided their diction. Newlove talks about historical "images" in "The Pride" and one of his source texts, G.E. Hyde's *Red Cloud's Folk*, asks its readers to "*picture* the little Teton camps" (18, emphasis added). Historians, like the poets who emulate them, have long striven to construct "a certain *picture* of the past" (Ankersmit 239), and as these metaphors took hold in historical writing, they became as much a part of the historiographic idiom of centennial-era Canadian poetry.

Poets' representations of the "historical image," however, are various. In shorter lyrics, "the image" might be a figurative idea or a metaphoric "glimpse" of history and/or a picture of the past described by an observer (i.e., in the manner of *ekphrasis*). Any individual image may be briefly discussed in a single line or meditated on at length throughout a section of a poem. The purpose and integrity of such images in lyric historiography vary from project to project, poet to poet. We've seen already in earlier chapters some concepts of images that are of little epistemological comfort to the historically conscious writer: an image can be distorted and synesthetic (Newlove), "fluid" or "moving" (Brewster), or so tenuous that it strains the poet's imagination (Purdy and Crozier). In the works of these writers, there is only an approach to the poetic image of history and not an apprehension of it. What I want to show in this chapter is that, for many writers, the familial past was a way to move past an "approach" and get closer to a direct treatment of the past.

Such poems are neither centred on epistemological struggle nor limited just to gestures toward new narrative content, because there is an implicit feeling of authority when individuals tell their own family history. It is, naturally, *their* story to tell. In family poems, therefore, the "I" is no longer simply a literary device to express uncertainty and scepticism: it is the source of knowledge. Broader stories of Canadian history surely remained of interest to writers after 1970, but mixed in among these poems were family lyrics, the latter of which generated a closeness to the past that mitigated the feeling of temporal and cultural distance engendered by grander historical frameworks.

Even if family history held such potential, not every poet found it especially appealing as poetic content; Newlove produced barely any family poetry. As I have, in earlier chapters, stressed his contributions to lyric historiography, it is worth pausing to explain his absence here and for the rest of this book. Newlove *was* interested in his family roots; he made the effort to obtain a copy of *The Newlove Family Tree*, which was published privately by an independent scholar in the United States.[3] For personal reasons, though, he was hesitant to discuss his family publicly.

Two exchanges between Andrew Suknaski and Newlove – one poignant, the other fiery – illuminate the point. After finding an old photo of Newlove's mother, Mary, in the possession of one Laura Dahlmann (a schoolteacher and Mary's friend), Suknaski mailed the picture to Newlove and urged him to write a poem about it. Newlove declined: "I've never before in my life seen pictures of my mother at that age. I loved her, but we couldn't talk; our family never did." He handwrote a postscript, "You will have to write the poem. I can't" (Newlove to Suknaski [1976]). Suknaski did, in fact, turn the letter into a poem, "Letters Between Two Prairie Friends," and published it five years later in *In the Name of Narid* without clearly identifying Newlove as the speaker's correspondent. In a more aggressive exchange, Newlove exploded at Suknaski over his planned documentary on the Regina riot of 1935, a riot in which Newlove's father was involved as a lawyer for the accused: "I would prefer that you do not make my father a character, a word I use after some thought, in [your film]. [...] I resent your intrusion into my life. He was my father. You know newspapers; I know flesh. I can't legally stop you from doing this, but, by God, if you go ahead you'll regret it" (Newlove to Suknaski [1985]). Despite Newlove's warning, Suknaski completed the project, which he later titled *The Disinherited*.[4]

In light of these exchanges, it should surprise no one that Newlove contributed virtually nothing to the enormous output of familial lyrics during and after the centennial era. There are only two notable poems about his family in his corpus, and neither is an actual, thorough exploration of his personal past. "The Permanent Tourist Comes Home" (1986) is an indirect account of his father's death, and a much earlier poem, "The Flowers" (1965), presents dreamlike glimpses of an older brother's lobotomy and institutionalization after a near-fatal accident – the fate of Newlove's own brother, Robert. Tellingly, Newlove chose not to reproduce the dedication that appeared in *Moving in Alone* ("for my brother") in either *The Fat Man: Selected Poems 1962–1972* (1977) or *Apology for Absence: Selected Poems 1962–1992* (1993); it was a decision that took readers' attention away from biography. That is not to say that Newlove didn't understand the narrative potential of familial writing. Poems like "Crazy Riel" or "The Pride" often focus on the unavailability of the past, but then, in the letters above, he speaks with an impassioned certainty about his knowledge of his family history. That line: "*I know flesh*." Newlove claimed ownership over his past, but he could not bring himself to explore it too deeply.

Other Canadian poets were more eager to experiment with what Marianne Hirsch calls "postmemory": an individual's attempt to experience or encounter a historical period that another subject close to them can actually recall. Hirsch specifically uses the term in the context of trauma theory. The grandchildren of those who lived through the Second World War, for instance, might draw on their grandparents' traumatic experience in order to obtain knowledge of the Holocaust. One generation relies on the personal memories of previous ones in order to establish concrete links to broader histories. She cites Art Spiegelman's *Maus* as an example of "postmemory," as the story demonstrates the illustrative "intersection of private and public history" (13).

Hirsch's concept speaks to some general assertions made in both Canadian history and literary criticism. When social history gained its footing in Canada in the early 1970s, the historian David Gagan was a major advocate of family history, which, he argued, offers the "building blocks" (124) for a larger narrative: "The more we come to understand the historical experience, the culture, the structure, and the historical identity of families and the dynamics of family life, the closer we come to recreating the social, economic, cultural, ideological, political, and perhaps even the psychic characteristics of whole societies" (124–5). For Gagan, the family is a microcosm of broader contexts. While he saw narrative potential and value in those family stories, he never specifically talked about those stories as testimonial in the way that Hirsch does. And while Hirsch's framework underscores the "I's" communion with and closeness to the past, she emphasizes traumatic experiences, which are surely not the only experiences to which one connects or reconnects through family. A fusion of these views is what I see in lyric historiography when the poems focus less on the state or region and more on the family: Gagan's microcosm of a broader world, but with Hirsch's lyrical lens. The work of two centennial-era poets, Florence McNeil and Dale Zieroth, is exceptional evidence of the potential such writing promises.

A badly neglected and fine, award-winning poet, Florence McNeil was mentored in Vancouver during the early 1960s by Earle Birney, who regarded her as "one of the best writers of poetry with a western base" (Birney to UBC). As a poet who lived on the prairies during the 1960s and 1970s, her writing is, in her own words, preoccupied with "W[est] Coast themes plus prairie interruptions" (McNeil to Birney) and centred on richly visual imaginings of history. McNeil regarded "the image" as "a (perhaps *the*) core technique" in her poetry (Letter from McNeil to Weingarten); scholars like Christopher Wiseman understandably claimed McNeil, in her time, had "no equal in Canada as a poet of visual metaphor" (40).[5] Her historical images may be an observer's reflection on large communities and ghost towns (*Ghost Towns* [1975] and *Barkerville* [1984]) or may be seen through the eyes of a historical persona (*Emily* [1975] and *The Overlanders* [1982]). McNeil said that her "historical impulse came early" in her career; her first full-length volume, which was rejected, was a "non-fiction history of Barkerville" (Letter from McNeil to Weingarten).

"Ghost Town" (1975; *GT* 2) succinctly establishes the fundamental features of her lyric historiography. As most readers are likely unfamiliar with the poem, I quote it in full:

How did we obliterate you
in a hundred years
you in your torn undershirts and hip boots

arms akimbo
by your muscular diggings
you with stumps for haloes
whose obsessed eyes
glitter through wavering lines
you by your wheels and rockers
with legs of stone   mountainous
in your temples   the flumes
pouring endlessly like blood

Here in the same mountains
there are new minted diggings
and tourists photographing themselves
in your rebuilt saloons
giggling at the barber shops   the gilded dance halls
and taking images of your plaster
replicas
oh but you have outwitted them
crude as the nuggets you sweated for
your past is missing from this landscape
leaves no trace on their negatives   their coloured screens
won't hold your five minute pose
which stopped the hills   the fumes with motionless energy
a century ago
and now defying immortality
declines a present
too secular
to be haunted.

A rich array of topics vie for the reader's attention: McNeil's secularism, the photograph and cultural memory, or the speaker's appeal to the history of "ghost towns." Especially interesting is McNeil's isolation of temporal markers through lineation, which emphasizes chronological distance: "in a hundred years" and "a century ago." The technique is identical to that which I noted earlier in Purdy's poems. The Purdyean search for "ghosts" is equally intriguing, and there is a potential gesture to Birney's infamous line about Canada's "lack of ghosts" lingering in McNeil's poem. Her speaker *wants* to be haunted. To encounter the past, however, seems impossible, as the plaster "replicas" of the ghost town are flawed, or at least unrevealing, homages to history. She thus draws a fairly grim conclusion: the "missing" past "def[ies] immortality" and no remnants of it survive. Her emphasis on temporal distance and distrust of "replicas" cumulatively suggest the irretrievability of the history to which she appeals. It seems perplexing that, in a poem so clearly driven by an effort to capture some image of the past, McNeil's speaker feels so little about the photographs. Tourists happily snap photos to memorialize their own visits, but the speaker seems largely unaffected by visual records of the site. "Images," "negatives," and "screens" do nothing to alleviate her overwhelming feeling that the past is absent.

In "Art Nouveau" (1975; *GT* 14–15), McNeil's speaker rummages through old photographs from the First World War and likewise finds historical images provide a mere glimpse of history: "there are photographs / blurred and unreal / the stiff geometric legs of dead horses / the abstract confusion of ordinary arms / and barbed wire / are reproduced poorly / and clarify nothing." The photos are not vivid: they are "blurred and unreal" representations of an "abstract" past. Pictures are equally blurry in "1915 Fighting Plane" (1975; *GT* 12), a poem in which McNeil's persona observes that the pilot in a photograph "sits / forever out of focus." Loss feels permanent in such poems. The poet cannot read into the pictures, and not just because they are blurry: her imagination, too, is blurry. The pastness of the past is too much with her; she is unable to conceive of more than she can see.

Yet, in "Society Notes: An Old Photo" (1979; *BA* 83), McNeil's persona more fully details a decades-old picture of her grandparents. Again, I quote the poem in full:

> My grandparents sit for their portrait in the garden
> and there is no trick of my imagination that can turn
> my grandmother's sagging lisle stockings
> into the svelte silk of the nineteen thirties
> beauties
> nor change my grandfather's rough plaid shirt
> his thick braces   the sailor stance
> (arms rolled as if he were always about
> to burst into the hornpipe)
> into the tux and tails of Fred Astaire
> the graceful patterns of
> New Yorker ads
> and I know they will turn from their picture
> from the spare brown frame
> into the orchard where trees are heavy with fruit
> up unpainted stairs
> into hidden rooms doomed by striped wallpaper

and rickety chairs
and I will refuse to admit them to my diary

I who had grown up facing the other side of
their country
had consciously drowned out the Hebridean music
had seen them as old people with dimes and dollars
they gladly shared
as embarrassing people flawed with serious accents
who lived with untidy dogs in a house
that smelled faintly of urine
Now that they are gone Now that I can go
through the old brown pictures at leisure
(having nothing to do but assess)
looking past the surface scratches
the pale unclear gloss
I can make out indistinctly
how kind and intelligent my grandmother's eyes
were
how my grandfather's hands seemed capable of
re-arranging any milieu
and the vitality in their faces suggesting
they might spin away at any moment
into a fast quadrille.

The tone of this poem is markedly different from that of "Ghost Town" or "Art Nouveau." The speaker is so much less defeated here, so much more willing to talk about the past, to speculate and wonder, to recover images and even the "smell" of the past (sadly, though, it is the charmless smell of "urine"). McNeil's persona has a different relationship to a familial past than to one more removed from her ancestry or personal experience. Here she diligently maps the photograph of her grandparents and provides perspective on the historical era it represents.

Lorraine York's note that "[p]hotography and possession [...] are often synonyms" (*Other Side* 144) sums up what family pictures can mean to writers like McNeil. *These* photos are neither "blurred" nor "forever out of focus"; they justify her authority over the past, an authority made more obvious by the persona's frequent repetition of "my" in the poem above. In another poem from *Ghost Towns*, "Heredity," McNeil's speaker looks through her "father's / brown bewildered photographs" and says that, when she "least expect[s] it," she "clarifie[s] our relative / positions" (31). McNeil's enjambed pun on "relative" is notable, because it reaffirms her heredity, but, in context, it specifically means that she believes she can accurately position characters from the past in relation to each other, capturing the nuances of a complex familial relationship and thus elaborating on the image. In "Society Notes," she asserts a comparable authority by claiming ownership of the "old brown pictures."

There also appears to be a more abstract claim over history, because McNeil's speaker is able to look "past the surface" of the photograph and "make out" details that the picture could not possibly reveal to any other observer of this particular image of the past: her grandmother's intelligence and kindness, her grandfather's strong hands, and even the rough textures of the 1930s that challenge her imagining of a Hollywood-like glamour. Even though her emphasis on "were" (the word is isolated and enjambed) near the end of the poem implies her awareness that the past is past, she "go[es]" into and "assess[es]" history. She is willing again to elaborate, even though she had once distanced herself from her family's "Hebridian music" and omitted them from her "diary." Now she rummages through the fine details of the picture, the scene, and her family. It is the persona's genealogical link to history in "Society Notes: An Old Photo" that permits this deeper historical engagement.

What McNeil's poem also shows is that historical "images" in centennial-era Canadian poetry were not strictly figurative. While history is the search for figurative "images" of the past that convince us of the reality of the past – Arthur Lower once said that "mental cameras" are among the historian's chief tools (13) – photographic images are natural and useful complements. The historical interest in photography during the 1960s and 1970s often translated to a creative one, partly because the financial situation of publishers who benefited from Canada Council grants permitted the production of more expensive books in which visual aids were used to enhance the poetic content. The incorporation of photographic material was not purely aesthetic or an issue of luxury; the historical power of photographs inspired many writers. Eli Mandel, for example, recalls an epiphany he had in 1946: "Those awful *photographs* towards the end of the war [...] the evidence of the camps began to manifest itself before the eyes of the astonished and horrified world" ("Auschwitz" 4). The emotional weight of the pictures stuck with Mandel, and around the same time that he discovered these particular photographs, he visited Estevan (his birthplace) and wrote his first poem, "Estevan, Saskatchewan" (1946).[6] Mandel's experience parallels that of Mavis Gallant, who was similarly shaken by "the first concentration camp pictures" and the unsettling sensation

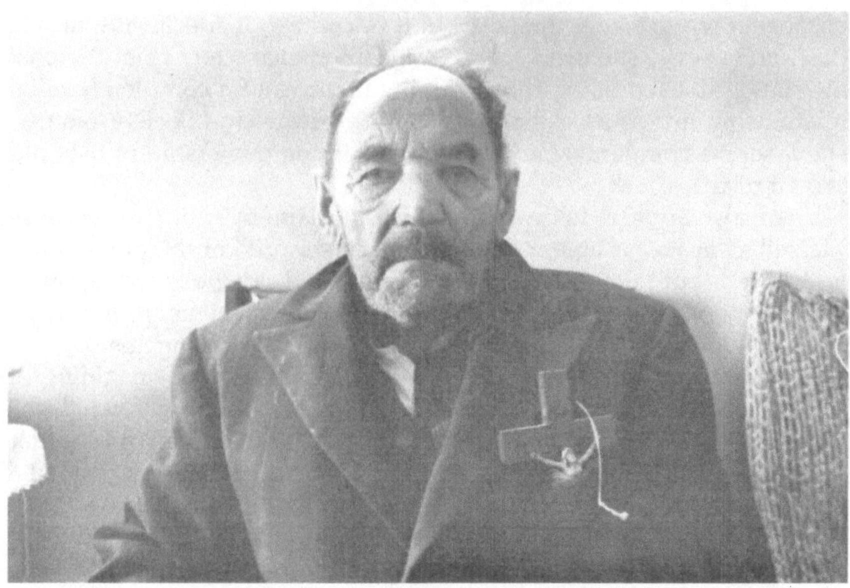

1 A portrait of Andrew Suknaski's father, used as a photographic insert to accompany the title page of *In the Name of Narid*.

of knowing that, she, as a young journalist, would have "to write the *explanation* of something [she] did not [herself] understand" (Gallant and Hancock 39). Pictures of the Holocaust demonstrated to many the psychological impact of photographic testimony – just as Hirsch argues. The Holocaust, she says, gave "rise to new aesthetic questions" (12) because the photograph was now a "witness" to atrocities and to history (13). An entire generation found something affirmatively historical in those pictures.

Roland Barthes has written that "we have an invincible resistance to believing in the past, in History, except in the form of myth. The Photograph, for the first time, puts an end to this resistance: henceforth the past is as certain as the present" (87–8). What a picture or past *means* can always be debated, but Barthes is right that a picture can affirm the *existence* of the past. A photograph is an epistemological aid, and thus also an evident relief to poets searching for an authoritative historical image. Some of these same writers thus saw the family photo album as a good place to start or continue that search. Some writers included family pictures on the covers of or in their books (see figs 1–3)

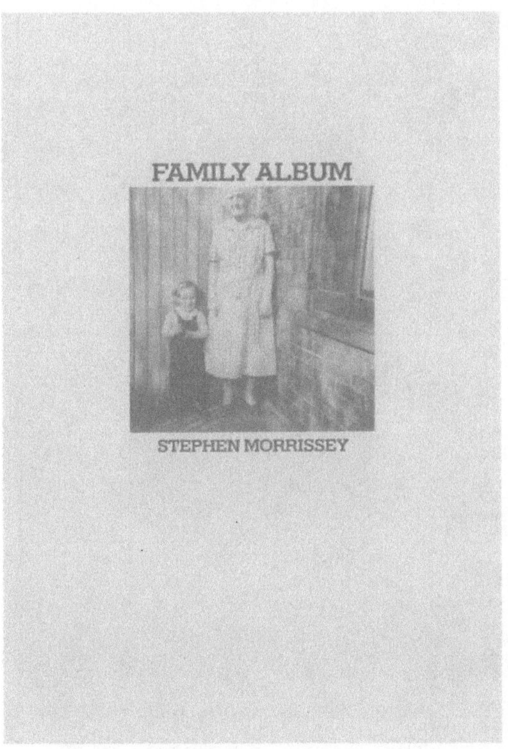

2 A family portrait used as the book cover for Stephen Morrissey's *Family Album*.

or implicitly acknowledged the link between photography and family (see fig. 4). While many poets continued to understand the concept of "image" as a modernist experiment or historians' metaphor, they also appreciated images more literally in the form of photographic family histories.

That is not to say, though, that these poets worked strictly within familial frames of reference. McNeil's willingness to push past the "surface" image admittedly yields only a fuller study of her family, but that impulse to go *further* can be read more abstractly. The poetic image of the family, literal or figurative, can be a stepping stone to a broader history. Critics in the 1970s saw this potential: Ian Underhill wrote that Canadian history "has been so recent that our grandparents are scarcely removed from the pioneer generation and are often the spokesmen for 'old-world' values. In this sense, the family portrait may also

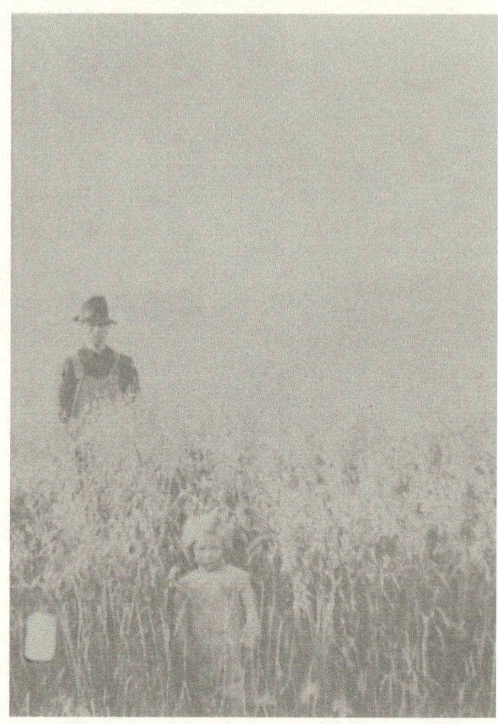

3 Pictured are Barry McKinnon's aunt and grandfather, whose images were used in *I Wanted to Say Something* and, here, on the cover for *Carcasses of Spring*.

be a portrait of Canada itself" (7), a statement that usefully pre-empts a later one from Susan McDaniel and Wendy Mitchinson ("The family is a topic which abounds with imaginative potential. [...] It is universal, perhaps not in structure, but in providing a microcosm of people's realities and dreams" [24]). Underhill, McDaniel, and Mitchinson acknowledge that the "I" is not necessarily insular, because its post-mnemonic or personal experiences can extend to consider a broader narrative in which the family is implicated. These suggestions parallel the hypotheses of centennial-era social historians like Gagan.

These possibilities for extension are integral to some of Dale Zieroth's family poems, but the effect of his familial writing is better recognized if prefaced with an example of a more Purdyean poem. Interestingly, Laurie Ricou once wrote that Purdy's "influence [on 1970s poetry] is perhaps best summed up in the poetry of Dale Zieroth" ("Poetry" 12);

Peter Stevens
Family Feelings
&
other poems

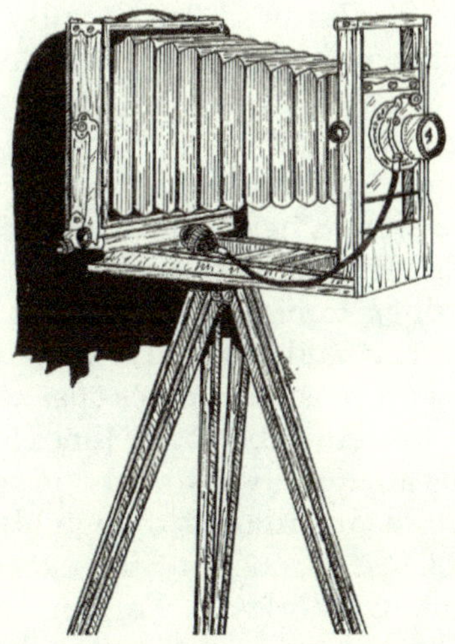

4 The cover of Peter Stevens's *Family Feelings & Other Poems* makes an implied connection between photography and family.

Zieroth himself has said, too, that he felt "validated" by Purdy and Newlove, both of whom legitimated his "impulse to look back to the prairies and rediscover it" (Email from Zieroth).[7] Zieroth's early volumes are the work of an assured young poet (George Woodcock, in fact, twice called him one of the best emerging poets of the centennial era) working under Purdy's influence.[8] The older poet's style and idiom are readily observable in Zieroth's "Looking at It Now: Summer '58–Winter '79" (1981; *Mid-River*, 58–60). In the opening lines, Zieroth's speaker notes that he "[l]ook[s]" at the past "from behind / this barricade of years." The obstructed past exists only in "pieces":

> All is gone, the barn pulled down, the horses dead,
> even the train is replaced; now what is not held in my head
> is lost, it never was

strong or clear enough to strike its line
across my brain. I remember, I remember, I remember
rats in the barn
the drake on the hen
miles of walking half-lost through poplar and bush [...]

The Purdyean motifs are unmistakable: the adult reflecting on a region he knew as a child recalls Purdy's "The Country North of Belleville," the "pulled down" barn resembles the "torn down" mill in Purdy's "Roblin's Mills," and Zieroth's emphasis on the past as "gone," "dead" or "replaced" is basic Purdy. Zieroth's enjambment highlights this absence: the broken phrase "it never was" suggests a past that is not just "lost," but also one that seems never to have existed in the first place.

Even the speaker's defiant repetition of "I remember" protests too much. The line rings ironically of Thomas Hood's sentimental "I Remember, I Remember" and possibly also of Charles G.D. Roberts's *The Tantramar Revisited* (in which Roberts's speaker claims in moments of mnemonic struggle to "remember it all" [lines 51, 54]). The speaker's repetition feels like his attempt to restore the past through an incantatory chant. His mantra seems fruitless, though; the speaker repeatedly introduces symbols of loss throughout the excerpt above, including in the final line ("walking half-lost"). Furthermore, the anomalously sharp rhyme, "dead" and "head," implies that *death* and loss predominate in the speaker's "head" (i.e., mind). Moreover, the rhyme itself serves as a mnemonic device for readers, thereby ensuring that they, too, will focus on the "dead," rather than on the more weakly remembered farms, evoked by the faint half-rhyme of "barn" and "hen." As a poem that shares Purdy's fascinations with local geography and the tactile erosion of its past, Zieroth's "Looking at It Now" exemplifies a lyric persona's meditative engagement with history, impeded by his distance from the era.

As a point of contrast, Zieroth's twin poems, "1) 120 Miles North of Winnipeg" (1973; *Clearing* 7) and "2) Detention Camp, Brandon, Manitoba" (1973; *Clearing* 8) are more exacting in their depiction of the past. Unlike "Looking at It Now," these two poems focus on the poet's familial past. The consequent difference in tone is immediately obvious:

My grandfather came here years ago,
family of eight. In the village,
nine miles away, they knew him as
the German and they were suspicious, being
already settled. Later he was

somewhat liked; still later
forgotten. [...]
The little English he spoke
he learned from the thin grey lady
in the one-room school, an hour away
by foot. The oldest could hunt, the youngest
could read. They knew nothing of
the world he'd left, and forgotten,
until 1914 made him an alien and
he left them on the land he'd come to
120 miles north of Winnipeg.

Even if some lines are vague ("came here years ago"), the majority of the poem shows off intimate knowledge: the grandfather may be misunderstood by others, but the speaker believes he has the knowledge to make him intelligible. His faith in his own ability establishes a sense of ownership akin to that in McNeil's "Society Notes." And Zieroth's persona *does* provide genuine insight into this misunderstood man: his ethnicity, his fluency in English, the company he kept, the size of his family, and so on. There are gaps, of course; the story provides a mere fragment of the grandfather's entire life. But the persona nonetheless convincingly positions himself against those who "forgot" his grandfather by claiming superior knowledge of this man's life.

There is, too, a larger narrative seeded in Zieroth's "1) 120 Miles North of Winnipeg," which he grows in its companion poem, "2) Detention Camp, Brandon, Manitoba." In the latter poem, Zieroth uses his grandfather's experiences to write a brief, but much broader, history of Canadian detention camps during the First World War. From the outset of the war, the Canadian government used these camps to imprison enemies of the state who engaged in treasonable acts or who allegedly intended to defect. The war had fostered generalized fear and xenophobia among Canadians, and so the criteria and reasons for arrests and imprisonment became increasingly unregulated during the 1910s. By the end of the war, these camps housed thousands of European immigrants of German, Austrian, Hungarian, and Ukrainian descent. The history of these camps has been told primarily by those who escaped them. The historian George Buri has studied testimonies from escapees such as Mitro Mahoumnuk, who was held at an "alien detention centre" overseen by Major-General William Otter, whose long career in the Canadian military included a decisive attack on Poundmaker during the 1885 Métis uprising. Mahoumnuk lived at the centre in Brandon, Manitoba, for two years with nearly a thousand others. (It is almost certain that Zieroth's grandfather would have been among them.) "Mitro's experiences are known today," Buri writes, "only because he managed to escape from the Brandon alien detention centre" (Buri).

Mohoumnuk's experiences parallel those of Zieroth's grandfather, who shared his own knowledge of these events with his grandson:

> Bodies at night would moan, asleep
> with others somewhere who dreamt
> of them. The sunrise on the wall
> became a condition, the sunset a way
> of counting days. The prisoners carried
> these things close to their bodies.
> This my grandfather came to know
> before leaving.

This detailed and emotional scene shows just how well Zieroth's twin poems model narrative development (in contrast, of course, with the random accumulation discussed in previous chapters). Zieroth establishes, for instance, a sequential narrative, since the numbering of each poem ("(1)" and "(2)") insists that one *must* follow the other. The order of the poems implies that, for Zieroth, history *begins* with one's family experiences. Familial memory is an entry point, the first stop in a narrative that strives toward a broader history inclusive of other people's experiences (hence the repeated plural nouns above, "bodies," "others," and "prisoners," which make this a shared experience and not just one belonging to Zieroth's grandfather). This process epitomizes the post-mnemonic past that Hirsch theorizes, in so far as Zieroth's lyrical impulse – his first-hand account of his grandfather's first-hand account – is what gives him the authority to explain an event that is simultaneously intimate (particular to his grandfather) and broad (known to or experienced by others).

It is also worth stressing that these Manitoban camps were largely unknown to many Canadians in 1973 (when Zieroth published the poems) because all of the "official government records dealing with internment operations" were destroyed in the 1950s (Buri). Not until the 1980s, when survivors began demanding an official apology from the government, did these detention centres receive press, and it was only in 2005 that the Canadian government made an official pledge to educate Canadians about the camps – with the caveat that it would neither compensate nor apologize to victims (Luciuk 52). More than thirty years before that official announcement, Zieroth had offered this unwritten history that, in light of the government's destruction of official records, could only be told by the people who "kn[e]w" the camps.

I draw on the examples of McNeil and Zieroth because they show that family history inspired some measure of confidence in these poets. It is interesting to think about ancestry as poetically and historically valuable not just because such content inherently challenges historians' principles of objectivity, but also because of how starkly this attraction to family contrasts with earlier attitudes toward genealogy in modern poetry. The rise of psychoanalysis and the generally combative qualities of Anglo-American modernist writing as anti-Victorian drove many twentieth-century authors to regard the family as a source of anxiety, a metonym for an earlier generation they wished to bury. To youthful modernists, the Victorians appeared "outmoded, not only in their professions, but in their ways of thinking, their emotional needs and responses" (Quinones 154); "old experience," in other words, did "not apply to new conditions" (153). For later Canadian writers, family history spurred no such anxiety. Family symbolized something else entirely: it was, and continues to be, a way for the historically minded writer to claim some measure of knowledge about the past. In other words, it offered a way to write authoritative histories less disrupted by – though not dismissive of – modern scepticism.

Once poets recognized the aesthetic, historical, and epistemological possibilities of familial poetry, they began to push beyond the boundaries of an isolated image[9] (whether literally a photographic image or a figurative image of history) and to connect one snapshot of the past to others in the service of a grander and more fully articulated history. They experimented with longer lyrics markedly different from the brief lyric meditations of poems about the nation. With few exceptions (only "The Pride" and "Under the White Hood" come to mind), brevity is typical of accumulative lyrics: Purdy's "Roblin's Mills" is fifty-six lines, "Remains of an Indian Village" is fifty-five lines, and "The North West Passage" is sixty-eight lines; Newlove's "Crazy Riel" is sixty-four lines, and "Ride Off Any Horizon" includes only one section (about twenty lines) that tackles the history of the nineteenth-century Northwest Uprising; Lorna Crozier's "Drifting Towards Batoche" is twenty-five lines; Brewster's "At Batoche" is, at eighty-three lines, one of the longer examples of an accumulative lyric. The brevity of these lyrics betrays the curbed and cautious poetic treatment tolerant of, though epistemologically unsettled by, an insurmountable feeling of the kinds of distance I described in previous chapters (temporal, cultural, and so forth). These distances represent the limits of a historically conscious lyric. And so if a writer conscious of those distances still wants to write a history, then they have to imagine ways to work within the limits of lyric to achieve narrative without appearing intellectually blinkered or, worse, foolishly authoritative. There must be some Eliotic return to belief. Family history offered that return. Those stories have been writers' means to relieve their scepticism and to contemplate new reasons to believe in history.

6 The "Edge of the Photograph": Developmental Long Poems

In 1978, ten years after [my father's] death, I wrote a poem called "The Witnesses" ... I called that poem "The Witnesses" because that's what I was doing, witnessing an event out of oral history, writing down what I imagined ... building ... the possible history of my father ... that's what history is to me, something personal ... My father and mother and the fathers and mothers before them have a right to exist in our imaginations.

Lane, "The Unyielding Phrase" 58–64

I carry these poems in my skull forever. Newlove's *Black Night Window* – that too is "pamiat."[1] Till McKinnon comes along with photos and lines chronicling a single place – Alberta.

Suknaski, "Prairie Graveyard" 119

By the end of the 1970s, the work of almost any Canadian poet alive and publishing would have proven D.G. Jones's claim in *Butterfly on Rock* (1970): "One of the characteristic preoccupations of [1960s] poets is a concern to possess [...] their father's or grandfather's world" (171). Jones's androcentrism aside, his statement affirms a familial impulse so widespread that scholars were motivated to publish anthologies and teaching guides addressing it.[2] The change in content provoked other changes: long poems – structured through orderly development, as opposed to the random accumulation of shorter lyrics – became a favoured form for poeticizing these familial explorations.

"Development" is a foil to "accumulation," and, like the latter, the term is tied to imagism. John T. Gage writes that a "developmental structure" signifies "those modes of organization ... in which the reader is drawn from one part to the next by transitions which involve a sense of necessity, whether by logical, chronological, or causal means." These structures, as Gage observes, contrast with imagistic accumulation by making "the order of the parts [...] significant" (108). One could achieve this developmental structure by claiming a creatively imagined (and sometimes superficial) authority over history; that would, I think, be fair to say of historical long poems by E.J. Pratt, Dorothy Livesay, and Don Gutteridge, and we can add to this list poems like Raymond Souster's *Jubilee of Death* (1984), Dennis Cooley's *Bloody Jack* (1984), and Gwendolyn MacEwen's *Terror and Erebus* (1965). But the writers of greater relevance to my study are those who found authority through their genetic link to the past. The structural and conceptual achievements of family poetry that I want to explore in this chapter thus suggest strong ties between lyric historiography in Canada and the developmental long poem, and those ties are equally suggestive of the intellectual and creative fertility inherent in histories that locate their centres within, rather than outside of, the world of the "I." "Genealogy," Robert Kroetsch has said, "is a primary version of narrative" ("Beyond Nationalism" 64).

The link between lyric and long poem that I am proposing requires some rethinking of what Eli Mandel doubtfully regarded as the "primary opposition" between that mode and form ("Death" 11).[3] Mandel questions the opposition, but not all critics have. Smaro Kamboureli, for example, contends that long poems such as Kroetsch's *Seed Catalogue*, Bowering's *Allophanes*, and Ondaatje's *The Collected Works of Billy the Kid* prove that long poems are "parod[ies]" of their "own lyrical impulse" (*Edge* 64). In my introduction, I took issue with these kinds of arguments, which treat "parody" as *the* sophisticated response to historiographic relativism. Kamboureli's points are, of course, completely true of those specific poets, but other poets did not indulge in play. Some, like Barry McKinnon, sincerely valued the narrative power of lyrical long poems.

That transformation in the context of lyric historiography is of particular interest to this chapter, but the inclination toward long poems during the centennial era was not due only to the narrative potential of family history. Long poems were of pressing concern to poets of the era. They were fashionable; epics (especially those of Ezra Pound, Louis Dudek, Charles Olson, and William Carlos Williams) were cutting edge. Writers who wanted to participate in this aesthetic innovation, however, needed compelling content to sustain their long poems. Given Canadians' growing obsession with historiographic writing after 1960, the past provided a rich landscape to mine for such content. From that wealth of stories, earlier writers like E.J. Pratt extracted content for long poems from moments of great consequence in Canadian and British history: the settlement of New France, the battle at Dunkirk, and the building of the Canadian Pacific Railway. But in an era of scepticism, poetry that romanticized the national past was a less inviting path for modern poets to follow. Something had to supplant that brand of long poem.

An exemplary case of what was thus a necessary innovation on the long poem is McKinnon's *I Wanted to Say Something* (1975),[4] which he wrote after discovering Newlove's work: "I sensed because of John," McKinnon says, "that the prairie experience, historical or otherwise, could be a 'subject' for poetry" (Email from McKinnon [Aug. 2011]). McKinnon's statement reaffirms a point I made in my previous chapter: the more attention poets paid to region, the more likely they were to write about their families. McKinnon's *I Wanted to Say Something* is therefore evidence of developments in lyric historiography: a move from national/regional history to family history and, relatedly, from accumulation to development.

Working mostly within a narrative of the poet's family, McKinnon's *I Wanted to Say Something* takes up prairie history in two closely related sections: (1) "The Legacy," a lyric history of McKinnon's grandparents, and (2) "The Moving Photograph," which showcases the lyric persona meditating on the accessibility of history. As the poet pieces together his familial past through photographs and text, he expects that his investigation will yield a private history that is a microcosm of a broader and distinctly prairie history. But the speaker's initial effort to celebrate his family history provokes his recognition of various historical injustices in which his family was complicit. McKinnon's poem is a benchmark: elegantly written, structurally innovative, evocative in its portrayal of his family history, and thoughtfully questioning of unambiguous celebrations of history.

In assigning heavy importance to McKinnon's *I Wanted to Say Something*, I am tasked with explaining why no one else has done so. First, McKinnon's readership has been small; his book has enjoyed an almost cult popularity and mostly among prairie-born writers who instantly identified with his work. In 1980, Lorna Crozier was the first to acknowledge McKinnon's critical neglect. She lamented that *I Wanted to Say Something* had "received very little critical attention, yet it has influenced a number of poets who have felt the same need to define their roots." "I offer my analysis as an apology to McKinnon," she wrote, "for the lack of attention paid in the past to a beautiful, well-crafted book" ("Edge" 106). Crozier was not alone in making this kind of proclamation, and even in a fairly recent publication, Dennis Cooley describes *I Wanted to Say Something* as "one of the first, one of the best, and one of the least-known of the post-modern [i.e., post-war] long prairie poems" ("Documents" 204). There are also frequent echoes of McKinnon in familial long poems written throughout the centennial era: both Suknaski's rhetoric of "geography" and "failure" in "Indian

Site on the Edge of Tonita Pasture" (*WMP* 78) and Douglas Barbour's rumination on the "lovely geometric patterns" of his grandfather's era (*Visions* sec. 9 n.p.) echo McKinnon's descriptions of Alberta's agricultural "geometry" (*IWSS* 28). Even Purdy borrowed from McKinnon: the opening lines of *In Search of Owen Roblin* ("Open the album / it is a cage of ancestors" [lines 1–2]) evoke McKinnon's photographic scenes and admiration of the family photo album. And yet, *I Wanted to Say Something* has garnered little attention outside of these circles since its original publication in 1975.[5]

Part of the reason for that neglect is that McKinnon's book had poor circulation. He published the book with his own small-press venture, the Caledonia Writing Series, which was based in Prince George, British Columbia. He founded the series in 1972 after learning the publishing trade through a summer job with Talonbooks that same year. Although the press was publishing the work of talented writers such as Brian Fawcett, Patrick Lane, Dorothy Livesay, Al Purdy, and Andrew Suknaski, it was still very much a *small* press with limited distribution and funding. McKinnon never did "huge mail-outs" (Telephone interview) and so his published books were infrequently circulated outside of British Columbia. Print runs rarely exceeded a hundred copies. In the specific case of McKinnon's *I Wanted to Say Something*, the book was printed on large brown broadsheets in a run of about one hundred that McKinnon glued by hand, with a binding that was, like the broadsheets themselves, quite fragile; the material conditions of the edition thus further limited its durability and distribution.

Hence, while the book was well regarded by McKinnon's contemporaries and had an impact on those to whom he sent it directly, *I Wanted to Say Something* could not and did not circulate widely enough to influence readers further east, especially anthologists and academics. In Michael Ondaatje's canon-forming publication, *The Long Poem Anthology* (1979), he lists McKinnon among those he could have included in the volume, but his "Further Reading" section shows that, in making that statement, he was apparently thinking of two other books by McKinnon: *Sex at Thirty-One* (1977) and *Songs and Speeches* (1976).[6] Even when Red Deer Press reissued *I Wanted to Say Something* in 1990 as a small paperback, McKinnon's poems failed to reach a larger audience because the press "poorly marketed the book" and primarily sold it only to libraries (Telephone interview). McKinnon's absence from major studies of the long poem only made his book harder for potential readers to discover. Although *I Wanted to Say Something* has traditionally existed outside the canon, it is nevertheless vital to understanding the aesthetic and conceptual development of lyric historiography, especially in the context of the familial long poem.

Drafted in 1969–70, *I Wanted to Say Something* was the result of several simultaneous events: McKinnon's discovery of Charles Olson and modernist long poems more generally, his reading of Newlove's *Moving in Alone* and *Black Night Window*, and, most importantly, Fred Dalton's (McKinnon's grandfather) decision to bequeath his collection of family photographs to his grandson. McKinnon read Olson's *Maximus Poems* "early on" in his career; it led him to consider "a long span[ning]" lyric poem, as did other long poems such as Pound's *Cantos* and William Carlos Williams's *Paterson*. In fact, the original page dimensions of *I Wanted to Say Something* were modelled on those of Olson's long poem (Email from McKinnon [Jan. 2012]). Unlike the near-pocket-sized 1990 version, McKinnon's 1975 edition has pages approximately 8.5 x 14 inches with abundant blank space between stanzas. The physical size of the 1975 version of *I Wanted to Say Something*, like Olson's full-sized *Maximus Poems*, embodies the conceptual size of the story. Modernist long poems, McKinnon recalls, were "lurking somewhere in the unconscious, but on the surface, I felt I was on my own, being pushed by some need to get [*I Wanted to Say Something*] down" (Email from McKinnon [Apr. 2012]). At the same time, he remembers that Purdy and Newlove (especially the latter) shaped his ideas about poetic composition: "Newlove was of interest to me for his lyric power [...] Newlove would have given me some sense that my 'subject matter' [prairie history] was legitimate" (Email from McKinnon [Feb. 2012]).

McKinnon's project, above all else, was inspired by his grandfather's penchant for photography. McKinnon recalls the genesis of his poem:

> At some point in the late sixties [Fred Dalton] started to clean the attics and disperse various items to family members. I remember seeing his photographs early on and said that I'd like to have them. [...] Dalton unknowingly documented his experience and the landscape – the life of a farm family as they went about the daily chores, harvesting, et cetera, and gave evidence of the seasons. One of his motives, again, the need for money, was to use his old Kodak camera to take pictures of men who worked on the railroads. These photographs, in many instances, were printed as post cards that could be mailed back to wherever "home" was. [...] [I]n the summer of 69 I wrote a one-page fragmentary piece – some kind of young poet's prairie/home nostalgia. I put the fragment away, and some time later could see that I had started something and that the pictures and stories could be used in the composition and that the photographs seemed as important as the text I was generating. In other words, not decoration, but illustrative in their own right – to act as a break in the text, breathing points for contemplation, but integral to what was now becoming a large concept – the poem to contain a family history. (Email from McKinnon [Aug. 2011])

McKinnon's specific phrasing above echoes Pound's description of his *Cantos* as "a poem to include history" – another link between McKinnon's project and Anglo-American modernist long poems. But I am also struck by the fact that his first "fragment," the brief lyric he drafted in the summer of 1969, inspired him to go further; the poem represented possibility, not an epistemological impasse as one finds in accumulative poems. And so he added to that small poem throughout 1969 until the spring of 1970, at which point he divided his book-length poem into three parts, only two of which remain in the published version.[7] I want to discuss McKinnon's *I Wanted to Say Something* by examining a tonal shift, whereby his book begins with his persona's feeling of secured confidence and faith in his literary and historical vision; by the book's end, however, this authority gradually deflates and the poet expresses profound scepticism about his vision.

The persona of "Part 1: The Legacy" tends to speak confidently and firmly about history. The poem begins with a look at "the photo album," and the speaker begins to craft a story around the pictures with the help of his family. As a complement to the poems I discussed in my last chapter, McKinnon's story is a further example of "postmemory":

> they thumb thru history and give
> us names to place on the distorted shapes (mothers, uncles and
> those who've died: photos continue   and we all laugh in the
> innocence – that it's all past that nothing lasts once the
> dream ends.
>
>   I trace the ignorance / blunt men
>   with plump wives
>   dragging themselves thru prairies
> and dust storms
>
> (15)[8]

McKinnon's persona pieces together a fragmented past: "distorted shapes" seem clarified once they are named, photographs "continue" history, and even the suggestion that "nothing lasts" seems disbelieved by the poet-persona who decides nonetheless to "trace" the historical narrative. Confident that he lacks the ignorance of his ancestors, the speaker finds in these photographs a palpable history, "frozen" in pictures (42) and waiting to be explored.

Initially, McKinnon's persona relies heavily on the aesthetic power of and information contained in such photographs. He differs from

Newlove's persona in this respect, even if it is hard to ignore an obvious influence:

image: arikaras
with traded spanish sabre blades
mounted on the long
heavy buffalo lances

("The Pride" *BNW* 105)

images:
nature (prairie, hills
rivers, trees, sun,
Indians

(*IWSS* 31)

Newlove's single, powerful image is, as I have earlier explained, one that he eventually questions: the image, he knows, derives from careless histories. McKinnon's persona, however, has faith in his catalogue of potential poetic images; they inspire him to write a developmental lyric. His language becomes noticeably deictic as he confidently guides the reader through pictures. Of the first photograph, for instance, he writes,

the train ended here right
by the house. you can see the
men – and there, the crane just past
the house

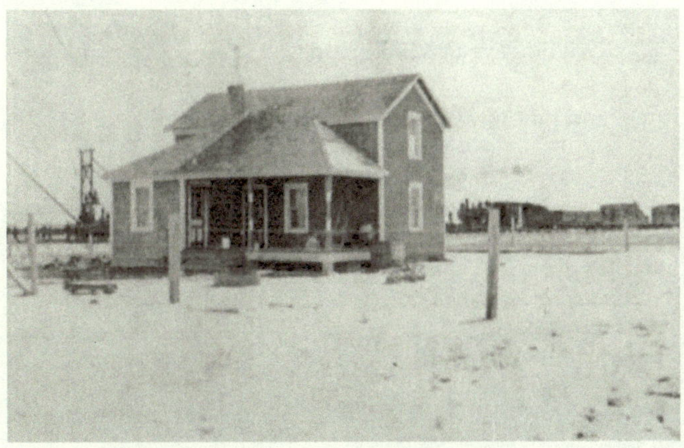

(16)

For Barthes, one of the most important qualities of a photograph is its ability to create an inhabitable landscape: "I want to live there, en finesse," Barthes writes, "and the tourist photograph never satisfies that *esprit de finesse*. For me, photographs of landscape (urban or country) must be habitable, not visitable. [...] Looking at these landscapes of predilection, it is as if I were certain of having been there or of going there" (38–40). McKinnon's photograph is not only a testament to an inhabitable landscape (marked quite literally by the pristine home), but his deictic language makes the photograph itself inhabitable. Photographs, Barthes notes, are always "an antiphon of 'Look,' 'See,' 'Here it is'" and other similarly "pure deictic language" (5). These aren't just connotations of McKinnon's pictures, they are the actual language of his poem: "here right / by the house" and "there, the crane just past / the house." The effect is a habitable landscape made more compelling by a photograph that readers are explicitly asked to enter and navigate. For brief moments, readers live in the photographic past with McKinnon's persona.

There is, too, an apparent promise in Part 1 that whatever appears hidden is or will be made plain to the reader. This revelatory quality of the text is readily apparent when McKinnon's persona examines a photograph of his grandfather and aunt (though the text momentarily mixes the aunt up with McKinnon's mother):

And here, your mother/your aunt
hidden in the grass, the oats
brushing
her shoulders

(who gave this life to me,

the legacy: pictures/and ignorance and love
to look back
upon:

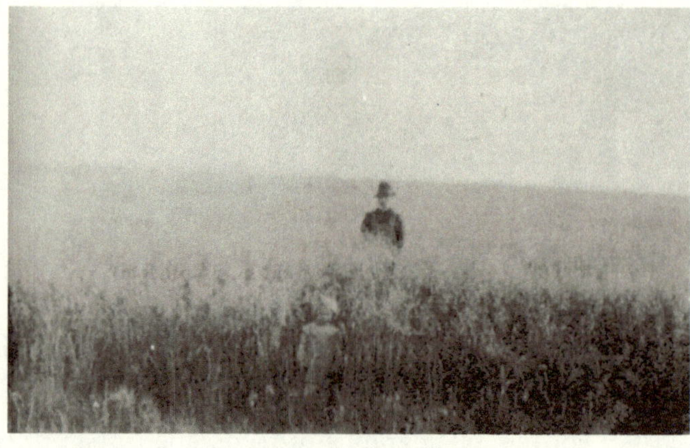

(17)

McKinnon again adopts deictic language ("here"), but he also draws the reader into relation with the photograph by – and this is unusual in the briefer poems of lyric historiography – incorporating a second voice. Given the basis for the poem, the voice is presumably his grandfather's voice, marked by the second-person pronouns ("your mother/your aunt"). The shift draws in the reader, putting them in the position of the poet-persona looking back at his familial past, which is another instance of inhabitation. The implicit promise that what is "hidden" can be made plain to the reader is also striking: without McKinnon's lyrical navigation, a reader might miss the aunt hiding in the grass. That promise of revelation contrasts with the straining speakers of lyric historiography who wait for clarity to come to them or who can only *attempt* to conjure up clear images. The inheritance of a "legacy," of a "dream lived in the genetic structure" (19), at times makes it seem as though the speaker's full apprehension of the past is possible.

Yet as the persona delves further into this history, he discovers that his grandparents' experience was one of confusion and failure, a discovery that noticeably affects the speaker's tone. McKinnon's persona refers frequently to the family's wish to take control of a chaotic landscape: "they came to conceive the land as enemy and fought / back with god and muscle and stupidity until the first winters / are thru, then spring and the promise enters again, the natural / cycle of trees beginning to bud" (26). Nature is indifferent to Dalton's "geometr[ic]" conception of "the land" (28), the "angles / in his head" (31). The farmer imagines the land, but his "meditation lack[s] // clarity" (28; the phrase repeats on 29), his "suffering lack[s] / clarity" (29). Incapable of ordering, shaping, or even understanding their experience, the family exists "amidst the chaos" (32), a chaos that the persona tends to observe in nature ("trees die on purpose" [34]).

As often, he observes chaos as social injustice: female farmhands and mothers who – unlike male farmers – "never" took breaks from their work (23) and the Indigenous communities "pushed further east / by the government" in order to make room for new settlers (26). As the persona discovers the correlation between these histories and the "ignoran[t]" (15, 17) vision of prairie settlers, he learns to distrust his musings on the past, and he proclaims his scepticism about halfway through the collection: "I emerge to destroy my own dreams / and the tricks of / memory" (30). It is a cruel and ironic epiphany: whereas an epiphany spiritually enlightens a romantic persona, McKinnon's revelation compels him to "destroy" his knowledge and question his certainty. At that moment, the poem shifts; for the remainder of the poem, McKinnon's speaker explores fissures in his narrative. The inevitable truth he confronts is that his poem, like the aspirations of his grandparents and their contemporaries, "beg[an] in innocence" (27, 28) but exposed ignorance.

Some subtle suggestions of this epiphany occur prior to the persona's declaration. One can find hints of this emerging scepticism in the photograph of Dalton below. I noted earlier the sense of involvement that McKinnon's deixis engenders in the reader. This photograph, conversely, produces a different effect. McKinnon's spacing before and after the picture is substantial, so I have shrunk the structure somewhat for purposes of reproduction:

Then, the man's task: horses, plows, and hired strangers –
and the fields stretched
                    natural before him
                                        (the thick soil. the enemy
lying flat
        and Indians pushed further east
by the government:

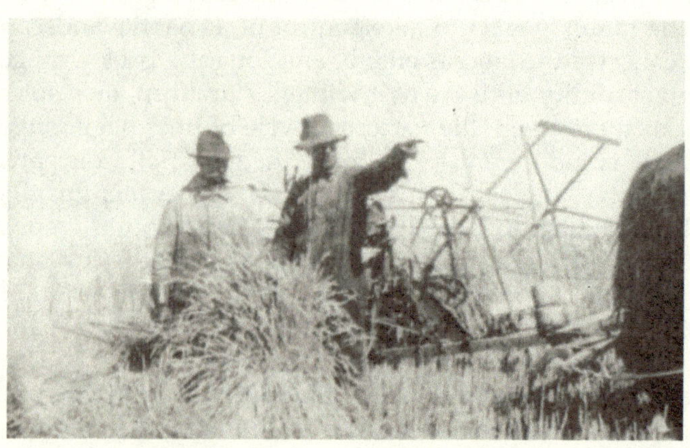

it all begins in innocence: the old news reels,
the chronicles. shots of the plow, and
black earth cut deep
                    thru the grass
                                beneath the roots – earth
split in
    furrows
                    a trench for the
seed.

(26–7)

The persona's criticism of colonialism introduces the picture of Fred Dalton with a colon, a punctuation that establishes a relationship between two ideas – in this case, the displacement of Indigenous communities and Dalton's settlement. The photograph that denotes "the innocence" of a farmer's dream also connotes the tragedy that befell other people in order for that dream to take form. Dalton's pose supports this reading: whereas the persona brings the reader into earlier photographs with deictic language, here Dalton is pushing the reader out with a deictic gesture. There are at least two possible (and not necessarily mutually exclusive) readings here: (1) Dalton may be pointing "east" to usher Indigenous peoples off the land or (2) there is some event or object beyond the frame of the photograph, the unavailability of which exposes the boundaries of McKinnon's perception. In the latter case, the persona asks readers to look beyond the edge of the photograph, which, of course, we cannot do (at least not within the confines of McKinnon's poem). This wonderfully enigmatic photograph hints that something lies outside the poet's narrative and photographic frames, which ideally encourages the reader to look for the story McKinnon realizes must also be written: the story of colonialism and resistance, the story to which pictures of prairie farmers only gesture and in which they are complicit.

The speaker's subsequent "root" metaphor reinforces the underlying and obscured narrative of conquest: the farmers destroy whatever is rooted in the land (or, whoever first occupied prairie spaces) in order to make room for a new "seed." This moment is decisive in McKinnon's text. It is the moment in which the speaker loses confidence in the reliability of photographic representation. Photographs once offered him certainty; suddenly, they symbolize boundaries. He begins seeing only the limits of pictures, stories, and poems, a realization that leads to his declaration that he will "destroy" his "dreams" and the "tricks of memory" and "begin to speak only of the failure – and difficult / love" (36). In this vein, Part 1 ends with "whispers," "scattered history," and a poet who realizes that he is beginning to "counter the mechanical / accuracy" of his family's stories (42). Things are quieter, the narrative now feeling less coherent. McKinnon's poignant conclusion to Part 1 undermines the epistemological certainty and lyric confidence that began it.

Part 2, appropriately titled "The Moving Photograph" (which was, in fact, the original title for McKinnon's book [Telephone interview]), continues this line of investigation into the authenticity of images and stories. The most obvious difference between Part 1 and Part 2 is the absence of photographs in the latter, as the speaker has come to doubt their promise of a complete historical image. The persona of the second section is full of such doubt, as he contemplates the "dust / in his lungs" – which may be an allusion to Newlove's "The Pride" (the "dust in our eyes"). McKinnon's contemplation makes him wonder, "where does he want the poem / to go / (thru angular history, / and names, the dates running as / a line / thru our lives," even though "the journey is not simple" (48). This realization that history cannot be neatly ordered into a straight (or, for that matter, poetic) line leads the humbled persona to offer his titular phrase: "I wanted to say something / is wrong and provide an / alternative" (49). Crozier posits that McKinnon's line is evidence of a persona "more interested in the process of his own telling, the movement from the desire to say something to the words actually said" ("The Edge" 106).

McKinnon's line says more than that, though. At first glance, the title of McKinnon's book might denote his inability to speak ("I wanted to say something, but I can't") or his intention to speak ("I wanted to say something, and, between these covers, I will"). When the full phrase actually appears in the poem, though, it artfully conveys humility: the displacement of Indigenous peoples, the ignorance engendered through colonialism, the belief that history can be displayed simplistically or understood in simple terms are all morally or epistemologically "wrong." The moment is an impasse in McKinnon's thinking: what alternatives to this history exist? How does one celebrate what is both joyful (a familial connection) and "wrong" (the related displacement of cultural others)? The more seriously McKinnon considers these implied questions, the more his poem feels diagnostic, more reminiscent of accumulative lyrics than developmental ones. The assured poet becomes a sceptical one as his desire for a narrative of "ecstasy" (49) turns into a much less romantic image of "decay[ing]" narratives (50) and, by implication, decaying authority.

Though that shift exists, McKinnon's ending isn't quite so dire as it may appear. His persona comes to terms with and finds value in this doubt. Part 2 begins,

with innocence the land
bore me. the cultivated
  womb became my
  skin. images pushed
inside the eye. the legacy of
        elevators and angles and
grass to get lost

in

hear the wind against his
        skin

the decay begins as he hears the mystery,
a whisper thru the trees, and voices
in the rooms
                below

(47)

As a bit of an aside, McKinnon's introduction to Part 2 is magnificently crafted: stirring imagery, precise diction, and an unmistakable ear for rhythm. The lines sing with alliteration and faint rhymes and sibilance – it still amazes me that McKinnon has fallen by the wayside of the Canadian canon. To come back to history, though: the opening line reinforces the fact that the poet was, obviously, born out of his family history. At the same time, "innocence" is, according to the poet, only where stories *begin*. Beyond that "innocence" is a much more dynamic history that inspires the poet's contemplation and reflection.

The section's title, "The Moving Photograph," carries several meanings associated with epistemology, emotion, and McKinnon's scepticism: the ultimately unrevealing and unstable photograph that "moves" away from meaning, the affective (i.e., "moving") photograph that inspires McKinnon's "difficult love," and the poet's limited ability to make an unmoving (earlier he uses the word "frozen") historical scene "move" again. I think all three of these readings function here simultaneously, clouding the past and creating a sense of "mystery." And now that the past is mysterious, it feels increasingly distant from the persona; the past "decay[s]" and appears buried (the obvious connotation of "below"), while voices become barely audible "whispers." He regards these voices as part of a "mute history" (55). History quiets, and once-promising photographs are now "fragments of / the dream I imagine going bad" (55). What the reader hears, instead of history, is the poet's voice. He impels readers to "hear" his crisp rhymes ("skin," "in," "skin," "begins"; "land," "and"), repetition ("skin") and much fainter echoes of consonants ("land," "cultivated," "pushed," "and," et cetera). Readers engage with the second part of McKinnon's poem much the way they would with accumulative lyric historiography: by focusing on the poet's voice and self-doubt rather than on a coherent historical image.

McKinnon concludes *I Wanted to Say Something* by emphasizing this lyric quality of his poem. He writes of himself,

he will sing before he disappears.
the history, people sustain him.   the voice taught
by birds, the meadow lark
                                        cutting the air
    with a sound/
                                he imitates
in his vision requiring the elements
    to balance and cohere

and now he sings again
here

    where we reach
                                the edge
    of the moving photo

graph

(61)

McKinnon's persona once again deploys deictic language, but he does so in order to draw attention to the presence of a poet-figure. The poem and poet, not the photograph, become the focus of the reader's attention. The persona insistently foregrounds himself: the distinctly prairie bird imagery, like the repeated image of a singer, recalls the "songbird" motif of romantic lyrics – Keats's "Ode to a Nightingale" or Shelley's "To a Skylark." Yet this foregrounded poet-figure is not a self-celebrating romantic. He is unoriginal; he "imitates." More importantly, he strives for an unrealized coherence with which to end the poem: not even the purposefully artificial rhyme of "cohere" and "here" can fool the reader into feeling a sense of closure, especially because the rhyme is preceded and followed by an enormous gap. It may be a gap in the text and in history, which explains why the poem concludes at the "edge" of an image, not at the "end" of the narrative; there is more to be discovered, but the poet's range of sight cannot fully account for the larger past in which his family played a small part. The final and broken word, "photograph," further stresses the incompleteness of his historical image, but it also signifies the poet's faith in the process of recording these images, because McKinnon "places emphasis on 'graph,' the Greek suffix for writing"

(Crozier, "The Edge" 108). The concluding line, isolated and broken, potentially feels like an image of defeat: the poet giving up on the fragmented past, the broken picture, and the isolating act of writing. Yet the last line also seems to be an imperative through which the speaker invites the reader to "*graph*," to write some other history now that this specific poem has reached its end. That reading would indicate that the poet-persona sees the documenting of postmemory as an essential and shared creative act: every familial memory enriches and adds diversity to our understanding of a broader history, no matter how quickly or often each writer encounters the edge of their own knowledge.

The end of McKinnon's poems, his epistemological impasse, is in keeping with the trajectories of most modernist long poems. Margaret Dickie observes a similar arc in the work of Hart Crane and William Carlos Williams, both of whom "started out with [...] a celebratory impulse, and a desire to write a long poem of synthesis [...] [but] came nevertheless to question the validity of their initial visions" (109). Careers continued with a confidence earned by the aesthetic success of the imagist movement and ended with the modernist long poem, a "fuller confrontation with [...] problems of representation" (155) and an intensified "awareness of [modernism's epistemological] limits" (161). Dickie's narrative is a compelling model of the move from accumulation to development: once modernists found the "authentic" image, they overcame the doubts inspired by inauthentic images, only to learn that whatever meaning they discover is momentary and not sustainable when interrogated ceaselessly. The sceptical mind, it appears, simply cannot allow a unified poem or a readily coherent vision of history to take shape; to do so contradicts every critical impulse behind sceptical writing and philosophy.

In many respects, the relationship I have been proposing in this chapter between the brief lyric and the long one resembles the relationship between imagism and the long poem. Dickie argues that the long poem was a "second stage" of one particular trajectory of Anglo-American modernism (2): "[T]he rapidity with which Modernism revolutionized American poetry [via imagism] left [modernist] poets to live out the greater parts of their careers in a revolution that had succeeded. Self-conscious experimenters, they had either to try new experiments or to repeat themselves" (3). The long poem, she therefore notes, was not a "unique accomplishment," but rather an indication of "a long history of composition in which Modernism changed and developed" (4): it was the result of a move from the "Imagist program of 1913" (2) to the longer pieces that drew their élan from "an image, a symbol, a fragmented translation, a mood of ecstatic affirmation" (11). Reflecting on twentieth-century poetry, Louis Dudek likewise notes that the successful apprehension of "the isolated image led to a new conception of the extended poem – the long poem composed completely of images. This development was of prime importance for literature" ("Theory" 268). An analogous development occurred during the centennial era: when poets discovered the narrative potential of the individual family images they accumulated, those images were arranged developmentally to create long poems that adhere to "some basic principle of continuity" and strive "toward a larger interpretation" (Dickie 109), a project that matched the literary ambitions of great modernist writers such as Pound and Olson.

This is the literary history into which McKinnon fits, and his example gives reason to question Sam Solecki's criticisms of contemporary Canadian lyrics. Solecki laments that poems adopting the "inclusive 'we' [...] have been replaced in the work of the younger poets by pronouns referring almost always only to a lover, a family member, or a personal relationship," which he feels is a "reduction in scope and ambition" (216). But that "reduction of scope," for some poets, *is* their pursuit of greater literary "ambition[s]": McKinnon's poem aspires to the "largeness" of Olson's *Maximus Poems*, Williams's *Paterson*, or Pound's *Cantos* while attending, simultaneously, to the experiences and personal history of the "I." That reduced scope is also one way of alleviating – to one degree or another – the epistemological crises in lyric historiography; the family photo album is personal and empowering, and it enables sceptics to claim a degree of knowledge about the past, a past that, even if familial, still serves as a microcosm of and/or a gateway into larger stories. But the more deeply poets probed those histories, the more they came to realize that having superior knowledge is not the same as having absolute knowledge. Even if these investigations yielded much longer and more visually intense collections of lyrics that presume to have the authority at least to explore and narrate the past, the poets still struggle to find closure. McKinnon's *I Wanted to Say Something* typifies this process.

Further, McKinnon's poem stirred his contemporaries, and it did so in ways that prove influence is not unidirectional. Purdy's *In Search of Owen Roblin* (1974), for instance, documents the settlement of Ameliasburgh by Owen Roblin in the nineteenth-century, though the poem is as much an exploration of Purdy's own family history; in relating the history of Roblin, he cannot help but locate his grandfather in the same era and attribute to that ancestor, accurately or inaccurately, the same pioneering spirit he sees in Roblin. *In Search of Owen Roblin* is a more overt attempt to connect the personal with the national than one finds in a book like McKinnon's *I Wanted to Say Something* – a difference of degree, not one of kind.

Purdy recognized the epistemological power of family history. He said in his 1993 autobiography, *Reaching for the Beaufort Sea*, that the world of his grandfather, "eighty years back of me in time," was paradoxically the world "closest to [him]" (16): "Even from a long time and distance, I can transport [people] back into here and now. As if they were pictures in my own brain, as if they are real now as they were real then. And I know they are true people, because when I compare a photograph that may exist of their faces and bodies with the one in my mind, then the photograph is nearly identical" (36). These were some of the feelings behind Purdy's *In Search of Owen Roblin*, a book that began taking shape in his mind as early as October 1972.

The timing is hardly coincidence. McKinnon had mailed Purdy a draft copy of *I Wanted to Say Something* sometime in 1970 or 1971 (Letter from McKinnon to Weingarten); McKinnon recalls that he was "sending Purdy everything" he wrote after they began regularly corresponding in the late 1960s (Telephone interview). Later, in the summer of 1972, Purdy was working on a radio play about his grandfather (Ridley Purdy) and Owen Roblin, which he performed on CBC Radio in 1973. Several months before that performance, he decided to redo the play as a book and enlisted the help of the photographer Bob Waller. Purdy suggested their collaboration on an "Ontario book" (Purdy to Waller), and he later described *In Search of Owen Roblin* to his publisher, Jack McClelland, as "a book of photographs of rural Ontario along with some of my poems" (Purdy to McClelland). Much of the material was from earlier poems (e.g., "Roblin's Mills" and "Roblin's Mills [II]") that he fused with writings about Ridley Purdy (such as "Elegy for a Grandfather," a poem from the late 1950s). This fusion led some reviewers to observe that, despite the title of Purdy's long poem, his "search is not only for Owen Roblin, but for Purdy himself, his identity, and the source of his being" (van Steen 68). Purdy's turn to the familial long poem, as well as his decision to make it a photographic collection, are obvious hints of McKinnon's influence.

Purdy's narrative arc is as much a reflection of McKinnon's impact as his form. The opening lines of *In Search of Owen Roblin* suggest that, like McKinnon's speaker, Purdy's persona finds the photograph album inviting: "Open the album / it is a cage of ancestors / locked in by metal clasps and stiff cardboard / released by my own careless fingers" (*BR* 238). The fact that only the speaker's "careless fingers" can "release" his ancestors undermines what seems at first to be Purdy's opening imperative. The reader, in other words, cannot "open the album," but not because of any lack of intelligence or imaginative ability; the reader lacks the intimacy with the past that the persona owns. That intimacy is what allows the persona to open the album even with "careless fingers." His intuitive possession of the past also explains the necromantic animations of the opening sections: the "frozen faces" (Purdy's image recalls McKinnon's description of "frozen" faces in *I Wanted to Say Something* [42]) suddenly have "bulging eyes" (*BR* 238) and the speaker, in keeping with his "careless" persona, makes the impossible claim that "the people literally fling themselves / out of the book into your eyes" (*BR* 238). The latter phrase conveys an intimacy with the past that cannot be replicated, because it exists in the "eyes" and, through a self-implicating pun, the "I."

This section of Purdy's poem foregrounds an unusually precise (unusual for Purdy, that is) and photographic rendering of the grandfather:

> his face the fresh ruddy face of a farm boy
> smeared with grease to protect himself
> against wild black flies and blazing sun
> sweating dust on a road leading into the sky
> with a single black cloud near the horizon
> a red kerchief wrapped around his head
> biscuits and dried deer meat for lunch
> six feet tall but only 200 pounds then (*BR* 241)

The numerical precision sharpens an already vivid scene, and that visual confidence is conveyed through the aurality of the scene, too: Purdy's persona says repeatedly that he "can hear" his grandfather's voice and the past more generally (*BR* 241) with striking clarity. That aural and visual certainty is something that seems impossible in earlier poems like "Remains of an Indian Village" or "The Battlefield at Batoche," where the past sounds faint and seems virtually irretrievable. The connection between "now" and "then" is less tenuous in *In Search of Owen Roblin* than in Purdy's earlier poems; the past is the present, extended forward by the speaker himself who has "somehow become" the embodiment of familial "memory" (*BR* 243). The poem conveys an insistent willingness to discover that parallels McKinnon's own instinct to explore: the frequent feeling of "discovery" (Purdy uses the word several times) anticipates the later claim of Purdy's speaker, that he is "unafraid of darkness or failure" as he ventures into the past (*BR* 270).

That is not to say, however, that Purdy's speaker sustains this confident feeling of having carried the past into the present and embodying it. Purdy's speaker uses his grandfather's life as an inroad into the settlement history of Ameliasburgh, but the more deeply he probes into that past, the less he seems to know or hear. He remembers "the slight shock of surprise / I felt to learn that Roblin was not the first man here" (*BR* 261), but his investigation into Roblin's predecessor, John Way, yields very little: "about him I know nothing / to that name I add nothing more" (*BR* 261). The lyric reaches its imaginative limits, drawing a line between the narrative wandering through a familial past and the careless, uncertain stumbling through the life of Roblin and the broader history of nineteenth-century Ontario. He "travel[s] still farther back" to flesh out this narrative, but inevitably hits an impasse because "1803" is "as far as the records go" (*BR* 262). After all of the fact-gathering about his grandfather and about Owen Roblin, Purdy reverts to the uncertain and tentative language that colours his earlier poetry: he knows that "names and dates say very little" about the things buried "underneath a village" and switches from the "personal family myth as real as a hamburger" (*BR* 240) to more speculative writing: as he imagines "two people / who never lived but surely existed," he extends his confession to say, "If they never lived dammit they should have / but I believe they did / nameless and unlisted in record books" (*BR* 264). There is none of the precision here that one finds in earlier sections of the poem. The details and factual accounts are replaced with the speaker's recognition of the limits of "the records" and his imagination.

Still, he is compelled to turn his attention to the era around his grandfather despite the fact that, no matter how many names, dates, artefacts, memories, and photographs he encounters, he recognizes that he is now supplying only "wild speculations" and "elusive unverified facts." Finally, Purdy's speaker wonders what everything he knows "add[s]" up to as a picture of the era in which his grandfather lived: "not very damn much" (*BR* 270). He ends the long poem by integrating one of his more ambiguous poems about the past, "Roblin's Mills [II]," into the narrative: the inclusion conjures up images of "fragments," "discarded" stories, and "forgotten" people who "had their being once / and left a place to stand on" (*BR* 273–4). The existence of the present is the only concrete proof of the existence of a vague and indistinct past.

Purdy's epiphany is not exactly the image of confirmation one might expect, given his assured introduction to the book. Increasingly uncertain about his version of history, he accepts that he is "a piece of the main" (*BR* 271) and finds that while "[i]n search of Owen Roblin" and Ridley Purdy, he "discovered a whole era" (*BR* 270).[9] The enormity of those images of "the main" and "the whole era" leads the reader away from the familial narrative and outward to the characteristically Purdyean poem: the reader learns something of Owen Roblin or Ridley Purdy, but then that knowledge pushes him outward, urging him to imagine a provocatively amorphous era in place of a more specific past.

What strikes me about Purdy's *In Search of Owen Roblin* versus his earlier work is that it demonstrates the same willingness to explore history in the way that McKinnon does in *I Wanted to Say Something*: as a history of narrative possibility that, even when it eventually looks outward to see a "whole era," establishes its narrative footing first with a precise rendering of the family.

As much as such writing was poetically progressive, it was also progressive history. A common criticism levied against the historical profession in Canada has been that innovations on content have rarely resulted in methodological innovation. Even as historians like David Gagan advocated for deeper engagements with social history and the history of the family (Gagan called this "uncharted territory" in the field of Canadian history [124]), they did not – as I explained in my introduction – do much to change their methods. Remember Steven High's argument: "The rise of the new 'Social History' in the 1970s and 1980s," he writes, "did not fundamentally change [historians'] relationships to our pasts or to our publics. ... The subject matter changed, but not the research process or our authorial voice" (22). The fundamental problem of historical writing in Canada – historians' pretention to unqualified narrative authority – went largely uncontested. In the years after Ramsay Cook and J.M.S. Careless advocated for "limited identities" and seeded interest in regional and familial pasts, historians continued to explore family history as they had any other kind of history. They held themselves to impossible standards of "objectivity," professional distance, academic disinterest, and intellectual authority.

Lyric historiography offers something else entirely: narrative ambiguity and sincere, self-implicating questions about authority. McKinnon, for instance, appreciates both what the "I" knows and what it cannot know by acknowledging the stories he must leave for others to tell. That movement inward and outward is a productive paradox in all lyric poetry: as "lyric poet[s] ... imagine for us a ... dynamic inwardness," they also "let us contemplate for ourselves our own memories" (Johnson 74). Insularity is not a necessary consequence of lyric because the empathetic act of reading another "I" may be validating. When McKinnon read Newlove's regionalist lyrics, for instance, he felt empowered to write his own story; evidently, the poet felt that if Newlove could lyrically argue for the importance of his locale, then McKinnon could himself argue for the importance of his own local story. Thus, in a community of lyric poets, no one can assume the value of their own story without, by implication, acknowledging that any other individual story is as important; as McKinnon values his grandfather's history, he also gestures to the value of an Indigenous family's story of displacement. And so rather than insularity, readers find in lyric historiography this tidal inward/outward movement that acknowledges the legitimacy of every story from every "I."

If that is indeed a quality of these poems, then there is something inherently democratic about the lyric as a historiographic method. To come back to what Solecki argues about the insularity of the "I" in contemporary poetry: his "we" is potentially the more troublesome poetic tactic. "We" is an exercise in homogenizing experience and identity in a country (and world) that has been, since the end of the Second World War, on an irreversible path to undermine, tirelessly, myths of unity and sameness. Through their emphasis on personal and familial experience, poems such as *I Wanted to Say Something* escaped this tired fad of unifying literature that hurries past or altogether ignores theories and histories of difference. Arguably, the "we," not the "I," is the site of insularity and exclusion.

That reading of familial poems offers greater evidence for one of the central arguments I have been building: poets have been vital to the reinvention of history as a social discourse invested in the experiences of all individuals. Their projects have unsettled conservative definitions of "legitimate history," whereby the lyric poet, like Walter Benjamin's historical materialist, values "the fullness of the past" (256). All experiences possess value and meaning, and so history becomes discourse, rather than dogma.

7 Sharing Authority

One of the major successes of Barry McKinnon's *I Wanted to Say Something* is the paradox it explores: a personal history inspires a sense of narrative authority and exposes an individual's epistemological limits. Andrew Suknaski's *Wood Mountain Poems* (1976) is, in many ways, an extended delineation of McKinnon's paradox. That McKinnon had an impact on Suknaski is clear enough. In 1990, Suknaski spoke of his work fondly:

> There is so much I could try to say about *I Wanted to Say Something*. But I can't articulate it. All I can say is this seminal poem was there before me. And where I went with *Wood Mountain Poems*, Barry's poem was a beacon for me. And I am sure something of Barry's vision of the early west – with all its hopes, dreams and losses – flared in Sid Marty's imagination when he wrote his poems about the Marty family in Southern Alberta [*The Tumbleweed Harvest*]. ("Foreword" n.p.)

In the same piece, Suknaski goes even further and credits McKinnon with seeding the search for family in the minds of Robert Kroetsch (*The Stone Hammer Poems* [1975] and *Seed Catalogue* [1977]) and Eli Mandel (*Out of Place* [1977]). Like these writers, Suknaski was keen to find out where his family history might take his literary career.

While this chapter focuses on Suknaski's lyric historiography, his corpus comprises much more than such poetry. Between 1965 and 1990, he undertook a huge number of projects: he founded presses and magazines, produced films, experimented with ideograms and visual art, began numerous long poems, made several unpublished attempts at writing historical texts such as *In Search of Parinti*, and wrote numerous unpublished poetry volumes such as *Divining West*, the last of which Suknaski described as his "nightmare [...] because it's such a spread eagled [long] poem. It keeps going off on tangents" (Suknaski and Hillis 117) – a reasonable claim, given that Suknaski's drafts of *Divining West* fill nearly an entire box in his archive at the University of Manitoba. All of this is to say that Suknaski's artistic endeavours are too varied and too numerous for me to cover adequately in this relatively short space; I do not want to give the false impression that my focus in this chapter on *Wood Mountain Poems* (1976) draws out any comprehensive conclusions about his career. His familial writing, however, is voluminous, and it was evidently of profound importance to him personally (he writes of his family in several books, especially *Wood Mountain Poems* and, much later, *In the Name of Narid* [1981]). Nonetheless, Suknaski's early creative work had little to do with such themes. He only began to write poetry seriously at the end of the 1960s, after leaving Wood Mountain, Saskatchewan, for Vancouver.

In Vancouver, Suknaski met Earle Birney and Al Purdy, both of whom became his mentors. Under their influence, he experimented with fairly conventional verse poetry, but also with ceramic pottery, ideograms, and visual art. These experiments were obviously influenced by his studies at the Kootenay School of Art, the place where Suknaski first met other Canadian poets such as Birney, Lionel Kearns, and Fred Wah. Suknaski began developing diverse types of poetry that developed his own sense of the "poetic image": inscribed sculptures, concrete poetry, imagistic poems, lyric historiography, and so forth. He called this writing his "word/picture" vision (*Rose Way in the East* n.p.),[1] which he developed with great enthusiasm after his discovery of Ezra Pound's *Cantos*; Suknaski even published a small chapbook in honour of Pound (*These Fragments I Have Gathered for Ezra* [1973]), and he makes nods to Pound in *Silk Trail* (1985). By the end of the 1960s, Suknaski recalls, he was attempting to write along "Imagist lines, trying to simply write a good little poem" (Suknaski and David 10). Suknaski's early poetics was thus firmly rooted in his personal interpretations of "the image"; he disliked his "documentary poet" label and instead regarded himself as a maker of "lyric images" (Suknaski and Melnyk 32).

For almost fifteen years after Purdy introduced Suknaski to Canadian readers in *Storm Warning* (1971), the young writer was unstoppably prolific in his experiments with these "lyric images." And then his career ended almost overnight. In the late 1980s, Suknaski suffered a series of breakdowns, which were foreshadowed in his diaries from that decade. Over those ten years, his entries became increasingly disordered on the page and in thought, and in an undated entry in the last of his archived diaries (circa 1990), Suknaski stabbed a pen through the page and scrawled in bold, large letters, "KIN WRITE NO MORE" (Diary entry). It appears to be the last thing he ever wrote, though he lived for two decades longer. It was during Suknaski's most productive period (from about 1970 until the mid-1980s) that his "lyric images" took on historical meaning for him. His poetry during this era concentrated mostly on his family history; this was, as Suknaski's foreword to *I Wanted to Say Something* suggests, partly because of his exposure to McKinnon's poetry.

Suknaski's deeply personal poetry about his family was encouraged not just by his literary circle, but also by the announcement of an official policy on multiculturalism on 8 October 1971. The policy had an impact on writers who, like the Ukrainian-Canadian Suknaski, were ethnically other to the hegemonic English-heritage Canadian, and that impact was both financial and personal.

The most immediate basis for Canada's multiculturalism policy dates back to the Pearson government's willingness to promote cultural dualism as a way of allaying tensions between French- and English-speaking Canada during the early years of the Quiet Revolution. These tensions prompted Pearson – at the suggestion of the Quebec politician and journalist André Laurendeau – to establish the Royal Commission on Bilingualism and Biculturalism (1963). The "very structure" of the commission, Kenneth McRoberts writes, "was deeply rooted in the idea of dualism. The co-chairs were a francophone and an anglophone: Laurendeau and Davidson Dunton, president of Carleton University. Of the other original members, three were francophone (two from Quebec) and three were anglophone (two from central Canada)" (40). That emphasis on dualism, however, attracted criticism because it excluded Canada's other communities.

The growing dissatisfaction with the commission on those grounds should have been anticipated. By the end of the Second World War, Canada was becoming an inescapably multi-ethnic country. Media coverage of the Quiet Revolution certainly raised awareness about cultural dualism; increased immigration since 1900, however, made cultural pluralism much more visible especially by the 1960s. For the first time in history, non-British peoples outnumbered those of British descent in Canada. The margin was relatively small in 1951, but in 1961, the population numbered approximately 10.5 million Canadians of non-British origin and approximately 7.9 million of British origin (StatsCan A125–63). John Diefenbaker therefore denounced the dualism of the B&B commission, and such critiques were echoed by public intellectuals like the historian Paul Yuzyk (McRoberts 122). Various cultural groups were "rejecting their subordinate positions" and calling for "new histories that would give them greater recognition in the country's past" (Berger, "Writings" 294).

Swayed by such arguments, the B&B Commission later, if somewhat hesitantly, published an entire volume titled *The Cultural Contribution of the Other Ethnic Groups,* which concluded that "the presence of other cultural groups in Canada is something for which all Canadians should be thankful" (14). The commission's December 1967 report laid groundwork for a reconstruction of Canada's domestic and international image. It is remarkable to think how quickly Canada's government moved from promoting a strictly English identity in the 1950s to the biculturalism of the 1960s and then to the multiculturalism of the 1970s. "It is certain," Peter Henshaw contends, "that the reports of the Royal Commission did much to popularize a term that had been brought to its attention by western Canadians who often spoke of 'multiculturalism' or 'the Canadian mosaic'" (204).

While these terms became popular by the late 1960s and early 1970s, the values for which they stood were in tension with documents like the Canadian Official Languages Act (1969). Naming only French and English as Canada's official languages, the act "reinforced the notion that the French and British were the two founding nations of Canada" and nurtured a "long-standing resistance to bilingualism" among numerous groups, "notably Ukrainian-Canadians" (Kamboureli, "Introduction" 10). The consequent outrage from Canada's marginalized ethnic communities provoked Trudeau's later announcement of an official policy on multiculturalism in 1971, which later gave way to Bill C-93 (1988) under Brian Mulroney's government.

The point of this historical detour is to substantiate James Struthers's statement made in 1982: "Ottawa has encouraged members of Canada's non-British and non-French minorities ... to retain rather than abandon their cultural heritage" (4). This was true for Canadian writers like Suknaski, and it gives some additional context for his eagerness to explore his family history in his writing. He directly benefited from the 1971 policy; *In the Name of Narid* was financially backed by the Secretary of State's Multiculturalism Directorate, an organization established the year after Trudeau made his announcement. The directorate assured financial support for many programs or publications that promoted a multicultural Canada.[2] Multicultural literature served federal policies backed by budgets (even if modest ones) that enabled writers like Suknaski to publish books about their heritage.

Equally important to Suknaski's familial writing was his loose apprenticeship under Purdy, who helped him find his poetic voice. That mentorship culminated in *Wood Mountain Poems,* a massively restructured and revised version of an earlier text of the same name (privately published in 1973); Suknaski also added poems from other chapbooks such as *Leaving Wood Mountain* to his revised edition. In late 1974, Suknaski solicited Purdy's help because he was unable to find a publisher for *Wood Mountain Poems*. Anansi rejected his manuscript for unclear reasons, and Macmillan's editors had kept silent for months after Suknaski sent them the same draft. He wrote to Purdy on 9 October: "if Macmillan does nothing [with *Wood Mountain Poems*], I'll send you old & new stuff if you still wanna do the book" (Suknaski qtd Weingarten, "Stories" 68). Purdy collaborated with Suknaski on the volume and edited it substantially during May 1975, more than a year after Suknaski had first sent it to Macmillan.

Working independently, Purdy exercised extensive control over *Wood Mountain Poems* and was largely responsible for the final shape of the volume. In fact, Purdy's vehement objection to Suknaski's intention to remove familial poems (specifically, several sections of "Homestead") from *Wood Mountain Poems* had a serious impact on the volume and Suknaski's career. Initially, Suknaski felt the poems about his family were too "heavy" to be included (qtd Weingarten, "Stories" 76), but Purdy convinced him to keep them: "'Homestead' is your central basic poem, and if you leave out 'epilogue' you cut something vital, real, tragic, and human. We all live with that sort of thing, in ourselves and others. [...] My reasons for including it are both literary and human: I just don't believe you or I or anyone should sweep unpleasant things under the rug. Because that 'epilogue' and the following 'suicide note' adds [*sic*] up to a magnificent poem. Possibly a masterpiece" (qtd Weingarten, "Stories" 78). Suknaski said that Purdy, in letters like this one, taught him that the poet must "reveal" even the most difficult "things" (Suknaski et al. 86). He accepted Purdy's suggestions and, later, regarded the revised *Wood Mountain Poems* as a breakthrough in his career: "I'm really grateful that I have come to some kind of voice of my own in *Wood Mountain Poems*. That's a particular space and time that really moves me now" (Suknaski and David 12).

Suknaski's opening poem, "Homestead, 1914 (Sec. 32, TP4, RGE2, W3RD, SASK.)" (*WMP* 19–26), is the major accomplishment of his book. "Homestead" likely appealed to readers like Purdy because it was one of few pieces in the collection that noticeably diverged from the accumulative lyrics that had become fairly commonplace as of the mid-1970s. Critics such as Stephen Scobie could be forgiven for finding accumulative poems somewhat repetitive by the end of the 1970s; in his review of Suknaski's *The Ghosts Call You Poor*, Scobie criticized (and not unfairly) Suknaski's "Dreaming of the Northwest Passage" as "a rather dull and standard exercise in the documentary mode" so typical of writers like Purdy (4). But the unique content of Suknaski's "Homestead," that intimate family saga he crafts, showed critics his inventiveness.

"Homestead" is also one of the few poems in *Wood Mountain Poems* sustained solely by Suknaski's lyric persona. The locational title immediately harkens back to the traditional romantic lyric, with the "I" rooting itself in a specific time and place to generate for the poet and reader a feeling of geographical or temporal immediacy. The poem is, if nothing else, about location: the poet strives to bring himself closer to the past and to live within a specific place, time, self, and poetic vision. Getting there took time. Suknaski wrote and rewrote the poem for several years. In the 1973 version of *Wood Mountain Poems*, he divided "Homestead" into nine parts. In Purdy's personal copy of Suknaski's 1974 draft, the poem was expanded to fourteen sections. Purdy finally reduced "Homestead" to eight sections, assuring Suknaski that it was necessary to cut the poem almost exactly in half for inclusion in the 1976 version of *Wood Mountain Poems*. Even with Purdy's edits, the poem is quite a long lyric made up of tightly rendered familial images that build on one another, thereby creating a sense of development. The poem begins with Suknaski's persona gradually delving into his family past:

> *i returning*
> for the third spring in a row now
> i return to visit father in his yorkton shack
> the first time i returned to see him
> he was a bit spooked
> seeing me after eleven years –
> a bindertwine held up his pants then
> that year he was still a fairly tough little beggar

Whereas many of Suknaski's poems depict his speaker's deferral to a second speaker, "Homestead" foregrounds its lyric speaker. Even Suknaski's use of the Roman numeral "*i*" to introduce this section implies an "I" that is "returning." Suknaski reuses the same verb, "return," in line two, and then again in line three. Suknaski's polyptoton creates a melodious repetition ("I return, I return, I return"): this is a speaker intimately and affectedly connected to the content of the poem. And the sprinkling of verbs throughout section i further indicates the liveliness of his engagement: "i note," "i think," "i buy," "i watch," and "[i] remember," the last of which is repeated once more before the section ends. The curt, poised verbs contrast with the hesitant declarations in other pieces in *Wood Mountain Poems* such as "Indian Site on the Edge of Tonita Pasture," in which the speaker can only "try to imagine" a past (an identical phrase appears in "The Teton Sioux and 1879 Prairie Fire") or "stand" and wait for "ancestral voices" (*WMP* 62). Because the persona's family is his subject, Suknaski's speaker begins "Homestead" as an active agent in the recovery of his home.

The poem also displays narrative confidence. In section ii, Suknaski's persona assuredly relates his mother's emigration from Poland:

ii mother
her ship sails for the new land
and she on it
the fare paid by her brother in limerick saskatchewan

dancing in the arms of some young farmer
she remembers the polish village
the day her mother is fatally struck
by a car –
she remembers being 14
when world war one begins
remembers how she and another girl walk 12 miles
to work every three days
shoveling coal onto flatcars for sixteen hours
before returning home
along the boundaries of wolves (their eyes glowing
like stars on the edge
of the dark forest)
she remembers the currency changing as the war ends
her money and several years' work
suddenly worthless one spring day

all these things drift away from the ship carrying
her to the unknown
new land

Many common traits of Purdy's poetry are evident here: the persona's geographic naming ("limerick"), compulsive numerical detailing ("14," "12," "three," "sixteen"), and active participles ("dancing," "shoveling," "returning," "changing"). Yet the overall tone of the section hardly resembles the self-doubting Purdy persona. Note, for example, the incantatory flow of memories here: "she remembers her polish village," "remembers being 14," and "remembers the currency changing as the war ends." Repetition (in this case, anaphora) is one of Suknaski's favoured techniques in his writing perhaps because of its mnemonic force, enhanced here by his choice of repetend, "remember." The mother's memories add to the narrative and emotional dimensions of the central image of the section, which is the mother's emigration. Her memories (which become Suknaski's postmemories) are glimpses of the old world that explain the desire and need to move to a "new land." The organized storytelling here contrasts with the frenetic gathering of image fragments in the accumulative poems I studied in previous chapters: the section begins with his mother "sail[ing] for the new land" and then logically concludes with "the ship carrying / her to the unknown / new land." "[C]ircling back," Barbara Herrnstein Smith writes, is "one of the simplest and most effective closural devices" (256): Suknaski's language ("new land") and imagery ("sails" and "ship") return the reader to scenes of exploration, which nicely parallels Suknaski's own familial searching. The energy of this section is predicated not on ambiguity as it might be in an accumulative poem, but rather on an orderly development of glimpses that stem from and advance toward the operative image of the mother's sailing to Canada. These are narrative strategies indicative of assured knowledge of the past.

While each section in "Homestead" hinges on this kind of narrative development, each also functions as part of a larger whole. Even if the circular structure of section ii suggests a closed-off fragment of history, it nevertheless segues directly into section iii. Section ii ends with the persona's mother sailing for the "new land," presumably to meet her brother in Limerick; section iii begins with his father's arrival in Limerick. Were it not for suggestion of "movement" and emigration in section ii, section iii would appear to start *in medias res*:

iii father
arrives in moose jaw fall of 1914
to find the landtitles office
is given the co-ordinates for the homestead east
of wood mountain village –
and he buys packsack and provisions for the long walk south
sleeps in haystacks for the first few nights
(finally arriving in limerick
buys homesteader's essentials: axe saw hammer
lumber nails shovel gun bullets food
and other miscellaneous items)

Originally titled "homestead," section iii was retitled "father" by Purdy. His editorial intervention reflects the fact that section ii and section iii are tightly associated by the various binaries they ponder: emigration/arrival, East Central Europe/Limerick, Saskatchewan, old/new, settlement/movement, mother/father, and so on. Suknaski's persona remains at the fore as he relates dovetailing stories of prairie immigration and homesteading.

It would be overstating the case to draw on further examples of the ways in which "Homestead" swiftly renders images of family history and tethers them together, but a brief overview of the remaining sections helpfully demonstrates the poem's broader drive toward closure. Section iv details the disintegration of the family (and picks up where an excised section, "marriage," leaves off); section v documents "the death of sister eve"; section vi briefly describes the persona's search for personal identity; section vii concludes the primary narrative about the persona's father, as the speaker comes to terms with the violent and unpredictable man who beat his wife "with a rolling pin"; and section viii offers a brief and ambiguous prayer. The effect of this structure is analogous to that of the circularity of section ii: "Homestead" begins with Suknaski's persona "returning" and meditating on his relationship with his father and ends with his climactic admission in section vii, "father / i must accept you and that other dark man within you." The parallelism of sections i and vii provides closure as the reader witnesses the speaker's epiphanic acceptance of his family's past and present. Just as Suknaski's individual sections use a circling-back structure, so does his full poem: "Homestead" begins and ends with an image of the persona reconciling with his father. Section vii is Suknaski's realization of a complex and emotionally demanding narrative that illuminates his persona's family history.

That reconciliation with his father inspires section viii (a "suicide note"), which serves as a coda to "Homestead." It is a mere four lines: "silence / and a prayer to you shugmanitou / for something / to believe in." I hesitate to accept section viii as more than a figurative "suicide note," a way of marking the death of a more naïve persona and the emergence of a more mature one who is ready to chronicle (or at least ready to attempt to chronicle) the history of the region in which he was born, which explains why Purdy made "Homestead" the opening poem of *Wood Mountain Poems*. But it is also the hopefulness of section viii that leads me to distrust a literal reading of the "suicide note." Section viii represents a moment in which the speaker finds himself capable of "belief" for the first time in the poem. His prayer and implied appeal to a higher power may seem to deflate him, but the concluding image of a praying poet was hardly a possibility at the beginning of "Homestead": he comes to prayer through a clear understanding of the history of which he is part. He can approach "belief" only after he has reconciled his past with his present. His poignant compromise with his father gives him faith enough to pray for the arrival of belief. "Homestead" thus differentiates itself from the parlous historical excavations of accumulative lyric historiography; the genuine sense that Suknaski's poet-persona has encountered a moment of structural and emotional resolution, however tenuous it may seem, should not be underappreciated.

At the same time, that modest moment of closure is what leads Lindy Ledohowski to read the persona's prayer to an Aboriginal deity ("shugmanitou," Suknaski tells readers in a footnote, was the Dakota peoples' word for "coyote") as a sign that he is ready to understand his place in history without relying strictly on "familial, principally paternal, relations" (92). That reading of Suknaski fits with the structure of the book: "Homestead" simultaneously functions as the front door to Suknaski's collection and as his back door into something bigger, his push beyond the edge of lyric.

In one way or another, Suknaski understood this aspect of his poetry: "[*Wood Mountain Poems* is] a personal search, yes, a movement into myself. But it's also a movement outwards, an outward expansion beyond the immediate sense of self" (Suknaski and Hillis 109). Suknaski himself says he aspires to "chronicle the meaning of these vast plains" ("Indian Site" 78). And yet, even as Suknaski claims to work toward that grander meaning, his historiographic authority is anchored by geographical and genealogical conditions, as in "Homestead." The poems in which his relationship to the past is strictly geographical resound with scepticism: the broader past of Wood Mountain eludes his grasp in ways that his familial history does not. While it may be true that family pictures and the histories they contain "retrieve a past that is ours but not ours alone" (Miller 51), there still seems to be, at least for Suknaski, a differentiation between a personal history and a broader one.

"Prairie Photographs" (*WMP* 82–4) illustrates my point, because it is a reminder of the fact that photographs, when not illustrative of the poet's familial past, elicit scepticism and resist closure. "Prairie Photographs" is thus more inclined toward accumulation than development. In approximately seventy lines, Suknaski's persona details four pictures: (1) a landscape photograph, (2) a picture of the "tall and beautiful" "kae turner," (3) "harry thomson['s]" picture of a 1933 dust storm, which conjures the persona's thought of a wife lighting a "coal oil lamp" at "12 noon" (an allusion, I suspect, to Sinclair Ross's short story, "The

Lamp at Noon" [1968]),[3] and (4) a photograph of a bedroom "papered with newspapers." Only in the original 1973 publication of *Wood Mountain Poems* did Suknaski include the actual images.[4] Suknaski's lines in the 1976 version are, like the poem itself, brief, his images abrupt:

> *i dust drift scene, manitoba*
> summer of 1930
> another dust storm has passed
> someone with an eye for remote beauty
> leaves a sagging shack
> to arrive somewhere –
> frames the dust drift scene
> with an old camera:
>
> spray of black leaves across a delicate tree
> hunched against a dust drift
> powerful arcs
> mirroring intense light
> where all green things begin
> to vanish
> and all remaining will too
> when the grasshoppers arrive

Although the speaker's ekphrastic natural scene is confidently rendered in a flowing, oscillating haiku-like verse (in tone, if not in structure), he struggles to contextualize the photographic image and thus finds himself more readily inclined to accumulate, rather than to develop, the images on which he meditates. Like the dust drift, the moment is fleeting, and the photograph, a mere fragment of the past, can only reveal so much: "someone" builds a homestead and then arrives "somewhere" to capture this moment. Suknaski offers similarly vague commentary on his fourth photographic image: the picture "tells something of poetry," contains an "embroidered pillow" that "suggest[s]" the "gentle love" of "some grandmother," and includes a "haunt[ing]" image of "the patch" on an anonymous and "proud" man's eye. In fact, the only significant deviation from purely photographic information in "Prairie Photographs" is the persona's rather flat allusion to Sinclair Ross's "The Lamp at Noon" in section iii; the image is more literary than historical. The general sense that Suknaski's speaker is confined to the image is what creates his uncertain tone and language: "somewhere," "someone," "some grandmother," "something of poetry."

The vagueness of these scenes pre-empts an ending that lacks closure. Even if "Prairie Photographs" obviously lacks the forceful juxtaposition that drives an imagist poem, it retains the resistance to closure and accumulation vital to imagism. Section iv helps illuminate the disconnection among Suknaski's four sections and creates a feeling of irresolution:

> one is haunted by the patch
> on the man's eye
> and must praise and love him
> this proud man
> turning one good eye to a new life
> weaving baskets to survive
> the lonely winters

Suknaski's four images contribute to a structure based on an apparently random accumulation: the image of a figure awaiting the "arriv[al]" of "grasshoppers" (section i), another person pondering "another winter" (section ii), a family lighting a lamp at noon (section iii), and a family facing a "lonely winter" (section iv) only tenuously connect to each other. Lacking concrete connections to one another, these photos could have been arranged in any order without noticeably affecting the paratactic structure of the poem. None of these observations is meant to devalue Suknaski's poem: his speaker's taciturn speculations nicely texture a welter of anonymous geographies and figures that offer glimpses of the past.

But "Prairie Photographs" is unstructured. There isn't closure here, at least not as Barbara Herrnstein Smith defines it: "We tend to speak of conclusions when a sequence of events has a relatively high degree of structure, when, in other words, we can perceive these events as related to one another by some principle of organization or design" (2). "Prairie Photographs" is not sequential, and a reader would be hard pressed to argue for any binding "principle of organization or design." Neither the images nor the narratives to which they allude guarantee the poetic power of "Prairie Photographs"; only the persona's generally thoughtful meditation on an era from which he is estranged gives meaning to the scenes. Both Suknaski's fragmented structure and limited sense of authority in such poems return us to the fundamental desire for poetic authority in lyric historiography. Lisa Grekul summarizes the challenge of Suknaski's writing astutely: "*Wood Mountain Poems* reflects [Suknaski's] interest in recording the past authentically: he is, in this collection, predominantly the poet trying out his role as historian. What he discovers, however, is that in the process of transcribing history, he cannot help but alter it because the process of writing is necessarily selective and subjective" (96). Suknaski's subjectivity comes to the fore through his methodical ambiguity, apparent in poems such as "Prairie Photographs." The accumulation of details and images is haphazard, the broader historical narrative left vague.

What especially interests me is how Suknaski handles the limits of his knowledge as he gets further and further from his inaugural familial poem, "Homestead." In "Indian Site on the Edge of Tonita Pasture" (*WMP* 78–81), Suknaski's wandering persona intends, but ultimately seems unable, to "chronicle" the history of the titular site. Near the beginning of the poem, he insists, "this is my right / to chronicle the meaning of these vast plains / in a geography of blood / and failure / *making them live*" (emphasis added). Patrick Lane too readily accepts these lines as evidence of "a man secure in his power and vision" ("Poetry" 94); the majority of the poem actually undermines Lane's reading. Overwhelmingly, the poem evidences Suknaski's scepticism about his persona's ability to keep history alive. Echoes of Purdy and Newlove are obvious here: lines such as "i try to imagine those who passed here so long ago" and "i stand here listening for the possible / ancestral voices" sound much like the struggling Purdy persona of "Remains of an Indian Village," and the image of the dead "possibly becoming this dust / i breathe" seems like a borrowing of either Newlove's "The Pride" (the image of "breath[ing]" in the "dust" of the dead) or McKinnon's *I Wanted to Say Something* (the "dust" in the speaker's "lungs"). More generic qualities of these earlier models also permeate Suknaski's poem. He uses recognizable Purdyean techniques to foreground his persona's scepticism: rhetorical questions ("who were the ancestors / that camped here?"), tenuous qualifiers ("perhaps here / a few santee families gathered"), an abundance of ellipses (including those which actually conclude the poem), and the struggling speaker frenetically gathering fragments from the past. In the absence of a familial connection, Suknaski experiences his relationship to the past quite differently and without the intellectual authority to organize what he discovers into narrative.

Perhaps that is why Suknaski finds himself drawn in such poems toward other voices; he gradually begins to wonder what others may know about this history. His speaker recalls "a grandmother's story" about "a whiteman / named isaac cowie" who in 1838 "went to old breland a metis / whose grandchild had been vaccinated [against smallpox] / and begged him for a lymph from the child's arm" in order to create "a healthy vaccine" for the residents of Fort Qu'Appelle and surrounding regions. Reflecting on the health workers who helped stop the spread of smallpox on the prairies, the persona is incapable of containing the full breadth of the history:

and remote places like touchwood hills
and wood mountain
these people doing their work so well
that not a single case of smallpox
occurred among them –
the northern plain
was another story ...
and maybe the santee grandmother knew
the story of the christ child
and was able to give it still
another meaning
making it live

The speaker is following an unsustainable line of development (the story about smallpox), and so he accumulates a different image of a different place: Suknaski's dash disturbs the story at a moment when the persona realizes there is "another story" that he cannot tell, and so he trails off with ellipses. And as the speaker returns to the imagined storytelling grandmother, he draws attention to his lyric as he begins to consider what the grandmother "maybe" knew. There is another storyteller, one more capable than the speaker, who will make the history of these people "live" again, which seems to contradict the persona's earlier insistence on his right and ability to do so. Suknaski's self-contradiction might be interpreted two ways: either the speaker has deliberately misled readers with regard to his abilities or he recognizes toward the end of the poem, when he thinks on the grandmother figure, that his ability extends only so far. The first possible reading seems unlikely, because deceit is uncharacteristic of Suknaski's poetry; self-doubt, however, is not. In poems that ponder histories to which he lacks an intimate connection, his persona often seems epistemologically lost.

There are more overt examples of poems in which Suknaski, facing those epistemological limits, turns to testimonies and histories. In "Jerry Potts" (*WMP* 97–105), Suknaski's persona begins to describe a photograph of Potts, a legendary nineteenth-century Métis guide, only to withdraw from the poem in section 2. Suknaski's speaker details the "famous photograph" of Potts, "better known as kehyokosi," or "bear child," and "born somewhere / before 1840." Inspired by the photograph, the speaker attempts to piece together Potts's life. He speaks fairly confidently of the historical facts he has gathered, but at line 50, when the speaker concludes the story of Potts's father's death, the narrative begins to cloud: "bear child's story / becomes vague at this point / some claim he is then adopted by alexander Harvey / [...] / others tend to believe the more colourful story: / bear child a young boy / skilful with a rifle / and how the evening his father dies / he follows / the murderer's trail day and night." There are already signs here that Suknaski's persona is becoming increasingly uncertain of the story he tells: history is now "vague," and he finds himself relaying competing, even contradictory, stories. Later in the poem, another shift: the speaker withdraws, replaced by the testimony of an anonymous speaker, a contemporary of Potts who in turn quotes Potts at length and sustains almost the entire remainder of the poem: "a few of us rode / down to fort benton in 1874 / we had heard of potts / that he was the finest guide / one could hope for" (100). Whether or not this testimony is Suknaski's fabrication or "found" material is unclear; I've found no source material for the poem, and Suknaski never mentions this piece in interviews. Purdy's drastic edits to Suknaski's book have also made it much more difficult to locate any source material on which the younger poet may have drawn. Still, in light of Suknaski's general attraction to found poems and testimonials, it seems unlikely that he fictionalized these voices and their recollection of events. *Wood Mountain Poems* is filled with found poems that lack proper acknowledgement: the poem "Louis Leveille," for instance, is actually material lifted from an obscure article about a Wood Mountain resident, Louis Lavallee, which appeared in the *Edmonton Journal* in 1929.[5] My point in drawing attention to poems like "Jerry Potts" and "Louis Leveille," though, is to show that in poems that hinge initially on accumulation, Suknaski invites new voices into the poem, to benefit from the intellectual authority of another speaker and to be as close as he can to the historical moment that captivates him.

In some poems, Suknaski's persona takes on the role of what Stephen Scobie calls a "listener" (4). "Dunc and Babe McPherson" (*WMP* 112–13) is exemplary in this regard. The poem begins with a photograph that the speaker himself cannot explain, and so the poem moves between Suknaski's voice and that of the titular characters who sit with "andy" and help him understand the pictures and history:

something in the picture turns the mind to the visit
and how we entered their house [...]
then he recalled their first experiences

when he and philip well were blacksmiths east of the old post:
i was shaping shoes when i heard the horses whinnying
i looked up and there was babe
holding the reins of her father's team
that moment i said to myself "this lil lady's my wife"
and i tell you the honest God's truth andy
i've never looked at another woman since

The content of Suknaski's poem isn't particularly revelatory and I don't pretend that the specific history it conveys is as powerful as, say, the history of Sitting Bull's time in Wood Mountain or of the Suknaskis' settlement. Still, I am struck by that image of someone else "holding the reins," quite likely a metaphor for Suknaski's own willingness to hand his poem over to Dunc: he relinquishes authority over the past and evidently appreciates the perspective of Dunc's "I" as much as he values his own. Suknaski's use of pronouns further proves the point. Remember how incredibly active Suknaski's "I" is in "Homestead," and then notice that here Dunc is the active "I": "i was," "i heard," "i looked," "i said," "i tell." Agency and authority in the poem rest with Dunc (and, to a lesser degree, Babe, who speaks only a handful of lines), not with Suknaski, the poet who obscures himself by using definite articles in place of first-person pronouns: "something in the picture turns *the* mind to the visit" (emphasis added). The poem exemplifies something Purdy remarked on in his introduction to *Wood Mountain Poems*: "More than anything else, [Suknaski's] poems are a clear look at people ... The poem-viewpoint shifts abruptly ... the dead are raised, in the sense of re-creating them on the now pinpoint of here: after which they return to the past, having lighted up a little place in the mind of *whoever knows about them*" (11, emphasis added). In that statement, Purdy captures something essential in Suknaski's poems, and it is something I proposed already when reading McKinnon's lyric historiography: developmental (i.e., familial) poems showcase a lyric persona content to assert intellectual authority, whereas many accumulative (i.e., non-familial) poems show a capacity to relinquish that authority and to acknowledge (to one degree or another) the lyric power of another speaker. Admittedly, that quality of lyric historiography is only implied in the works of Purdy, Newlove, and McKinnon, but it is demonstrable in and central to Suknaski's writing.

Operating throughout *Wood Mountain Poems*, then, are several personas: the self-doubting Purdyean speaker, the withdrawn "listener," and the active poet-figure who collects images of his personal past, a past that intersects however tangentially with broader histories.

Suknaski's exploration of his own past implicitly connects his story to those of other East Central European immigrants whose families came to Canada in huge waves at the turn of the twentieth century; other poems, though, acknowledge the potential narrative power of other storytellers (e.g., "the santee grandmother" in "Indian Site on the Edge of Tonita Pasture"). Those acknowledgments are often unsatisfying – especially because Suknaski does not question at all his appropriation of Indigenous figures, words, and myths throughout *Wood Mountain Poems*. In other cases, though, the acknowledgments are deeper. There are poems ("Jerry Potts" and "Dunc and Babe McPherson") that better capture what Dennis Cooley calls the "virtue" of Suknaski's poetry: his willingness to bring "unassuming voices into the poem, acknowledge their power," and allow "them weight, their dignity and integrity." He is, Cooley says, "humbly attentive" to other people's stories and histories ("Vernacular Muse" 61), a poetics that Suknaski would continue experimenting with in *East of Myloona* (1979). His poems show the potential for a reinvention not just of historical content but also of the very ways in which one may assign the intellectual authority to write history.

Suknaski, in turn, impressed upon younger poets the importance of this poetics.[6] Whereas Mick Burrs's writing in the 1970s deals with broader events in Canadian history (e.g., his Riel poems that were explored earlier in my study), *The Blue Pools of Paradise* (1983) focused on his family: poems such as "Zady," "Stanzas for My Grandmother," "My Great Aunt Sarah's Treasure," and "My Birth and Early Development" were marked departures from his earlier historiographic writing. Burrs explains his turn as a direct effect of his friendship with Suknaski:

> More than anyone else, [Suknaski] inspired me to go deeper into my roots. And he was quite persistent about it. He used to say: "Mick, you've got to write about your ancestry." After a few years, I got tired of hearing it, and so I applied for and then received a grant from the Saskatchewan Arts Board to write a full-length manuscript exclusively about my roots, my family history, my ancestry. The result was *The Blue Pools of Paradise*. I dedicated it to him. It still means a lot to me that he truly helped inspire a particular stream of my work – not only by his words of constant encouragement, but also by his own example, especially in his *Wood Mountain Poems*. It is this book in particular that inspired many Canadian poets to write about family and ancestry. (Burrs and Weingarten)

Not only does Burrs's successful grant application further indicate an active governmental commitment to nurture multicultural literature, but his comments also show the wide-ranging impact of a nexus of influential literary relations. It was with Suknaski's support that Burrs began work in the early 1980s on a sequence of poems titled "A Document of Secrets." The second part of this sequence, "Of the Unknown and the Unseen" (1983; *Blue Pools of Paradise* 4–7), concerns a poet-speaker who self-identifies as "Steven Michael Burrs, maker / of images, composer of songs." His mention of music denotes his inclination toward lyric, and he also makes explicit the link between "poetry" (the Greek *poiesis*, "maker," is the root of the word) and "images"; he goes on to describe in detail "three images" of his grandfather. Burrs adopts a nearly identical structure in "Unlike Father, Unlike Son" (1997), in which his persona, remembering the family patriarch, exclaims, "I am left only with images": he finds connections between these images of his father's past, from a time "before [the poet-speaker] was born" (65), and develops them into a long sequence of poems. "A Document of Secrets" is the first of Burrs's poems to focus so intensely on the idea of the image: the speaker explains at length the context and meaning of a photograph of his grandfather, which Burrs reproduces twice to bookend *The Blue Pools of Paradise*.

In one of Burrs's later additions to "A Document of Secrets," "Missing Persona Report" (1993; *Dark Halo* 33–9), Burrs's persona "summon[s]" the "image" of his father, grandfather, and great-grandfather in order to imagine the experience of nineteenth- and twentieth-century pogroms in East Central Europe. The bodies of these victims, his speaker explains, have been buried beneath a "communications centre / erected" during the postwar era. Suknaski directly inspired Burrs's poem; reading about Eastern European history in the *New York Times*, he sent Burrs a clipping of an article about this construction project and urged him to write a poem, "partly lyrical," that engaged with the "objective facts" of the news story (Burrs and Weingarten).[7] Suknaski was encouraging Burrs to see family history as a gateway into a larger – in this case, an international – historical sphere:

I believe this is what happened
to the remains of my great-grandfather:

how his cold blood underground
later was joined
by the warm red stream

of others slaughtered
in a ravine nearby
the year after I was born

the bodies of entire families
sanctified by bullets

their bones blessed and bulldozed
in mud and barbed wire

by the Nazis' elite Einsatzgruppe C
in that dark and hungry mouth
known as Babi Yar[8]

Although Burrs seems aware of his limited ability to narrate his great-grandfather's fate ("I believe this is what happened"), he little doubts his interpretation of events. And the detail here is exceptional. The poem admittedly lacks nuance, but its lyricized narrative style offers a reasonably interesting depiction of a literal and figurative confluence: the somatic fusion of Jewish ancestors and the intersection of private and public history. Only the persona's story of his great-grandfather allows him to discuss Babi Yar and "the old Jewish cemetery in Kiev" that was "obliterated" by construction crews. The family story becomes, as in Suknaski's writing, a path to a broader history and, as "Missing Persona Report" is only one section of a much longer piece, to an extended lyric project that bears obvious resemblance to Suknaski's poetry.

For Eli Mandel, Suknaski's example was equally guiding. In 1977, Mandel wrote, "I remember how moved I was when last year I first heard Andrew Suknaski read [...] I thought: [*Wood Mountain Poems* is] the book I should have written, its terrible authenticity, its powerful directness, its voices and places echoing in its time and truth" ("Writing West" 26). Look at Mandel's language: it conveys his appreciation of historiographic authority (the "authenticity" of Suknaski's work), of imagism (the "directness" of his images), and even of the frequently recurring motif – which I have noted in poems throughout this study – of history as a sound that poets struggle to hear (the "echoes" of voices in *Wood Mountain Poems*). Mandel's phrasing is a testament to the evident power of lyric historiography as a genre that conveys the immediacy of experience in ways that close, or at least appear to close, the gap between the past and present. He also understands such writing as the correlation between "the west" as a region and a "personal mythology" that, together, yield "the sounds and rhythms of a voice, images, definition" ("Writing West" 25). It was Suknaski's "powerful" expression that motivated Mandel to use the "first poem" he ever wrote ("Estevan, Saskatchewan" ["Auschwitz" 5]) as the seed for his long poem *Out of Place* (1977). Mandel's return home from Europe generated that first poem; describing its composition in a prose essay, Mandel cannot help but chant the incantatory phrase, "I had come home ... I had come home" (3–5). During that trip in August 1945, ruminating on what he had learned of the Holocaust, Mandel was compelled to bear witness to the past: "I had become fragmented, broken into many pieces – now and then, here and there. Toronto, 1970; Europe, 1944; Estevan, 1930. And the photographs. Family albums" ("Auschwitz" 9). In this essay and in *Out of Place*, Mandel has an obvious yearning to connect a very personal history to a much larger one in which he feels implicated. One way in which he dealt with that bridging was to understand the legacy of Jewish immigrants in the Canadian context, which constituted the basis of *Out of Place*.

In some ways, Mandel's book feels like an extension of Suknaski's work as much as of that early 1946 poem about Estevan. There are some noteworthy, if minor, overlaps here: Mandel's book begins with part "I" followed by its title, "Return." The proximity of the Roman numeral "I" and the word "return" plays the same pun that Suknaski uses in "Homestead": the lyrical "I" "return[s]." Also like Suknaski's poem, the reader bears witness to the return; the events and encounters unfold as we read, which replicates the feeling of exploration embraced by Mandel's lyric speaker. In moving beyond an isolated image, that early poetic fragment, Mandel's speaker expects to achieve a deeper understanding of his own family history. That longing for a confident grasp of the past, a feeling realized through an exploratory narrative, connects Mandel's project to that of Suknaski, especially because these searches ("journey" is the word Ann Mandel uses in her preface to *Out of Place* [n.p.]) are always metonymic of a broader search for a distinctly familial past and, sometimes only through hints or the readers' inferences, a broader history. Mandel's first lines capture that metonymic relation, because as the speaker notes the "appear[ance]" of his father and mother, he also notices the awakening of "all / the ghostly jews / of estevan" (13). The speaker enacts that negotiation throughout the book: he remembers Riel's rebellion at Batoche (15) and poeticizes the infamous 1931 coal miner's strike in Estevan (24). Mandel's title perhaps explains why he is drawn to these events. I doubt that his title, *Out of Place*, celebrates displacement; the length to which his speaker goes to find a place in which he fits suggests quite the opposite. He is, indeed, trying to place himself geographically, temporally, and genealogically. This is another quality of such developmental lyrics, in which there is always a desire to find something – Purdy, for instance, is "in search of Owen Roblin." The motif will become even more apparent when I discuss the work of Atwood and Crate, but it is no less obvious in the work of poets like Purdy and Mandel. They yearn to position themselves in the past, in their families, and in the world. That hopeful search brings Mandel to Estevan, as he situates himself in a history simultaneously contracted and broad, just as Suknaski does in *Wood Mountain Poems*.

However hopefully Mandel begins that search, his poem nevertheless ends at an epistemological impasse. The book begins confidently: the speaker assertively "name[s] / remember[s] and recite[s]" as he wanders a town that "lives" (14). That exploration continues until halfway through the poem, at which point Mandel's persona includes a letter from "Mrs. Feldman." Feldman writes that she is "surprised" to hear Mandel on the radio promoting a new book "about the Jewish Colony of Hoffer (or Sonnenfeld Colony which is the correct name)" (36). The crisp, authoritative beginning to Mandel's poem contrasts with these later revelations that have the speaker reflecting on the accuracy of his memories and information. He realizes that Mrs Feldman has shown him that he's "got the ghosts wrong": "were we in the wrong place? / who is mistaken?" (37). That shaken confidence concludes Part I and the book continues with Part II, "The Double"; here again the Roman numeral functions symbolically, this time to reiterate the doubleness of an "I" who has come to doubt his own identity or even his sense of time and place. He imagines multiple doubles (I/other and past/present) and finds himself trapped in an existential quandary: "This clock is a shadow of that real clock. When / I look at my clock I have no way of knowing whether I am in / the first or second universe" (53). Mandel's speaker is unable to distinguish between reality and the Platonic shadow. The past becomes blurrier as Mandel's speaker grapples with the intelligibility of his memories, pictures, scenes, and artefacts; it is a quality of the poem enhanced by the photographic images of false fronts and gravestones.

Tellingly, Mandel ends his poem with these gravestones, images of death that contrast with the lively and energetic language that commences *Out of Place*. The fact that Mandel's photographs are of names such as "Hoffer" shows his reach outward: he thinks beyond his own family to imagine a grander community and history of Canadian Jews living on the prairies. The stones offer little more than evidence that the past "had its being once" – to adapt Purdy's phrase in the concluding lines of *In Search of Owen Roblin* – even if its character remains somewhat ambiguous in the present. Mandel's poem thus brings the reader to other names and other histories with the sense that his own lyrical narrative has concluded at the point where others might begin. It is another exemplary case in which a writer imagines what narratives exist beyond those of the lyric "I."

An epilogue on Suknaski: I've championed Suknaski's *Wood Mountain Poems*, as well as the writing it directly shaped, as poetry that locates authority in the "I" and that tests the strength of its own authority by moving historically outward. When read alongside Purdy's *In Search of Owen Roblin*, Mandel's *Out of Place*, Burrs's *The Blue Pools of Paradise*, others I have not discussed (Douglas Barbour's *Visions of My Grandfather*, for instance) and others to which I will turn in later chapters, Suknaski's collection suggests that modern Canadian poets' scepticism and their attraction to history (as well as their influences on each other's work) draw out at least one obvious conclusion about lyric historiography: poets found intellectual authority in developmental writing about the family and willingly deferred or questioned that authority in accumulative lyrics. And in Suknaski's case, it appears that he had a preference for lyric insistence over lyric withdrawal, confidence over scepticism, the realized image over the desired one.

I like Grekul's interpretation of "Suknaski's transformation" over the course of the 1970s and 1980s. She says that his poetry negotiates "his ambivalent identity – his simultaneous sense of belonging to and alienation from Anglo-Canadian, aboriginal, and Ukrainian communities" (106). I agree with Grekul that this negotiation led him to meditate with a greater sense of vocation on his familial past in, most especially, *In the Name of Narid*, the collection in which he renamed himself "andrei suknatskyj" and included many poems dedicated to or written about family members: "andrew suknatskyj [sr.]" (76–9), "julia suknatskyj" (65–7), "eve suknatskyj" (91–4), "peter suknatskyj" (83–4), "aunt maria" (26–8), and so on. While I admit that Grekul's argument is a very plausible reading of that transition, I suspect, too, that Suknaski's early tactic of deferring his poetic voice partly influenced this trajectory. His consistent attraction to testimonial poems that draw attention away from the poet-persona had to have led him to reflect on questions about authority: of what history can the sceptical and historically conscious poet write with conviction and without deferral of authority or voice? "Homestead" surely provided Suknaski with an answer to this question, and I can only assume that the death of both his parents in 1978 bolstered his commitment to familial writing in later books like *In the Name of Narid*, which he published three years later.

This intensified focus, however, came at the expense of Suknaski's provocative bridging of histories, which led many to criticize his later poems as too lyrical and too insular; it is interesting to think of this as a constant risk in such writing. An effective lyric history is one that can reach and briefly transcend the limits of a lyrical perspective: *Wood Mountain Poems* earned widespread praise for its remarkable depiction of not just Suknaski's life but also of Wood Mountain. It was, as Purdy wrote in his introduction to the volume, neither "a history" nor an "autobiography" (11). *In the Name of Narid* was received less enthusiastically because it did not achieve such balance. Anne Montagnes reviewed *In the Name of Narid* negatively and called it "alienat[ing]": "There is no glossary and some of his core words don't occur in dictionaries. What, for instance, is the Narid of the title? What is wilia, bahbokolie, pysanky? Or is part of Suknaski's intention to force the alienated but captivated reader into the kind of learning by immersion our forefathers forced on his people? And is this poetry?" (E14). Robert Attridge similarly expressed his distaste: he wrote that Suknaski's work "may be making an important statement about Ukrainian culture in Canada, but as poetry [*In the Name of Narid*] seems almost unreadable. [...] Suknaski seems trapped by his own heritage" (33).

These aren't unfair criticisms. The opening to Suknaski's elegy for his mother, "Dominion Day Departures," exemplifies some of what provokes them:

north of lac la ronge
a saturday
clear blue sky
stanley mission road
suknatskyj
back in boyhood magic
tries to snare a pike
with wire loop
and willow
when two young
native women
going west in an old hack
stop

'hey you seen an ole woman
come by here?
woman wit fishin pole?'
'no i've only bin here
bout an hour why?'
'she wen west dis way
yesserday never come back' (65)

Suknaski's visually distracting structure only compounds the slow beginning to this poem, where little effort is made to ground the reader. Were it not for the dedication at the beginning of the poem, I doubt any readers would even recognize this as a lyric elegy, let alone one for "julia suknatskyj." "Dominion Day Departures" never gains its footing; when read alongside a poem like "Homestead," it appears abstruse and unfocused. Suknaski obviously saw in family poetry the potential for personal and creative growth, and so his complete embrace of such writing is understandable. But the more inward the poetry became, the more he limited his audience. It is certainly worth questioning how strongly his unwavering focus on family history and growing inattention to broader histories in his published works could appeal to readers still reeling from the various national identity crises and multiculturalism debates of the 1960s and 1970s.

Regardless, even if Suknaski's later writing alienated some readers, *Wood Mountain Poems* offered them an original, exciting, and influential interpretation of lyric historiography. As well, in the context of my own interest in examples of familial lyric historiography, *Wood Mountain Poems* evidences several key points: (1) the personal ownership of and connectedness to the familial past provided a means of narrating history with a strong sense of authority, (2) such a provision allowed longer developmental lyrics that softened or delayed the epistemological impasses that necessarily kept the lengths of accumulative lyrics about the past understandably brief, and (3) poets who recognized the poignancy and value of familial pasts were sometimes enticed to engage not just with their own story but also with those of others. In the last case, that openness signals something more: a gesture, one might say, to a collectively written history in which authority is shared and decentralized. Of course, Suknaski's specific product is imperfect. Heavily filtered and, at times, flippant in their handling of Indigenous peoples and history, his lyrics abound with evidence that he struggled to escape his own worldview. Those concerns notwithstanding, Suknaski's *Wood Mountain Poems* is a powerful statement, a case for exploration, as he recognizes that every individual must listen to other stories with a passion equal to that which drives them to tell their own.

8 Figurative Families and Feminism

How intriguing that America had forefathers and we had foremothers.

Atwood qtd Sullivan 209

Margaret Atwood's *The Journals of Susanna Moodie* (1970) is, in a manner of speaking, a "family history." As the epigraph above shows, however, she imagined family figuratively, seizing on Susanna Moodie – the nineteenth-century English emigrant to Ontario and author of the Canadian classic *Roughing It in the Bush* (1852) – and positioning her not just as a poetic subject, but also a "foremother." Atwood's construction of a figurative genealogy can be explained by piecing together her early perspectives on nationalism and feminism. She said, in 1978, that she was "really not very interested in a personal mythology," because "[y]ou can only indulge in the luxury of figuring yourself out when you're oriented in space and time" (Atwood and Hammond 110). Atwood's terms here are vague, but her distinction seems to be between a genetic history (a kind of "personal mythology") and a national or cultural one (a broader "space and time"). Atwood's apparent preference was for a project that found family through a broader history, rather than doing things the other way around, as male poets like Suknaski and McKinnon were doing around 1970.

Atwood's unusual route to the family is more than likely her reaction to the fact that the history of Canada circa 1970 was predominantly, if not exclusively, a history of men. No writer needed to demonstrate the importance of men in a broader national or literary past. It was implicit. Perhaps that is why so many male writers found it sufficiently fulfilling to explore androcentric family histories; it was comfortably and conveniently metonymic for male writers to imagine and heroize the pioneering father or grandfather figure. Female writers, in contrast, did not have a larger framework inclusive of women's history to which they could gesture through smaller-scale family portraits. It was this general absence of women in history and literature that writers like Atwood needed to address before any kind of "personal mythology" could be written.

Some of Atwood's female contemporaries did nonetheless write more literally about family. Florence McNeil's *Balancing Act* (1979) and Leona Gom's *Land of the Peace* (1980) both contain family poems, and, looking past the 1980s, Lorna Crozier recalls her father in *Inventing the Hawk* (1992) and Atwood muses on both her father and her distant ancestor, Mary Webster, in *Morning in the Burned House* (1995).[1] Daphne Marlatt's *How Hug a Stone* (1983) and Di Brandt's *questions i asked my mother* (1987) both have clear ties to the genre I'm exploring if only by way of content: Marlatt writes that her key themes are the "haunting family," the feminist writer's realization that history is "[c]ollective and personal," and the act of writing as women "without models (or so we think)" (viii) while also trying, as she puts it, to "understand [her] mother" (n.p.), and Brandt searches for her mother's stories and connects them to the "old wives' tales" that "sustained the women in [her] culture" (*Wild Mother* 4). Marlatt and Brandt bridge a personal history with a collective one to challenge the exclusive frameworks of Canadian history, literature, and theory. I won't talk more about these poems here, though, because I want to show the transformations within lyric historiography – hence my move past literal families to figurative ones.

Whether literal or figurative in content, feminist poems about family grappled with similar concerns. Throughout Brandt's early career, for instance, she lamented that existing theoretical praxes in Canadian literature were "useless for coming to terms with maternal experience" (*Wild Mother* 3). "Where," she had once asked herself, "were the mother stories?" (4). Whereas Brandt's poetry evokes literal maternal ties, Atwood saw greater literary potential in the figurative foremother as a way of filling the same void in literature and history; the pivot perhaps seemed natural to Atwood, given second-wave feminism's widely deployed rhetoric of "sisterhood" and "foremothers." As examples of lyric historiography, her poems realize the genre's potential for culturally subversive writing.

I underscore that point because as much as I can and want to appreciate the ingenuity of lyric historiography in works by Purdy, Newlove, McKinnon, and Suknaski, I am also aware of the fact that none of these writers sufficiently challenges conservative social frameworks (e.g., the role of patriarchy in shaping and structuring both history and society) as often as they challenge historiographic methods. Atwood challenges these same methods while also rejecting the long-standing patriarchal systems of power built into those methodologies. The opportunity to do such work is inherent in lyric historiography because the genre promises, of course, a relocation of perspective. An empowered "I" wrests narrative power away from those who claim the unchallenged academic authority to create and preserve predominating narrative frameworks. Atwood says that politics "really has to do with how people order their society, to whom power is ascribed, who is considered to have power" (Atwood and Brans 87), and the same could be said of history. Those who organize society in particular ways naturally shape the views of those who organize history in equally specific ways. Atwood works from that premise in *The Journals of Susanna Moodie* by interrogating and relocating power, questioning the politics of historical representation as much as the mode one adopts when writing that history. In this way, she writes in contrast with many of her male contemporaries.

Atwood's urge to locate narrative and political power within female experience is connected to the centennial-era feminist movement, which gained momentum in Canada after the establishment of the Royal Commission on the Status of Women (RCSW; 1967–72). The movement had, however, already been well underway before 1967 with the formation of groups such as the Voice of Women (VOW; est. 1960). That non-partisan organization advocated peace and nuclear disarmament while also bringing Canadian women into conversation with each other. VOW was one of many feminist formations that fused anti-war messages with distinctly feminist arguments for equality in society. The energy behind these formations was fed by "an influx of female students into universities, the debut of the birth control pill, and the advent of a 'New Morality,'" all of which brought women's issues to the fore in Canadian politics (Sethna 289). As various groups and organizations formed, many of them expressed overlapping beliefs: an insistence that the gendered balance of power be equalized in the workplace, the home, and society.

Especially because feminism was wrapped up in discussions of workplace fairness, its advocates readily identified with leftist politics. This was an era of propitious intersections that nurtured the development of progressive political movements: as centennial-era feminism gained momentum in the 1960s, its concerns with regard to women's wages, access to employment, and work conditions naturally coincided with the general concerns of the New Left movement (its own momentum bolstered by the founding of the New Democratic Party in 1961). Pearson's Liberals, fearful of losing voters to the NDP, thus found themselves under tremendous pressure to demonstrate their own investment in addressing feminist issues: the Liberal government's decision to launch the RCSW was proof that it understood the importance of feminism to modern Canada, and the RCSW report itself, once it was published, included recommendations that were attentive to many ongoing debates about the massive restructuring of gendered power relations in the workplace, better representation of women in unions and in politics, and abortion rights.

These particular demands culminated in the founding of the National Action Committee on the Status of Women (NAC) in 1972 – a direct outcome of the RCSW report published at approximately the same time. At first funded entirely by the Canadian government, the NAC was founded in order to make sure that the Canadian government addressed and implemented all 167 recommendations from the RCSW report. The NAC's particular emphasis on union and labour reform substantiates Ian McKay's claim that the "languages of socialism" lingered in 1960s political movements, even if adopted for purposes that might have appeared unconventional to socialists of an earlier era (184). The language was, ultimately, about redistributing power, hence Sandra Burt et al.'s imagining of 1960s feminism as the effort to dismantle conservative "system[s] of power" (10). A rhetoric of power was written into many movements of the era: second-wave feminism, Black Power, and Red Power capture, in complementary ways, the rebellious attitudes of the era manifested in history, creative literature, and broad social movements. While the dismantling of "systems of power" was integral to such movements, activists believed the sensible reaction to their scepticism was not just to "dismantle" but also to relocate power.

Those related tasks were as essential to writing new histories as to restructuring society. That is to say that groundbreaking books like Marylee Stephenson's *Women in Canada* (1973) and Jean Johnston's *Wilderness Women: Canada's Forgotten History* (1973) were arguments for the impact of women in Canada's past, which implicitly suggested their potential to shape the country's present. Johnston's text, for instance, repurposed common terms, phrases, and tropes of Canadian history in order to stress women's contributions to the state: "Women [...] *were the colonizers*" (vi, emphasis added), "women were *adventurers* [like] Champlain" (vii, emphasis added), and "women planted the roots of *settlement* in the New World" (viii, emphasis added). Johnston's idiom obviously lacks a language sensitive to decolonization, and she trivializes those movements further by gleefully portraying colonization as an "adventure." In context, though, her narrative presents a basic effort to portray strong women who possessed a "fearless resolution" as they built the country (237). For such writers, these stories were historical evidence of women's capability as leaders and visionaries.

The search for these historical foremothers was as much a literary concern as an academic one. It might, though, be better to regard this "search" as a "recovery" operation, which is how Atwood's generation understood it. Di Brandt and Barbara Godard have recently remarked on the importance of rediscovering the "radical cultural reform" of modernism by recovering female writers whose contributions to modernist art may have been overlooked because their projects were specific to the "aims [of] women writers" (13). Likewise, Lorraine McMullen elsewhere admires the "rescuing [of] nineteenth-century women writers from anonymity" (3) for the purpose of establishing a literary tradition for female writers. This is the project in which I see Atwood taking part: rediscovering, recovering, rescuing.

That Atwood needed to find positive, encouraging examples of female artists is understandable. Rosemary Sullivan describes a formative moment in Atwood's life: her viewing of the film *The Red Shoes* in the late 1940s. The film portrays a talented dancer, Victoria Page, who is forced to choose between her art and her lover. Overwhelmed by the dilemma and expelled from her dance company, Page throws herself in front of a train and, with her dying breath, asks her lover to take off her dancing shoes. Atwood understood the film's message: "that a girl could not be an artist without great suffering, without, in a sense, being unnatural" (55). Atwood understandably felt discouraged to write, concerned that she would be judged as a woman in an overwhelmingly male profession. Her experiences with some Canadian writers confirmed those fears: in 1980 while reading at Convocation Hall in Toronto, Atwood noticed that the poet Irving Layton "fell asleep and began to snore" (Pietkiewicz qtd Cameron 441). The scene is vaguely reminiscent of an earlier one in 1969, when Layton "made a point of reading his own poetry from the audience in an audible tone while [Atwood] read on stage" at the Bohemian Embassy and then "snor[ed] loudly" (Sullivan 104). Rather than being wholly discouraged by these experiences, Atwood instead realized that she "needed ... to find a place for herself as a woman [writing in Canada]. If the tradition of writing excluded women, there had to be something wrong with the tradition" (131). That early epiphany anticipated the writing of major feminist scholars such as Elaine Showalter, who emphasized the importance of undermining such traditions: "Women," Showalter said in 1971, "are estranged from their own experience and unable to perceive its shape and authenticity, in part because they do not see it mirrored and given resonance in literature" (856). Echoing Showalter, Patrocinio P. Schweickart would later say that "feminist readings of female texts are motivated by the need 'to connect,' to recuperate, or to formulate [...] the context, the tradition, that would link women writers to one another" (48). Atwood intuited the necessity of such work from a young age.[2]

When she began writing *The Journals of Susanna Moodie* in the 1960s, she had already realized that the building of this new tradition entailed recovery work. She spoke openly of this idea only after she had published *The Journals* (her first noteworthy mention of it was in 1972 in a comment on Purdy's poetry [*Survival* 112]), but various hints of her "archaeological" impulse were evident in her poetry of the 1960s. She was then writing partly under the influence of Frye, with whom she studied at Victoria College in Toronto, and his "garrison" theory had an evident impact on her writing. In literal terms, Frye described the garrison as a fortified and structural defence against the "deep terror" of nature (227) – like a cabin in the woods. Frye was, however, open to more metaphorical interpretations of the garrison as common social "moral[ity]" (233). Traditional gender roles, for instance, could be considered "fortified" norms. D.G. Jones and Malcolm Ross helped broaden Frye's more metaphorical interpretation: the garrison may be used as a "defensive isolation of our scattered pioneer communities" or, when read metaphorically, to suggest the enduring dominance of particular "moral and social values" (Ross 131). However, the "moral and social values" outside the garrison may represent something "vital and authentic" (Jones 36), a liveliness perhaps lost in a sheltered society. Jones, in that vein, sees Leonard Cohen's *Beautiful Losers* as a story about the "overly exclusive and overly mechanical rationalism" of a psychologically garrisoned society that is threatened by "the outcast irrational world" (81). Whether literal or figurative, the garrison symbolizes any system intended to be "exclusive rather than inclusive" (36).

In poems from the 1960s, one finds Atwood experimenting with these literal and figurative "garrisons" often. She uses these poems to expound upon her own theorizing of a broadly conceived inclusion/exclusion binary: an object or individual may be excluded from a picture, a society, or a time and place. In *The Circle Game* (1966), that binary takes different forms. In "This Is a Photograph of Me" (11), the speaker describes a picture and is attentive to the boundaries of the image: she draws the reader's attention to "the left-hand corner" and says she exists outside the frame of the photograph, "just under the surface" of the poem. Atwood's poems of the period commonly return to images of submersion when portraying exclusion: "sunken / bones" ("After the Flood, We" 4) or buried "wooden people" ("Some Objects of Wood and Stone" 58). In other poems, she explores boundaries, the perimeters that individuals and communities draw as symbols of control. Even the title of "The Circle Game" speaks to this interest of her writing, and the speaker interrogates and challenges these boundaries throughout the poem, which culminates with the speaker's proclamations that everything must be "broken," "erased," and "cracked" (44).

Poems in *The Animals in That Country* (1968) make much more explicit nods to Frye's garrison theory than those in *The Circle Game*, as in "Progressive Insanities of a Pioneer" (*TATC* 36–7). "[P]roclaiming himself the centre" of a "green sheet of paper," Atwood's pioneer figure refuses the chaos of the natural world. He prefers to impose himself on the landscape, even as nature speaks defiantly to him in a language of unimpeded growth: "a tree-sprout, a nameless / weed, words / he couldn't understand." The amorphousness of the fertile and ever-growing natural world is incomprehensible to the pioneer, who tries to bring order to a landscape defined by "an ordered absence" of boundaries and perimeters (37). The pioneer's garrisons fail him; the landscape refuses to submit to his idea of order, a resistance that culminates with the concluding image of "the unnamed / whale invad[ing]" the pioneer's cabin, his mind, and the poem. Atwood's pioneer perceives the natural world as threatening only because he is unwilling to learn its language and accept its concept of order. "Order" has a specific and fairly conventional meaning for him: order means naming, structures, centres, and peripheries. Nature is indifferent to such notions of order, and so when it invades the garrisoned pioneer's space, he believes nature is an unrelenting aggressor. The exhausted pioneer is eventually driven to madness because he cannot accept any terms or forms of existence except his own.

And yet, while Atwood's speakers may see the world external to the garrison as a threat, it is not necessarily so. Take "A Fortification" (*TATC* 16), in which Atwood's speaker is stuck inside the garrison and made mechanical by it: "voice[s]" are "airdrill[s]" and "eyes" become associated with "hydraulic / doors." The world outside of this one is unfamiliar:

> But there is a thing, person, a blunt groping
> though the light denies it: what face
> could be here among the lamps and the clear edges?
> Still for an instant I
> catch sight of the other creature,

the one that has real skin, real hair,
vanishing down the line of cells
back to the lost forest of being vulnerable

Although the garrisoned community conditions its inhabitants to prefer this orderly and mechanized world, the speaker hints at their desire for "vulnerability," which exists beyond an illuminated perimeter. The boundary is tenuous and arbitrary, and it is accepted only because the authorities within the garrison will it so. Those same authorities mechanize sensory experience, which is likely why they fear the non-mechanical world that exists beyond the perimeter of their world: past the edge is authenticity, a "real[ity]" that the garrisoned world "denies." The otherness of this reality compels the speaker to regard it as a "thing" and a "creature." Underlying Atwood's portrayal of a potentially threatening external force is her speaker's surprising epiphany: what lives outside the garrison is actually *alive* and reminds the speaker of their own living feelings by provoking their fear. Their fear is therefore ironic: the outside wilderness recovers the community's sensation of being alive, which may actually comfort a speaker so used to the dehumanizing experience of living without feeling inside the garrison. If these portrayals of the garrison are any suggestion of Atwood's general thinking at the time, then she evidently considered "exclusion" not as protection but rather as the denial of life and enlivening things.

Nevertheless, Atwood's personas often fear the world outside the garrison and thus sometimes uphold its barriers. In *The Journals of Susanna Moodie*, these Frygean garrisons manifest in ways reminiscent of "Progressive Insanities of a Pioneer." Moodie sees the wilderness as a threat to her safety; anyone alert to "these trees, to this particular sun," she believes, "would be surrounded, stormed, broken // in upon by branches, roots, tendrils, the dark / side of light" ("The Planters" 17). Atwood's diction recalls both the iconoclasm of "The Circle Game" and the fear of an invading external force in "Progressive Insanities of a Pioneer." Her speedily accumulating catalogue also communicates anxiety, and the length of the list underscores the "size" of the supposed threat that exists outside the garrison. This fearful Moodie predominates in "Journal I": she builds a garrison against nature that continually fails to repel the external force.

In "Journal III," however, Moodie recognizes the futility of garrisons. Perhaps she experiences that epiphany because, at this point in the poems, *she* has been excluded. Her burial is of course literal (given that "Journal III" appears to take place in modern-day Toronto), but she is also "outside" in other ways: she has been excluded from time and history, and she wants to be recovered. When the reader encounters this subterranean Moodie, she surfaces triumphantly to announce that she knows now what she never knew in life: whatever can be excluded can still be alive and irrepressible. Those excluded things – again, like her – have "ways of getting through" (60).

"A Bus Along St. Clair: December" (*JSM* 60–1) – Atwood's final poem in the volume – is about the inevitability of that resurfacing: Moodie "get[s] through" the soil, and the poem ends with a vision of the city turned into a "forest." This revenant Moodie at last grasps the illusion of the garrison and finds value in reconciling the closed, urban space with the external world toward which it is needlessly antagonistic: the "concrete" (and thus deadened) city is potentially reinvigorated by the living forest. The garrison is more than the shutting out of nature. It is also a productive metaphor for historical study as Atwood may have imagined it: history closes out any force that threatens the coherence of a predominating narrative. If the return of the forest is the return of life to the city, then we can infer what kind of impact Moodie's return to history might have on the predominating narratives of Atwood's era. And that return is a defiant act: in her afterword to the collection, Atwood writes that Moodie "refuses to be ploughed under completely" (64). Atwood's decision to dramatize that refusal pushes past Moodie's "conscious voice" in an effort to get closer to her "other voice" (63), a voice Atwood says she found in "gaps between what was said and what hovered, just unsaid, between the lines" ("Introduction" viii). Filling those gaps and unearthing Moodie, Atwood is disrupting both conventional history and literary canons.

But the archaeological images in Atwood's writing of the 1960s were much more to her than a simple homage to Frygean theory. Archaeological metaphors were also built into feminist literature. The anthology *Sisterhood Is Powerful* (Morgan 1970), for instance, held personal meaning for Atwood, and Connie Brown and Jane Seitz's introduction stresses the importance of recovery: "Women [have throughout history] writ[ten] novels, essays, poems, magazine articles, but most of these are long out of print, and the task of *digging up* those old sources is still ahead of us" (3, emphasis added).[3] Feminists, they write, want "direct contact with the lives and ideas of the nineteenth-century feminists" and desire "to know much more [...] in order to reclaim our past from obscurity, to rediscover our heroines, to understand our present" (4). The motif endured for decades: the essayist Tillie Olsen described the problem of women's literary "silences," and later critics responded directly to her by saying that the recognition of such silences necessarily "fostered" acts of "recover[y] and recuperat[ion]" in creative and critical writing (Hedges and Fishkin 10). Decades later, Carla Kaplan wrote of a "recuperative paradigm of recovering lost, silenced, or misunderstood, or devalued women's voices," which has, underlying it, an "archaeological imperative" (169). Writers like Atwood yearned to unbury silenced traditions. "We read writing by women," she said in 1990, because doing so shows "something ... basic ... It was ... a feeling that you too could do it because, look, it could be done" ("If You Can't Say Something Nice" 17). Hence, when I talk of "archaeology" in Atwood's work, it is as much a feminist term as it is a Frygean one.

For Atwood, though, the idea of "archaeology" had even wider associations. In an unpublished speech Atwood gave at the PEN Conference in June 1986, she commented on "archaeology" as a distinctly Canadian curiosity: "English Canadians of my generation did not study much Canadian history or politics in school [...] my generation reacted to this vacuum by becoming quite archaeological in their interests." "The Canadian writer," she said, "felt compelled to excavate, to dig up what had been buried and forgotten because no one had considered it important enough to save [...] a Canadian writer may set more store by an old photograph or two, or a broken bottle, than others might set by a whole castle" (PEN speech). This speech both evidences the centrality of "archaeology" in Atwood's thinking and captures some basic aesthetics of lyric historiography: the search for historical fragments ("a broken bottle") and thumbing through photographs. In that same speech, Atwood again names Purdy as a central figure in the tradition. Fourteen years before her speech at PEN, Atwood more explicitly noted Purdy's significance to this kind of writing: "There is a distinct archeological [*sic*] motif in Canadian literature – unearthing the buried and forgotten past – that for me is epitomized by Al Purdy's poems about poking around in the foundations of old Ontario farmhouses, graveyards, remains of Indian villages and other likely sites" (*Survival* 112).

Those statements insist upon Atwood's unlikely place in the web of writers that this book has established. "Unlikely" because I expect linking Atwood's feminist poems to the projects of a writer like Purdy could seem preposterous given that no one would mistake Purdy for a feminist. Neither on nor off the page did he show any grasp of or affection for feminism; he called Susanna Moodie a "bitch" and "not quite human" ("Atwood's Moodie" 83) in his review of Atwood's book, and he added that he could never share his thoughts on the book with Atwood "personally" because "she's a woman, even though very intelligent" (84). Atwood, in fact, once quipped to Margaret Laurence that although she liked Purdy and admired him as a poet, she felt, upon first meeting him and Irving Layton, that neither knew whether to "shake [her] hand or grab [her] ass" (Atwood to Laurence). And yet Atwood also felt that, despite Purdy's chauvinism, he offered an important literary precedent. After Purdy wrote to Atwood in praise of *The Journals of Susanna Moodie*,[4] she wrote back to him, "I'm very glad you like the book – if there was one Can. poet I'd dedicate it to it would be you (The Country North of etc.)" (Atwood to Purdy). Atwood's reference to Purdy's "The Country of North of Belleville" and, implicitly, *The Cariboo Horses* is vague, but it does prove that Purdy's poems and opinion mattered to her.

The fact that Atwood could be both highly critical of Purdy and literarily indebted to him epitomizes the "ambivalent legacy of modernity" of which Rita Felski writes. Felski says that the "dethroning of the white bourgeois male as privileged subject of history ... re-open[ed] and le[ft] unresolved the question of what modernity might mean for women and other subaltern groups." For Felski, modernity signifies the clash of "hierarchies of sexual difference" while offering, at the same time, an "extended tradition of questioning and contesting dominant gender norms" (*Gender* 208). In other words, female writers working within a Western tradition internalized modern scepticism as a revolutionary tool and then used it to express their distrust of a modern society predicated on patriarchy. Therein lay the paradox: feminist writers have "been highly critical of the concept of the modern," but they have "also been deeply influenced by it" (16).

In the context of lyric historiography, the paradox is best explained by returning to Atwood and Purdy. Both understood lyric historiography as a complex nationalist expression, and for writers of Atwood's generation (especially female writers), nationalism and feminism were correlative. Atwood knew this. Discussing her early career, she notes, "all [nationalists are] saying is, 'We exist.' Not that we're better, just that we're different. Similarly, women have been saying, 'We exist. We don't wish particularly to be defined by you'" (Atwood and Hammond 109–10). Feminism and nationalism, she would say in a later interview, "connect" (Atwood, Crabbe, and Fitzgerald 139). In exploring that connection, Atwood was able to identify in broad strokes with Purdy's historically conscious poetics (she cites him as the source of a poetics insistent on "digging up [...] buried things" and counts her Moodie poems as another example of this literary "digging" [*ISOAG* 20]) because his writing offered evidence of a dynamic Canadian past. At the same time, she distanced herself from his example by refusing to endorse his misogyny or replicate his androcentric literary vision. Atwood is, in other words, both a part of and apart from the lyric historiography that predated her Moodie poems.

So while Atwood connects herself to this tradition, she was not simply mimicking Purdy's archaeological poetics or the work of those who followed his example. She was cultivating her own interpretation of a literary genre, even as she borrowed some of its conventions – namely, the developmental structure of her poems (they are vaguely chronological and build to a climax), as well as her intensely visual book design (the cover sports a sideways photograph of Moodie, and, at William Toye's suggestion, Atwood included in the text several sketches of Moodie's family).[5] In some ways the aesthetic and poetic overlap of Atwood and other writers of lyric historiography is logical, because she shared her contemporaries' sensitivity to the era's nationalist fervour and the related resurgence of Canadian history. Atwood was, however, understandably less interested in male historical figures than male writers were; after airing a radio version of *The Journals of Susanna Moodie* in 1969, the CBC invited Atwood to write poems about John A. Macdonald, an offer she refused.[6] That incident could only have confirmed Atwood's sense that there was something wrong with the literary and historical tradition in Canada: write an empowering treatment of a female historical figure, and then you're invited to write an empowering treatment of a male one. This is what Atwood faced as a female Canadian writer, for whom – to adapt the words of Emily Dickinson – a foremother was a miracle.

Atwood's politics were not the only way in which she distinguished herself from earlier examples of lyric historiography; she was also experimenting with a different kind of lyric. Because Atwood dramatizes Moodie's actual voice instead of her own, it may seem reasonable to call *The Journals of Susanna Moodie* a sequence of "dramatic monologues" rather than a set of lyrics. At the same time, I don't think these labels are mutually exclusive. The dramatic monologue is a flexible mode closely associated with lyric, if only because the poet's shadowy presence underlies the dramatic voice. The performative "I" comes to the reader through the poetic "I" whose agency, though masked, is essential in the crafting of that performance. The effect in dramatic monologues is what Alan Sinfield calls a "divided consciousness" because "we are obliged to posit simultaneously the speaking 'I' and the poet's 'I'" (32). The implied connection to the lyric "I" seems especially true of more modern dramatic monologues, in which the speaking subject and the poet are drawn into much closer relation.

Esther Loehndorf uses Eliot's "The Love Song of J. Alfred Prufrock" as an example of this relation. The fact that "the very real threat of madness" that Eliot communicates in "Prufrock" "is perceptible also in other poems Eliot wrote at the time" implies a much less strict division between speaker and poet in his dramatic monologues (133). In other words, "the poet's presence behind the mask can still be felt," and, in modern poetry especially, it can be felt quite strongly (121). The examples on which Loehndorf draws demonstrate the flexible relationship between the speaking subject and the poet, a flexibility that led Glennis Byron to claim that "the [dramatic monologue] form is now considered to allow for various positionings of the speaking subject with respect to the writing poet" (19). In this vein, part of what aligns *The Journals of Susanna Moodie* with lyric historiography is Atwood's intricate conflation of Moodie's historical "I" with her own lyric "I" – hence Purdy's use of the hyphenated "Atwood-Moodie" when he names Atwood's poetic subject (83).[7]

Atwood herself insists that the poems are "lyrical" (Atwood and Struthers 58) and observes an ineluctable link between her lyric persona and that of Moodie: "[*The Journals of Susanna Moodie*] aren't so much 'about' her as written by me, but 'by' her as written through me, I'd as soon keep 'her' work separate from 'mine'" (Atwood to Toye). That labyrinthine statement communicates both Atwood's closeness to and detachment from Moodie's "I," a paradox to which Atwood gestured later in her career by saying that her poems showcase "a lyrical form," even if it is not the traditional "subjective lyrical" mode (Atwood and Struthers 58). What a reader can extract from these muddied statements is that Moodie's "I" is dual: it is the personal expression of Atwood and Moodie simultaneously. I read that strategy as symptomatic of Atwood's scepticism: the modern "I" cannot be present in a recovery project without knowingly colouring the portrayal of a historical "I." Atwood's description of *The Journals of Susanna Moodie* as "lyrical" suggests to me that this is a deliberate encroachment on the past that purposefully stresses the historical construction as interpretation, rather than as fact. Atwood never insisted upon the sanctity of truth. In reality, she often proposed the inverse: "I am not one of those who believes there is no truth to be known. But I have to conclude that [...] truth is sometimes unknowable" (*ISOAG* 37).[8] Scepticism, in other words, has been essential to her writing and can be observed in *The Journals* through portrayals of lyric duality.[9]

"The Double Voice" (*JSM* 42) is one of Atwood's more explicit performances of that doubleness. Sid Stephen argues that the poem "acknowledges the presence of Atwood" (34), a fair assumption as Moodie's persona sees herself in double: "Two voices / took turns using my eyes." A literal reading of this wonderfully synesthetic line calls to mind Atwood's own vision of Moodie as a "divided" self who curbs her thoughts and feelings and thus expresses sometimes competing versions of herself (62). At the same time, another reading might emphasize the possibility that the line hints at Atwood's lyric presence: she is one of the two voices sharing Moodie's "eyes." It can get more complicated: if Atwood is punning on "eyes" to suggest two selves ("I's"), then that would mean two voices speak through multiple Moodies. The line encapsulates the intense layering of authorial voices, perspectives, and identities in Atwood's poems.

The speaker continues to distinguish among these multiple selves, and, in this particular excerpt, Atwood contrasts conservative and modern verse:

> One saw through my
> bleared and gradually
> bleaching eyes, red leaves,
> the rituals of seasons and rivers
>
> The other found a dead dog
> jubilant with maggots
> half-buried among the sweet peas.

In the penultimate stanza, the stanza structure, the weak slant rhyme of "my" and "gradually," and the faint sibilance of "leaves" and "rivers" emulate the epical verse form of the heroic quatrain. But the persona's deficient metre and poor ear suggest a lack of commitment to or inability to write this romantic epic. This voice loosely conforms to the structures and content of nineteenth-century poetry; to break from these expectations would be unimaginable for Moodie, who says earlier in the poem that she feels obliged to speak in "hushed tones" and write "uplifting verse." Atwood's concluding tercet hardly resembles this hushed voice: the looser haiku-like structure, free verse, and juxtaposition of jubilation and death feel modern and even imagistic. Here are two competing poetic voices: the struggling and tentative romantic (Moodie, whose poetry in *Roughing It in the Bush* does tend toward heroic couplets) and the modern poet in search of a distilled and complex image (perhaps Atwood herself, who notes that her poems always "start with images" [Atwood and Levenson 25]). This poem epitomizes the duality of Atwood's entire book.

Sometimes this Atwood/Moodie duality manifests itself in Atwood's political messages, which are much more explicit in her early drafts.

In the unpublished "Letter to Descendants," Atwood uses Moodie to speak directly to modern Canadian women:

> If you think everything has changed since then
> look into the mirror
>
> or out
> the window. It's the same thing
>
> If you think you know more
> because you have been here
> longer, look out the
> the window. Or into the mirror.
>
> These give you borders
> and corners; keep life
> cut to a pragmatic size (n.p.)

In some ways, Atwood's poem would have fit perfectly with her collection: the mirror image (one of Atwood's favourite symbols throughout her career), the Frygean "border" that keeps women "cut" down to "pragmatic size," and the terseness of the lines and speaker are key features in most poems from *The Journals of Susanna Moodie*. The persona's political message, however, hardly resembles Moodie at all; in fact, there's no trace of Moodie. While the poem effectively sustains some of Atwood's key motifs and imagery, it is too modern in its message to maintain the vocal duality she threads throughout the rest of the collection. That inconsistency might explain Atwood's decision to cut the poem from her final draft.

"The Wereman" (*JSM* 19) more effectively balances Atwood's modern voice with that of Moodie; it epitomizes Atwood's self-conscious fashioning of a very specific image of Moodie as a mother. In this poem, Moodie watches her husband disappear into the forest and wonders how their experiences in the bush have transformed or will transform them: "My husband walks in the frosted field / an X, a concept / defined against a blank; / he swerves, enters the forest and is blotted out." Diana Relke's note that this scene is Atwood/Moodie "quickly writ[ing]" Moodie's husband "out of the poem" (40) can actually be pushed further: his exit from the poem is, in fact, his exit from the text. He never returns in later poems, even though Moodie says "he will / return." Yet, while Mr Moodie is walked out of the text, others are introduced and reintroduced: Moodie's children appear in multiple poems such as "The Two Fires" and "Death of a Young Son by Drowning." Atwood's creative choices denote the boundaries of her historical narrative: some characters work within her frame, others don't.

The overtness of her inclusions and especially her exclusions is a self-reflexive gesture. Even if Atwood's content is progressive, that doesn't mean that her writing has somehow overcome subjectivity. Exclusion is a basic quality of historical writing. The preferential treatment of one figure can precipitate the exclusion or unequal treatment of another. This is not necessarily a problem in history, unless a historian believes that a personal preference correlates to an objective assessment of history. For instance, a historical narrative that uses Confederation as its anchoring event is, in and of itself, harmless. That narrative becomes problematic, though, when its author claims objectivity in structuring history around that event; Confederation, in other words, becomes not just one historian's anchor, but *the* historical anchor for all narratives of Canada. Both the lyric duality of Atwood's writing and her exclusion of characters from her framework guard her against accusations of such dogmatism. Her version of history is only one possible version of the past.

Atwood's willingness to explore beyond the known facts of Moodie's life is further evidence of that subjectivity. "Death of a Young Son by Drowning" (*JSM* 30–1) illustrates the point. The poem is a response to the death of Moodie's son, which Moodie herself never discusses: "There is [the] Susanna Moodie we get by reading her texts, which never go into things like what she thought about her husband; she just never mentions it. The prime example is the story she tells about the boy who drowned, who wasn't related to her at all." The drowning of Moodie's own son, Atwood concludes, "is contained in the metaphor that she has given previously of this other child" (Atwood and Castro 216). The sketch to which Atwood refers is from Moodie's *Life in the Clearings* (1853), in which Moodie declines to discuss her son's death: "I will not dwell upon that dark hour, the saddest and darkest in my sad eventful life" (1989; 46). Moodie is equally evasive in *Roughing It*: "This feeling [of unease around fire] was greatly increased after a second fire, when, for some torturing minutes, a lovely boy, since drowned, was supposed to have perished in the burning house" (1989; 395). Moodie may refuse to dwell on this event, but Atwood shows no such restraint. Even just her simple willingness to elaborate on this narrative shows a modern persona taking over Moodie's historical "I," and the anachronisms that litter the poem are further evidence of this persona (e.g., the mention of a "bathysphere" at line 11, a word coined in 1930 [*OED*]).

Atwood's allusions are equally enlightening:

He, who navigated with success
the dangerous river of his own birth
once more set forth

on a voyage of discovery (*JSM* 30)

> Fresh ships and new honours were bestowed upon [Christopher Columbus], that he might once more set forth on a voyage of discovery. ("Life and Voyages" 63)

Like the word "bathysphere," Atwood's obvious allusion to "The Life and Voyages of Columbus" (her echo of Columbus's "voyage of discovery") is anachronistic: "The Life and Voyages of Columbus" (part of a collection of nautical stories, *Sea Stories* [1855]) was published after Moodie's *Roughing It* and *Life in the Clearings*. The allusion itself points to a more modern voice, but so do some possible interpretations of its function. Atwood implies some correlation between Moodie's drowned son and (in some histories) the American forefather. But the correlation is obscure: is Atwood drawing another boundary in the text by drowning a "Columbus" figure and focusing on Moodie's tenacious survival? Or is she merely using this event to show that Moodie has been to Canadians what Columbus has been to many Americans? The allusion is inscrutable, but either of these interpretations would suggest a modern ingression that shows the degree to which Atwood's history is self-consciously constructed.

Further, Atwood's allusions to her own work in *The Journals of Susanna Moodie* reveal her presence behind Moodie's voice. There is Atwood's intertextual linking of *The Circle Game* with "Alternate Thoughts from Underground" (in which Moodie contemplates life "outside the circle" [57]). Or there is the echo in "Visit to Toronto, with Companions," when a frustrated Moodie confesses that "[t]he landscape was saying something / but I couldn't hear" (50), and a careful reader will be reminded of Atwood's "Progressive Insanities of a Pioneer," in which nature speaks in "words" the speaker can't "understand" (36). Yet another allusion surfaces in "Departure from the Bush" when Moodie declares, "I was not completed" (*JSM* 27), which the maddened protagonist of Atwood's later novel, *Surfacing* (1972), expresses verbatim (149).[10] Atwood's feminism, anachronisms, and allusions to her own works indicate that the revenant Moodie who partly guides *The Journals of Susanna Moodie* is an entry point for Atwood's persona as much as it is a recovered voice.

Still, I don't want that reading to undermine Atwood's powerful recovery of Moodie's "I," because her project was to recover Moodie and portray her as the inaugurator of a Canadian literary tradition inclusive of women. If Atwood had simply used her own voice and written a more straightforward set of lyric poems, then there would be no actual recovery. The dramatic "I" creates the illusion of having unearthed not just Moodie's life, but also her silenced voice. This was a conscious choice. Atwood's earliest handwritten drafts of the book were written impersonally from the perspective of a contemporary speaker, but she crossed out all of the third-person titles and replaced them with titles suggestive of Moodie's presence: "Her Arrival" became "Further Arrivals," "Her Neighbours" became "First Neighbours," "Daguerreotype Taken in Her Old Age" became "Daguerreotype Taken in Old Age," and "Her Solipcism [*sic*] While Dying" became "Solipsism While Dying."[11] Her revision signals one of many moments in Atwood's career when the recovery of an "I" seemed essential: one might point to the return of the "I" in the third part of *The Edible Woman* (1969) or to Atwood herself, who published *The Circle Game* as "Margaret Atwood" after releasing *Double Persephone* (1961) as the semi-anonymous "M.E. Atwood" – and she used the latter, as well, in poems published in *Fiddlehead* throughout 1963 and 1964. Atwood's onomastic history implies, as her literature does, that the recovery of identity and voice was something of which she was very conscious during her early career.

Atwood evidently wanted, though, to do more than simply recover Moodie's voice. There was a very specific "Moodie" she had in mind. Consider "Ghost," a poem Atwood cut from the final version of *Journals*. In it, Moodie describes herself as

> less than a voice
> at times   unheard by most
> a thin shiver
> in the air, a white vibration (n.p.)

Atwood's speaker meditates on the aurality of the past – the loss of a sound, a voice – and thus enacts the same motif on which I have earlier remarked in the writing of her contemporaries (such as Purdy, Burrs, and McKinnon). There are, though, other links to those writers. One finds as much an anti-Birney subtext here as in Purdy's poems, and the conclusion Atwood draws is similar to that which Purdy draws in his poetry: rather than a "lack of ghosts," there are (perhaps many) "unheard" ghosts. Atwood's spacing mimics the silence that Moodie laments: the gap between "times" and "unheard" signifies silence, just as the curtness of the third line reflects the "thin[ness]" of the voice. There are other disruptions: the jagged lines broken by caesurae and enjambment fragment this voice and contribute to the reader's feeling that this aural past has been lost or disfigured. Atwood's motive for cutting this poem is unclear, but I suspect her decision had something to do with the inevitable suggestion of silence inherent in a whisper. Atwood presumably wanted Moodie's voice to be audible and present, and that voice would be undermined by any depiction of Moodie as a whispering ghost. A quieted Moodie is certainly not what readers see when Moodie triumphantly emerges into modern-day Toronto in "A Bus Along St. Clair: December" (*JSM* 60–1). In that poem, she is not a whispering apparition, but rather "the old woman sitting across from you on the bus." She does not sit passively or inaudibly: "secret hat-pins" shoot from "her eyes," "destroying the walls." That living and interactive Moodie contrasts with the ghostly vision of her as "less than a voice" or a "vibration" fluttering ambiguously "in the air."

In recovering Moodie, Atwood clearly wanted to present a voice more defiant than the one in "Ghost." By the end of *Journals*, a buried Moodie ruminates on her literal and figurative burial. In "Alternate Thoughts from Underground" (*JSM* 57), she finds herself "Down. Shovelled." "[S]uperstructures" have paved over her and made her feel as absent from modern life as the "giant reptiles" of prehistory. Generations are "invade[d]" and buried by the subsequent era that redefines what makes an acceptable history. The androcentric structures of modernity become as powerful as the destructive force that killed the "great reptiles," which leaves little hope for Moodie. Even still, Moodie's long-dead "I" is indefatigable in Atwood's final poem, "A Bus Along St. Clair: December":

> It would take more than that to banish
> me: this is my kingdom still.
>
> Turn, look up
> through the gritty window: an unexplored
> wilderness of wires
>
> Though they buried me in monuments
> of concrete slabs, of cables
> though they mounded a pyramid
> of cold light over my head
> though they said, We will build
> silver paradise with a bulldozer
>
> it shows how little they know
> about vanishing: I have
> my ways of getting through.

While the first mention of a "monument" might sound optimistic, the actual image that emerges is a chthonic and neglected Moodie. The concrete monument ironically memorializes forgetfulness by paving over her. The image is a stabilizing one that has historical implications because the concrete slabs are monuments to the building of Toronto – a literal and symbolic foundation for the city. They are, by implication, equally symbolic of a foundational history now set in stone and from which Moodie is excluded. The image recalls the urges for order and stability inherent in the garrison mentality, which is what makes Moodie's triumphant eruption through the surface so shocking and rousing: she has an irrepressible urge to "get through" and fight her extinction. She wields tremendous power in this scene not just because she emerges from underground, but also because she communes directly with readers and metapoetically assumes control of their reading experience. Her stern imperatives demand the reader's obedience: we are directed to "look up" and, later, to "look down." Unmistakably, this is the speaker who "refuses to be ploughed under completely," the one who breaks through the garrisons constructed to repel her, whether these garrisons are the city threatened by "the forest," the concrete slabs breached by Moodie's ghost, or the histories into which she inserts herself.

In many ways, that final scene exemplifies Atwood's philosophical development as a poet over the course of the 1960s. The moment in which Moodie triumphantly bursts into modern life ties together Atwood's various understandings of "archaeology" and "garrisons" (Frygean, feminist, and nationalist): a female Canadian icon, cut from histories, invades the world that has forgotten and buried her. Karen Stein's claim that *The Journals of Susanna Moodie* is, structurally speaking, a departure from Atwood's earlier poetry (24) is reasonable, but, conceptually, the poems are, as Gwendolyn MacEwen said to Atwood, "the culminations" of themes the latter was exploring throughout the 1960s. The other thing about MacEwen's letter to Atwood that catches me is that she says Atwood's *Journals* "ma[d]e so much more sense to [her] re Canada than x number of other things" she'd read (MacEwen to Atwood). If those poems made more "sense" to MacEwen, it was probably because Atwood had offered a viable alternative to the androcentric lyric historiography of Purdy and the male poets on whom he had the greatest impact.

MacEwen wasn't alone in feeling that way. Numerous critics noted Atwood's apparent influence on Florence McNeil's *Emily* (1975), which is understandable given that the book is, like Atwood's poems, both lyrical and dramatic.[12] McNeil assumes Carr's voice to show the struggle a female artist faces in a society intolerant of her aspirations. Carr's worldview is in direct tension with that of her father: "I see Victoria as masts and mud and great green lawns / and my father's hand guiding me / round the unattractive bits of history" ("History Lesson 1879" 13). The opening phrase of the poem, "I see," instantly draws attention to perspective, variously conceived. One perspective, of course, is that of

Carr's father, the man who tries to sanitize her historical knowledge. McNeil's Carr, however, refuses guided evasion. She wants to discover her own ways of seeing and knowing, and so she continually tries to unlearn her father's worldview, if only for the sake of her art. For much of McNeil's book, Carr grapples with this tension between the world her father taught her to see and the one she wants to experience.

That tension is paramount in the poem "London I," in which Carr takes a "life class" at the Westminister School of Art and feels scandalized by the nude model:

I am my father's daughter
he was a puritan   respectably wore
the tight high collared morals of
his peers

and in the life class still
I wonder should I set aside
my eyes
cover up my nose my mouth my ears
close out the beautiful naked
symmetry of
the model   lending her body to
        my pencil and pad
look at the ceiling   study my feet
recall that the body's curves and
                creases
are intrinsically bad (20)

The poem weaves worldviews. First, there is Carr's father, whose perspectives are social performances: he dresses up and wears "the tight high collared morals" of others. As in other poems that use roman numerals, I am tempted to read the titular "I/1" as a suggestion that the London "I/me" will be somehow divergent from the "I" that is a "father's daughter." As a point of record, it was in London that Carr felt a shift in her personhood as she overcame her Victorian sense of modesty. In her autobiography, she recalls that when she "looked up" from her canvas during class, the nude model "swallowed every bit" of her "shyness": "I had never been taught to think of our naked bodies as something beautiful, only as something indecent, something to be hidden. Here was nothing but loveliness ... only loveliness" (Carr 132). In McNeil's poem, Carr's father adopts a worldview that is socially inscribed, whereas Carr's view derives, both in the poem and in her autobiography, from an aesthetic sensibility that she intuits through personal feeling and observation rather than learning, as her father had, through social conditioning. Her initial instinct to look away from the model is undermined as soon as she realizes that the body is reassuringly "symmetr[ical]," even if the body "curves" and "creases." The dynamism of a nude body is more real to Carr than the order achieved by covering it with clothes. This epiphany leads McNeil's Carr, at the end of the poem, to sketch lines that "are soft and real and unembarrassed" (21). McNeil's poem is fundamentally about her escape from the "orderly" and "polite" "victorian vision" that once led her to believe "the coast forest was always a threat" ("In the beginning ..." 25). You can hear the Frygean echo here: the colonial distinctions between the orderly city and the chaotic forest. McNeil's text, as much as Atwood's, negotiates conservative traditions and modern thought.

What's interesting about McNeil's text is that it showcases a reassuringly figurative familial connection between the poet and Carr, while the poems themselves struggle against a literal familial legacy that, in ways reminiscent of Anglo-American modernists, induces anxiety in Carr: "I am a name now / but it is still my father's name" ("Awards" 8). While McNeil's poem, more than others, offers a deeper consideration of why the literal family could be a burden for modern women, that same sense of burden, especially because it is experienced by an artist figure, connects McNeil to Carr. And Carr's social context is no less accepting of a female artist: the repression of the female self in a Victorian system of patriarchy is a continual source of struggle for Carr, who wants to articulate her self-discovery. In a moment reminiscent of Atwood's "I, who had been erased" (*JSM* 26), McNeil's Carr declares, "I who wrestle with words [...] now plod / by invitation / to the Authors Association" ("Being a Writer" 62). Describing the Canadian Authors Association in ways surprisingly similar to those in F.R. Scott's "The Canadian Authors Meet" (1927), Carr watches "old women / with forced petals" who "tell about juvenile love" and who stand for the same Victorian repression as her father. "I do not despise you o literati," Carr says in this poem; "[I] would like only to baptize you / with scalding rain" ("Being a Writer" 63). As an independent artist, Carr fits in with neither her family nor her society, and that defiance is something that McNeil emphasizes.

While in many ways an accurate and authoritative portrayal of Carr, McNeil's book is still cautious in its conclusions. Her closing poem, "1945," is a conflicted effort at narrative closure. On the one hand, McNeil's final poem is an account of Carr's death as the end of her life narrative – a fitting "end" to the book. On the other hand, that poem also suggests that, in death, Carr's identity becomes amorphous. The poem meditates on the ambiguity of representational images, whether those are the product of the self or of someone else. In particular, Carr repeatedly speaks doubtingly of "mirrors" in the poem: after Carr "declare[s] war on mirrors," she then "turn[s] around the mirrors" in her room (72). That act of protesting her mirror image might be Carr looking at an aged version of herself and not recognizing her own face; she says that "there is a deep gash where a mouth once was" and that "my hands ... hold skin like a sense of duty" (72). At the same time, McNeil is seeing herself in Carr: both are West Coast writers whose impulses are progressive and fundamentally feminist. This moment feels like one in which the mirror McNeil holds up to herself to see Carr begins to seem inadequate. The crisp mirror image is replaced by a much more ambiguous image of landscape:

> I turn around the mirrors
> say to my landscapes   You reflect me
> there is some spirit here
> and life (72)

What endures after Carr's death is not a sustainable mirror image, but rather the nebulous landscape paintings that have "some spirit" and some "life." In death, only Carr's abstract art mirrors her self, and those are hardly concrete images offering definitive interpretations of the artist or her life.

McNeil's final lines reinforce the suggestion that Carr's life is a work of art to be endlessly interpreted: "at the top of the Canvas / there is only room to grow" (72). Like the photograph, the canvas is a literal framework with references and narratives outside its boundaries. That final scene, like the forested West Coast, conjures up for me the images of Frygean garrisons that permeate Atwood's poems, the idea that a past, as much as a landscape, can be only tenuously contained and framed.

McNeil's poems are only one instance of Atwood's literary influence.[13] Many poets learned from *The Journals of Susanna Moodie*, including contemporary poets such as Nadine McInnis, whose *Two Hemispheres* (2007) – a photographic collection of poems about ten nineteenth-century women – is a reaction to historical attitudes toward depression and specific cases of women's institutionalization. McInnis felt that these women were "familiar, in every sense of the word" ("Afterword" 87) because her own depression led her to see them as "foremothers"; Atwood's poems were, McInnis recalls, "an influence" as she drafted the book (Email from McInnis). There are numerous other examples to which one could point and find evidence of Atwood's impact: Anne Carson's homage to Emily Brontë, "The Glass Essay" (1995), Florence McNeil's *The Overlanders* (1982), and Lorna Crozier's *A Saving Grace: The Collected Poems of Mrs Bentley* (1996), the last of which is a reimagining of the sexuality and proto-feminism of Sinclair Ross's fictional narrator in *As for Me and My House* (1941), Mrs Bentley.[14] As book-length poems that recover historical (and sometimes fictional) women, imbuing them with presence and life and making their lyrical experiences immediate for readers, these texts bear obvious traces of Atwood's influence.

In providing these various accounts of lyric historiography, I do not want to give the impression that Atwood's impact has been limited to creative writing; her influence has extended even to re-releases of Moodie's *Roughing It in the Bush*. In 1959, Robert MacDougall edited Moodie's *Life in the Clearings*, and, in his introduction to the volume, remarked that the source material for his edition "does not [always] have Mrs. Moodie's authority" but rather the authority of "an independent judgment," that is, the New York–based editors of DeWitt and Davenport who published their edition of *Life in the Clearings* in 1854 (xxiii). Like MacDougall, Carl Klinck demonstrated little interest in Moodie's authority when he edited *Roughing It in the Bush* for McClelland and Stewart: in his 1962 version of the text, Klinck claimed that the reading public "of the 1960's" had no patience for long texts (x).[15] The back of the book also frames Moodie's text as a "large fund of ironic observations on pioneer life in Canada" and a "lively re-creation of an era that is past in this country"; the author of the blurb regards the text as a historical document of Canada's pioneer era and makes virtually no mention of Moodie's strong character or her authorial voice. These editions took readers away from Moodie and were invested in representing her era more than her self.

Those goals markedly contrast with those of later editors. The back-cover blurb of the unabridged 1989 edition of *Roughing It* (published again by McClelland and Stewart) is adequate proof: the blurb summarizes the book as a symbol of Moodie's "firm determination to puncture the illusions European land-agents were circulating about life in Canada." "This frank and fascinating chronicle," it continues, "details her harsh – and humorous – experiences in homesteading." The blurb ends by claiming that Moodie's text, "[p]art documentary, part psychological parable," is "an honest account of how one woman coped not only in a new world, but, more importantly, with herself." None of Klinck's nostalgic nationalist rhetoric is here; there is only Moodie, a "woman cop[ing]" with a difficult landscape and being. If Moodie's *Roughing*

It appeared to be a "psychological parable" to the editors of this later edition (and surely to the editors of several other editions that came out in the 1980s and thereafter), it is hard to imagine that Atwood's enormously popular poems and her commentary on Moodie's psychological condition in her afterword had no effect on the framing of these texts. Even Susan Glickman's afterword to the 1989 edition obviously replicates Atwood's claim in the afterword to *The Journals of Susanna Moodie* that Moodie is psychologically complex and "divided" (62): "Susanna cannot make up her mind. She presents herself (as a character) arguing that 'God has been very good to us' and yet she closes the book (as its narrator) declaring that her sole purpose [...] has been to deter others from making the same terrible mistake her family did" (535). The echo is unmistakable.

As an example of lyric historiography specifically, *The Journals of Susanna Moodie* evidences the degree to which the genre was capable of being both repurposed and politically subversive. Atwood adopted the aesthetic and philosophical qualities of lyric historiography that appealed to her own project and then consciously deviated from the content that poets like Purdy explored. Her relationship with Purdy is a valuable case study of the ways in which poets with utterly incompatible worldviews can influence each other. And, equally important, is the fact that each writer, their differences notwithstanding, could recognize in each other's work similar goals that fostered a sense of community among them, which is why Purdy could say of Atwood's poems, "this [book] is very fine, certainly the best that will come in Canada this year" (Purdy to Atwood [March 1970]). But the model that Atwood provided, the example of family imagined figuratively and the past imagined intimately, made it possible to propose a history rooted in the belief that cultural nationalism could be analogous to and informed by modern feminism. The way in which this recuperation generated new discourses on Moodie and influenced other creative writers may prove to be the enduring quality of her sequence; her work, indeed, left a place for later writers to stand on.

9 Indigeneity and Performance: The Fictions of Nations

The long poems about literal or figurative families that appeared in rapid succession after 1970 each, in their own way, showed that the Canadian poetry community valued lyric as a historiographic method and as a subversive mode. Atwood's poems, for instance, stood against the widespread indifference to women's historical perspectives and experiences. And yet, however progressive Atwood's poetry may have seemed in 1970, its appeal to an intersectional community of feminists was limited. It, like many early entries into centennial-era feminist discourses in Canada and elsewhere, did little to capture women's ethnic and cultural diversity. Indeed, Atwood's writing belongs to a generation of feminist literature that the American author Alice Walker criticized for normalizing white middle-class experience and disregarding other women's experiences.[1] Her claim is just one example of how trademarks of the 1960s – scepticism, revolt, self-empowerment – carried forward, ensuring that later readers would continue to critique and refine the movements, ideologies, and histories that seemed, if only for brief moments, suitably progressive.

Many of these critiques – and certainly this is true of Walker's work – stress the importance of grasping "intersectionality." While that term would not enter common usage until the late 1980s (via Kimberlé Crenshaw's speeches and writing), the concept for which it stands was well understood by activists long before then: "intersectionality" insists on understanding the different ways in which each individual's intersecting ethnic, gender, and political identities affect their position and agency in society. A Canadian example would be the range of feminisms the Royal Commission on the Status of Women outlined in their 1970 report. RCSW representatives understood feminism to embrace the unique challenges Indigenous women face, and it was the report writers' attention to those challenges that led them to recommend that federal and provincial governments "provide expanded, comprehensive courses for all public officials and employees and their spouses, working with Indians and Eskimos; to familiarize them with the cultures and traditions of the native people, including training in the native languages" (215). The report went further and recommended that Indigenous communities "should be involved in the changes that are taking place not only in their lives but also in Canada" (217).[2] In making these recommendations, the RCSW showed its readers that Canadian feminism was, to be sure, a movement intersecting with the Red Power movement of the 1960s and 1970s.

During an era in which publishers, scholars, and readers generally "privileg[ed] ... the native male voice" (Harjo and Bird 22), an Indigenous feminist literature was badly needed. With *Pale as Real Ladies* (1989), Joan Crate (Métis) participates in that intersectional conversation through her recovery of the nineteenth-century poet E. Pauline Johnson/Tekahionwake (Mohawk).[3] As a poet and stage performer, Johnson has been regarded by many as a cultural hero because of her willingness to speak out against settler society. To Crate, Johnson is a foremother who worked with and against the conventions of Victorian acceptability and of the authorized "Other" in a colonial society. Crate's poems thus ruminate on the performances demanded of Indigenous women by settlers, and, in that way, *Pale as Real Ladies* is a commentary on colonial coercion and violence.

Crate's example is, therefore, further evidence of the subversive potential in lyric historiography. I speak of Crate as a poet situated within the literary web that I have been charting because of proven connections she has to Atwood. That said, there are numerous writers I have not included in this chapter whose impulse to challenge and write against conventional colonial histories is informed by different influences and knowledge, some of which can be located more immediately within the cultural traditions of specific Indigenous communities (here I am thinking in particular of writers like Louise Halfe [Cree], about whom I will say more in my conclusion). Crate's lyric historiography, though, was heavily influenced by Atwood. When Atwood said that women read women because to do so inspires "a feeling that you too could do it because, look, it could be done" ("If You Can't Say Something Nice" 17), she could never have imagined that an emerging writer like Crate would have that exact reaction to *The Journals of Susanna Moodie*: "I was quite influenced by Margaret Atwood's *The Journals of Susanna Moodie*. But I wanted to give a different take. I wanted to give what I considered a more Canadian perspective because Moodie comes over from Britain. I was pretty influenced by that: the idea of it actually. And that's often where writers start, don't you think? They take someone they like or they hear someone who's getting attention and they go, 'Hey, I can do that'" (Crate and Beach).[4] Atwood's impact on Crate may explain some of the latter poet's creative and structural choices: she adopts a developmental structure for her lyric sequence that concludes with Johnson's quasi-afterlife, includes visual aids (and, in addition to pictures of Johnson on the front and back cover of the book, there are ekphrastic poems about Johnson's photographs), and conflates her lyric "I" with Johnson's dramatic "I" to show her identification with Johnson as a personal and cultural foremother. The parallels between *Pale as Real Ladies* and Atwood's *Journals* are palpable.

Bringing Crate into a discussion about lyric historiography, I find myself at an unanticipated moment in my own study. When I began this book about ten years ago, it had not occurred to me – at least not with the same force it now does – that every scholar, including myself, has limits to and gaps in their knowledge. I draw attention to this point because Indigenous scholars have often outlined the danger of holding firmly onto knowledge without questioning or recognizing one's own position. While writing this book, a colleague had advised me to emphasize my expertise over my openness to correction, but I felt then – as I do now – that such an addition would be disingenuous in a study so concerned with the value and limits of individual knowledge. Intelligence, like compassion, is not achieved through assertions, but rather by making a genuine effort to reach a deeper understanding of a time, place, or perspective. While it may be necessary in a scholarly study to assert expertise, it seems equally important to acknowledge that a persistent problem in settler-authored studies is the deployment of uncontested, imperialistic interpretations. It would be irresponsible to pretend that I, as a third-generation Canadian and as a scholar entrenched in settler traditions of language and literature, could fully step back from those personal and academic positions. Hence, my discussion here – informed by years of research, interviews, and thought – will still surely invite expansion and possibly correction. Those outcomes seem to me ideal, because my critical efforts in this chapter, and in this book, are determined encouragements of further conversations, not assertions of rigid conclusions.

Crate may prove to be an important figure in those conversations, if only because she illuminates the danger of interpretive imperialism that I mention above; she is also the only writer in this study so far to contest in any substantial way an essentially colonial framework for Canadian history. Other writers discussed in this book challenged important issues in historical study: Purdy articulated the limits of subjectivity in the writing of broad histories, Newlove helped destigmatize regionalist writing, McKinnon and Suknaski demonstrated the conceptual power of familial poetry and testimony, and Atwood validated feminist recovery projects by showing the remarkable achievement of "family" imagined figuratively. Yet, their scepticism about the veracity and integrity of historical narratives, however acute, never led any of them to genuinely question their colonial positions. In poems like *In Search of Owen Roblin*, Purdy comfortably celebrates the "place" on which the present stands, which for him is undoubtedly a place of settler privilege built on a history of oppressing Indigenous peoples. In "The Battlefield at Batoche," Purdy also says that Batoche is where "the Metis [*sic*] nation was born and died" (*S&D* 42), which disregards Indigenous-authored histories that treat the Métis uprisings as historical tipping points, catalysts for a deeper historical consciousness and the "long journey of the Métis people," rather than as their birth and death (Lischke and McNab 1). Likewise, Atwood's *Journals of Susanna Moodie* entirely sidesteps Moodie's problematic portrayal of her so-called "Indian friends" in *Roughing It in the Bush*. Put simply, there is not even a hint of colonial self-awareness in these poems.

Other poets draw relatively more attention to the impact of colonialism. McKinnon, for instance, gestures to forced relocation in Canadian history, "resist[ing]," as one reviewer noted, "the tendency to romanticize" his family's past in the context of a larger history (Blackburn 225). Newlove similarly acknowledges the cultural devastation wrought by European settlement in "The Pride," even as that same poem evidences Newlove's own problematic adoption of colonial tropes and motifs. These poets appear, however briefly and however at odds with themselves, contemplative of their genetic or spatial connection to horrific cultural trespasses. Suknaski is similarly reflective. In the afterword to *Wood Mountain Poems*, he says that his writing "deal[s] with 'a vaguely divided guilt; guilt for what happened to the Indian (his land taken) imprisoned on his reserve; and guilt because to feel this guilt is a betrayal of what you ethnically are – the son of a homesteader and his wife who must be rightfully honored in one's mythology'" (124). Suknaski's uncomfortable dilemma is less resolved in this passage than readers today might hope, and while I argued earlier that his poems respectfully attend to other voices, there is the evident problem that, in so doing, Suknaski appropriates the stories and languages of the communities toward which he feels his unproductive guilt.

Even if admiring of each poet's effort to reinvent historiographic methods, I am hard-pressed to find among them an unambiguous indictment of colonialism. The past is never as progressive as we, in the present, need or want it to be, and this makes it difficult to be unequivocal when studying poets as products of their eras. And yet, these cases – especially those of McKinnon, Newlove, and Suknaski – show that some centennial-era writers were grappling with, if not resolving, the political, cultural, and philosophical challenges brought on by the historical positions of their "I's": the lyric mode liberated Canadian poets of the need for a romantic nationalist vision of the nation, but, as they looked more closely at the past, some noticed historical and social inequality. Those writers were either too ill-equipped or too unwilling to address such issues at length in their poems.

Nevertheless, I am still struck by the fact that those poems bear a basic methodological relation to the works of writers, such as Joan Crate, who challenge colonial histories. The specifics of each writer's positioning and poetry set them apart, but the implications of a shared methodology are there: the self-reflexive and sharp lenses of lyrical writing lend authority to the individual and implicitly prevent any one writer from claiming an apprehension of a whole history. The poets share in exploring lyric perspectives that allow them to celebrate the historical experiences of which they are certain (their own literal or figurative legacies) and then to find themselves, inevitably it seems, at the fringes of other lyric centres that bespeak pasts of which these writers have (sometimes self-admittedly) too little knowledge or too little claim – remember Crozier's line from "Drifting Towards Batoche," "these were not my people" – to continue writing and exploring.

It is only because every poet in my study celebrates, equally, the knowledge, experience, feelings, and limits of the lyric "I" that I can read them side-by-side. They are always imagining, even anticipating, other contributions to a larger and insistently dissonant past. Purdy, as a case in point, notes that he is merely a "piece of the main" and not necessarily the proverbial "everyman" – this despite Sam Solecki's claim that Purdy is the "central poet of [Canadian] experience" (10).[5] Rather, what happens in Purdy's poems and in the other writing I've presented in this book is the constant, paradoxical centring and decentring of the "I," the mark of discourse rather than of unambiguous and romantic valorizations of individual perspectives. And so while scholars can and should identify and justifiably criticize the apparent limitations of the settler frameworks within which some of these lyrics work, and while the authors here under discussion have been at times insensitive to the particular projects or circumstances of their contemporaries, I still value their collaborative effort to reinvent history as a cacophony of individual positions, politics, and experiences.[6]

The transformative quality of lyric historiography is an essential feature of the genre to note if I am going to connect authors who may seem at odds intellectually, ethically, or politically. I spoke in my last chapter of Atwood's repurposing of lyric historiography, which is also a useful way to think of Crate's project. It seems counterintuitive to imagine Crate, an author of Métis heritage, finding inspiration in the poetics of Atwood, who once said that Canadians have "a better track record" than Americans in their treatment of Indigenous peoples (*Survival* 92) and who almost entirely elided Moodie's encounters with Indigenous communities in *The Journals of Susanna Moodie*. And yet when Crate first read Atwood during her undergraduate years at the University of Calgary in the early 1980s, she felt that *The Journals of Susanna Moodie* marked literary and historiographic possibility: "In the past, it has been both acceptable and common to almost completely erase the Indigenous presence when writing about Canada, even when doing so in a historical context. [Atwood's] omissions [of Indigenous groups from *The Journals of Susanna Moodie*] did leave an absence in the portrayal of a foremother for Canadian women and I saw the opportunity to address that" (Letter from Crate to Weingarten).

At the same time, Crate was critical of Atwood's work, even as she admired it. The motifs common to Atwood's poems didn't resonate with Crate as well as their recuperative function had:

> I thought of writing about Pauline Johnson in a way similar to Atwood's first-person poems. Except Johnson's alienation came primarily from the expectations imposed by the colonizing society who (arguably) regard Johnson first as an Indigenous woman ("sauvage"), then as a curiosity. In contrast to Moodie, Johnson experiences no alienation from the land itself as it has been Johnson's paternal family home for generations. *Pale as Real Ladies* is meant to reveal an Indigenous woman's familiarity with the land but estrangement from the imposed culture. (Letter from Crate to Weingarten)

Crate's comments here complement those of Margery Fee, who has recently observed that Indigenous "discourses of autochthony ... differ from those produced by settlers" (*Literary* 7). Fee notes that English Canada's most celebrated centennial-era critics – namely, Frye and Atwood – associate nature with the experience of "deep terror" (Frye 227) and "victimhood" (e.g., Atwood's *Survival*). I would add that non-Indigenous Canadian poets have tended to regard nature's indifferent state of being as a conscious aggression against humanity. Case in point: Atwood's afterword to *The Journals of Susanna Moodie* echoes

Frye's belief that "to enter Canada is a matter of being silently swallowed by an alien continent" (217); "[w]e move," Atwood says, "in fear" of the enormous wilderness (*JSM* 62). The motifs of terror, fear, alienation, and an indifferent natural world resonate, too, in Atwood's "Progressive Insanities of a Pioneer" or – to draw on earlier examples – Earle Birney's *David* and "Bushed." Yet those depictions, Fee observes, contrast with "Indigenous epistemologies" (8): "Indigenous people," she writes, "have not characteristically described themselves as transfixed by a deep terror in response to nature or as heroes for overcoming it" (7). Indigenous relationships to nature often appear reciprocal; the Assembly of First Nations describes the spiritual relationship between the individual and the Earth as a dialogue through which "Mother Earth teaches" and "provides" for those who share and respect the Earth ("Honouring Earth").[7]

But I am interested, too, in Fee's note on heroism. For Crate, the act of overcoming alienation and achieving some measure of heroism occurs not in the natural world, but in the social one. Granted, Atwood's Moodie is, as a proto-feminist, an indefatigable social figure, but much of what seems to compel Atwood to heroize her is Moodie's distinctly Frygean survival: surviving the bush, surviving a garrisoned history, and so on. The Frygean alienation and terror, the Atwoodean trope of survival – these are the frames of reference for heroism in *The Journals of Susanna Moodie*, a heroism achieved in environments that spur feelings analogous to the fear that both Atwood and Frye first portrayed as a response to an indifferent Nature. Crate, alternatively, explores resilience in the face of violence: heroism is surviving cultural trauma, not the natural world. This is what Crate depicts in a loosely chronological portrayal of Johnson's life ("Part I") and a subsequent series of "legends" that serve as Johnson's quasi-afterlife ("Part II").

Throughout her book, Crate emphasizes the continuity of Johnson's struggles with her own. Like Atwood in *The Journals of Susanna Moodie*, Crate blurs the "I" in her poems: her book is a lyric meditation on the personal conditions and experiences of a contemporary "I" fused with the historical "I" of a figurative foremother. There is obvious evidence of this reading in Crate's opening narrative poem, "Prairie Greyhound" (n.p.). The poem depicts Crate's persona riding a Greyhound bus to an unknown destination at two in the morning: "Pauline, you are with me. Your face stares through the bus window, and I no longer know where I end and you begin. ... Tonight on this bus, I am half me and half you." The scene is gothic: the ghostly foremother reanimating in the middle of the night, her uncanny apparition unexpectedly emerging in the present and partially manifesting in the reflection of the lyric speaker.

Crate is not, though, the possessed victim of a ghost story; she is its architect. She imagines herself as Johnson's mirror image and progeny in order to justify taking possession of Johnson. This is Crate's deliberate search for familial ghosts rather than some accidental stumbling, and the scene evinces spatial and temporal movement, a forging ahead suggestive of discovery. Most obviously, the bus stands for both Crate's search for a destination (the past) and for the simultaneous travelling of her "I," her move deeper into Johnson's "I"/"eye."

That descent seems intuitive for Crate's persona. In Johnson's life, Crate sees familiar struggles:

> Emily Pauline Johnson, Mohawk Princess, the Chief's youngest daughter. Poet, patriot, author, actor, lover, spinster, lonely. ... Your mother insisted you be schooled white, taught her spotless manners. Yet it was the mottled history of your father's people you recited, his pride you adopted, your grandfather's Indian name, Tekahionwake, you took. "Hey squaw," they called from the foot of the stage. These relics were not enough to protect you from voices in the dark.

Crate reflects on the stark binary of "two worlds," a colonial presumption that one cannot maintain a coherent identity if one's heritage is too "mixed"; of course, many Indigenous writers have vehemently rejected that claim.[8] In colonial interpretations, the mixed-culture self can only be divided, and in Crate's poem the division is between the "mottled" (i.e., dirty or spotted) history of the Mohawk and a "spotless" English culture. Those experiences parallel what Crate's persona experiences on the bus as she hears men yelling "Hey Babe!" and "Squaw." Crate's persona stares into the window as she listens to the catcalls, and there is – as her look into the window suggests – a kind of mirroring: the scene is almost as if Crate is being heckled while on stage, performing or being asked to performed as both a woman ("Babe") and an Indigenous person ("squaw"). Instantly the scene associates performance with violence.

Indeed, the history of Indigenous-settler relations in Canada has been, partly, a history of performance. Settlers invented and still perpetuate the misleading image of what Daniel Francis calls the "imaginary Indian," which signifies the "manufactured" (21) colonial image of the Other as uncivilized and primitive, who might otherwise be represented as the "noble savage." This manufactured identity fails to capture the inherent complexity of individual or community identities, which are rarely so monolithic; when I use "Indigenous" or other contemporary terms like "Aboriginal" in this chapter, I do so to get away from these monolithic and artificial identities and closer to self-determined ones. Colonialism, however, demands performance, not self-definition.

In Homi Bhabha's imagining of colonial performance, settlers possess the authority to shape identities. Performance is obviously not just a colonial concern; Judith Butler famously theorized performance as "the gendered body acting ... within the confines of already existing directives" (526). In Butler's thinking, women learn to accept gendered identities as "normal" behaviour and thus they perform those identities, sometimes wholly unaware of their performance. In so far as these identities are taught through political and social conditioning, they are symptomatic of power dynamics: heavily gendered roles are often portrayed as "normal" by those in power and are therefore not always consensually self-guided performances. That is not to say that performance is always masking someone's "true self," because every identity is a performance; no identity transcends all others. The performances we adopt are always responses to specific contexts, but one must consider the privilege of agency: do we safely modify our self-definition(s) as we engage with our environment or is our environment a place in which some coerce others – through speech acts, visual representations, and laws – to adopt non-negotiable and authorized performances?

Bhabha calls the latter process "mimicry," which "is at once resemblance and menace" (86). For the colonizer, mimicry signifies "narcissism" (their perceived superiority over the Other) and "paranoia" (their continued recognition of the Other as deviantly or threateningly other), whereas for the colonized, mimicry emptily promises social acceptance (91). It is, in Jacques Lacan's view, a protective "camouflage" (qtd Bhabha 85), but an "ambivalent" camouflage in so far as its wearer is always "almost the same, but not quite" (86). To one degree or another, mimicry makes difference visible even as the individual aspires to and performs sameness.

Naturally, Bhabha's theory opens itself up to interpretations of what it means to be, in Bhabha's terms, an "authorized" other:

1. *Performing "whiteness."* The most literal interpretation of Bhabha's term is the material or social performance of whatever appearances or actions constitute, in the mind of the colonizer, "whiteness." Maria Campbell (Métis), for instance, recalls her mixed feelings about "Indians in suits" (166), the people whom she initially judged as traitors to their culture only to empathize later with their effort to emulate images of "whiteness." Such performers desire acceptance within settler society, but remain, in Bhabha's terms, "*almost the same but not* white" (89, emphasis added). The risk of Bhabha's

paradigm of *"almost, but not white"* is that one could read it as a suggestion that Indigenous societies cannot evolve without somehow also signalling their lack of agency – in other words, as a suggestion that "authentic" Indigenous peoples are somehow socially, culturally, and politically static, stuck in the past. This would be a misreading of Bhabha: "mimicry" is a power play in which the colonizer determines the avenues (creative, social, political) available to the colonized (thereby limiting their agency to self-define). In cases where survivors of colonization wilfully explore their own agency by adopting and experimenting with creative, social, or political platforms encountered through colonialism, however, Bhabha speaks of "hybridity," which carries with it a subversive potential, as in the case of Emma LaRocque (Métis): "I have sought to master this language [English] so that it would no longer master me" ("Preface" xxvi).

2. *Performing "authorized versions of otherness"* (Bhabha 88). Bernice Loft Winslow toured as a "representative" of the Iroquois nation through the 1930s (C. Morgan 81), wearing an "Indian" costume purchased from a store (82). Smithsonian scholars "verified" her authority to perform as an "Indian" (79), which assuaged doubting audiences on the lookout for fakes. Winslow felt no such relief. Her stage performances muddled her sense of self. At one point, she explained, "I almost don't know whether I'm me or not" (qtd Morgan 80). Increasingly, Winslow felt that she was an outsider not just to English Canadians (from whom she'd always felt estranged) but also to her own people (83). Her audience, however, was sure she was "the real thing" – an authorized other, in Bhabha's terms or, in Marilyn Dumont's (Cree-Métis) terms, an "authentic" Other (47). The parallels to Johnson and her career are remarkable. Both women were talented poets and wished to represent their cultures and challenge popular opinions about "Indians"; they had to perform a prescribed stereotype in order to do so, and agonized over their stymied agency. In this case, Bhabha's "almost-but-not-white" paradigm is not so straightforward; one might actually amend Bhabha's phrase to "authorized, but still not equal to white." Settlers feign tolerance while still demanding performances that reinforce a dynamic in which the performer is relatively powerless.

Mimicry – whether conceived of as performing "whiteness" or performing "Otherness" – ignores the possibility of genuine dialogue or an empathetic discovery of the Other. Mimicry is an emblem of political, social, and economic power in so far as its orchestrators force or tempt the Other to perform while remaining comfortably at a distance – so far, in fact, that they see no reason to question their definition of "authenticity" or to recognize it as an act of psychological violence. Self-definition, however, demands that the colonized be seen on their own terms and up close.

For Indigenous communities, self-defining within Canada has been a work in progress after centuries of cultural silencing. The concept of silence in feminism, as I explained it in my last chapter, corresponds in many ways to the concept of silence as a colonial affront to the colonized, and for Indigenous women these silences intersect. In Canada, the power to speak freely and self-define has historically been denied to Indigenous communities partly because of widespread assumptions about their "primitiveness." Critics like Kateri Akiwenzie-Damm (Anishinaabe) have explained the silencing of Indigenous peoples much more compassionately and sensibly. Akiwenzie-Damm points out that silence occurred in these communities not because they "had not yet learned how to write 'literature' or to use foreign art forms" but because Indigenous "artistic traditions had been banned, denigrated, and even outlawed" (170).[9] That is why Jeanette Armstrong (Syilx Okanagan) says it is erroneous to regard Indigenous literature as "'emergent'" (180): such literature may have only begun to reach a widespread audience in the late twentieth century, but its existence – written or oral – was never doubted within Indigenous communities.

Those communities, however, were constantly at risk of or subject to cultural devastation, especially during the era of the residential schools – the late nineteenth century until the late twentieth century – because these schools "forbade the use of original languages, did not actively teach English or writing or any other academic subject for that matter" (Maracle 78). The history of these schools has been well chronicled in recent years[10] and has revealed the degree to which literacy and language skills in Indigenous communities were catastrophically affected: children attending these schools were forcibly removed from their homes, were denied the right to speak their own language and even to learn English effectively, and were repeatedly, and violently, shamed or punished for practising their own culture at school.[11] The cultural damage wrought by the residential school system was compounded by numerous amendments to the Indian Act between 1884 and 1951, which limited Indigenous peoples' right to perform various ceremonies such as the potlatch, gather in groups (especially for any political purpose), fundraise, and obtain or make use of a lawyer. The function of these amendments was to ensure that any effort toward self-definition or political organization within Indigenous communities was minimalized, if not fully eliminated. Such circumstances ensured that, as LaRocque notes, there would be "an absence of Native presence in Canadian culture from the 1870s to the 1970s" (*WTOM* 15).

LaRocque observes some of the assumptions associated with silence, where settlers make silence synonymous with illiteracy, and "illiteracy is often associated with lack of literature, even lack of intelligence" ("Preface" xv). A representative example of these frameworks can be found in Donald Graham French and John Daniel Logan's *Highways of Canadian Literature* (1924): writing in praise of Johnson, they said that the "Indian people ... had been dumb or inarticulate" before her (202). "Johnson," they held, was "the 'Voice' of her inarticulate Indian fellows, but the voice itself was that of a woman cultured in the forms and music of English poetry" (198). In their view, Johnson began as "Indian" but "became Canadian" (202), and that transition accounts for her discovery of her own genius, because – again, in their thinking – there were almost no examples of "literary gifts" in "Indian" culture: "her taste for literature ... must have come from her mother's side" (198). French and Logan discount entirely the possibility of a literate or articulate voice from within an Indigenous society, and their claims for Johnson exemplify a common assumption among many non-Indigenous readers: silence was a symptom of "Indian" primitivism, which could be alleviated only through assimilation into English culture.[12]

These are examples of a concerted effort on the part of settlers to devalue Indigenous knowledge and literature, and the consequent silencing of those communities is something that Indigenous activists and writers have worked tirelessly to undo. Essential to understanding the poetry of Johnson and Crate is an elaboration on the efforts of Indigenous writers to pursue those goals, and so I want to dwell for a long moment on the Red Power movement. If my aim is to challenge the settler frameworks of other poets in this study (as well as my own), then I feel it is necessary to say more about what the centennial era looked like as an era of Red Power – even though, in this small space, my account of the era will hardly be comprehensive.

The Red Power movement hit its stride at a time when multiculturalism was becoming increasingly associated with Canada's public image. The promotion of that image was the job of numerous organizations such as the Centennial Commission. The commission's members believed that the centennial would help "build a stronger and more harmonious Canada" (*Handbook* 3), and so in 1964 they distributed a guide that declared the government's "widest encouragement of the fine arts" and the right of "*[e]very citizen* [...] *to participate*" in centennial celebrations (7); the guide's italicized text reveals how centrally this participation figured in the mindset of the organizers. After the centennial, the authors believed, Canada would enter its "second century of Confederation with a proud heart and in unity" (2). Similarly, the Canadian Centenary Council (est. 1960) sought to "reach as many Canadians as possible and to involve all of them in Centennial preparations" (Hanna 8), and the Canadian Interfaith Conference (CIC) undertook "every effort [...] to present Canada as a country where all faiths were equally welcome and given equal recognition in Canadian public life" (Miedema 202). While such gestures were relatively progressive, they were driven by naïve ideals of national unity. Gary Miedema notes, for instance, that the CIC emphasized the things that dominant religious groups "held in common" (e.g., single-deity religions), which "effectively excluded a number of faith groups from public life." In keeping with the sentiments Pierre Trudeau espoused after his election in 1968, centennial "public officials interpreted the inclusion of religious diversity in public life to mean the inclusion of those religious voices that would contribute to their vision of national unity, not endanger it" (204).

But that vision *was* endangered by the push for inclusion, because what Kristy A. Holmes calls the "politics of sameness" proved divisive (45). For example, the Expo 67 "Indian Pavilion" shocked visitors with its "written and pictorial indictment[s]" of colonialism (Miller and Rutherdale 161). Surprised by the organizers' rebellious message, Arthur Laing – then minister of the Department of Indian Affairs – fought to shut down the pavilion, but halted his efforts once he realized such measures would garner bad publicity.[13] This incident is evidence of Armand Garnet Ruffo's (Ojibway) recent argument that government funding for Indigenous-led initiatives was not intended to aid "self-determination"; the funding was an attempt to "civilize" and "assimilate" ("Where the Voice" 174).[14] And yet those attempts failed, because the government's support gave marginalized communities the means to contest social inequality and systemic racism.

By the 1960s, there was a strong base for Indigenous activists to expand their movement. Political groups were permitted to organize after the passage of amendments to the Indian Act in 1951; the Federation of Saskatchewan Indians (est. 1958), the National Indian Council (est. 1961), the National Indian Brotherhood (est. 1969), and the American Indian Movement (est. 1968) were among the best-known groups.[15] The 1966–7 Hawthorn Report made public many of the issues these groups confronted. Published under the editorial supervision of Harry Hawthorn, the two-volume *A Survey of the Contemporary Indians of Canada: Economic, Political, Educational Needs, and Policies* posited that the "[c]ontinuation of the present situation of internal colonialism is unacceptable" (292).[16] Rejecting "assimilation," Hawthorn proposed that "Indians should be regarded as 'citizens plus'; in addition to the normal rights and duties of citizenship, Indians possess certain additional rights as charter members of the Canadian community" (13). The report was "the first formal challenge to the longstanding and ineffectual federal policy of integration"; it promoted the "preserv[ation] and promot[ion]" of Indigenous cultures (Behiels 263).[17] The report also came at an ideal moment: it fanned the flames of a movement that was already underway after the end of the Second World War, at which point Indigenous peoples felt that, through their wartime efforts, "they had proven their right to speak for themselves" (Hoefnagels 236). While Hawthorn's report was revolutionary, there were also powerful voices from within Indigenous communities, some of whom observed the potential inherent in political intersections. An exemplary case is *Prison of Grass* (1975), in which Howard Adams (Métis) recalls that his "experiences in the black civil rights struggle and the Berkeley campus revolt" taught him "a great deal about civil disobedience" (177).

Deeply concerned about the political organization of Indigenous communities, Indian Affairs used Hawthorn's report as an opportunity to propose new federal policies, which led to the inauspiciously named White Paper (1969). The paper aggravated tensions between Red Power activists and the Trudeau government because it recommended "the gradual elimination of reserves" and "ignored the desire of Native peoples to retain their identities"; all Indigenous groups would be subject to "the jurisdiction of the provinces" without any federal assurances (Finkel 249).[18] This proposal led Harold Cardinal (Cree) to draw parallels between Red Power and the Quiet Revolution, specifically with regard to English-Canadian assimilation tactics: "It is difficult to envision any responsible Indian organization willing to participate in a proposal that [...] attempts to define and legislate Indians out of existence" (137).[19] In 1970, the Indian Chiefs of Alberta published a reply to the White Paper that used the title *Citizens Plus* as a clear nod to Hawthorn's report and demanded the preservation of Indigenous cultures: "What Indians asked that the Canadian Constitution be changed to remove any reference to Indians or Indian lands? [...] As representatives of our people we are pledged to continue our earnest efforts to preserve the hereditary and legal privileges of our people" (1–3).[20] Responding to overwhelming criticism, the Trudeau government withdrew the White Paper in 1971, the same year that it proposed an official policy of multiculturalism, which led to the Multiculturalism Act of 1988.[21] The proposal of the White Paper and the later endorsement of multiculturalism only further convinced Indigenous activists that there needed to be a rewriting of Canadian politics, history, and literature.

And if the White Paper hadn't been enough to encourage this re-writing, there was ample motivation in the field of history. Standard history texts say much about the institutionalized racism of Canada's education system. A particularly stunning example is *The Great Adventure* (1950), written by the Governor General's Award winner Donalda Dickie, who was a curriculum adviser and children's writer.[22] *The Great Adventure* was a stock textbook for many Canadian elementary schools until the 1960s. In it, Dickie writes very briefly of Indigenous communities, noting that their people "all looked more or less alike" (12). Even just that simple phrase teaches harmful lessons: her agglomerating "all" disregards national diversity among Indigenous groups; her suggestion that sameness defines "Indians" means that any person who looks *different* should not be considered "authentically" Indigenous; and the past-tense language shows her dismissal of contemporary Indigenous communities. This is how easily history and cultural definitions are mediated and controlled. If scholars did not reinforce stereotypes, they tended to say nothing at all; not one of the twenty chapters in George W. Brown and Edgar McInnis's major 1971 publication, *Canada*, deals with Indigenous peoples.

At the same time, this was also the era in which Indigenous authors challenged these standard approaches. Harold Cardinal published *The Unjust Society* (1969) as a direct response to Trudeau's White Paper and in it rejected Trudeau's popular notion of "the just society." Cardinal identified issues such as land claims, assimilation policies (what he calls at one point "the development of good Christian brown white men" [85]), residential schools, and the Indigenous political awakening of the 1950s and 1960s in order to make his audience see that Aboriginals "will not be silenced again" (162). That breaking of silence was well realized in Waubageshig's (Ojibway) edited collection of essays *The Only Good Indian* (1970), which was published with the intention of overturning long-standing assumptions about what constituted a "representative opinion from Canada's native people" ("Introduction" v). Several years later, Howard Adams published the polemical *Prison of Grass: Canada from the Native Point of View* (1975), in which he bluntly describes contemporary Canada as "a white racist society" (3) in which the government negotiates "with gunfire" (199) and the alleged "ugliness of things non-white deeply affects native people" (167). These books worked against the long-standing silencing of Indigenous perspectives on Canadian history and society, and what each author reveals in their own way is the importance of self-definition.

Some of the most spirited revolts of this sort took place in centennial-era literature. Although "mainstream trade or literary publishers" were unavailable to most, if not all, Indigenous writers during the centennial era, there was a flourishing Aboriginal magazine culture, and in these "newspapers, magazines, and tabloids" (Ruffo, "Where the Voice" 181) appeared numerous "occasional poets" (184).[23] Their poems offered progressive examples of an "autonomous authority" in poetic explorations of Indigenous life and history under a colonial power (186). As important as this poetry has been, it is widely accepted that the most groundbreaking publication of the era was actually Maria Campbell's *Halfbreed* (1973), an autobiography that continues to resonate with contemporary Indigenous historians and artists. Campbell's best-selling book was revelatory in its detailed account of what it was like to grow up as a Métis woman in Canada: she provided insight into the experience of residential schools, systemic prejudice against Indigenous peoples in Canadian society, and the epidemics of suicide, drug abuse, alcoholism, poverty, and depression that have beset Indigenous communities since colonial contact.

This literature – and the Red Power movement more generally – shared with many other political movements of this era what Myrna Kostash calls the "cross-fertiliz[ation]" of decolonizing idioms among movements such as Black Power, the New Left, and so on (154). As "a political project," decolonization meant "more than merely achieving political independence." It "symbolized a rejection of a habit of passive submission to society's dictates, demanded a democratization of market forces, mobilized poetry and cinema, liberated sexuality, and led to a search for an entirely new way of living and thinking" (Mills 151). While the rhetoric of decolonization permeated Canadian books, television, and radio, there was also political collaboration: various national and international decolonization movements interacted with one another and shared their political philosophies. The Black Panthers, for example, visited Montreal and Halifax in 1968 to raise awareness about the US civil rights movement (Kostash 149; see also Palmer 356). The Black Panthers did not reserve these visits exclusively for Black communities: "Black Panther spokesmen received a warm welcome among Native activists in the Canadian west, where they were embraced as fellow revolutionaries" (Palmer 400). The philosophies and politics of decolonization were ubiquitous.

Advocates of decolonization looked to the past for inspiration, which is why E. Pauline Johnson became a vital figure in the thinking of many writers who lived through or identified with the Red Power movement. Her appeal to later generations has to do with the fact that, unlike most poets writing in Canada, Johnson was internationally renowned and therefore able to spread to an enormous audience a message of tolerance and respect for Indigenous communities. The importance of that audience and voice should not be underestimated. Even if there were "a number of very fine Native writers by the later 1960s to the mid-1970s" (LaRocque, "Preface" xvi), it was difficult for them to find a wide audience. The magazines about which Ruffo writes had modest readerships,[24] and LaRocque notes that many Indigenous writers experienced "ghettoization," speaking primarily to each other ("Preface" xviii); first-rate Indigenous authors had virtually no "access to the publishing world" until the last half of the 1970s (xix). Johnson's audience and popularity were therefore remarkable. Her achievement is even more remarkable when one considers the nineteenth-century society in which she lived.

A tangled part of this history, however, is Johnson's on- and off-stage identities. Johnson gained overnight celebrity status in January 1892 after reading at an event with several prominent Confederation-era poets such as William Wilfred Campbell and Duncan Campbell Scott. She showed a natural ability to engage her audience; she was the only one of the readers to be called back for an encore. After that night, she became a headlining performer and toured from 1892 until 1910, often wearing an "Indian" costume for the first half of her performances and switching into an English-style evening dress for the last half. Whereas Johnson's Victorian outfit is an instance of performing "whiteness" as Bhabha would have it, her Indian costume indulged Victorian audiences' conception of the "authorized Other": it consisted of various items such as "fur pelts, Iroquois silver medallions, wampum belts, and her father's hunting knife," and she later added "a necklace of bear claws" and a "Sioux scalp," among other decorations (Gerson and Strong-Boag, *Paddling* 110). Like Johnson's costumes, her poetry represented opposing identities: some of her poems boldly condemned the colonial theft of land that "Indians" owned "[b]y right, by birth" ("A Cry from an Indian Wife" 15), questioned the will of "the white man's God" ("A Cry from an Indian Wife" 15), and demanded that colonialists "Give back our land and our country" ("The Cattle Thief" 99). Other poems, however, celebrated "old England's throne" as a power that "serve[s] her subjects best" ("For Queen and Country: May 24th" 59).

More complex still is the fact that Johnson "shared many of the racial attitudes of her day" (Fee and Nason 17). She drew, for instance, on stereotypical motifs such as "the vanishing race" and the "noble savage" in her poems and essays: images such as a "waning nation" ("The Re-Interment of Red Jacket" 11) and a warrior calling out with a "savage eloquence" ("The Death-Cry" 32) are not uncommon in her writing – nor are sweeping generalizations about "Indians," such as her note that "No Indian man ever asked or permitted his womankind" to do farm work as Eastern European women did in the "Canadian North West" ("The Stings of Civilization" 283–4).[25] Her ambivalent performances and writing did not hurt her reputation during her lifetime.[26] Late twentieth-century critics like George Lyon, however, would unsympathetically accuse her of appearing "politically incoherent" (144), and from Johnson's death in 1913 until the end of the twentieth century she was continually subjected to similarly hostile preconceptions about women, romantic writers, and Aboriginals.[27] Her various self-representations have given readers plenty of angles from which to argue selective interpretations that distort or reduce her legacy, and the enormous gaps in knowledge about her own political or moral philosophies have led others to take creative leaps in explaining her core beliefs – working from the problematic assumption, of course, that one has static core beliefs.

Until recently, most scholars upheld a traditional portrayal of Johnson as a conservative poet and maudlin Canadian nationalist. In 1981, Betty Keller was the first to remark on the ways in which earlier editors and writers had constructed that portrayal. Keller argued that most of what had been written on Johnson amounted to "misrepresentations" and "fairy tale[s]" (*Pauline* 2), especially in Mrs W. Garland Foster's biography of Johnson, *The Mohawk Princess* (1931). One of the "fairy tales" of Foster's biography is the romantic Canadian nationalism into which she tirelessly folds Johnson: "she laid the whole of her genius at the service of her country [Canada]" (154). Foster disregards the rebelliousness of Johnson's writing, preferring instead to create an inoffensive image of a dedicated Canadian nationalist whose works united Indigenous groups with British-descended Canadians.

Foster is so eager to slot Johnson into this skewed, romantic legacy that she concludes her study by publishing a series of letters evidently intended to deepen the reader's sense that Johnson had been a true Canadian patriot. It's a remarkable story about Johnson's unusual connection to the Great War: after her death, Johnson left her sister just over two hundred dollars, which her sister passed on to a respected editor, John Nelson, "with the suggestion that [the money] be devoted to some purpose which would be in keeping with Pauline's ideas" (156). At first, Nelson considered using the money to support Vancouver General Hospital by funding medical services for artists. When that plan proved too complicated, he decided on what he thought to be an even more fitting tribute: he used the money to buy a machine gun. The gun would eventually carry the dutiful inscription "Tekahionwake" on its side and would be sent to the front lines during the latter half of the First World War (159). This was what Nelson believed would be "in keeping with Pauline's ideas," despite the fact that some of her most famous poems, such as "A Cry from an Indian Wife" (1885), carry distinctly anti-war sentiments and that her father was shot in 1873 by one of six men who brutally beat him – not to mention the disturbing colonial history inherent in the production and trade of firearms. The fate of Johnson's bequest shows the degree to which supporters and readers made Johnson's personhood a contortionist's act: she was wrenched to fit into frameworks that appealed to, as in the case of Nelson and Foster, a romantic nationalism without any apparent acknowledgment of the many denotations and subtexts in her poetry that disclosed her distrust of such cultural chauvinism.

These perverse postmortems on Johnson's "ideas" affected her reception among later literary critics. Her editorial construction has been appalling. Until the late twentieth century, Johnson seemed unimportant to non-Indigenous editors.[28] If they were able to spell her name correctly – Edward S. Caswell names her "John*st*on" in his *Canadian Singers and Their Songs* (1919) – then editors tended to take one of three approaches to her work: they represented her as the embodiment of successful assimilation (the "Indian" turned English), portrayed her as a superficial romantic (the sentimental poet), or decided against representing her at all.[29] A.J.M. Smith included one poem by her in *The Book of Canadian Poetry* (1943), but he was, to put it mildly, unenthusiastic about her work; in his 1943 introduction, he says that her poems "are as empty of content as any devotee of pure poetry could wish" (21).[30] Smith was writing as a modernist critic, and modernism, in his conception of it, distinguished itself from poetry that centred on local and lyrical experience; this was the basis for his famous distinction between "native" (i.e., writing that potentially limits its impact by focusing on the local) and "cosmopolitan" (i.e., a literature that escapes the local and enters "into the universal, civilizing culture of ideas" [*Book of Canadian Poetry* 5]). Given Smith's effort to encourage his co-editors (namely, F.R. Scott) to include Dorothy Livesay in their groundbreaking 1936 anthology *New Provinces*, I can't say for certain that Johnson's gender further reduced her stature in Smith's eyes.[31] He did, however, consider Indigenous poetry "primitive" (*Book of Canadian Poetry* 35), and so his antagonism toward Johnson's poetry was fuelled at least by assumptions about both her romanticism and ethnicity. His attitude was characteristic of many modernist editors such as Desmond Pacey and Earle Birney, the latter of whom was infamously unkind toward Johnson's poetry, remarking once that he didn't read her.[32] Johnson's appeal, as a talented poet and an Indigenous woman who publicly critiqued colonialism, was lost entirely on these editors.[33]

One of the key concerns in the editorial construction of Johnson since the 1950s has been the authenticity of her identity. In some cases, Johnson risked seeming "too Indian" for some audiences (hence French and Logan's effort to portray her as a poet assimilated into English Canada). In other cases, she was not "Indian" enough: in *The Evolution of Canadian Literature: 1867–1914* (1973), Paul Denham, Mary-Jane Edwards, and George Parker claimed that Johnson's "life and works seem less typical today of a Canadian Indian" (191). That kind of comment epitomizes a trope in colonial discourses that implies an identity can be authenticated through testable particularities: a name, skin colour, style of writing, social performance, or any other arbitrary characteristic. If one "fails" these tests, then they are, in the eyes of settlers, "inauthentic."

My point in perusing this biographical and editorial history is to show just how negotiated and distorted Johnson's identity and reputation were by the 1980s, when Crate began writing her poems, a time at which critics began to notice that Johnson was "fast disappearing from anthologies" (Harry 152). For some centennial-era Indigenous readers and writers, it was important to prevent that disappearance and to take the historical figure of Johnson out of the hands of non-Indigenous editors, scholars, and writers who were working within colonial frameworks. While Johnson is not universally celebrated among Indigenous scholars,[34] many regard her as living proof that the silence settler societies have historically imposed on Indigenous communities can be overcome.

Johnson's influence on younger writers was, as I suggested earlier, intersectional: writers like Beth Brant (Mohawk) note that Johnson "drew a map for *all* women to follow" by contesting social norms of the Victorian era as a powerful female performer (7, emphasis added) and by serving as "a spiritual grandmother" specifically to female Indigenous writers (5). Brant's intersectional reading parallels the impressions of non-Indigenous writers such as Atwood, who said that Johnson's "The Pilot of the Plains" (1912) had an influence on her own conception of strong women in literature.[35] Ruffo recently expanded on Brant's statement and claimed Johnson as "the spiritual grandmother to all Native writers" ("Introduction" xxx).[36] What Ruffo and Brant express is born partly out of a widespread sentiment among Indigenous writers since the 1970s: just as non-Indigenous feminist writers were looking for foremothers, Indigenous writers, especially women, "needed to hear the words of Aboriginal women in order to understand this country, its history, and its present" (Perreault and Vance xii).

Sympathetic recoveries of her work thus portray Johnson as the figure who "began a movement that has proved unstoppable in its momentum" (a movement marked by its unsilencing of "First Nations women" [Brant 5]) and, in more general ways, as a "staunch defender of Indian actions and rights" (LaRocque, *WTOM* 122). These reflections offer the means to counter Johnson's legacy in the context of romantic nationalism: her literary fame modelled some of the potential of Indigenous artists, her career demonstrated possibilities to Indigenous and non-Indigenous female writers, and her "staunch" defence of "Indian actions and rights" spoke to the nationalism underlying the Red Power movement and other like-minded initiatives. I argued earlier that Atwood was drawn to Moodie because she appealed to Atwood's literary, political, and nationalist sensibilities; Johnson has been an analogously vital foremother in the imaginations of writers like Ruffo, Brant, LaRocque, and Crate. Few, if any, of these reclamations of Johnson, however, portray her career as an unqualified triumph over colonial silencing; she is, in the words of LaRocque, one of "the most interesting examples of the colonized adopting or internalizing colonizer terms and images" (*WTOM* 122).[37] Johnson was surely a stymied revolutionary.

An oft-discussed aspect of this ambiguous image is Johnson's "Indian costume." Scholars have interpreted the significance of this costume, and Johnson's performances generally, in wildly different ways. Daniel Francis argues that her costume was evidence of her "capitaliz[ing]" (127) on common stereotypes of "Indians" and that her general "pandering" to white audiences "limited her effectiveness as a spokesperson for Native people" (132). Rick Monture (Mohawk) goes further and raises the possibility that her costume change midway through numerous performances, from "Mohawk Tekahionwake to the Victorian Pauline," might actually imply "that all Native people would simply be better off if they would just adapt to Euro-Canadian ways like the poet" ("Beneath" 129) – a symbolic act of assimilation performed on stage to win her audiences' favour.[38] Carole Gerson and Veronica Strong-Boag, alternatively, read her costume as subversive: "Johnson seemed to ... contribute to the homogenization of the Native in modern culture. However, this strategy may well have enhanced her political positioning. By claiming the universal Indian subject, her dramatic persona effectively engaged with the whole history of imperialism in North America. ... Johnson played 'the trickster,' carefully manipulating her audiences" ("Championing" 50). To me, this claim seems dubious and it also draws too readily for my comfort on the "trickster" trope used often in scholarship on Indigenous writing.[39] Gerson and Strong-Boag's argument for such heroism in Johnson's on-stage performance makes sense in so far as it evidences a sympathetic effort, but their argument is ultimately more wishful than realistic: there is no evidence to suggest that Johnson used her costume strategically, at least not in the way Gerson and Strong-Boag imagine. LaRocque's assessment rings truest to me: "I would like to think she engaged in subversive mimicry, but I do not think these are sufficient explanations. ... In order for her to have an audience, she had to acquiesce to dominant requirements" (*WTOM* 124–5).[40] Johnson's writing, LaRocque points out, is comparably ambiguous: "Johnson had internalized White stereotypes of 'Indians.' ... It may, in part, be that she took to poetic licence, or that given the political climate, she had little choice but to latch onto popular stereotypes to gain an audience" (123–4).

Johnson knew well this pressure to perform. When her friend Harry O'Brien accused her of "debasing herself in her recitals" by performing a disingenuous identity and unskilled poetry (Keller, *Pauline* 71), she was initially defensive, but she later confessed to him in February 1894, "I hate and despise brain debasement, literary 'pot-boiling' and yet I have done, will do these things, though I sneer at my own littleness in so doing. ... Ye Gods, how I hate [the audience's] laughter at times, when such laughter is called forth by some of my brainless lines and business. I could do so much better if they would only let me" (qtd Keller 72). Later that year, in September, she wrote another letter to O'Brien and resentfully recollected performances in which she had "laughter on [her] face and tears in [her] heart" (qtd S. Johnston 126). These were the performances that made Johnson feel, in her words, like "the mere doll of the people and slave to money" (qtd S. Johnston 126). Johnson was hardly oblivious: she wanted to be a better poet and to "sing the glories of [her] own people" (qtd Seton 6), but she was constantly negotiating "the options available to her to produce and refine a particular standpoint while also trying to earn a living in a society full of prejudice against independent women and those marked as racially Other" (Fee and Nason 17). And yet, she could just as easily write lines that deny both her gender and Indigenous heritage: "we, the men of Canada, can face the world and brag / That we were born in Canada beneath the British flag" ("Canadian Born" 125). These lines are from the title poem of Johnson's second book of poetry, which she published almost ten years after she had written O'Brien about her longing to do better. Even at that point in her career, she was still (it seems) writing verses to meet her audience's expectations.[41]

Critics have long debated what kept Johnson working within these conventions: it may have been the appeal of "the limelight" (York, *Literary Celebrity* 44), the impossibility of breaking "long established role[s]" for Indigenous women (Lyon 140), the nationalistic urge to "write down [Indigenous] stories of history" to whatever degree was possible (Brant 5), the emboldening feeling that came from those occasions when she "'talked back' to the dominant culture" (Gerson and Strong-Boag 3), the necessity of earning money to publish her poetry (see Keller's biography), or the feeling of responsibility to spread a message of tolerance that would "ensure her people survived the transition to modernity" (Collett 160). Some of these explanations are inspiring; some are reductive. None is definitive. But whatever her reasons for performing (a debate I doubt anyone can resolve), she did so in ways that have befogged her intentions and beliefs and offered an unsettling example of the kind of "co-opted" performances engendered through colonialism.

Of course, performance is as much a social issue as a theatrical one, and this parallelism is one on which Crate remarks in representing Johnson's life. In Crate's "The Party" (*PARL* 36–7), Johnson's brother Allen hosts a private gathering at his home and wears "[b]eads," "feathers," and a "scalp" in front of "[t]he boss's daughter." The daughter, horrified, exits the party, and Allen is "fired / from his white collar job at the bank."[42] More than a biographical account, the poem is a study in unauthorized performances. When Allen replaces his "flannel suit" and "white collar" with the clothes of "an Indian," he is punished; his transformation inspires revulsion and fear in those who exercise formal power over him. Allen's punishment is exclusion, but Johnson's father, George Johnson, suffers much more violent retribution in "The Death of My Father" (*PARL* 31–2): a "lead ball that broke both jaws," "crushed ... ribs," a gunshot. These events happened: non-Indigenous locals attacked Johnson's father in retaliation for his efforts to control whiskey in his community and to protect his people from settlers thieving their timber. George's later death left his family in poverty. Both poems, like the true events on which they are based, portray the consequences of saying the wrong words or performing the wrong role – the risks, in other words, of being the unauthorized Other.

Johnson herself understood very well the ways in which stage performances had much in common with social ones. In 1892, she published an essay in the *Toronto Sunday Globe*, in which she stressed that even as communities share "peculiar characteristics ... it scarcely follows that every individual of a nation must possess these prescribed singularities, or otherwise forfeit in the eyes of the world their nationality" ("Strong Race" 177). She would later publish another essay that stresses the damage of performance on especially the Indigenous mother, whose "entire code of existence must be shattered" and who "must teach [her son] to go the wrong way according to her standards." To do otherwise, Johnson says, would ensure that "her child will fail in the race with civilization" ("The Stings" 284). The politics of performance, as well as the implicit power structure behind those politics, are a legacy of colonialism, a legacy made more obvious to Canadians by investigations into its lingering impact: since 2001, the "Where Are the Children?" campaign has collected interviews with residential school survivors like Lorna Rope (Nakota), who said in 2013 that she lived without her own identity until "about 5 or 6 years ago." Before that, she says, "I would never admit to be a First Nations person" (Rope). The outpouring of Indigenous memoirs, interviews, and testimonies that have appeared in and outside of Canada since Campbell published *Half-Breed* supports Bonita Lawrence's (Mi'kmaw) recent assertion that questions about personal and collective identity are "much larger than that of personal or even group identity – [they go] directly to the heart of the colonization process and to the genocidal policies of settler governments across the Americas toward Indigenous peoples" (16). This deep-rooted racism is not just a part of a past of which many Canadians have been unaware, or, worse, to which they have been indifferent. It is part of Canada today and affects not just Indigenous communities: a study conducted in 2016 by the Angus Reid Institute and CBC showed that 68 per cent of Canadians "said minorities should be doing more to fit in with mainstream society instead of keeping their own customs and languages" (Proctor).

Crate's poems address these issues by situating Johnson within that culture of silence and mimicry and by retrieving a perspective that is simultaneously past and present; yet, Crate raises doubts about her own portrayal of Johnson precisely because of that temporal conflation. Some of that doubt surfaces in "Prairie Greyhound" (*PARL* n.p.), which is partly a self-reflection addressed directly to Johnson:

> I write poems for you. I re-invent you. It is not your words I want, your books of verse, your stories and legends. It is the sound of your voice, your breath cool on my cheek, your insistent geniality, your travel, your toughness, your pretense. And your loneliness, your stretched-thin days, desolation, illness, suffering. Your death.

I have stressed in other chapters the idea that the absence of sound painfully captures the unavailability of the past to the present, and that motif recurs here. It is understandable that sound is what Crate's persona desires. The writer Janet Marie Rogers (Mohawk) expresses an identical yearning in the brief prose piece "Pauline Passed Here" (2014): "I want [Johnson's] voice in my ear" (39). The desire for closeness is one that neither Crate nor Rogers can possibly fulfil, and so the dramatic lyric is (as it was for Atwood) a sensible mode to adopt: it brings, even if in somewhat illusory ways, both Crate and her audience closer to Johnson's voice. At the same time, Crate's first-person pronouns undermine any possibility of mistaking this reclamation for an objective rendering since it is clearly her persona speaking: "I write," "I re-invent," "I want." This is Crate's personal "re-invent[ion]" of Johnson, and so the identity that she recovers may conflate her self with that of Johnson. I would imagine that is why when Crate's persona "reach[es] for [Johnson's] face," she only "scratch[es]" the "glass" of the Greyhound window. At times, Crate seems distant from and close to Johnson.

Johnson's self-censored performances make that distance feel more acute, as in "The Poetry Reading" (*PARL* 18–19), which begins with Johnson on stage, promising to tell her audience a story:

> Tonight let me tell you of
> a world swallowed in one quick gulp
> with only crumbs remaining,
> while in one stale memory-corner
> a small girl shivers on the steps
> of a tar-paper shack.
> Her daydreams are bruises behind her eyes,
> oozing songs of suicide
> children mouth in her unfinished womb.

Johnson vows to use her stage presence to educate her audience on the negative impact European contact has had on Indigenous communities. Atwood's Moodie will not be "ploughed under" (*JSM* 64), and Crate's Johnson is similarly rebellious: "I will not return to silence. / Do you hear me?" Yet Crate's lines are hardly unambiguous as obdurate avowals. They depend on the reader's emphasis: the last line might be read assertively ("do *you hear* me?") or it might connote a vulnerable moment of hesitation ("*do* you hear me?"). She might be insisting on evidence that her interlocutor has understood or she might be unsure she has anyone's ear. Whether or not Johnson can fully embrace her revolutionary temperament is always ambiguous in Crate's poems.

This ambiguity plays out more evocatively in the latter half of the poem, when Johnson locks eyes with a "[p]owdered woman in the first row." This woman is as much a performer as Johnson: her make-up, first-row status, and consumption of entertainment all point to her wealth and class. But her powdered face and "plucked eyebrows" suggest that "pale ladies" are not, despite the title of the book, so easily categorized as real. It is an interesting scene: both women are performers, and readers can safely infer that, to varying degrees of course, both roles do harm to each individual's sense of agency in a colonial and patriarchal society.

And yet there is no camaraderie here. Even if the powdered woman's performance denotes her own painful conformity, the scene nevertheless also shows her willingness to use that role to exercise power over Johnson; she invites Johnson into her own performance by asking her from the audience, "will you have tea now?" Tea, of course, is an appropriate symbol here: Britain's seventeenth-century merchant tea trade is a standard study in colonial exploitation. In this particular scene, the woman's offer of tea is itself exploitive, because her invitation is her entertainment. Johnson does, after all, comply from the stage. She never descends from it to meet the powdered woman as an equal. The poem ends with a fuller expression of this power dynamic through images of Johnson's commodification:

> You dust biscuit from the corner
> of your mouth, and I remain
> onstage in front of you.
> I stare at the pelts
> Hanging from my shoulder,
> and sip from fine bone china.

The scene complements Crate's opening to the poem, in which Johnson envisions an entire "world" consumed: there are "only crumbs remaining," and a "bruise[d]" child occupies a "corner" of people's minds. In the excerpt above, that scope has shrunk from a metaphorical ravenousness that defines generations since European contact to a focus on the powdered woman, who gobbles down a biscuit and unknowingly leaves crumbs in the corner of her mouth. The enjambed line, "of your mouth, and I remain," is striking: the crumbs linger at the corner of the woman's mouth, and Johnson lingers on stage, her self consumed as though she were, too, edible. (Relatedly, I remember Crate telling me that she first encountered Johnson as a picture on a box of Vancouver-made chocolates [Letter from Crate to Weingarten]).[43] Crate's poem, like her memory, exemplifies colonial commodification.

Performing to satisfy her audience, Johnson cannot uphold her earlier vow (that she will not "return to silence"). The final image of her sipping tea is, in fact, a moment of silence, her mouth muzzled by the luxurious mug forced onto her by the powdered woman. The poem is admittedly unnerving because it simultaneously emphasizes Johnson's powerful presence and then undercuts that emphasis by showing Johnson's acquiescence (to redeploy LaRocque's term). It's a difficult scene. The poem both heroically memorializes Johnson and marks the limits of her heroism. This is the conundrum of an authorized Other.

The contrasting sections of a later poem, "The Naming" (*PARL* 39–41), present a more overt example of this ambiguity. At the beginning of the poem Johnson rebelliously rejects the name "Emily Pauline" and calls herself Tekahionwake after her great-grandfather, but by the end of the poem she appears to offer up her agency to her audience:

Bill me as the Mohawk Princess.
Exhibit me buckskinned on a platform,
chanting, my skin bitten
by teeth, quills, clawed.
To have you hear my voice,
I will turn any trick at all.

Johnson's publicist Frank Yeigh came up with the name "The Mohawk Princess" as a promotional strategy, and it was also Yeigh who pushed her to wear an Indian costume in her performances (hence the imperatives, "[b]ill me" and "[e]xhibit me"). The name stuck, its endurance assured after Johnson's death when Mrs W. Garland Foster used it as the title of her 1931 biography. According to Betty Keller, Johnson approved of the name (*Pauline* 20), but the sincerity of her consent is impossible to know, and the letters I introduced earlier prove that Johnson had many secret misgivings about her public persona that likely extended to include her name and dress. I offer this context because Crate implies Johnson's involuntary performance, and this portrayal is to me much more meaningful than the wishful image of contrapuntal performance that Gerson and Strong-Boag describe when they argue that Johnson "manipulat[ed] her audience" to "enhance" her "political positioning." The problem with Gerson and Strong-Boag's well-intentioned claim is that it downplays a more nuanced (and more likely) interpretation, which Crate proposes: Johnson's contradictory performances capture the many ways in which her poetics, self-representation, and politics were stifled and coercively guided by Yeigh and others.

That claim is not an attempt to reduce Johnson to a "victim." While I agree with Myra Rutherdale and Katie Pickles, who have stressed the importance of "mov[ing] beyond viewing either Aboriginal or white women as passive victims" (5), it is still important to appreciate that not every courageous act has an ideal outcome. Johnson was not "passive": she supported herself financially, maintained a public life, enjoyed a prosperous career as a poet and performer, and even occasionally altered her audience's perception of Indigenous peoples and causes in Canada.[44] Those qualities of her historical self have had an immeasurable impact on writers in Canada and abroad. Still, Johnson's letters to Harry O'Brien also indicate that she was vividly aware of the ways in which the expectations of her era hindered her ability to self-define, and I therefore worry that exaggerated claims about Johnson's naming, costuming, and private or public performances mask potentially edifying, if unsettling, questions about silence and performance still pertinent to Indigenous communities. To tie this back to Crate's poems, appreciating Johnson's courage does not relieve the poet from acknowledging that there were many moments in Johnson's life when speaking was still paradoxically a kind of silence. "The Naming" epitomizes that disconcerting conclusion.

So does "I Am a Prophet" (*PARL* 59–60), the poem that concludes Part I of *Pale as Real Ladies* and that is, in the words of Tanis MacDonald, a "grisly" (176) and "disturbing" poem (177). The poem begins with the speaker having been "chosen by Tyee / to tell of the beginning," but it turns slowly into a performance with distressingly erotic overtones:

> My feet tell the story of the lost tribes
> who wandered in their own darkness.
> When they reached the Promised Land
> they did not know it, but fell
> down its wet, green gullet,
> emerged as ravens, whales, eagles.
> You may see their names written across my toes
> for just one dollar.
>
> But wait!
> There is more. Here, along
> my thighs are the virgin births.

The cultural pride Johnson feels at the outset of the poem devolves into a perverse infomercial ("But wait! / There is more"), and then Johnson's marketing of her body actually overshadows the stories with which she has been entrusted. The stories won't hold her audience, so she resorts to using her body to regain their attention. The invitations become increasingly desperate. She invites her audience to look at her breasts, to "kiss" her body, to buy her "a drink," to pay ten dollars to see "every scar" on her body. For twenty dollars, she finally offers, "you can make your own [scars]."

Johnson's scarred body is a devastating image. Before discovering Crate's poetry, I had always imagined scars as proof of the past, as invitations into stories or *aide-memoires*. When Odysseus returns from the Trojan Wars, the scar above his knee – a memento from a boar during a hunt with his grandfather Autolycus – proves his identity to his former wet-nurse, Eurycleia. His scar is his identity, a testament to his entrance into manhood and to painful lessons from which he has gained wisdom and strength. If a scar is a part of our individual story, as it was for Odysseus, then what story accompanies scars inflicted for entertainment? Crate's Johnson performs in order to avoid the physical violence inflicted on unauthorized Others, and yet here is a poem in which performance is physical violence: it obliges the performer to follow a script of dress, gestures, and expressions written by someone else.

Arguably, "I Am a Prophet" is something of a thought experiment: what if the psychological trauma of performance could be represented as physical trauma? Would the audience then better understand its lasting impact? Intangible psychological scars, like a scar above the knee, signify stories, and Johnson's story (at least, this particular aspect of it) does not mark the liberating growth that Odysseus's story does. Her scar instead invites readers into a story about oppression and commodification. The inherent violence of such acts is evident in Johnson's performances of either Victorian "whiteness" (e.g., Johnson's evening gown) or authorized otherness (e.g., the "pelts hanging" from her "shoulder" and her label of "Mohawk Princess"). Johnson wrote once that "it is not always the great scars that hurt the most, some of the lesser customs of the Whitemen wound ... vitally" ("The Stings" 286). There is something of that in Crate's poem, in which Johnson's audience is as likely to dismiss her as they are to consume or scar her.

What should readers make, then, of Crate's title, "I am a Prophet"? It carries the suggestion that the poem is, itself, a prophecy: Johnson's experience foretells the future experiences of her descendants, and MacDonald agrees that the "prophecy of the poem is undeniably a warning about the future" (177). That reading is in line with Crate's prologue, in which her persona is heckled on the bus in the present, just as Johnson was sometimes heckled on the stage in the past. Yet I am uncomfortable with the assumption that Crate's poem can be reduced to a "warning" for Indigenous readers, because it seems perverse to task a victimized readership with action. Crate's poem is also – perhaps even primarily – a warning to non-Indigenous readers, reminding them that the spectacle they observe in the poem is one in which they may be historically complicit and of which they should be aware. It is a fitting, if unsettling, end to Part I that shows Johnson coming up against her era and experiencing moments of both empowerment and oppression.

The tone of Part II is very different. Whereas the epigraph in Part I is somewhat deferential and self-censoring, the epigraph that begins Part II shows Johnson listening to a "history" that "unwinds" and allows her to "climb words back to a beginning" (62). Five poems that reimagine several Indigenous stories then follow: "Beaver Woman," "Blue Sky how you won your wife," "Woman who married a ghost," "Wife of Son of the Sea," and "Siwash Rock." The movement here is not forward into a sphere of performance (as in Part I) but back to a set of stories that are, for Johnson/Crate, only the "beginning" of a new exploration of an individual identity and its ties to a larger community. Lee Briscoe Thompson finds this section affirming, as the poems "seem to suggest, by the potency of their narratives and the vibrancy of their imagery, that Pauline's Mohawk heritage will have the last word" (130). Thompson's reading mostly aligns with my own in so far as I also read these five poems as Johnson's exploration and assertion of her Indigenous heritage as imagined by Crate.

But Thompson's claim that these are Mohawk stories is actually inaccurate. Crate drew from different traditions to write Part II: "Siwash Rock," for instance, recognizably descends from Johnson's *Legends of Vancouver* (which includes the story "The Siwash Rock") and has roots in the Squamish tradition, whereas "Wife of Son of the Sea" appears to be Crate's interpretation of the Samish story of "The Woman Who Married the Sea." For Crate to end with these stories is chronologically appropriate, as the poems symbolize a late period in Johnson's actual life when she was living in Vancouver and learning some of these stories from Chief Joe Capilano (Squamish). One key difference, though: Johnson's *Legends* foreground her perspective as a listener to Chief Capilano's stories, whereas Part II of *Pale as Real Ladies* is told from a lyrical perspective (I presume Johnson's) as she navigates a series of dream-like scenes.

That portrayal of Johnson raises a concern: whereas Johnson explicitly attributes the stories she includes in *Legends of Vancouver* to Chief Joe Capilano (she had, in fact, wanted to call the book *The Legends of the Capilano*, but her publishers rejected the title), Crate's poems contain no such reference, and in the absence of attribution, Crate's decision to include and alter the content of these stories is problematic. I am highlighting this concern because the last few decades of

Canadian criticism and postcolonial theory have generated thoughtful conversations about the ethics of storytelling, and those discussions have heightened critics' sensitivity toward the safe handling of Indigenous stories, given what readers should now know about cultural appropriation. In the absence of acknowledged sources, Crate risks having these stories misattributed (e.g., Thompson's note that these are "Mohawk" stories) and risks, too, more general criticisms about her use of stories that may be considered the property of a particular storyteller or community.

These issues are made more complex by Crate's "ambiguous and highly negotiated" identity and her complicated reputation among some Indigenous writers (MacDonald 179). Crate made no mention in her first two books of poetry (*Pale as Real Ladies* and *Foreign Homes*) of her heritage, and this has partly led "some Indigenous authors [to] believe that Crate is not Indigenous enough to be rewriting the subjectivities and voices of First Nations women" (MacDonald 179). MacDonald challenges those assessments by arguing that centuries of assimilation tactics and genocide have resulted in complex reactions to the "suppressed, disconnected, or historically denigrated racial backgrounds of people living in Canada at the beginning of the twenty-first century," reactions that include "mut[ing] or in some cases even hid[ing] their heritage" (180). Marilyn Dumont usefully explains, too, that one must add nuance to models of "traditional experience in native culture": "some of us have been more exposed to [that experience] than others," and that, she writes, "is one experience of nativeness and there is a multiplicity of experiences out there" (49). As a non-Indigenous scholar, I want to be as mindful of that multiplicity as possible, and that leads me to consider Crate's personal history: even though her "father's influence ensured a strong cultural connection," her immediate family was entirely cut off, socially and geographically, from almost all other relations (Letter from Crate to Weingarten).

Whereas MacDonald uses those contexts to understand Crate's adoption of Johnson's "I," those personal circumstances also help readers understand Crate's early interpretation of the relationship between stories and Indigenous communities. An additional point to consider is that Crate studied literature at the University of Calgary, where she was taught that poets could freely take creative liberties with stories (a Western model of creativity against which Margery Fee persuasively writes)[45] and that too much self-reflexivity (i.e., positioning and attribution) in a text risks conflating a creative work with an academic one. With the benefit of hindsight, Crate now feels very differently about her decision to incorporate these stories into her work. "Knowing now what I didn't know then [about the importance of stories as property]," she says:

> I would have reconsidered using those stories or at least added an afterword to *Pale as Real Ladies* to give a clearer record of where the stories came from. At the time, it seemed too 'academic' to do that kind of thing and I had come across many of these stories in books without fully understanding at that point in my life what it might mean to some communities to have me rewrite them or share them. (Telephone interview)

In trying to understand and give voice to Crate's perspective on her creative choices, I do not mean to dismiss valid critical concerns. I can appreciate, though, that Crate's first effort to reconnect with a broad set of Indigenous communities was done independently. As part of that discovery, she wrote Johnson's life and incorporated various stories into her poems in order, she hoped, to overturn the degrading portrayal of Johnson that she encountered during her time at the University of Calgary (Letter from Crate to Weingarten). She thus uses these final poems to show that, after a lifelong effort to negotiate multiple and conflicting identities, Johnson gains "the ability to transcend her era and be a voice in the landscape of sacred stories" (Letter from Crate to Weingarten); in acknowledging the critical challenges of reading Part II, I do not want to detract from Crate's powerful rendering of that voice.

Crate's poems imagine Johnson living within and outside of the stories she tells. Sometimes, she speaks at a distance ("Young woman cleaning salmon on a rock / counts her silvery selves multiplied on scales" ["Wife of Son of the Sea" 68]) and at other times she has somehow become a character in stories as they unfold ("lost lover / come home, come home to me" ["Siwash Rock" 69]). That tidal mode potentially risks appearing as a lyrical incongruity in Crate's book; the movement in and out of stories contrasts with the consistently foregrounded "I" in Part I. In a section, though, that constructs an image of a liberated Johnson, this ghostly movement is a logical contrast to her manacled performances in Part I; it also parallels the heroic image of Atwood's ghostly Moodie rebelliously bursting through the ground at the end of *The Journals of Susanna Moodie*. That analysis is double-edged, because, like Moodie, Johnson achieves freedom and agency only in death. Still, these literal deaths can be optimistically read as figurative transformations: the death of one self and the birth of another, or the abandonment of one world in which the individual is fettered in exchange for another. This reading aligns well with some interpretations of Johnson's retirement in 1909 from stage performances and the time she spent as friends with Chief Joe Capilano, which was surely a period of "rebirth" for Johnson in some respects.

It seems odd, though, that Crate would counter this hopeful act of discovery with a destructive one. Her ominous sixth poem, "My brother saw the first sailing ship" (*PARL* 70) dreamily portrays European contact:

> I look into a piece of the moon
> and see the dirty smudge of my reflection.
> I fling it over water, watch it spin
> the sky, glinting cloud
> and hawk wings plucked suddenly
> by the pale hand that catches it –
> tin plate –
> tearing the moon from sky.

Up until this moment in Part II, the speaker has said nothing of her skin colour. It is not until she witnesses a "pale hand" reaching to ravage the land – it "pluck[s]" "hawk wings" and "tear[s] the moon from sky" – that she suddenly remarks in a disparaging way on her own appearance. Racial binaries only occur to the speaker after she encounters Europeans; she has seen herself through the colonizer's eyes. Then comes an ambiguous finale to Crate's collection. The last lines, quoted above, might be extensions of Crate's insistence on the speaker's full agency: she has, perhaps, "fl[u]ng" away her negative self-image and thus disburdened herself of the shame that the settlers attempt to inspire in her. But what should readers make of the final image, in which a "pale hand" is apparently now holding the speaker's "dirty ... reflection"? Does the hand control her self-image (her face is, after all, in his hands) or does it hold proof of her defiance, given that she is throwing away a "dirty" identity bestowed upon her? These are unanswerable questions that point to a fork in Crate's own thinking. Neither she nor the speaker knows where this new exploration of her roots will lead.

I have been reading Crate's *Pale as Real Ladies* as further evidence of the subversive potential in lyric historiography. Her poetry adopts some fundamental features of the genre: like other "familial" poems, it follows a developmental structure, imagines a figurative kinship, shows self-awareness, considers and creatively interprets the historical fragments and images tied to Johnson's life and writing, and, through its recovery of Johnson's "I," brings readers closer to a historical experience.

As a subversive act, Crate's poems tear down rituals of mimicry even as she portrays them. She repurposes the genre in which she works to bring readers closer to Johnson's experiences, and she does so in ways that ironically put her poems at odds with other examples of lyric historiography working more comfortably within colonial frameworks.

In considering Crate's poems more deeply, I also extract from them a profound meditation on the consequences of performance. Identity is more than the perennial question, "who am I?" or "who are we?" Those questions have correlatives. No, I am not about to reignite the rhetorical TNT of Frye's "Where is here?" (222). I think we need to be more specific about the questions implied by "who am I?" and reach beyond basic individual personhood or Frye's rhetoric of spatial ontology in order to do so. Identity is relative in every sense of the word: it is a negotiation of and response to our genetic inheritances, our cultural communities, and our sociopolitical contexts. In balancing and exploring those pillars, individual identity is always a set of identities, some of which may be channelled secondarily in one context or made primary in another. We are different selves in different environments.

In that way, as I said earlier in this chapter, we are always performing various selves. Because our identity is always tied to our environment, the correlative question of interest to me is not "what different selves do I perform?" or "in what worlds do I perform?" but rather "to what degree do my performances suggest my *agency* as I experience the world?" That is a question that goes far beyond "who am I?" or "where is here?" It begins with introspection: "[b]y looking critically at how we have been constructed as 'Indian,'" Gloria Bird (Spokane) writes, "and by interrogating the ways in which we become complicit in the perpetuation of both the stereotyping and the romanticizing of Indian people, can we take the first step to undoing the damage that colonization has wrought. If we are not attentive, we can easily be swayed into accepting notions of ourselves as vanishing or somehow inferior, doomed, and tragic" (47–8). Examining and interrogating the literary or historical tropes to which Bird alludes is certainly part of the conversation, and that is important work for those who acknowledge the ways in which their performances are evidence of having been "swayed." Introspection is also the responsibility of those who sway, as are the social questions implied by such work: to what violence (psychological, verbal, or physical) is the unauthorized Other subjected because of those interrogations and those "first steps"? And there are other kinds of aggressions that impinge on self-definition, including political and legal challenges – acts of constitutional violence.[46] The right to self-define, socially or politically, has never been adequately addressed by the Canadian government, and that is because, historically, that government has seen identity as threatening to the philosophies of sameness made to sustain what Adele Perry calls "the fiction of the nation" (133): a myth of romantic unity and a celebration of narrative and cultural coherence, which comes at the expense of narrative and cultural diversity.

Perhaps it is distance that has made such fictions possible. I have spoken of distance in various ways throughout this study. Some distances are logical and provoke self-reflection: temporal distance (the inevitable feeling of distance that time inspires in us as readers of history) and cultural distance (the recognition of an ethnic or social separation that compels poets to recognize their limits in writing about cultural pasts of which they have too little knowledge). Other distances are wilfully and needlessly divisive: objective distance (conservative historians' conscious aversion to resources too heavily indebted to personal experience) and colonial distance (the refusal to engage in genuine dialogue with or to consider the perspectives of authorized or unauthorized Others). The latter pairing sustains the assumption that the Other can only ever be unbearably other, and that assumption, like these wilful distances themselves, is a failure of imagination. And when judged at a distance, any person will wish they could simply be seen up close. Lyric is seeing. Lyric declares difference as much as it encourages a basic willingness to admire the human face of experiences. What Canadians have now is a more diverse record of historical experiences, each of which is an opportunity to attain closeness to the individual and the past, and to reimagine the concept of nation as something other than a coercive fiction.

Crate's *Pale as Real Ladies* is a contribution to that record. Her unsettling resurrection of Johnson reminds contemporary audiences what it looks like to negotiate an intersectional identity in a society that enforces and polices performances. While there is heroism in that portrayal of Johnson, the ominousness of Crate's ending is equally vital; it suggests that reclaiming agency does not necessarily end others' efforts to deprive you of it, just as Johnson's will to speak in Crate's other poems "does not ensure reception" (Verwaayen, "Appropriate" 46). Those tensions in Crate's text parallel tensions manifest in Canada's past and present, and her portrayal of them pushes her readers to resist any "fiction of the nation" that insists on making fictions of its people.

10 The Future of History

Nous connaîtrons-nous seulement un peu nous-mêmes sans les arts?

(Could we ever know each other in the slightest without the arts?)

Gabrielle Roy, *Hidden Mountain* 120

The past is always as we imagine it; history is a personal exploration, no matter who writes it. This book connects some of the many constellating dots that link ground-breaking Canadian poetry published since 1960 in order to show how different writers laid that process bare for their readers. Those poems make up a collection of lyric historiography in dialogue with itself, a genre nurtured by the interminable movements that have, since the centennial era, reinvented the writing of history and, in many cases, relocated the sites of social, political, and narrative authority. And while the particular narrative I have crafted includes dialogues among writers of lyric historiography, the personalism of their poems, even as poets spoke to one another on or off the page, ensured that the genre never stagnated: each poet's form and content reflect their own experience. Still, there are enough consistencies in the poetry to suggest a group coherence, the primary similarity being that many writers since 1960 have been drawn toward lyrical, developmental, and familial poetry. Despite the many influences and inheritances, I wonder if the idea that had the greatest impact on these poets' projects was that gravitational lure of the familial past. Perhaps the true magic of genealogy – when it is available to someone in the first place – is the authority and insight it promises any writer finding their place in larger narratives, movements, and nationalisms.

During an era in which it was fashionable to question and even disbelieve in historical endeavours, many writers returned to belief by tracing these literal or figurative genealogies. In so doing, they created and perpetuated the kind of history that social historians have imagined since the 1970s: histories that are transparently subjective, productively indeterminate, anti-essentialist in their thinking about identity and the past, and considerate of different epistemological positions. No individual writer's oeuvre can prove what I have argued here about such literature; it takes a generation's collective body of writing to show the intellectual profundity, methodological value, and narrative potential of historical writing that achieves closeness to the past.

And their era ensured near-constant influence and evolution within the genre. Purdy's brief accumulative poems gave way to McKinnon's long developmental one, Atwood's figuratively familial poems reimagined the concept of genealogy, Crate's interrogation of colonial performance innovated on the revolutionary tenor of Atwood's poetry about gendered politics, McKinnon's experiments with literal photographs complemented Newlove's figurative historical images, Purdy's epistemological impasses contrast with Suknaski's willingness to listen to others' stories, and Zieroth's poems share McNeil's lyric method. Much came together, and had to come together, for this poetry to appear. It was a symphony of politics, histories, poems, communities, mentorships, apprenticeships, and explorations that made an ever-evolving genre possible.

Those internal developments and that range of influences gesture to the daunting task that poets faced: they strove to relate a historical experience authoritatively while still acknowledging that the past can be variously, and no less truthfully, imagined by others. There is something seemingly self-reflexive in Atwood's "Paths and Thingscape" from *The Journals of Susanna Moodie*: "there are some who have dreams / of birds flying in the shapes / of letters; the sky's / codes" (20). While Atwood's Moodie hints at the foolishness of reading meaning into the inherent randomness of nature, Atwood is finding meaning in lives randomly traced in the dust behind her. She is, like Moodie, a writer on foreign land, wandering the landscape of the past in hopes of understanding it. Atwood's effort to chart Moodie's life ironically parallels Moodie's own mapping of "trail[s]" among the "trees" (20): both should see that the trail is, in fact, the absence of a trail. So it is with the past. We can speak ontologically of the past, but to speak with an unthwarted confidence of what patterns or meaning reside in an era or event or figure is impossible.

That point is neither defeat nor dissuasion. It is not the death of history. Everyone shares in the temptation to organize, correlatively, experience and time, to conceive of the past (the personal or the communal) as a foundation for the present. We thrive on such structure because we are hardwired to find patterns. That cannot be controlled. What is controllable, however, is our purpose in offering structure to the past. One can aim to achieve something more in history than some monolithic notion of "the past as it really was." The faith in that model of history is fading, and for good reason: it alienates, excludes, and devalues those who do not fit the moulds on which it insists. So we must find some other reason to write history, where one can look for an empathetic framework to replace those conventional assumptions of absolute authority and knowledge. This is what lyric historiography offers. It asks writers to assert and relinquish authority in every instance, in every utterance. This paradoxical position bestows authority on individual readings of the past, even as it simultaneously relieves poets of that authority in order to encourage and ensure diverse perspectives on the worlds in which we live and in which those before us lived.

Lyric historiography shows something else, too: identity still matters. The concept is not some tired relic of Canada's nationalistic 1960s or a modern romantic hangover. It is still very much with us. Its endurance may be because, as Gerald Izenberg has recently said in a general context, we "can't do without identity." "[W]e are not," he says, "nothing and nowhere" (457). As long as an individual is of a place and time, they hold onto that basic impulse to identify and define the "I." And as they do so, they may also have a compulsion to explain their identity or identities by articulating location: the location of perspective, of their families, of themselves. Such questions most assuredly still capture the imagination. And the unexpected irony of lyric historiography of the centennial era is that the more closely poets looked at their position, the more willingly they disbelieved in the sanctity of their own knowledge. They learned to appreciate particulars, and identity is predicated on particulars. This is why I think A.J.M. Smith had it wrong when he distinguished so rigidly between the local ("native") and the global ("cosmopolitan") in his introduction to *The Book of Canadian Poetry* (1943). As centennial-era poets turned to the local, it became clear to them that the local is not a disconnection from broader and intersectional frameworks. The local – the lyrical – is a starting point, the foundation on which one builds the epistemological confidence and narrative momentum necessary to enter into contact and dialogue with the external world.

I began this book by gesturing to those qualities of lyric through a brief mention of Margaret Prang's 1977 address to the Canadian Historical Association, in which she said that Canadian literature was leading the way for historians as they transitioned from political history to social history – and that sentiment was captured, too, by the social historian

H.J. Hanham, who said that wherever Canadian literature has gone, "Canadian history has been slow to follow" ("Canadian History" 17). To come back, though, to the line I singled out in my introduction: Prang said she admired poets because they enrich the general public's "capacity to comprehend and feel" Canada's diversity. She wanted historians to "accept, *intellectually and emotionally*, the remarkable diversities of this country and finally abandon our apologetic stance toward regional and local history" (emphasis added). We need more, she says, than intellect to understand the past. We need to *feel* the experience of having been there. The poets I've discussed in this study demonstrate an intellectual grasp of historical events, but there is also something affectively historical in their writing: there is the hopeful, if blemished, "innocence" of McKinnon's grandfather, the "kind[ness]" in the eyes of McNeil's grandmother, the "moan[ing]" bodies of prisoners among Zieroth's grandfather in a Manitoban camp, the "real, tragic, and human" – Purdy's words – quality of Suknaski's "Homestead," the psychologically divided Moodie of Atwood's poems, and the conflicted voice of E. Pauline Johnson in Crate's *Pale as Real Ladies*. These poems generate histories at once intellectual and felt, histories that reinvent form and content by relocating narrative power. For those reasons, a shared history may be a more definite feat of poetry than of academic history.

Admittedly, that claim is contentious. Yet, ongoing debates in the academy support it. A truly social history (that effort to get closer to the "experiences of people") has many advocates in the historical profession: it had trailblazing supporters in the 1970s like Barry Broadfoot and the founders of the Multicultural History Society of Ontario. In more recent years the historian Steven High has become co-director of the Centre for Oral History and Digital Storytelling at Concordia University and the emerging historian Jesse Thistle (Cree-Métis) is researching intergenerational trauma by drawing directly on his familial history. Even with these voices in the field, over the last several decades there have still been spirited debates about who possesses the authority to write history. And because the method, if not always the content, of social history has remained overwhelmingly conservative, non-academics have often been excluded from the conversation.

That distance and exclusion have resulted in an alienating academic discourse. In 1991, for example, Carl Berger questioned social historians' tendency to work with "anonymous social patterns, with groups and classes, rather than with individuals," which "tended to make access to the past difficult for the general reader" ("Writings" 296). That same year, Christopher Moore said that "academic social historians do little to seek or welcome readers who neither have PhDs nor aspire to them ... [they] have yet to find a language that would let them both do their work and share it with the wider society of readers" (53). Even if historians had added to what David Gagan and H.E. Turner called in 1982 the "limited inventory" (92) of social history and recognized the potential for individual or community experiences to provide insight into "larger populations" (92), conservative political histories "outweighed the literature of the 'new' history" (Berger, "Writings" 332). The "decentralized" Canadian history that David Jay Bercuson had optimistically anticipated in *Canada and the Burden of Unity* (1977; 15) had not yet been achieved by the time Berger wrote his retrospective on the field.

The debate was picked up again in 1994 by Veronica Strong-Boag who, unlike Berger, criticized not the craft but rather the content of history, which she believed still reflected "[n]eo-conservative efforts to frame a consensus history" (6) and too seldom meditated on "power relations" both in history and in the writing of history (5): "If it is to be fully told, our history needs many interwoven narratives where none, as has too often been the case in the past, excludes the others. ... We must make room for other voices who have so often been silenced. Such humility is challenging if our expectations of privilege are considerable" (6). Two years later, Evelyn Légaré would criticize what she thought to be a truth of Canadian society and culture: "Full inclusion within the nation demands 'sameness'" (351). In 2000, Timothy Stanley wrote against J.L. Granatstein's polemical *Who Killed Canadian History?* (1998), and he wondered why the "grand narrative of Canada as a nation has been remarkably stable since its invention at the beginning of the twentieth century" in various forms as "the stuff of popular and official histories, Heritage Minutes, beer commercials, public school teaching." "Some people who live in Canada" he wrote, "can claim this history, and hence the status of being 'Canadian,' as their own. Others cannot. By making Europeans and their activities the subject of the narratives, ... the grand narrative makes it difficult for non-Europeans to claim membership in the imagined community that it purports to explain" (83). Instead of broad "nationalist frameworks," he concluded, historians should consider "'small'" histories and capture "multiple pasts" so that the history of one era or region can be received "in multiple ways" (102). Less than a decade later, both Adele Perry and Steven High wrote seminal articles that asked historians to "rethink the relationship between communities and their historians" (Perry 124) without mistaking inclusion for a sign that historians have overcome neoconservative (to return to Strong-Boag's term) histories still working within "the same national conventions" as earlier ones

(Perry 132). Only now, Steven High argues, are historians truly beginning to "bridge the community-university divide" (23). This is merely a snapshot of the struggle to reinvent from historians' point of view.

Meanwhile, Canadian poetry has told a different story: "Whoever tells you that history is not about individuals, only about large trends and movements," Atwood once said, "is lying" (*ISOAG* 7). The stories to which Atwood gestures can be found in a body of literature much larger than the one presented in this study. My focus on a particular group of poets who were, to one degree or another, affiliated with each other is not a suggestion that their accomplishments are unique to their circle. After all, lyric historiography denotes a method, not specific writers from particular regions or nations – one of the many darlings I had to kill in drafts of this book was a proposed chapter on the American poet Robert Lowell's *Life Studies* (1959). And so lyric historiography might be studied through the community I have represented, but it can and should also be understood in relation to other specific traditions in and outside of Canada.

There are, for instance, many Indigenous poets working toward what Daniel Heath Justice (Cherokee) has called a "sovereignty of expression" (69), a sovereignty that further complicates whatever one means when one speaks of "national identity." My analysis of Joan Crate's poetry recognizes only one example of a much larger discussion going on in Canada right now about the dehumanizing effects of colonialism. That dehumanization is, in Emma LaRocque's view, one of the reasons that autobiography has appealed to Indigenous writers: the "facts of biography ... humanize[d] the much dehumanized 'Indian'" ("Preface" xviii). The more attention critics pay to the "sovereignty of expression," the easier it is to feel confident that Canadian literature has moved beyond, or is moving beyond, those early caricatures of "the guide, helper, or shaman" (Fee "Romantic Nationalism," 29). To offer that attention means resisting any temptation to generalize Indigenous literatures as working strictly – if at all – within the kinds of frameworks that I have constructed, and instead listening to Lee Maracle's (Sto:lo) insistence that scholars should pay close attention to "the study of the original culture from which [an] author arises" (84).

That is not to say that we must read Indigenous-authored literature as separate from the literary circles that I've studied throughout this book. Scholars can still find connections, but they must heed the advice of Kateri Akiwenzie-Damm: "Although contemporary Aboriginal literatures incorporate forms that may be recognizable from other traditions ... many of these forms, as used by First Peoples writers, are influenced as much by our own traditional forms as by these more recent ones" (170). Deanna Reder (Cree-Métis), too, points out that "it is possible to recognize ... Western conventions" in Indigenous-authored works while also acknowledging conventions specific to the author's nation and to do so "without being drawn into discussions of cultural contamination or authenticity" (159). These intersections can be part of new critical conversations.

One place for those conversations to begin is by thinking more broadly about lyrical histories as imagined by different literary communities. As a case in point, Neal McLeod's (Cree) work on "body poetic" captures the somatic intimacy of poetry much more directly than my own study, though his model is, in other ways, analogous to lyric historiography.[1] The parallels are, I think, self-evident: according to McLeod, a body poetic "connects our living bodies to the living earth around us" (109), and thus entails an exploration of "the connection of contemporary storytellers and poets to the ancient poetic pathways of [Cree] ancestors" (110–11). McLeod explains that

> the process of poetry ... could be described as mamâhtâwisiwin (the process of tapping into the Great Mystery), which is mediated by our historicity and wâhkôhtowin (kinship). Because of this connection to other generations, there emerges an ethical dimension to Cree poetic discourse, namely, the moral responsibility to remember. (111)

McLeod says that this approach enables a "narrative genealogy" (112), through which "individual experiences" build toward a "larger narrative structure" that contributes "in a small way" to "the larger collective memory" of a community (113). This, he says, is a "poetics of empathy": a "web of understanding of our embodied locations" that can "stretch ... outwards to a wider context of collective historicity" expressive of a "poetics grounded in dialogue and an open-ended flow of narrative understanding" (114). The opportunity for open-endedness in such discourses, he continues, is where a respect for tradition intersects with "a radical questioning" of it (117). This is one of many possible discourses that could be read as complementary to the scepticism about inherited knowledge I have been tracing throughout this book.

For McLeod, the poetry of Louise Halfe / Sky-Dancer (Cree) exemplifies a "body poetic" in so far as her poems link "a contemporary understanding to a past understanding" (117) by articulating the past with full appreciation for the "embodied present" (118).[2] Halfe's long poem *Blue Marrow* (1998) further embodies what McLeod identifies as the "narrative genealogy," emphasis on the living body, and open-endedness of a body poetic. Halfe's poetry was inspired by dreams she had in the early

1970s. She dreamt of her grandfather teaching her "syllabics" and of her grandmothers guiding her toward "a vision quest": "My Elder said after a fast that I would write from the daily pages of the universe. And an Elder asked: 'what will you write next, Louise?' I laughed and said, 'I'll rewrite history.' I did not take it seriously then, but the obsession only grew." The poems born out of that epiphany balance her recovery of stories that exist within a Cree tradition that long predates colonial contact with her urge to understand how colonialism has damaged her connection to that tradition:

> I so wanted to hear the stories of my grandmothers, their lovers, their lives and I had to reconstruct the small memories I had and experienced. Residential school robbed so much that I was left to flounder in my thoughts and reconstruction. I needed and wanted the guidance of my parents and my grandfolks, but my parents were too damaged already by residential school and the impact of destroyed livelihood. ... I still, at times, have difficulty going back to these stolen years where memory collects the fragments of what is left. ... The damage was huge and irreparable for my parents and for my kin. In a sense, their voices were silenced. I wanted and needed to break those thick silences. (Email from Halfe)

Her excavation of those silenced voices yielded *Blue Marrow*, a book-length poem that moves among numerous voices as Halfe's "I" navigates the stories of her Grandmothers. The poetry is visceral, corporeal in its representation of perspective and voice. The body is the story. Sometimes that relationship is beautifully sublime: Halfe locates songs and narrative power in "the bones" of her Grandmothers (19). She finds stories written on the body, measured by figurative and literal scars: "I am a large scab" (20), "So many scars. / So many sewed mouths" (46), and "Did our Grandmothers know we would be scarred / by the fists and boots of men?" (98). Halfe explores these intimate and somatic pasts, but also imagines a broader history told through those bodies. Her Grandmothers reveal to her generations of Indigenous women traded to "Frenchmen" ("mistikôsiwak"), "Englishmen" ("âkayâsiwak"), "Ukrainians" ("opîtatowêwak"), "Norwegians," "Irishmen," and "Scotsmen" (61). These scenes support Méira Cook's reading of Halfe's work as a search "for a past that is both personal and communal" (85).

Additionally, there are emerging writers whose poetics has been shaped by a range of lyric traditions. Cara-Lyn Morgan's first book, *What Became My Grieving Ceremony* (2014), navigates her Trinidadian and Métis roots, and the poetry of both Halfe and Suknaski spoke directly to her as she began planning the book. Because of literary encounters with these poets (as well as Gregory Scofield, Al Purdy, and John Newlove), Morgan felt fully alerted to the possibility that "the small towns, barns, and kitchen counters of [her] childhood could be microcosms for what larger histories surrounded those humble places" (Email from Morgan).[3] These were the microhistories that seeded poems in which Morgan's persona rejects her father's claim that "[t]here are no stories" of their familial past worth telling. In "From Genesis to Revelations," her father repeats that phrase, over and over, until the speaker has her "revelation": "There are. She knows. There are" (13). Here is a testament to the continuing appeal of lyric historiography in Canadian poetry, one that also embodies the unexpected connections among different poetic and cultural traditions in Canada.

I began my career tracing modernism through the Western tradition, but through that work I have realized how much more there is than those legacies: more narrative authorities and locations, more history and knowledge. There is still so much to say. There are many cultural and literary traditions that show, provocatively, intensely, poignantly, what it looks like to wrest power away from an academy that has spent most of the last century upholding conservative histories rather than advancing shared ones.

But I am drawn back again to the question of identity and of nationalism. The examples of lyric historiography, McLeod's body poetic, or any other comparably self-reflexive (and self-reflective) texts complicate the related concepts of "national history" or "national identity" or, more simply, "nation." Without an anchoring centre to which historians, poets, or literary scholars can point, those terms become increasingly slippery. By the end of the 1990s, that slipperiness provoked hostility from some scholars: in literary criticism, Solecki lamented that Al Purdy would be "the last Canadian poet" as Canada transitioned into a multicultural state rather than a united nation and, in history, Granatstein bemoaned that Canadian history had been killed by progressives. These are examples of what happens when a twentieth-century country attempts to live out a nineteenth-century nationalism: its critics and historians struggle against modern realities, namely the diversity that comes with increasing efforts toward decolonization and self-definition.

While today's critical currents are shifting, there is still a long history of noteworthy critics conceiving of national identity as a concept tied primarily to the Canadian state. Robert Kroetsch presciently argued once that the "task of criticism, now, is to examine ... new directions without recourse to an easy version of national definition" ("Beyond

Nationalism" 66), but in one form or another that easy definition continues to reign. Throughout this study I have said much about the conservatism of Canadian historians, but one could easily make similar claims for some literature scholars. Take Jonathan Kertzer's provocative question from 1998: "What happens to a national literature when the very idea of the nation has been set in doubt?" (5). That question, as Kertzer has phrased it, suggests that the concept of nation, rather than the concept of the *Canadian* nation, has been doubted, which is not quite accurate.

Admittedly, that assessment of Kertzer's work risks seeming like my own semantic quibbling, but I would counter that the conflation of *a* nation with *the* nation is too widespread to be regarded so innocuously. Laura Moss noted in 2003 that "many scholars question the very concept of nationalism in Canada because it is so often predicated on the dissolution of the First Nations" ("Is Canada Postcolonial?" 10). And, certainly, what she says is true. In his recent study of Canadian literature anthologies, Robert Lecker recalls facing "uncertainty" and questioning his own nostalgia for an era in which "the nation cohered" (19) and remembers that he found relief only in the realization that "there was no need to resolve the tension, and that it was the very existence of that tension keeping [him] energized when it came to the study of Canadian literature" (19). I appreciate Lecker's efforts to spin his own dilemma positively, but the "tension" he appreciates still poses a methodological problem: Canadians once believed in the unity of the nation, and now they believe only in the "tension" inherent in that earlier, flawed belief, and so, still, the idea of a whole Canada (even if that idea is represented as an absence) anchors their discussions. This is a convenient critical loophole that allows academics of a particular generation to continue speaking of concepts in dire need of a theoretical overhaul.

As a point of comparison, Frank Davey attacks earlier models of nationalism by wrenching our definition of "national" to make the word interchangeable with "multicultural." In so doing, he allows himself to read culturally or ethnically diverse poets as "more 'national'" than earlier ones ("Al Purdy" 54). At the same time, Davey has also said that Canadian fiction "announce[s] ... the arrival of the post-national state ... a world and a nation in which social structures no longer link regions or communities, political process is doubted, and individual alienation becomes normal" (*Post-National* 266). Lecker is energetically tense about the wholeness of Canada; Davey is peaceably complacent with either (or both?) redefining the nation as one unified through diversity or experiencing a "post-national" condition in which "alienation" is "normal." Neither critic imagines that beyond these limited nationalist frameworks could be more than an impasse.

We cannot simply and conveniently redefine "nation" to make the concept of a unified Canada relevant again, and I don't think cultural communities in Canada need to live and write history and literature under the assumption that they exist (and should do so as enthusiastically as Lecker does) in tension with or (as Davey claims he does) in the absence of "social structures." This is the wall that Desmond Morton hit in 1979 when he said that the absence of an "over-arching sense of what Canada is" necessarily means that every history would be "an argument for ... antagonisms" (7), and, much more recently, Renée Hulan has reiterated a version of this interpretation of Canadian history: "Canadians suffer either the domination of a master narrative in need of unsettling or the total lack of a unifying narrative" (781). Why is the only option in this framework of a nationalist or a post-nationalist Canada, to antagonize or "suffer"? Why haven't Canadian historians or literary critics been able to imagine more consistently something other than blinkered nationalism, convenient rewritings of national identity, or painful epistemological deadlocks? And, most importantly, of what use to the many nations and communities within Canada are those reactions to what Jo-Ann Episkenew (Métis) calls "the authorized national collective myth," in which "the colonizers function as both authors and protagonists" as they "invest in themselves the authority" to speak and write of the past and of identities (71)? J.M.S. Careless insisted in 1954 that we "must think beyond [romantic] nationalism" ("Canadian Nationalism" 12) and yet some critics and historians still clearly struggle to do so; romantic celebrations have been replaced by mournings for romanticism.

In that vein, Kertzer's declaration that "the problem today [in 1998] is that ... [w]e have endless diagnoses of the national malaise but too little 'promise' ... to give confidence in the future" (167) is an assumption on which he puts too little critical pressure, because whatever its philosophical or cultural basis, lyric historiography attests to the fact that one can be post-romantic without also being post-nationalist or post-community. Scholars can, as well, frame discussions in ways that resist the rhetoric of postmodernist tension and suffering. In dwelling on – and sometimes enjoying the critical potential of – failure, scholars blind themselves to the other frameworks and epistemologies that might inform new literature, histories, and selves. I agree with Neil Besner when he says that "ideas of nation and ideas of the postcolonial are neither so successive nor so opposed" (44) because although many critics have chosen to read nationalism as an antiquated concept, it can be a decolonizing or decentring act: Beth Brant, for instance, says that E. Pauline Johnson "was a Nationalist. Canada may attempt to claim her as theirs, but Johnson belonged to only one Nation, the Mohawk Nation" (7). It is a challenging task to negotiate that kind of statement with those of Davey, Kertzer, Hulan, or Solecki.

No one needs to work under the assumption that once a conservative nationalism is outmoded, then the broader concept of nationalism is universally impractical. That is a conclusion that restricts our ability to defamiliarize and reimagine the definitions and rhetoric associated with national communities. Likewise, as I said in my introduction to this book, scholars and writers should also be wary of any declaration that, as Bowering has said, "history is impossible" when they reflect on decades in which communities within Canada were, for the first time, self-defining – some remaining within a colonial framework, while others worked and are working outside of and against those same frameworks.

Maybe communities need concepts of nation now more than ever before to sustain those new narratives, but it cannot be the concepts to which Canadians have become accustomed. These claims make me think of Laura Gillman's unequivocal note that "[i]dentities matter." "[P]articularly," she adds, "for those whose visible identities (of race and gender) place them disadvantageously with respect to social power, and who therefore have a stake in claiming and exploring their identity" (4). Gillman's attentiveness to the power of identity complements Daniel Heath Justice's work, in which he has pointed out that "a great many scholars ... have concluded that nationalism is an unredeemable blight on history," which is an unreasonable conclusion to "Indigenous peoples, for whom collectivist assertions of peoplehood have been at the centre of political resistance against the onslaught of Eurowestern colonialism, imperialism, industrialization, and commodification." Nationalism "in Indigenous contexts," he reminds readers, is "often very different from the assimilative and assaultive consumerist patriotism that fuels the modern nation-state" (63).

The lyric centres to which readers are privy in contrapuntal poetry and other writing should divorce them from those assimilationist myths of the nation and guide them to consider instead the self-defining nationalists speaking and writing from places of familiarity, in every sense of the word. There is something off in Hulan's claim that "historians [have] worked to *give* voice to history's voiceless" (784, emphasis added), because it implies that the voiceless are *still* unable to speak for themselves, even as they assert the right to speak from their own centre rather than be read from that of another authorized perspective. "Nationalism" or comparable expressions of community can be the decentralizing acts of public memory that, in the words of Henry Giroux, "mak[e] connections that are often hidden, forgotten, or willfully ignored" and that ask an audience to "critically examin[e] [their] own historical location amid relations of power, privilege, or subordination" (68).

In Canada, those connections are becoming increasingly visible. But this is not the nationalism of which mainstream critics and historians have known and spoken in the past. Historically, when mainstream creative writers, historians, and nationalists have spoken of "nation," they have almost always meant something familiar – geographically, socially, culturally – and thus local. Was the Canada First movement of the 1860s and 1870s anything more than a movement to celebrate Ontario? Did historians like Donald Creighton or Donalda Dickie mean anything more than their own frames of reference when they used the word "nation"? One reader of the popular Canadian magazine *Saturday Night*, Michel Dagenais, got to the issue more directly in a 1969 letter to the editor. He took issue with an earlier article by Robert Fulford about draft dodgers, in which Fulford generalized the Canadian character. Dagenais objected: "Mr. Fulford is not a typical Canadian, nor are Torontonians typical of Canada. Canada is a country of many people ... Does Canada consist of Ontario?" (4). Dagenais recognized something quite important: "nation" is narrowly and locally conceived, and yet the concept is often broadly applied. The local community evidently has valuable and sustainable narrative power, but it is deeply problematic to conflate the community with the country. Rendered with greater scepticism and self-consciousness, however, the local community is a place through which one may welcome oneself into the world.

If it is agreeable to imagine that the concept of nation is only ever self-reflexively local in such a sense, then I hope my study has shown that its iterations have been fiercely and exceptionally represented in Canadian poetry. If that argument seems surprising in any way, it is because we have not looked closely enough or done enough to trace the various literary legacies and traditions that have created and continue to nurture the conditions for transcultural discourses: the scepticism, the return to belief through images and photographs, the broken silences. Poets since 1960 have brought readers closer to a diversity of revelatory stories: the history of Albertan farmhands (McKinnon), of Ukrainian immigration (Suknaski), of Canadian internment camps (Zieroth), of colonial foremothers (Atwood), of feminist artists (McNeil), of the Jewish experience on the prairies (Mandel), of transnational Jewish histories (Burrs), of Ameliasburgh, Ontario (Purdy), of Indigenous foremothers (Crate), of Cree language, knowledge, and stories (Halfe), and of growing up both Trinidadian and Métis in Canada (Morgan).

There are so many other book-length lyrics to which I could turn to make my point about the enduring appeal of literal or figurative family poems and the local nation: reimaginings of Louis Riel from Indigenous perspectives (Scofield's *Louis: The Heretic Poems* [2012]), Renée Sarojini Saklikar's investigation into her personal connection to the Air India tragedy (*Children of Air India* [2013]), Souvankham Thammavongsa's poetry about the Cambodian refugee crisis told through her reading of her father's scrapbook (*Found* [2007]), Jordan Abel's meditation on ethnography studies in relation to his Nisga'a ancestors in *The Place of Scraps* (2013), Armand Garnet Ruffo's reflections on the lives of his great uncle and Grey Owl in *Grey Owl: The Mystery of Archie Belaney* (1996),[4] and Garry Thomas Morse's striving to "bear / witness / to every name" in *Discovery Passages* (2011) by exploring the history of the Kwakwaka'wakw nation from which he descends (26). As the literary community has grown, lyrical histories have increasingly moved away from predominantly colonial frameworks to consider a wider range of experiences in both the past and present. Canadian poetry has, more than I think readers and scholars have ever appreciated, been the principal site for histories at once progressive, diverse, and human.

When we read that poetry, when we find evidence of shared authority, there is suddenly so much more we can expect and demand from historical discourses too limited in their definitions of authority and expertise. The refusal in lyric historiography to ascribe narrative authority to any one individual is necessary to social history. And while some might argue that those lyrics risk insularity or solipsism, the poets in this study rarely model such alienation: they continually suggest or explicitly find connections to broader communities, enough to know and say that, to lift a line from Cara-Lyn Morgan, "if there is one / there are thousands" (49).

That writing gives voice. It gives authority and hope. It appreciates lyric as a method to permit genuine encounters with, rather than just discussions about, those whom we have not yet met. It makes it possible for readers to receive and experience each other, and it gives them the tools to do so without sacrificing or devaluing the distinctive histories and knowledge of individuals and communities. The social historians who have participated in the historiographic debates raging since the 1960s have imagined that kind of storytelling as one potential future for history. But that is also a future tested in Canadian poetry over the last fifty years. Poets have shown and are still showing what profitable historical worlds emerge from scepticism and lyric. They are showing readers what it means to believe in and share the past. And, in so doing, they have deepened our understanding of histories and identities more dynamic, more disputed and questioned, than many have realized. Much of that work began during a cultural moment in which writers and academics recognized the necessity of reinvention. They needed new histories then. We still need them now.

Notes

Introduction

1 See Karen A. Finlay's *The Force of Culture* (especially 218–37), Paul Litt's *The Muses, the Masses, and the Massey Commission*, and the last chapter of Maria Tippett's *Making Culture* for fuller articulations of this Royal Commission (also known as the Massey Report) and its recommendations. The report concluded with calls for more funding for universities, public radio, television, and the arts; the underlying fear of the report's writers was that, in the absence of that funding, American culture would assimilate Canadian culture. There are numerous examples of symbolic acts that took place alongside the publication of this report in order to signal Canada's developing sense of a fuller autonomy. During his campaign in 1945, for example, Mackenzie King promised to create an official Canadian citizenship and flag. In 1946, King's push for a flag proved unpopular, and he dropped the issue. A proposal to rename "Dominion Day" as "Canada Day" was also abandoned that same year for similar reasons (Igartua 16–17). Even though many politicians agreed with Louis St Laurent's move to abandon Canada's identity as a "Dominion," the commentary from some newspapers suggests that Canadian citizens still clung to the image of Canada-as-colony; the *Calgary Herald* and the *Ottawa Journal*, for instance, opposed abandoning the label of "Dominion." Much of the Canadian populace saw these symbolic gestures as needlessly hostile to Britain, a sentiment that was most inflamed by St Laurent's decision to deny the British military support during the Suez crisis in 1956.

2 Likewise, Harold A. Innis's *The Fur Trade in Canada: An Introduction to Canadian Economic History* (1930) focuses on trade economies established in Upper and Lower Canada. W.L. Morton questioned the Laurentian thesis in "Clio in Canada: The Interpretation of Canadian History" (1946), regarding Creighton favourably but noting that his work "affirms the Laurentian

dominance" (106). See Marlene Shore's anthology of essays on Canadian history, *The Contested Past: Reading Canada's History* (2002), in which there are numerous articles that contest these early methodologies. Donald Wright has also recently published a biography of Donald Creighton, *Donald Creighton: A Life in History* (2015), which addresses some of the backlash old-guard historians faced late in their careers.

3 My use of "the centennial era" is not a romantic nationalist endorsement or a "celebration" of 1967. The "centennial era" is, in my use of it, an ironic term, in so far as it suggests the celebration of a coherent national project, whereas the era itself evidences the degree to which the concept of "Canada" as a nation was challenged. That tension is explored throughout this study.

4 Ramsay Cook coined the term "limited identities" in "Canadian Centennial Celebrations" (1967). The term was popularized in J.M.S. Careless's "'Limited Identities' in Canada" (1969), and he later offered a retrospective on the term in "Limited Identities: Ten Years Later" (1980). Both Cook and Careless became increasingly critical of the concept, particularly because they believed younger historians had interpreted the term in ways that were fragmenting and dividing the historical profession in Canada. See John Herd Thompson's "Integrating Regional Patterns into a National Canadian History" (1990), in which Thompson considers the evolving use of the term and its relevance to discourses in Canadian history.

5 While I would argue that a distrust of history was unusually widespread during the centennial era, the concept of history's unreliability did not originate in this period. Ian Haywood's *The Making of History: A Study of the Literary Forgeries of James Macpherson and Thomas Chatterton in Relation to Eighteenth-Century Ideas of History and Fiction* (1986) is an exemplary study of early historiographic scepticism. Although eighteenth-century historians sought "factuality," Haywood notes that they seldom agreed on "what constituted a fact or historical truth" (16). His study explores various responses to this concern with historical truth.

6 The popularity of the novel has been affirmed by the frequent emphasis on novels in ground-breaking studies such as Hutcheon's *The Canadian Postmodern* (1988). There are numerous such examples: Robert Kroetsch's "Beyond Nationalism: A Prologue" (1981), Owen D. Percy's "Melting History: Defrosting Moments in Novels by Wayne Johnston, Michael Winter, and Robert Kroetsch" (2007), Sherrill Grace's "Calling Out the McLean Boys: George Bowering's Shoot and the Autobiography of British Columbia History" (2005), and Herb Wyile's "Attack of the 'Latté-Drinking Relativists': Postmodernism, Historiography, and Historical Fiction" (2010) and *Speculative Fictions* (2002) are evidence of a trend in Canadian criticism that suggests critics tend to privilege novels over poetry.

7 I am deliberately resisting the term "modernist scepticism" for two reasons: that term would suggest (1) that scepticism has its roots only in the aesthetic movement of modernism, which it does not, and (2) that later writers who used this tactic were themselves "modernists." This is especially important to understand as I begin to discuss Indigenous poets such as Louise Halfe in my conclusion, whose work is – as I note in that chapter – informed much more by what Neal McLeod calls a "body poetic" than by modernism.

8 Purdy's self-identification will be taken up in chapter 2. As far as Atwood goes: Robert Fulford, among many other critics, has noted her tendency toward coyness when it comes to specific labels: "She writes a feminist novel and then denies she's influenced by feminism, expressing resentment that feminists have taken her up" ("The Images of Atwood" 96). Take, for instance, Atwood's interview with Gail van Varseveld. Responding to van Varseveld's question about "a function for literature in relation to the women's movement," Atwood responded, "Oh, there are all kinds of functions for literature but I'm not sure they are something that the writer should be concerned with, or not any more than any other member of society" (66).

9 Yeats, Conrad, and Woolf are the primary figures in Manfred Weidhorn's *An Anatomy of Skepticism* (2006), Mark Wollaeger's *Joseph Conrad and the Fictions of Skepticism* (1990), Herta Newman's *Virginia Woolf and Mrs Brown: Toward a Realism of Uncertainty* (1996) respectively.

10 F.O. Matthiessen, drawing on Eliot's 1931 introduction to Blaise Pascal's *Pensées* (1670) – "every man who thinks and lives by thought must have his own scepticism, that which stops at the question, that which ends in denial, or that which leads to faith and which is somehow integrated into the faith which transcends it" – offered the same interpretation of Eliot's scepticism (100).

11 My notes on the postmodernist novel here stress the influence of Hutcheon, rather than that of equally important theorists. The reason for this emphasis is summed up nicely by Robert Stacey, who notes that – as I argue to be the case for centennial-era writing more broadly – Canadian postmodernism has been reduced often "to the fictional genre of 'historiographic metafiction' and/or to [Hutcheon's] favoured tropes of irony, parody, metafictional self-consciousness, and thematic 'ex-centricity'" ("Introduction" xiii). "[A]lternative understandings of the postmodern," he writes, "were overshadowed by Hutcheon's work, or else were absorbed by it" (xiv). By emphasizing Hutcheon's "favoured tropes," I am not endorsing this reductive model of "postmodernism." Rather, I am suggesting, as Stacey does, that this era of our literary history – as much as the term postmodernism, which is not my concern here – needs enlargement.

12 Jonathan Kertzer's summation of contemporary criticism in 1998 epitomizes the undue emphasis critics place on playful models of scepticism: "Today's critics, always vigilant against essentialist thinking, characterize our literature by the way it studiously/playfully/sensuously renounces all claims to authenticity" (22–3).

13 It is worth noting that *Clio's Craft* does include an essay on oral history by Russell G. Hann, which tellingly falls under a section of the book titled "Problems of Evidence." Even as Hann finds potential in oral history and testimony, he simultaneously says that oral history "is not history at all ... The evidence it produces does not rank high in the historian's hierarchy of primary sources" (42). His half-hearted defence of this approach is further evidence that, as of the late 1980s, Canadian historians distrusted any methodologies they considered unorthodox.

14 While Dummitt seems quite assured in his conclusion, Adele Perry has vehemently refuted his claim that the "inclusion" has been achieved in the historical profession. See Perry's "Nation, Empire and the Writing of History in Canada in English" (2008).

15 Raddeker does, however, note that Munslow and Rosenstone's *Experiments in Rethinking History* (2004) is a successful, though exceptional, attempt to write a self-reflexive and sceptical history.

16 I recognize, of course, that modernism is historically associated with intellectual elitism; one need only read Louis Dudek's 1975 interview with Michael Darling, in which Dudek exclaimed, "I damn well am an elitist!" (12); I came across this quotation in Brian Trehearne's *The Montreal Forties* (239). While modernist elitism is not an explicit concern of my study, the rise of the "working-class" poet (Al Purdy, John Newlove, Patrick Lane, etc.) is evidence that the intellectual elitism and academic poetry associated with high modernism was, like impersonality, of lesser concern to centennial-era poets. This will, I think, become increasingly evident as I gradually explain the politics of poets in this study.

17 Readers will notice that I have relied heavily on interviews with authors in order to establish or clarify links amongst writers. My use of interviews as part of my research is partly a reflection of my book's argument: when writing about the past, academics must consider the benefits of getting closer to the history they study. To me, it would have seemed hypocritical to remain entirely at a distance from writers in this study, given my argument for redistributing the authority to write history.

1 Al Purdy's Modern Scepticism

1 In making this claim, I don't mean to suggest that other topics in Purdy's poetry have gone unnoticed. Despite (or perhaps because of) the reductive

readings of Purdy as a nationalist, recent criticism has altogether moved away from his nationalism as a topic of discussion. Presenters at The Ivory Thought symposium in 2006 (published 2008), for instance, rarely address Purdy's nationalism: critics in that book propose reading Purdy in contexts of romanticism (Sandra Djwa and D.M.R. Bentley), of the picturesque (Robert Stacey), of elegy (Jeremy Lalonde), and of poetic authority (I.S. MacLaren and Janice Fiamengo). Although refreshing, such a cacophony of approaches does little to clarify Purdy's significance to Canadian literature, a conundrum signalled by D.M.R. Bentley's conclusion to the volume based on the conference proceedings: "the most pressing and important question now facing Purdy criticism is [...] whether his work is informed by [...] a consistent (or perceptively inconsistent) system of thought" ("Conclusion" 244).

2 The following criticisms of Purdy's early poetry denote his limited achievements as an imitative romantic poet, one who poorly replicates stereotypical tropes of accomplished romantic poetry, rather than the limitations of romanticism itself. In order to define certain aspects of romanticism, I emphasize the following features of romantic poetry: subjective emotional experience, the lyrical, the meditative, the nostalgic, the pastoral, and the concern with history and memory, and their relation to the present. George Bornstein has suggested that caricatures of romanticism stem from "the detritus with which imitative later poets and hostile later critics have encrusted original romantic achievements" (8). Certainly Purdy's early poetry falls into this category. The characteristics of romanticism identified in this chapter are general features that critics tend to emphasize. Sarah M. Zimmerman attributes such emphases to M.H. Abrams's scholarship, which "gained" "centrality" in the twentieth century: "Abrams's elaboration of the shared features of a handful of poems proved paradigm-making; as the period's 'poetic norm,' the lyric has been associated with solitariness, introspection, and a desire for transcendence" (16). Lamenting that "[e]ach critical generation since Abrams has built [...] on his suppositions" (19; she cites Jerome McGann, Marjorie Levinson, and Alan Liu as representative cases), Zimmerman rightfully seeks to broaden the frameworks of such limited models and their implications for literary and historical study (see 20–31 of her *Romanticism, Lyricism, and History* for examples of these alternative models). Significantly, critics such as Zimmerman are less sceptical about Abrams's descriptions of romantic poetry's features and more suspicious of the way in which such features have been read by Abrams and his successors (such as Frye, McGann, Levinson, Liu) to suggest that romantic introspection necessarily entails asocial and ahistorical poetics. As John Paul Riquelme noted in 1991, "There is currently no end in sight to the revaluation of Romanticism that

has been under way" (6); numerous critics like Zimmerman continue to reconceptualize the meaning of the term.

3 MacKendrick claims that *The Enchanted Echo* "hints" at Purdy's later "potential" (145), but Solecki vehemently disagrees: "MacKendrick's curious attempt to salvage something from the wreck strikes me as simply wrong [...] I doubt that, if challenged, MacKendrick could [find any value in the volume]" (52).

4 Solecki does, in fact, acknowledge that the "force of Layton's presence" was primary to Purdy's development" (77).

5 See Solecki's *Last Canadian Poet* for the date of composition (160).

6 The claim here parallels that of Linda Kinnahan, who notes "Dickinsonian dashes" in William Carlos Williams's poetry that "refuse closure" and signal "hesitancy and multiple possibility" (28). Naturally, Kinnahan's point also applies easily to Purdy's own "Dickinsonian" dashes. In "The Country of the Young" (1967), for example, a dash concludes the poem: "hear an old man's voice / in the country of the young / that says / 'Look here –'" (*NOS* 80). The dash obscures the location to which the "old man" gestures. His deictic imperative therefore frustrates the reader, and the unavoidable ambiguity of the line also fuels the persona's fear that one might "never find the place" (80) that he seeks.

7 I assume Purdy writes of the Gitxsan people because "Remains of an Indian Village" (written in 1961) is likely about Purdy's visit to Kispiox in 1960. He describes the British Columbian village in "The Cartography of Myself": "I managed to reach Kispiox on the Indian reservation, with its carved house fronts and rotting totem poles. The place seemed entirely deserted, so I drove past the village and down to the Kispiox River. Standing in the shallows, wearing hip waders and baseball caps, were some twenty American fishermen with station wagons parked nearby" (17). There are notable parallels between the poem and this prose piece, such as the descriptions of "rotting" things and of people waist-deep at the site, just as the speaker is "waist-deep in the criss-cross / rivers" at the end of "Remains."

8 "Uncle Louis" was first published in 1980 by Coach House in a slim volume. I have included page numbers from the version that appeared in *West Window* (1982) because it is much easier to locate. Bowering also published a slightly different version of "Uncle Louis" in 1981 in the American journal *Epoch*.

9 On 24 October 1961, Louis Dudek wrote to Peter Miller after he received Purdy's draft of *Poems for All the Annettes* (Dudek to Miller), but the manuscript was not finalized until summer 1962, and it was released in early fall that same year. There was, in other words, ample time for Purdy to make adjustments or additions.

10 Although the unpublished essay is undated, it was certainly written in 1962. Purdy quotes directly from two poetry volumes published in 1962 (James Reaney's *Twelve Letters to a Small Town* and Raymond Souster's *A Local Pride: Poems*). January or February is the likely month of composition because Purdy casually remarks that Pratt was "nearly eighty" at the time (he turned eighty on 4 February 1962).

11 Birney's poem first appeared in *Delta* (though not listed in its table of contents) and was reprinted in *Ice, Cod, Bell, or Stone* (1962).

12 My citation refers to the page on which Birney's poem appears in *Delta*. Birney altered the lineation of the poem in later versions.

13 Purdy not only read and contributed to *Delta*, but he also "irregularly [...] helped" Louis Dudek produce issues (MacKendrick 136).

14 "'Her Gates Both East and West'" should not be confused with Purdy's 1972 essay of the same name.

2 Developing a Lyric Historiography

1 Purdy also reviewed Helge Ingstad's *Under the Pole Star* in *Canadian Literature* 33 (1967). His letters to Ingstad are available at Queen's University (see 2071a Box 1 Folder 2). The letters elaborate on Purdy's curiosity about Farley Mowat's accusation that Ingstad "planted" archaeological evidence at L'Anse aux Meadows; Ingstad vehemently denied the accusation. Purdy briefly describes the controversy in *Reaching for the Beaufort Sea* (239).

2 Sam Solecki mistakenly attributes this last quotation to Captain Luke Fox's *North-West Fox or Fox from the North-West Passage* (234).

3 The unpublished manuscript is in the University of Saskatchewan's Purdy Collection.

4 Sandra Djwa briefly discusses Pratt's wish to go north in "Al Purdy: Ivory Thots and the Last Romantic" (2008): "Pratt had wanted to go north to write on Franklin's expedition, but F.R. Scott was the first modern poet to actually get there, followed by both Earle Birney and Purdy" (52). The contrast of Pratt's inability to achieve his poetic vision with Purdy's seemingly inexhaustible funding from the CCA points to another motivator in the latter poet's career: his historiographic impulse matured at a moment when funding was available for him to explore settings that opened up a vast range of topics. Such geographic and historical diversity will become obvious as I proceed with my discussion of Purdy's continued experiments with lyric historiography after 1962.

5 Although there is a long-standing myth that Canada's mid-century cultural boom can be boiled down to the Massey Commission report, there was much more happening. In *Making Culture*, Maria Tippett roots the voracious artistic spirit of the 1950s in the formation of various artistic groups

in previous decades, such as the Sculptors' Society of Canada (est. 1928) and the Canadian Authors' Association (est. 1921). These groups and many others promoted primarily "Canadian content" in order to "foster indigenous [that is, English-Canadian] activity" (Tippett 15). This example is one of many others that Tippett uses to explain cultural growth that occurred long before the Massey Commission. Her most frequent examples are of private philanthropy, as well as groups and commissions established to fund and sustain pre-1950 artists (e.g., Montreal's Contemporary Arts Society [est. 1939] and the Massey Foundation [est. 1918]).

6 Purdy does not capitalize "alters" in later versions of the poem; the capitalization of the word in *The Cariboo Horses* may have been a typo.

7 The poem first appeared, with an erroneous title ("The Battle of Batoche"), in *The Globe and Mail Weekend Magazine* 33.20 (1972).

8 Purdy first published "Winter Walking" in *The Blur in Between* (1960), but the line I've quoted first appeared in the 1968 version of the poem.

3 Lyric And Regionalism: Challenging Histories, Part 1

1 This chapter, specifically the sections dealing with John Newlove's "The Pride," appeared in *Studies in Canadian Literature* 38.1 (2013) in a different form. Readers of that article will notice some rhetorical shifts in the revised version provided here. In retrospect, my original article put too little pressure on Newlove and did too little to make him accountable for his problematic portrayals of Indigenous stories and people. Since 2011, when I wrote that article, I have gained new theoretical and historical perspective. Readers who compare that article to this chapter will therefore notice that I take a harder line here with Newlove than I did in *SCL*, even as I stand by my basic argument that Newlove did, in ways poets before him had not, inspire a generation of regionalist poets and that we should not read such poets in only one way. Nonetheless, I have made changes to this chapter, which signal my admission that my earlier publication did not go far enough in either acknowledging the shortcomings of "The Pride" or appreciating the arguments of scholars like Margery Fee, who was one of the first critics to do the important work of drawing attention to problematic portrayals of Indigenous groups in Canadian poetry.

2 Lorna Crozier and Gary Hyland point also to R.E. Rashley as an example of a modern poet on the prairies (245). However, Rashley's readership was minimal and much of his poetry was, until *Paso Por Aqui* (1973), largely romantic in its themes and concerns. I have found only two critics who directly mention Rashley as an influence. E.F. Dyck says that "the first significant books [of Saskatchewan poetry] appear in the fifties (Rashley,

Mandel) and sixties (Newlove)" ("Introduction" xvi). Alternatively, Don Kerr remarks that the publication of Rashley's selected poems is "an important event in Canadian poetry, though few will be aware of it" (169); he doesn't say much in the way of Rashley's influence on younger writers but instead focuses on Rashley's move from "embarrassing" poetry (170) to the more "powerful" poems of his later career (177).

3 While I use the term "regionalist" positively, some critics have vehemently rejected the term. The common critique of regionalist writing has been its presumed emphasis on shallow features of the local (i.e., landscape). These critiques can be found in the work of E.K. Brown ("regionalist art ... stresses the superficial and the peculiar at the expense [...] of the fundamental and universal" [25]), Edward McCourt ("True regional literature ... illustrates the effect of particular, rather than general, physical, economic, and racial features upon the lives of ordinary men and women" [*Canadian West* 56]), and Robert Wardhaugh (who says that regionalism uses "place" as its "'defining' element" and thus sidesteps "gender, class, and ethnicity" [5]). These attacks on regionalism, though, centre on a very specific definition of a term that can be more productively (or at least more variously) defined. I therefore agree with Jonathan Hart when he says that "regionalism itself is neither bad nor good. It can be used for positive or negative ends": it can "reinscribe stereotypes" or "provide alternatives" (115). Eli Mandel similarly wanted to destigmatize the concept of regionalism by thinking about it as "a region of the mind" ("Images" 50); in other words, an expression of an individual experience of the region from any perspective important to the individual. Mandel's model of regionalism is the one that has most influenced my own definition as I have outlined it in this chapter: I use "prairie region" not simply for the purpose of identifying one comprehensible space, but instead to acknowledge the multiple sites in which a heterogeneous literary culture flourished after 1960: in this context, the term denotes the geographical boundaries of Alberta, Saskatchewan, and Manitoba, the provinces in which many of the poets I study rooted their poetry and/or established themselves.

4 It is worth noting, too, that most prairie criticism exhibits a preference for fiction over poetry. Donald Stephens's *Writers of the Prairies* (1973), for instance, includes an article on only one prairie poet, Robert Kroetsch, whose poetry is eclipsed by a discussion of his novels.

5 The growth of these kinds of initiatives has been covered in spectacular detail by Crozier and Hyland (246) and, to a lesser extent, in the work of Nathalie Cooke (see "Lorna Crozier"). I confirmed many such details in this section by interviewing Mick Burrs.

6 While Careless is the sole author of this article, his paper was published exactly as he presented it at the CHA conference. Hence, Lower's

comments during question period were published alongside Careless's article, but not as a separate piece. For purposes of readability, I've cited Lower's comments as part of Careless's article.

7 See Louis Dudek's "Two Canadian Poets Who Are 'Raw, Exciting, Alive'" (1965) and Robert Weaver's "Three Canadian Books That Might Get Overlooked" (1965). Newlove tended to receive high praise from his critics. In a 1968 review of Newlove's *Black Night Window*, for instance, Weaver called him "today's poet": "*Black Night Window* isn't only an impressive book of poetry in its own right, it also has qualities of intelligence, ambition and generosity that make it a good omen for John Newlove's future career" ("Today's Poet" 39). Douglas Barbour, reviewing the same text, wrote that Newlove's best "poems rank with any that are being written in the world today" (Rev. of *BNW* 295).

8 Newlove met Purdy sometime in late 1963 at Roy Kiyooka's home (S. Newlove, Telephone interview). They continued a regular correspondence thereafter.

9 A.J.M. Smith included a revised version of "The Pride" in *Modern Canadian Verse* (1967) that is nearly identical to the one that concludes Newlove's watershed collection, *Black Night Window* (1968). Newlove revised and reprinted "The Pride" numerous times: two more versions appear in Andy Wainwright's *Notes for a Native Land* (1969) and Newlove's *The Fat Man: Selected Poems, 1962–1972* (1977).

10 John Ferns, for instance, championed "The Pride" as "an important Canadian poem," one destined to "become a staple of university Canadian literature courses" (73).

11 Some of this enthusiasm for Newlove can be found, among other places, in Dennis Cooley's "RePlacing" (1980), Gary Geddes's "The Site of a Loss: or, the Pleasures of Rewriting the Text" (1996), and Patrick Lane's "The Unyielding Phrase" (1989).

12 See E.F. Dyck's analysis of *The Green Plain*, in which he notes that Newlove "parodies" Eliot ("Place" 84).

13 Readers of "The Pride" and Newlove's other poems about history will notice the poet's general reluctance to capitalize names. He explained the habit in a letter to George Bowering from 2 November 1965: "Probably I made indian names, d'sonoqua, etc., with no capitals because caps in the middle of the line interrupt it, to me, clog the eye: anyways they have an effect, like any move, and I didn't want the effect. Actually only believe in caps for start of sentence, nowhere else. That's the greek in me. Coming out. Geek" (Newlove to Bowering).

14 In Andy Wainwright's anthology, *Notes for a Native Land*, Newlove added "again" to the last line of "The Pride." My discussion here, however, concerns Newlove's project as it took shape during the 1960s; I have therefore

relied on the version he published in *Black Night Window* and, where relevant, in *Tamarack*.

4 The Métis Uprisings: Challenging Histories, Part 2

1 As a representative of the Métis people, Louis Riel was the leader of two nineteenth-century uprisings. The first uprising, commonly known as the Red River Rebellion (1869–70), led to the creation of the Manitoba Act, which officially recognized Manitoba as a Canadian province. The execution of Thomas Scott, an Irish Canadian captured during Riel's raid of Fort Garry, Saskatchewan, intensified hostilities between Riel and the Canadian government. Consequently, Riel escaped to the United States, but he returned in 1885 to lead the Northwest Uprising (1885) in a second effort to resolve the discontent of the Métis people. Riel's forces were defeated at the Battle of Batoche in May 1885, and Riel himself was executed for treason in Regina that November.

2 Of course, Dales's argument is only one of many explanations for Riel's popularity; Douglas Owram argues that a pervasive attraction to "the ubiquitous American cowboy" (325) was equally responsible. As the passage is valuable for those interested in potential causes of shifts in Riel history, here is Owram's explanation of Riel's popularity during the 1960s: "The war itself had created a new awareness of the dangers of racial injustice and had made the former casual assumptions about race less acceptable. Equally, the previous orientation toward the expansion of the might of the British empire as a perspective for the writing of Canadian history began to seem less relevant [...] Finally, Canadians were absorbing more and more of their cultural standards and images from south of the border. Radio, newspapers, magazines, and even comic books brought home to Canadians the relative abundance of American heroes like Davey Crockett, Stonewall Jackson, and, of course, the ubiquitous American cowboy" (325).

3 See Souster's "The Heroes" (1977) and "Found Poem: Louis Riel Addresses the Jury" (1977); Kim Dales and Patrick Holland also note this trend in Souster's writing (Dales 9–12; Holland 226–7).

4 I am relying on a version of my interview with Burrs that was published on *Prairie Fire*'s website. As part of a site renovation, the interview has since been removed.

5 Although Newlove wrote this poem in 1965, my discussion draws on the version he published in *Black Night Window* for two reasons. First, the version he produced in 1965 is virtually identical to that which he published in 1968. Second, my discussion partly concerns Newlove's impact on his fellow poets. Since, based on archival evidence, it seems that only Roy Kiyooka saw his rough draft of "Crazy Riel," I have decided to focus on the version of the poem that reached a larger group of readers. The draft can

be found in Newlove's letter to Kiyooka (31 August 1965), which is stored in his archives at the University of Manitoba.

6 Letendre founded the village that became known as Batoche. He lived there during the decisive 1885 battle that ended the Northwest uprising and actively participated in the reconstruction of the community after the battle devastated local businesses and residences.

7 A version of Burrs's poem ("Mrs. Nicolas") originally appeared in *Going to War: Found Poems of the Metis People* (1975). The poem is based on Carol Pearlstone's discussion with Mrs Alexandrine Nicolas, who lived in Duck Lake, Saskatchewan, and witnessed the 1885 uprising. Burrs's poem "summarizes an entire tape" of interviews with Mrs Nicolas (*Going to War* 30).

8 In making this statement, I am thinking of Bryan Palmer's *Canada's 1960s*: "The great irony of the Sixties was thus that while it decisively declared the end of one Canada, it defeated, for a generation or more, the possibility of realizing a new national identity" (429).

5 Inheriting the Past

1 The admiration that Purdy, Cohen, and Mandel had for Layton has been acknowledged in, respectively, *The Last Canadian Poet* (Sam Solecki; 1999), *Various Positions: A Life of Leonard Cohen* (Ira B. Nadel; 2010), and *The Politics of Art: Eli Mandel's Poetry and Criticism* (Ed Jewinski and Andrew James Stubbs; 1992). Barry McKinnon studied under Layton at Sir George Williams University in Montreal in the 1960s.

2 See Newlove's letter to Jack David at ECW Press: "Can't use title "Permanent Tourist," or "Tourist," because it's Pat Page's. Just found out. Permanent memory" (Newlove to David).

3 The correspondence is in Newlove's archives at the University of Manitoba. J. Newlove offered to pay Thomas Vernon Newlove for a copy of the family tree once it was completed.

4 At the University of Manitoba, I looked for evidence that Newlove knew Suknaski finished his documentary project, but I found nothing. Newlove may never have known.

5 In fact, many reviewers of McNeil's era enthusiastically celebrated her writing. Lorraine Vernon admired the "fierce intensity" that lay "beneath [McNeil's] cold clarity" (36a) and Gary Geddes declared McNeil a "genuine poet" ("Celebrating" 38). Judith Fitzgerald goes further. She proclaims McNeil's *The Overlanders* (1982), a long poem about a nineteenth-century Canadian expedition, to be "perfectly conceived and executed" and "almost too good to be real" (17). I cite these reviews to remind readers that McNeil stirred her critics with an "exciting and impressive flowering of poetic talent" (Gasparini ,"Ghosts" 18), even if very little has been written about her work; several short review essays and a brief article, "Florence

McNeil and Pat Lowther" (1977) by Sean Ryan (a.k.a. Eugene McNamara), make up the only extended considerations of her poetry.

6 Mandel published the poem for the first time in *Trio* (1954), but he notes the date of composition in "Auschwitz and Poetry" as 1946 (4–5).

7 Zieroth drew further inspiration from Margaret Laurence, who was, like himself, born in Neepawa, Manitoba. He discovered her writing in the 1960s, and, too broke to purchase her books, he read her writing in department stores "a chapter at a time" (Laurence, "Books" 242).

8 See George Woodcock's "Swarming of Poets: An Editorial Reportage" (1971) and "The Meeting of Time and Space" (1987).

9 I am drawing this phrase – "isolated image" – from Louis Dudek's "Theory of the Image" (268).

6 The "Edge of the Photograph": Developmental Long Poems

1 According to Mandel, "Descriptions, inventories, and administrative records in [Russian archives] were all known as pamiati; epic tales were written down 'for the old to hear and the young to remember'" (qtd Suknaski "Prairie Graveyard" 116).

2 For instance, Ian Underhill published a teaching guide, *Family Portraits* (1978), and Kenneth Sherman edited *Relations: Family Portraits* (1986).

3 See, for instance, Northrop Frye's note that a large number of Canadian poets "have turned to narrative forms ... rather than lyrical ones" (242).

4 McKinnon completed and began circulating the poem in 1970, but he officially published it in 1975.

5 My biographical notes on McKinnon are derived from my personal interviews with him, as well as his memoir on the Caledonia Writing Series.

6 McKinnon's *Sex at Thirty-One* was later anthologized in the prairie-born Sharon Thesen's *The New Long Poem Anthology* (1991).

7 The third part of McKinnon's *I Wanted to Say Something* can be found in his fonds at the University of Northern British Columbia.

8 Because the original version of *I Wanted to Say Something* is an extremely rare text, all citations refer to the 1990 version (hereafter *IWSS*).

9 In his poem, Purdy attributes the line to John Donne, referring to Donne's "Meditation XVII": "No man is an island entire of itself; every man / is a piece of the continent, a part of the main" (lines 1–2).

7 Sharing Authority

1 In his biographical statement for the book, Suknaski titled it *Rose Far in the East*. I have used the title that appears on the front cover.

2 See Lorna Roth's "The Delicate Acts of "Colour Balancing": Multiculturalism and Canadian Television Broadcasting Policies and Practices" (1998).

The government also published a guidebook, *Publications Supported by Multiculturalism Canada* (1984), to demonstrate the vast networks supported by this initiative; Suknaski's *Narid* is listed as an example of a text funded by the agency (55).

3 Ross and Suknaski were actually very close, as Ross was a personal hero to Suknaski. In addition to the letters published in Ross's *Collecting Stamps Would Have Been More Fun*, there are many other exchanges between the two writers in Suknaski's archive at the University of Manitoba.

4 I have opted not to include Suknaski's pictures in this book due to their poor quality. Even in Suknaski's original text, the photographs are of extremely low resolution and are therefore virtually impossible to reproduce effectively.

5 I have been unable to locate the original article, but Suknaski kept a cropped photocopy of it, which can be found in his archive at the University of Manitoba (MSS 125 Box 11 Folder 11). "Louis Leveille" is well over four hundred lines long in Suknaski's 1974 draft of *Wood Mountain Poems*, and he replicates much of his source material verbatim. Al Purdy, seemingly unaware that "Louis Leveille" was a found poem, removed all but approximately twenty lines, which constitute the final version of the poem.

6 Suknaski also had an impact on novelists: upon meeting Suknaski, Margaret Laurence "immediately thanked him for *Wood Mountain Poems*, saying it validated her own project of writing the story of western Canada" (D. Morgan 31).

7 The article in question is Lucy S. Dawidowicz's "Babi Yar's Legacy," which appeared in the *New York Times* on 27 Sept. 1981. In Burrs's selected poems, *The Names Leave the Stones*, he introduced "Missing Persona Report" by quoting Suknaski's marginalia on Dawidowicz's article (45).

8 A revised version of this poem appears in *The Names Leave the Stones: Poems New and Selected* (2001).

8 Figurative Families and Feminism

1 In *The Red Shoes: Margaret Atwood Starting Out* (1998), Rosemary Sullivan recounts the history of Atwood's ancestor, Mary Webster, who was accused of witchcraft and sentence to hanging; she survived the execution (16). In *Margaret Atwood: A Biography* (1998), Nathalie Cooke speaks more on Atwood's representations of family (see, for instance, 270).

2 In fact, after 1960, there were many examples of female writers working through this same process and exploring figurative foremothers who were of both artistic and historical importance to them: Florence McNeil said "women poets have tended to identify more personally than men with [non-familial] historical figures" (Letter from McNeil to Weingarten) (an

identification she explores in *Emily* [1975]), Jovette Marchessault finds a figurative family among four female writers from Quebec's history in *Saga of the Wet Hens* (1981), and Susan Swan imagines her connection (even if only by name) to the nineteenth-century celebrity Anna Swan (whom she portrays as a writer) in *The Biggest Modern Woman of the World* (1985).

3 See Atwood's correspondence with Margaret Laurence (Thomas Fisher Margaret Atwood Papers, MSS 200 Box 160 Folder 11). Atwood mailed Laurence selections from *Sisterhood Is Powerful* in late 1970 or early 1971. In several letters from January 1971, Atwood and Laurence discuss the merits and flaws of particular articles from this anthology.

4 See Purdy's letter dated 24 March 1970 in Atwood's papers at the Thomas Fisher Library: "Just had a chance to look thoroughly at your Moodie (Moody?) book ... All sorts of thoughts about it, so asked George Woodcock to review it for CanLit. Already doing it for Wascana R. so Purdy swings into high gear or something" (Purdy to Atwood). Purdy's review appeared in the winter 1971 issue of *Canadian Literature*.

5 After seeing Atwood's sketches of Moodie in Jay Macpherson's living room, William Toye (Atwood's editor at Oxford University Press) convinced her to include these sketches in *The Journals of Susanna Moodie*. He wrote to Atwood, "Though I don't remember them clearly, I did see and like the pictures by you in Jay's living room" (Toye to Atwood).

6 Atwood mentions the project in an interview with Linda Sandler (27).

7 Purdy is not the only critic to make this observation: Sid Stephen calls the poems a "self-portrait of Margaret Atwood" (32), Sherrill Grace notes the duality of the Atwood-Moodie speaker (*Violent Duality* 34), Diana Relke identifies the speaker as "Atwood/Moodie" (43), and Faye Hammill senses something unmistakably modern about Atwood's "blunt, colloquial diction," which "contrasts sharply with the restraint and decorum of Moodie's own prose" (71).

8 Atwood offers comparable views in an earlier interview, in which she said "nobody can claim to have the absolute, whole, objective, total, complete truth" (Atwood and Castro 232).

9 This argument runs counter to one proposed by Coral Ann Howells, who connects Atwood's scepticism with postmodernist theory: "[T]he debates around historiography have induced [for Atwood] a general skepticism about the legitimating narratives of history" (111). Her tethering of "skepticism" and "postmodernism" leads her to conclude that the Susanna Moodie poems are somehow less sceptical than the later *Alias Grace*. But a careful reader would be hard-pressed to distinguish between the scepticism of these works in any way that isn't superficial. Laura Groening has made similar statements and regards Atwood's poems as an unfolding of "new truths" about Moodie (166).

10 Although publication dates suggest *Surfacing* is echoing *The Journals of Susanna Moodie*, it's difficult to say for sure which echoes which: Atwood wrote her early notes for *Surfacing* in 1965 (Atwood and Castro 218), whereas she began planning her poetic sequence in 1965 and began writing it sometime around 1967 (209).

11 See Margaret Atwood's papers at the Thomas Fisher Rare Books Library (MSS 200 Box 12 Folder 2).

12 From Gary Geddes: "*Emily* begs comparison with Atwood's *Journals of Susanna Moodie*, since both are about a woman's perception of the confrontation of wilderness and English gentility, and about the ego's struggle to control external data" ("Celebrating" 38). Numerous others observed parallels between McNeil's text and that of Atwood, as in reviews of *Emily* by Melanie Murray and Tanya Long.

13 Indeed, there were numerous responses to Atwood's poems in both fiction and theatre. Carol Shields rejected Atwood's image of a Moodie frightened by nature, but still recognized the value of her poems: "[Writers and historians are] all talking about separate readings and there's going to be a communal approach and a new Susanna Moodie, if you like, will rise from all this" (qtd Crowe, *Enduring Enigma*). In order to participate in this discourse, Shields wrote both a critical study of Moodie, *Susanna Moodie: Voice and Vision* (1977), and a novel, *Small Ceremonies* (1976), which detailed a contemporary scholar's attempt to write a biography about Moodie. Timothy Findley "reengaged" with Moodie's story in *Headhunter* (1993) after he "was reintroduced" to her through Atwood's poems (qtd Crowe, *Enduring Enigma*). Donna Smyth's play *Susanna Moodie* (1976) incorporated selections from both Atwood's poetry and Moodie's *Roughing It in the Bush*. There was, too, Beth Hopkins and Anne Joyce's *Daughter by Adoption* (1981), as well as Peggy Sample's *Love and Work Enough* (1984).

14 Nathalie Cooke also notes Atwood's influence on the structure of Stephanie Bolster's *White Stone: The Alice Poems* (1998; see Cooke's *Margaret Atwood: A Critical Companion* [26]); in an interview, Bolster recalls Atwood's book – her "first encounter" with the "book-length poetic sequence" – was a model for her own poems about Alice Liddell, a figure "who stood in certain ways as a surrogate" for the author herself (Email from Bolster).

15 Janet Friskney frames this editorial choice somewhat differently in *New Canadian Library*: "M&S decided substantial abridgement of *Roughing It in the Bush* would be necessary for financial reasons" (139). The editor, Carl Klinck, did not object; he had, in fact, "suggested the first significant excisions" before others at M&S expressed concerns about cost-saving (138).

9 Indigeneity and Performance: The Fictions of Nations

1 Laura Gillman's *Unassimilable Feminisms* (2010) takes up the various feminisms that emerged as a response to the feminist movement of the 1960s (Gillman's specific context is American), and in that book (see especially chapters 3 and 4) she offers a detailed account of the various political and cultural associations inherent in the term "womanism." Gillman's book more generally is a thoughtful reflection that offers "more nuanced frameworks for understanding intra-group differences" (6).

2 These comments from the RCSW report speak to the work of Ristock and Wine, both of whom stress that, after 1970, Canadian women became increasingly "aware of women's diversity" (12).

3 Margery Fee and Dory Nason note that the terms "Mohawk" and "Iroquois," while still commonly accepted, are gradually "being replaced by 'Kanien'kehá: ka' for the people, meaning People of the Flint" ("Introduction" 13). Like Fee and Nason, I use the term "Mohawk" because it is the same term Johnson used to identify herself.

4 As of spring 2016, the link to Kimmy Beach's interview with Joan Crate was non-functioning. I am indebted to Beach for sharing a digital copy of this interview with me as I revised my manuscript.

5 Purdy was, in fact, suspicious of Solecki's title, and expressed some doubt regarding its accuracy in a letter to Solecki dated 18 February 1997 (Solecki, *Yours, Al* 524–5).

6 In making this claim, I am not speculating on each author's reactions to the directions in which lyric historiography went. I acknowledge, of course, methodological overlaps, patterns of influence, and so forth – but none of these intersections guarantees that Purdy, for instance, would have regarded the poetics of Crate or other writers admiringly; earlier in my study, in an analogous case, I noted that Ramsay Cook and J.M.S. Careless regretted – to one degree or another – the discourse born out of their joint work on "limited identities" (see Careless's "Limited Identities – Ten Years Later"). Whether or not the political or cultural positions of writers in my study aligned, though, I caution readers against assuming that these differing positions necessarily suggest implicit antagonisms among them.

7 Winona LaDuke (Anishinaabe), in a related passage, distinguishes between the Anishinaabeg word "nishnabe akin" ("the land to which the people belong") and the European model of "the land belongs to the people." The former concept, LaDuke points out, presupposes connections and "responsibilities" to the land, rather than commercial or governmental ownership (23).

8 Chris Andersen (Métis) contests this reading of "mixed" identity in his recent history of the Métis people. For Andersen, the assumption that "mixed

blood" necessarily denotes dividedness is based on European concepts of blood quantum and cultural purity, whereas the Métis people themselves understand identity as fluid and intersectional. See *Metis: Race, Recognition, and the Struggle for Indigenous Peoplehood* (2014), in which he argues that the popular assumption that "Métis" denotes simply "mixedness" rather than a political national consciousness underscores "the relative inability of Canadian colonial administrators to think outside their own official binaries of 'white' and 'Indian'" (35–6). "Métis are classified as hybrid," he writes, "in ways that deny that which we seek most, an acknowledgement of our political legitimacy and authenticity as an Indigenous people" (38).

9 Akiwenzie-Damm's words here capture the spirit of the "appropriation debates" ongoing since the 1980s. An early articulation came from Lenore Keeshig-Tobias, who contributed to a CBC Radio panel on cultural appropriation, in which she reiterated for listeners that the "void" in Indigenous literature is the direct result of "outlaw[ing] native cultures" (*Morningside* 41). Keeshig-Tobias's statements in that transcript capture, in brief, the essential concerns that have sustained these debates about the liberal arts for the last several decades.

10 A recent study that offers an excellent and detailed account of these issues is Jo-Ann Episkenew's *Taking Back Our Spirits: Indigenous Literature, Public Policy, and Healing* (2009).

11 The effect of this process, as described by both Emma LaRocque ("Here" ix) and Lee Maracle (78), was widespread illiteracy in Indigenous communities across Canada. For both authors, that illiteracy partly explains the relative dearth of Indigenous literature between 1900 and 1990.

12 French and Logan's sentiments are quite common in Canadian anthologies published between 1900 and 1990. Denham et al., the editors of *The Evolution of Canadian Literature in English: 1867–1914* (1973), declared that "[Johnson's] poetry now seems more amusing and embarrassing than serious and patriotic." They conclude that the only way to appreciate Johnson is to value her education in English poetry: "Her best work is ... that in which she ... sings in her own voice and combines an English lyrical form with native Canadian imagery" (191). The obvious implication of such statements is that Johnson can only be a good poet when she writes from within a European tradition. This is the same sentiment Catherine M. McLay espouses in *Canadian Literature: The Beginnings to the 20th Century* (1974), in which she included fourteen poems by Johnson. McLay is generally affirming, but she makes overt efforts to convince her reader that Johnson is primarily descended from an English tradition: "Despite her Indian inheritance, Johnson shares with the Canadian poets of her generation the strong influence of Wordsworth, Keats and Shelley

and of their successors Tennyson and Swinburne. ... Even the Indian poems are not without evidence of her British education ... " (387). McLay speaks of Johnson's heritage and "Indian poems" as though they keep her at a disadvantage ("Despite ... even"), rather than acknowledging them as literarily valid and valuable. She seems concerned that her audience might "mistake" Johnson for a Mohawk poet rather than an Anglo-American one. It's a common tactic editors use to explain Johnson's inclusion: they propose, openly or unconsciously, that her absorption of Western literature is a symbolic success (a microcosm of colonial assimilation) that makes her a poet of worth, "despite," as McLay would have it, the intellectual and cultural 'disadvantage' that stems from her "Indianness." There isn't anything inherently wrong with acknowledging Johnson's literary education, which did include extensive reading in Anglo-American romanticism. The concern in so doing, though, is that that acknowledgment risks representing Johnson as the "Indian" who was civilized by her contact with that tradition, rather than suggesting that two (or more) equally valuable traditions informed her work to varying degrees.

13 The pavilion remained open and received extensive media attention: John Gray wrote in the *Montreal Star* that the display's "brutal frankness" about the horrors of colonialism undermined the "sweetness and pride of national achievement" that many expected from Expo 67 (qtd Miller and Rutherdale 167). See also Palmer's *Canada's 1960s* (391–2).

14 In making these claims, Ruffo is drawing on Sally Weaver's *Making Canadian Indian Policy* (1981).

15 In acknowledging this rapid expansion of political organizations, I also want to be clear that there were organizations in the early twentieth century, despite the laws intended to limit their development. There was, for instance, the Indian League of Canada (est. 1919). See Hoefnagels's "Native Activism and the Development of Powwows in the 1960s" (2009).

16 The rhetoric of Hawthorn's report was consistently condemnatory. "Something has gone wrong," Hawthorn concluded: "For a century public policy affecting Indians has suffered from the twin and related evils of widely agreed meaningful objectives, and by [*sic*] a relative failure of the Canadian people and their governments to provide the funds and the personnel to mount large scale positive programs of development for the Indian people" (400).

17 Some historians of course vehemently opposed conclusions drawn by the Hawthorn Commission. In 1983, Robert J. Carney wrote that the Hawthorn Report was propaganda used to end "public funding for Roman Catholic schools" (610); unsurprisingly, his piece appeared in the Canadian Catholic Historical Association's journal. Through an incredibly myopic analysis of early twentieth-century legislation, Carney argues that

the Canadian government had always admirably promoted Indigenous "enfranchisement" (612), though he seems curiously indifferent to the fact that Aboriginals were unable to vote in Canadian federal elections without sacrificing their "Indian" status until 1960.

18 Even before the announcement of the White Paper, however, Red Power had been gaining momentum. As well, these later groups drew inspiration from more than just Hawthorn's report: they were also partly inspired by the civil rights movements in the United States, which encouraged them to enact their own challenge "to constituted authority" (Finkel 243). Métis historian Howard Adams, for example, notes "there was a parallel between Red Power in Canada and Black Power in the U.S." (qtd Palmer 402).

19 Like activists of the 1960s, contemporary historians continue to view the White Paper as evidence of a desire to make Canada "white" (Newhouse 289; see also Palmer 393); the motif is common in much Canadian history of the last two decades.

20 David Newhouse covers these issues much more extensively in his work (see 290–1). The paper was also known as "The Red Paper."

21 While some celebrate Trudeau's 1971 policy, it did little to alleviate tensions in Canada. Kenneth McRoberts offers a solid critique of the policy. As Trudeau repeatedly stressed the policy's appeal to "individualism," many detractors felt that, for Trudeau, "the announcement of [multiculturalism] was more important than its implementation" (McRoberts 127). Greg Gauld likewise notes that Trudeau's notions of multiculturalism "largely left" communities "to organize themselves" (10). Such claims seem supported by the late prime minister's apparent indifference to the announcement of an official multiculturalism act, which came seventeen years later under Brian Mulroney's government. Furthermore, Trudeau funded multiculturalism programs poorly. In 1971–72, just under 80 million dollars were spent on bilingual programs, compared to only 2 million spent on multiculturalism. In 1981–2, 196 million dollars were spent on the former program, and only 14 million on the latter (McRoberts 128). Recent historians therefore criticize Trudeau's policy, which McRoberts contends was used to offset Quebec's push for biculturalism (McRoberts 120–90; see also Faurschou et al. 8–10).

22 I am indebted to José Igartua's *The Other Quiet Revolution* for pointing me to Dickie's work.

23 On the note of unavailability, Smaro Kamboureli points to the experiences of Lee Maracle (Sto:lo), who "began her writing career by publishing her own books because no Canadian publisher would publish her" ("Introduction" 3).

24 Ruffo estimates that the readerships numbered in the hundreds "if not thousands" ("Where the Voice" 181).

25 Citing Kim Anderson's *A Recognition of Being* (1997), Jo-Ann Episkenew contests this representation of Indigenous cultures: "In [some Indigenous] nations that engaged in agriculture, for example, farming was typically women's work. ... Indeed, some Indian societies considered the women to be the owners of the land. How shocked young Indian boys were when school officials ordered them to work on the school farms. By attempting to make them over into farmers, the school officials effectively emasculated these young men" (48).

26 Numerous biographers and critics such as Betty Keller, Carole Gerson, Veronica Strong-Boag, and Charlotte Gray have thoroughly proven that Johnson held the affection of contemporary poets such as Charles G.D. Roberts, her readers, and her audiences.

27 I want to make it clear that Lyon's position is deeply problematic. For instance, his evidence for Johnson's "incoheren[ce]" includes the fact that Johnson sometimes questioned the vanishing race myth, but then "had no children herself [and thus] embodied in her own life this theme" (146–7).

28 Johnson was best represented by in books edited by Theodore H. Rand, (*A Treasury of Canadian Verse* [1900]) and John W. Garvin (*Canadian Poets* [1916]), both of whom included a relatively diverse selection of poems to demonstrate her range of subjects and voice. Until the appearance of Terry Goldie and Daniel David Moses's *An Anthology of Native Literature in English* (1992) and Carole Gerson's *Canadian Poetry from the Beginnings through the First World War* (1994), Johnson was otherwise disregarded or poorly represented.

29 Johnson was, for example, excluded from A.J.M. Smith's *The Oxford Book of Canadian Verse* (1960), Alan Creighton and Hilda M. Ridley's *The New Canadian Anthology* (1938), M.G. Hesse's *Women in Canadian Literature* (1976), Ralph Gustafson's *The Anthology of Canadian Poetry* (1941), Gustafson's multiple editions of *The Penguin Book of Canadian Verse* (1958, 1967), Carl F. Klinck and Reginald E. Watters's three editions of *Canadian Anthology* (1974), and Malcolm Ross's *Poets of the Confederation* (1961).

30 Smith softened these criticisms in later versions of the anthology, but their core remained intact: "though her collected poems are still sold to tourists in Vancouver and Victoria, [Johnson] is likely to be remembered chiefly for one or two graceful lyrics which make no claim to national or racial significance. In the theatrical and once popular ballads of Indian life, her rhythm is heavy, her imagery conventional, and her language melodramatic and forced" (23; 1948). Smith republished this version of his notes on Johnson's poetry in the 1957 edition of his anthology.

31 See J.A. Weingarten's "Modernist Poetry in Canada, 1920–1960" (2015) as well as Peggy Kelly's "Politics, Gender, and *New Provinces*" (2003) for more

on Livesay's exclusion from *New Provinces* (1936). While Smith fought for her inclusion, F.R. Scott opposed it.

32 Birney's exact phrase was "I don't read her" (qtd Gerson and Strong-Boag 130). The context of the statement, as presented in Gerson and Strong-Boag's *Paddling Her Own Canoe*, is somewhat unclear, and perhaps overstated on Birney's part, given that he included Johnson's "The Train Dogs" in *20th Century Canadian Poetry* (1953).

33 That being said, Ruffo has argued that even if Johnson had been anthologized, her reception would still have suffered from the epidemic of illiteracy among Indigenous communities caused by residential schools, which "effectively severed whatever influence E. Pauline Johnson might have had on the next generation of Native writers" ("Introduction" xxii).

34 Margery Fee and Dory Nason give an excellent and thorough account of these criticisms with close attention to the work of Rick Monture (specifically, *We Share Our Matters*). See Fee and Nason's introduction to *Tekahionwake: E. Pauline Johnson's Writings on Native North America* (23–6).

35 Atwood writes that Johnson's "The Indian Girl in Modern Fiction" (1892), "tears strips off a number of white authors for dishing up, again and again, the same kind of Indian maiden in their books – a poor, doomed creature, who passionately loves the white hero ... and who usually ends her life by suicide. ... Johnson herself wrote a haunting poem in which it's the white man who dies for the Indian woman instead ... I'm willing to bet ['The Pilot of the Plains'] influenced more than one writer ... that is, besides me" (*Strange Things* 92–3)

36 Numerous writers attest to Johnson's impact on Indigenous writers. Lee Maracle has similarly called her "the mother of Indigenous literature north of the 49th parallel" (78).

37 In a similar vein, Gloria Bird, in conversation with Joy Harjo (Muscogee [Creek]), adds that there is often a "mental bondage" in Indigenous writing, which suggests that many such writers have "internalized the stereotypes and romanticisms" of colonial society (Bird and Harjo 25).

38 Mark Cronlund Anderson and Carmen L. Robertson also interpret Johnson's "transformation" in this way (105).

39 See, for instance, Fee's "The Trickster Moment," which explores the use of this motif in scholarly criticism.

40 Ruffo similarly captures LaRocque's conundrum when he says that "much of Johnson's work ... begs the question as to whether Johnson the writer was undermined by Johnson the performer. There is also the related question of her being co-opted into white Canadian society ... Johnson the Union-Jack-waving poet, extolling the virtues of a fledgling nation" ("Out of the Silence" 212).

41 Anne Collett gives a thorough account of this book's publication history in "Pauline Johnson-Tekahionwake: Trafficking Woman" (2008).

42 It is true that Allen Johnson hosted parties while wearing "Iroquois garments," to which some of his colleagues' daughters were invited, which eventually led to his dismissal from his job (Gerson and Strong-Boag , *Paddling* 52).

43 Mary Elizabeth Leighton writes about similar instances of commodifying Johnson; she notes, for instance, that promotional material for her performance occasionally appeared alongside advertisements for "Pocahontas cigars" (152).

44 Betty Keller, for instance, recalls a story in which a Canadian soldier came up to Johnson after she performed "A Cry from an Indian Wife" for her audience and conveyed to her that the poem had made him regret his own role in fighting the Métis during the 1885 Northwest Uprising (60).

45 See Fee's "The Trickster Moment."

46 Pamela Palmater (Mi'kmaq), for instance, has done much to expose the legal, social, familial, and psychological consequences of a system in which legal identity is determined not by Indigenous groups themselves but rather by the Canadian government. Palmater also talks about generations of repressed identities: "Despite my grandmother's ability to speak the [Mi'kmaq] language fluently, she told her children that speaking Mi'kmaq would only cause them harm in the outside world. She did not feel free to pass on her language to her children and grandchildren" (16).

10 The Future of History

1 While poetry is an obvious example for me to draw on here for purposes of comparison, there is a broader claim to be made for personalism in Indigenous writing. Armand Garnett Ruffo has said much of this: "Aboriginal people tended to gravitate towards political essay, memoir, poetry, and sacred story. At the risk of generalizing, we can understand why these genres might have been adopted. With so many grievances, the loss of traditions, the loss of lands and self-determination, Aboriginal people naturally sought to validate their cultures and seek redress, choosing forms that readily allowed them to express themselves" ("Where the Voice" 172).

2 As I entered the final editing phase of this book, a colleague brought to my attention Neal McLeod's history of domestic abuse. Naturally, this realization had me thinking about the ethical implications not just of including McLeod's work in a manuscript on its way to press, but also of using his work as a lens through which to look at Halfe's poetry. With regard to the latter issue, I consulted with Halfe, and she granted me permission to

draw on McLeod's work with reference to her poetry. With regard to the ethical implications of using his work in the first place, my invocation of McLeod's scholarship is a sign of respect for his extensive cultural knowledge and lucidity as a scholar, but it should by no means be interpreted as a disavowal of his wrongdoing or as a minimizing of the harm he has caused others.

3 Through her studies with Tim Lilburn at the University of Victoria, Morgan discovered many of the poets who had the greatest impact on her early writing. Lilburn, she recalls, "recognized something in my very early writing which he felt would be fostered by Andrew Suknaski and Louise Halfe." Morgan then read Al Purdy's "Say the Names," Newlove's prairie poems from the 1960s, and Gregory Scofield's *Singing Home the Bones*, the last of which, she has said, "threads its influence all through *What Became My Grieving Ceremony*" (Email from Morgan).

4 On the note of Ruffo and Grey Owl: "that's the reason I took on the project in the first place. If it hadn't been for the stories that I had heard about Belaney from my grandmother and great uncle, then I probably wouldn't have been drawn to the story ... the central thing that I learned is that it was my family, the Espaniel family ... who actually helped create Grey Owl" (Ruffo and McLeod 28).

Works Cited

ARCHIVAL SOURCES

Margaret Atwood Papers. Thomas Fisher Rare Book Library, U of Toronto.
"Ghost," MSS 200 Box 12 Folder 4.
"Letter to Descendants," MSS 200 Box 12 Folder 4.
Letter to Margaret Laurence 18 Jan. 1971, MSS 200 Box 160 Folder 11.
Letter from MacEwen, 2 April 1970, MSS 200 Box 160 Folder 23.
Letter from Al Purdy 24 March 1970, MSS 335, Box 76 (No Folder).
Letter to Al Purdy, 26 March 1970, MSS 335 Box 76 (No Folder).
Letter to Bill Toye, 25 Feb. 1969, MSS 335 Box 76 (No Folder).
Letter from Bill Toye, 9 Oct. 1969, MSS 335 Box 76 (No Folder).
PEN Speech. MSS 200 Box 91 Folder 30.

Earle Birney Papers. MS. Coll. 49. Thomas Fisher Rare Book Library, U of Toronto.
Letter to UBC, 14 Nov. 1971, Box 129 Folder 51.
Letter from Florence McNeil, 23 Oct. 1970, Box 129 Folder 51.

Contact Press Collection. MS COLL 69. Thomas Fisher Rare Book Library, U of Toronto.
Louis Dudek to Peter Miller, 24 Oct. 1961, Box 1 Folder 5.

John Newlove Papers. MS. 57. Thomas Fisher Rare Book Library, U of Toronto.
Letter from Al Purdy, 28 Aug. 1963, Box 10 Folder 40.

John Newlove Archives. MSS. 70. Dept. of Archives and Special Collections. Elizabeth Dafoe Library, U of Manitoba.
"History," n.d., Box 5 Folder 2.
Letter to George Bowering, 2 Nov. 1965, Box 18 Folder 14.
Letter to Robert Bringhurst, 14 May 1981, Box 18 Folder 16.
Letter to Jack David, 24 Feb. 1984, Box 23 Folder 12).
Letter to James English, 3 Nov. 1985, Box 20 Folder 15.

Letter to Roy Kiyooka, 31 Aug. 1965, Box 19 Folder 20.
Letter to Andrew Suknaski, 11 Feb. 1985, Box 21 Folder 2.
Letter from David Zieroth, 17 Sept. 1971, Box 21 Folder 14.

Al Purdy Fonds. Queen's U. Archives, Kathleen Ryan Hall.
Letter to Milton Acorn, 6 June 1974, 2071b Box 2 Folder 6.
Letter to Margaret Atwood, 21 Oct. 1970, 2071b Box 2 Folder 21.
Letter to Earle Birney, 7 Dec. 1969, 2071b Box 2 Folder 37.
Letter to Earle Birney, 27 Jan. 1979, 2071b Box 2 Folder 37.
Letter to George Bowering, 26 Sept. 1973, 2071b Box 2 Folder 43.
Letter to Jack McClelland. 26 Oct. 1972, 2071b Box 5 Folder 63.
Letter from Barry McKinnon, 31 Oct. 1972, 2071b Box 4 Folder 11.
Letter to Andrew Suknaski, 20 Oct. 1973, 2071b Box 5 Folder 22.
Letter to Bob Waller, 19 Oct. 1972, 2071b Box 5 Folder 63.
"Roblin's Mills [II]," 2071a Box 5 Folder 26.

Al Purdy Collection. MSS 4. U of Saskatchewan Archives, Murray Library.
"The New Poetry and the Old." Retrieved from: http://cdm15126.contentdm.oclc.org/cdm/compoundobject/collection/p201201coll1/id/1039.

Andrew Suknaski Fonds. MSS 125. Dept. of Archives and Special Collections, Elizabeth Dafoe Library, U of Manitoba.
Diary Entry. N.d. Box 10 Folder 8.
Letter from Newlove, 10 Nov. 1976, Box 12 Folder 3.

PRIMARY AND SECONDARY SOURCES

Abel, Jordan. *The Place of Scraps*. Vancouver: Talonbooks, 2013.

Adams, Howard. *Prison of Grass: Canada from the Native Point of View*. Toronto: New Press, 1975.

Akiwenzie-Damm, Kateri. "First Peoples Literature in Canada." *Hidden in Plain Sight: Contributions of Aboriginal Peoples to Canadian Identity and Culture*. Vol. 1. Ed. David R. Newhouse, Cora J. Voyageur, and Dan Beavon. Toronto: U of Toronto P, 2005. 169–76.

Amabile, George, and Kim Dales, eds. *No Feather, No Ink*. Saskatoon: Thistledown, 1985.

Andersen, Chris. *Métis: Race, Recognition, and the Struggle for Indigenous Peoplehood*. Vancouver: U of British Columbia P, 2014.

Anderson, Kim. *A Recognition of Being: Reconstructing Native Womanhood*. Toronto: Sumach, 2000.

Anderson, Mark Cronlund, and Carmen L. Robertson. *Seeing Red: A History of Natives in Canadian Newspapers*. Winnipeg: U of Manitoba P, 2011.

Ankersmit, Frank. "Statements, Texts, and Pictures." *A New Philosophy of History*. Ed. Frank Ankersmit and Hans Kellner. Chicago: U of Chicago P, 1995. 212–40.

Armstrong, Jeanette. "Aboriginal Literatures: A Distinctive Genre within Canadian Literature." *Hidden in Plain Sight: Contributions of Aboriginal Peoples to Canadian Identity and Culture*. Vol. 1. Ed. David R. Newhouse, Cora J. Voyageur, and Dan Beavon. Toronto: U of Toronto P, 2005. 180–6.

Attridge, Robert. Rev. of *In the Name of Narid*. *CV II* 6.4 (1982): 32–3.

Assembly of First Nations. "Honouring Earth." Retrieved 22 March 2014 from AFN.ca. http://www.afn.ca/en/honoring-earth.

Atwood, Margaret. *Double Persephone*. Toronto: Hawkshead, 1961.

– [as M.E. Atwood]. "Avalon Revisited." *Fiddlehead* 55 (1963): 10–13.

– [as M.E. Atwood]. "Fall and All: A Sequence." *Fiddlehead* 59 (1964): 58–63.

– *The Circle Game*. 1964. Toronto: Contact, 1966.

– *The Animals in That Country*. Toronto: Oxford UP, 1968.

– *The Edible Woman*. Toronto: McClelland and Stewart, 1969.

– *The Journals of Susanna Moodie*. Toronto: Oxford UP, 1970.

– *Surfacing*. Toronto: McClelland and Stewart, 1972.

– *Survival: A Thematic Guide to Canadian Literature*. Toronto: Anansi, 1972.

– "Introduction." *Roughing It in the Bush*. London: Virago, 1986. vii–xiv.

– "If You Can't Say Something Nice, Don't Say Anything at All." *Language in Her Eye: Views on Writing and Gender by Canadian Women Writing in English*. Ed. Libby Scheier et al. Toronto: Coach House, 1990. 15–25.

– *Morning in the Burned House*. Toronto: McClelland and Stewart, 1995.

– *Strange Things: The Malevolent North in Canadian Literature*. New York: Oxford UP, 1995.

– *Alias Grace*. London: Bloomsbury, 1996.

– *In Search of Alias Grace: On Writing Canadian Historical Fiction*. Ottawa: U of Ottawa P, 1997.

Atwood, Margaret, and Jo Brans. "Using What You're Given." 1988. *Waltzing Again: New and Selected Conversations with Margaret Atwood*. Princeton: Ontario Review, 2006. 79–89.

Atwood, Margaret, and Jan Garden Castro. "An Interview with Margaret Atwood." 1983. *Margaret Atwood: Vision and Forms*. Ed. Kathryn van Spanckeren and Jan Garden Castro. Carbondale: Southern Illinois UP, 1988. 215–32.

Atwood, Margaret, Kathryn Crabbe, and Gregory Fitzgerald. "Evading the Pigeonholers." 1987. *Margaret Atwood: Conversations*. Princeton: Ontario Review, 1990. 131–9.

Atwood, Margaret, and Karla Hammond. "Articulating the Mute." 1979. *Margaret Atwood: Conversations*. Princeton: Ontario Review, 1990. 109–20.

Atwood, Margaret, and J.R. (Tim) Struthers. "Playing Around." 1976. *Margaret Atwood: Conversations*. Princeton: Ontario Review, 1990. 58–68.

Atwood, Margaret, and Gail van Varseveld "Talking with Atwood." *Room of One's Own* 1.2 (1975): 66–79.

Bailey, Anne Geddes. "Re-visioning Documentary Readings of Anne Marriott's *The Wind Our Enemy.*" *Canadian Poetry: Studies, Documents, Reviews* 31 (1992): 55–67.

Bancroft, Hubert Howe. *History of the Northwest Coast.* San Francisco: History Company, 1884.

– *History of British Columbia 1792–1887.* San Francisco: History Company, 1887.

Barbour, Douglas. Rev. of *Black Night Window. Dalhousie Review* 49 (1969): 293–5.

– *Visions of My Grandfather.* Ottawa: Golden Dog, 1977.

– "John Newlove and His Works." *Canadian Writers and Their Works.* Ed. Jack David et al. Toronto: ECW, 1992: 279–336.

Barthes, Roland. *Camera Lucida: Reflections on Photography.* New York: Hill and Wang, 1981.

Bartley, Jan. "'Something in Which to Believe for Once': The Poetry of John Newlove." *Open Letter* 2.9 (1974): 19–48.

Behiels, Michael D. "Aboriginal Nationalism in the Ascendancy: The Assembly of First Nations' First Campaign for the Inherent Right to Self-Government, 1968–1987." *Canadas of the Mind: The Making and Unmaking of Canadian Nationalisms in the Twentieth Century.* Ed. Norman Hillmer and Adam Chapnick. Montreal: McGill-Queen's UP, 2007. 260–86.

Bell, Michael. "Thought, Language, Aesthetics, and Being, 1900–1940." *Encyclopedia of Literary Modernism.* Ed. Paul Poplawski. Santa Barbara: Greenwood, 2003. 419–30.

Benjamin, Walter. "Theses on the Philosophy of History." 1955. *Illuminations: Essays and Reflections.* New York: Harcourt, 2007. 253–64.

Bentley, D.M.R. *The Gay]Grey Moose: Essays on the Ecologies and Mythologies of Canadian Poetry, 1690–1990.* Ottawa: U of Ottawa P, 1992.

– "Conclusion, Retrospective, and Prospective." *The Ivory Thought.* Ed. Gerald Lynch et al. Ottawa: U of Ottawa P, 2008. 239–46.

– "Unremembered and Learning Much: LAC Alfred W. Purdy." *The Ivory Thought.* Ed. Gerald Lynch et al. Ottawa: U of Ottawa P, 2008. 31–50.

Bercuson, David Jay. *Canada and the Burden of Unity.* Toronto: Gage, 1980.

Berger, Carl. *The Writing of Canadian History.* 2nd ed. Toronto: U of Toronto P, 1986.

– "Writings in Canadian History." *The Literary History of Canada: Volume Four,* 2nd ed. Ed. W.H. New. Toronto: U of Toronto P, 1990. 293–332.

Berkhofer, Robert F. *Beyond the Great Story: History as Text and Discourse.* Cambridge: Belknap/Harvard UP, 1995.

Besner, Neil. "What Resides in the Question 'Is Canada Postcolonial?'" *Is Canada Postcolonial? Unsettling Canadian Literature.* Ed. Laura Moss. Waterloo: Wilfrid Laurier UP, 2003: 40–8.

Best, George. *The Three Voyages of Martin Frobisher*. London: Hakluyt Society, 1867.

Bhabha, Homi. *The Location of Culture*. London: Routledge, 1994.

Bird, Gloria. "Breaking the Silence: Writing as Witness." *Speaking for the Generations: Native Writers on Writing*. Ed. Simon Ortiz. Tucson: U of Arizona Press, 1998. 26–48.

Bird, Gloria, and Joy Harjo. *Reinventing the Enemy's Language: Contemporary Native Women's Writing of North America*. New York: Norton, 1997.

Birney, Earle. *David, and Other Poems*. Toronto: Ryerson, 1942.

– "Canada: Case History." *The Strait of Anian: Selected Poems by Earle Birney*. Toronto: Ryerson Press, 1948.

– *20th Century Canadian Poetry: An Anthology*. Toronto: Ryerson, 1953.

– "Canadian Literature." *Delta* 17 (Jan. 1962): 14.

– *Ice Cod Bell or Stone: New Poems*. Toronto: McClelland and Stewart, 1962.

Blackburn, William. Rev. of Barry McKinnon's *I Wanted to Say Something*. *Canadian Book Review Annual* (1990). 225.

Bliss, Michael. "Privatizing the Mind: The Sundering of Canadian History, the Sundering of Canada." *Journal of Canadian Studies* 26.4 (1991–2): 5–17. https://doi.org/10.3138/jcs.26.4.5

Bloom, Harold. *The Anxiety of Influence: A Theory of Poetry*. 1973. New York: Oxford UP, 1997.

Bolster, Stephanie. *White Stone: The Alice Poems*. Montreal: Signal, 1998.

– Email received by J.A. Weingarten. 16 June 2015.

Bornstein, George. *Transformations of Romanticism in Yeats, Eliot, and Stevens*. Chicago: U of Chicago P, 1976.

Bowering, George. *Vancouver*. Toronto: Weed/Flower, 1970.

– *Allophanes*. Toronto: Coach House, 1976.

– *Uncle Louis*. Toronto: Coach House, 1980.

– "Uncle Louis." *Epoch* 30.3 (1981): 161–74.

– "Uncle Louis." *West Window*. Toronto: General Publishing, 1982: 117–32.

– "A Great Northward Darkness: The Attack on History in Recent Canadian Fiction." *Imaginary Hand: Essays*. Edmonton: NeWest, 1988. 1–21.

– "Language Women: Post-Anecdotal Writing in Canada." *Imaginary Hand: Essays*. Edmonton: NeWest, 1988: 99–110.

Bradley, Nicholas. "Men with Guts: Al Purdy, Robinson Jeffers, and Geopoetic Influence." *Canadian Poetry: Studies, Documents, Reviews* 62 (2008): 44–63.

– , ed. *We Go Far Back in Time: The Letters of Earle Birney and Al Purdy, 1947–1984*. Madeira Park: Harbour Publishing, 2014.

Brandt, Di. *questions i asked my mother*. Winnipeg: Turnstone, 1988.

– *Wild Mother Dancing: Maternal Narrative in Canadian Literature*. Winnipeg: U of Manitoba P, 1993.

Brandt, Di, and Barbara Godard. "A New Genealogy of Canadian Literary Modernism." *Wider Boundaries of Daring: The Modernist Impulse in Canadian Women's Poetry*. Ed. Di Brandt and Barbara Godard. Waterloo: Wilfrid Laurier UP, 2009. 1–25.

Brant, Beth. "The Good Red Road." *Writing as Witness: Essay and Talk*. Toronto: Women's Press, 1994. 5–24.

Braz, Albert. *The False Traitor: Louis Riel in Canadian Culture*. Toronto: U of Toronto P, 2003.

Brewster, Elizabeth. *Lilloet*. Toronto: Ryerson, 1951.

– *In Search of Eros*. Toronto: Clarke & Irwin, 1974.

– *The Way Home*. Ottawa: Oberon, 1982.

– "The Moving Image." *Spring Again*. Ottawa: Oberon, 1990. 16–17.

– *Spring Again*. Ottawa: Oberon, 1990.

– *Invention of Truth*. Ottawa: Oberon, 1991.

– *Collected Poems of Elizabeth Brewster*. 2 vols. Ottawa: Oberon, 2003–4.

Broadfoot, Barry. *Ten Lost Years 1929–1939: Memories of Canadians Who Survived the Depression*. Toronto: Doubleday, 1973.

– *Six War Years 1939–1945: Memories of Canadians at Home and Abroad*. Toronto: Doubleday, 1974.

Brown, Connie, and Jane Seitz. "You've Come a Long Way Baby." *Sisterhood Is Powerful: An Anthology of Writing from the Women's Liberation Movement*. Ed. Robin Morgan. New York: Random House, 1970. 3–28.

Brown, E.K. *On Canadian Poetry*. Toronto: Ryerson, 1943.

Brown, George W., and Edgar McInnis, eds. *Canada*. 1950. Oakland: U of California P, 1971.

Brown, Robert Craig. "Biography in Canadian History." *Clio's Craft: A Primer of Historical Methods*. Ed. T.A. Crowley. Toronto: Copp Clark Pitman, 1988. 154–62.

Brydon, Diana. *Timothy Findley*. New York: Twayne, 1998.

Buri, George. "'Enemies within Our Gates': Brandon's Alien Detention Centre during the Great War." *Manitoba History* 56 (2007). Retrieved 23 August 2012 from http://www.mhs.mb.ca/docs/mb_history/56/aliendetention.shtml.

Burrs, Mick [a.k.a. Steven Michael Berzensky]. *The Blue Pools of Paradise*. Moose Jaw: Coteau, 1983.

– *Dark Halo*. Regina: Coteau, 1993.

– *The Names Leave the Stones: Poems New and Selected*. Regina: Coteau, 2001.

Burrs, Mick, and Carol Pearlstone, eds. *Going to War: Found Poems of the Métis People*. Regina: Dept. of Culture and Youth, 1975.

Burrs, Mick, and J.A. Weingarten. "Preservation in Poetry: An Interview with Mick Burrs." *Prairie Fire* Online (2010): http://www.prairiefire.ca/interview_jaw_burrs.html (link inactive).

Burt, Sandra, et al. *Changing Patterns: Women in Canada*. Toronto: McClelland and Stewart, 1988.
Byron, Glennis. *Dramatic Monologue*. New York: Routledge, 2003.
Cameron, Elspeth. *Irving Layton: A Portrait*. Toronto: Stoddart, 1985.
Campbell, Maria. *Halfbreed*. Toronto: McClelland and Stewart, 1973.
Cardinal, Harold. *The Unjust Society: The Tragedy of Canada's Indians*. 1969. Toronto: Douglas and McIntyre, 1999.
Careless, J.M.S. "Canadian Nationalism: Immature or Obsolete." *Canadian Historical Association* 33.1 (1954): 12–19. https://doi.org/10.7202/300357ar
– "'Limited Identities' in Canada." *Canadian Historical Review* 50.1 (1969): 1–10. https://doi.org/10.3138/chr-050-01-01
– "Limited Identities: Ten Years Later." *Manitoba History* 1.1 (1980): 3–9.
Carman, Bliss. *Bliss Carman's Poems*. 1922. Toronto: McClelland and Stewart, 1931.
Carman, Bliss, and Richard Hovey. *Songs from Vagabondia*. Boston: Matthews and Lane, 1894.
Carney, Robert J. "Aboriginal Residential Schools before Confederation: The Early Experience." *CCHA Historical Studies* 61 (1995): 13–40.
Carr, Emily. *Growing Pains: The Autobiography of Emily Carr*. Vancouver: Douglas & McIntyre, 2005.
Carson, Anne. *Glass, Irony, and God*. New York: New Directions, 1995.
Caswell, Edward S. *Canadian Singers and Their Songs: A Collection of Portraits, Autograph Poems, and Brief Biographies*. Toronto: McClelland and Stewart, 1925.
Cavell, Janice. "Arctic Exploration in Canadian Print Culture, 1890–1930." *Papers of the Bibliographical Society of Canada* 44.2 (2006): 7–43.
The Centennial Handbook: A Handbook of Information on the 1967 Centennial Organization, Their Constitution, Their Aims and Objectives. Ottawa: Duhamel Queen's Printer, 1964.
Certeau, Michel de. *Heterologies: Discourse on the Other*. Minneapolis: U of Minnesota P, 1986.
– *The Writing of History*. New York: Columbia UP, 1988.
Christensen, Peter. *Hail Storm*. Saskatoon: Thistledown, 1977.
Citizens Plus. Edmonton: Indian Association of Alberta, 1970.
Clayton, Jay, and Eric Rothstein, eds. *Influence and Intertextuality in Literary History*. Madison: U of Wisconsin P, 1991.
Cohen, Leonard. *Beautiful Losers*. Toronto: McClelland and Stewart, 1966.
Coleridge, Samuel Taylor. *The Collected Works of Samuel Taylor Coleridge*. Princeton: Princeton UP, 1969–2002.
Collett, Anne. "Pauline Johnson-Tekahionwake: Trafficking Woman." *Victorian Traffic: Identity, Exchange, Performance*. Ed. S. Thomas. Newcastle upon Tyne: Cambridge Scholars, 2008. 143–62.

Cook, Ramsay. "Canadian Centennial Celebrations." *International Journal* 22.4 (1967): 659–63. https://doi.org/10.2307/40200205
– "Good-Bye to All That." *Canadian Historical Review* 49.3 (1968): 275–7. https://doi.org/10.3138/CHR-049-03-05
Cooke, Nathalie. "Lorna Crozier (1948–)." *Canadian Writers and Their Works.* Ed. Jack David et al. Toronto: ECW, 1992. 77–155.
– *Margaret Atwood: A Biography*. Toronto: ECW, 1998.
– *Margaret Atwood: A Critical Companion*. Westport: Greenwood, 2004.
Cooley, Dennis. "RePlacing." *Essays on Canadian Writing* 18–19 (1980): 9–20.
– *Bloody Jack*. Winnipeg: Turnstone, 1984.
– "The Vernacular Muse in Prairie Poetry (Part 2)." *Prairie Fire* 8.1 (1987): 60–70.
– "Documents in the Postmodern Long Prairie Poem." *History, Literature, and the Writing of the Canadian Prairies*. Ed. Alison Calder and Robert Wardhaugh. Winnipeg: U of Manitoba P, 2005. 175–211.
Crate, Joan. *Pale as Real Ladies: Poems for Pauline Johnson*. Ilderton: Brick, 1989.
– *Foreign Homes*. London: Brick, 2001.
– Letter received by J.A. Weingarten. 17 June 2016.
– Telephone interview. 11 August 2016.
Crate, Joan, and Kimmy Beach. "A Conversation." 16 Oct. 2012. n.p.
Creighton, Alan, and Hilda M. Ridley. *The New Canadian Anthology*. Toronto: Crucible, 1938.
Creighton, D.G. *The Commercial Empire of the St Lawrence, 1760–1850*. Toronto: Ryerson, 1937.
Crowe, Patrick, et al. *The Enduring Enigma of Susanna Moodie*. Toronto: Upper Canada Moving Picture, 1997.
Crowley, T.A, ed. *Clio's Craft: A Primer of Historical Methods*. Toronto: Copp Clark Pitman, 1988.
Crozier, Lorna [as Lorna Uher]. *Inside Is the Sky*. Saskatoon: Thistledown, 1976.
– [as Lorna Uher]. "The Edge of the Page: A Response to Barry McKinnon's *I Wanted to Say Something*." *Essays on Canadian Writing* 18–19 (1980): 106–11.
– *The Weather*. Moose Jaw: Thunder Creek, 1983.
– "Drifting Towards Batoche." *No Feather, No Ink*. Ed. George Amabile and Kim Dales. Saskatoon: Thistledown Press, 1985. 184.
– *Inventing the Hawk*. Toronto: McClelland and Stewart, 1992.
– *A Saving Grace: The Collected Poems of Mrs Bentley*. Toronto: McClelland and Stewart, 1996.
– Email received by J.A. Weingarten. 1 March 2012.
Crozier, Lorna, and Gary Hyland, eds. *A Sudden Radiance: Saskatchewan Poetry*. Regina: Coteau, 1987.
Crozier, Lorna, and Elizabeth Philips. "Seeing Distance: Lorna Crozier's Art of Paradox." *Where the Words Come From: Canadian Poets in Conversation*. Robert's Creek: Nightwood, 2002. 139–58.

Culler, Jonathan. *Theory of the Lyric*. Cambridge: Harvard UP, 2017.
Cuthand, Beth. *Voices in the Waterfall*. Penticton: Theytus, 1989.
Dagenais, Michel. [No title]. *Saturday Night* 84.1 (1969): 4.
Dales, Kim. "The Art of Rebellion: Batoche and the Lyric Poem." *Prairie Fire* 6.4 (1985): 6–15.
Davey, Frank. *Post-National Arguments: The Politics of the Anglophone-Canadian Novel since 1967*. Toronto: U of Toronto P, 1993.
– "Al Purdy, Sam Solecki, and the Poetics of the 1960s." *Canadian Poetry* 51 (2002): 39–57.
Davis, Natalie Zemon. *Fiction in the Archives: Pardon Tales and Their Tellers in Sixteenth-Century France*. 1988. Stanford: Stanford UP, 1995.
Dawidowicz, Lucy S. "Babi Yar's Legacy." *New York Times* 27 September 1981: A.48.
Denham, Paul. "Celebration of Presence." *NeWest Review* 19.2 (1993): 26–7.
Denham, Paul, et al. *The Evolution of Canadian Literature in English: 1867–1914*. Toronto: Holt, Rinehart, & Winston, 1973.
Dickie, Donalda. *The Great Adventure: An Illustrated History of Canada for Young Canadians*. Toronto: Dent, 1950. Rpt 1957.
Dickie, Margaret. *On the Modernist Long Poem*. Iowa: U of Iowa P, 1986.
Djwa, Sandra. "Al Purdy: Ivory Thots and the Last Romantic." *The Ivory Thought*. Ed. Gerald Lynch et al. Ottawa: U of Ottawa P, 2008. 51–62.
Dudek, Louis. "Two Canadian Poets Who Are 'Raw, Exciting, Alive.'" *Montreal Star* 26 June 1965: 12.
– "The Theory of the Image in Modern Poetry." *Open Letter* 4.8–9 (1981): 263–82.
Dudek, Louis, and Michael Darling. "An Interview with Louis Dudek." *Essays on Canadian Writing* 3 (1975): 2–14.
Dummitt, Christopher "After Inclusiveness: The Future of Canadian History." *Contesting Clio's Craft: New Directions and Debates in Canadian History*. London: Institute for the Study of the Americas, 2009. 98–122.
Dumont, Marilyn. "Positive Images of Nativeness." *Looking at the Words of Our Peoples: First Nations Analysis of Literature*. Ed. Jeanette Armstrong. Penticton, BC: Theytus, 1993. 45–50.
Dyck, E.F. "Introduction." *Essays on Saskatchewan Writing*. Ed. E.F. Dyck. Regina: Saskatchewan Writers Guild, 1987. ix–xxi.
– "Place in the Poetry of John Newlove." *Canadian Literature* 122–3 (1989): 69–91.
Eliot, T.S. *The Waste Land: A Facsimile and Transcript of the Original Drafts*. 1922. Ed. Valerie Eliot. San Diego: Harcourt Brace, 1971, rpt 1994.
– *Four Quartets*. New York: Harcourt, 1943.
– *Notes towards the Definition of Culture*. 1948. New York: Harcourt, 2014.
Episkenew, Jo-Ann. *Taking Back Our Spirits: Indigenous Literature, Public Policy, and Healing*. Winnipeg: U of Manitoba P, 2009.

Faurschou, Gail, et al. *Canadian Cultural Studies: A Reader*. Durham: Duke UP, 2009.

Fee, Margery. "Romantic Nationalism and the Image of Native People in Contemporary English-Canadian Literature." *The Native in Literature* Ed. Cheryl Calver et al. Oakville: ECW, 1987. 15–33.

– "The Trickster Moment, Cultural Appropriation, and the Liberal Imagination in Canada." *Troubling Tricksters: Revisiting Critical Conversations*. Ed. Deanna Reder and Linda Morra. Waterloo: Wilfrid Laurier UP, 2010. 59–76.

– *Literary Land Claims: The "Indian Land Question" From Pontiac's War to Attawapiskat*. Waterloo: Wilfrid Laurier UP, 2015.

Fee, Margery and Dory Nason. "Introduction." *Tekahionwake: E. Pauline Johnson's Writings on Native North America*. Ed. Margery Fee and Dory Nason. Peterborough: Broadview, 2016. 13–30.

Felski, Rita. "Modernism and Modernity: Engendering Literary History." *Rereading Modernism*. Ed. Lisa Rado. New York: Garland, 1994. 191–208.

– *The Gender of Modernity*. Cambridge: Harvard UP, 1995.

Ferguson, W.K. "Some Problems of Historiography." *Historical Papers* (1960): 1–12.

Ferns, John. "A Desolate Country: John Newlove's *Black Night Window*." *Far Point* 2 (1969): 68–75.

Fiamengo, Janice. "'Kind of ludicrous or kind of beautiful I guess': Al Purdy's Rhetoric of Failure." *The Ivory Thought*. Ed. Gerald Lynch et al. Ottawa: U of Ottawa P, 2008. 159–72.

Findley, Timothy. *Headhunter*. New York: Crown, 1993.

Finkel, Alvin. *Our Lives: Canada after 1945*. Toronto: Lorimer, 1997.

Finlay, Karen A. *The Force of Culture: Vincent Massey and Canadian Sovereignty*. Toronto: U of Toronto P, 2004.

Fitzgerald, Judith. Rev. of *The Overlanders*. *Globe and Mail* 19 Feb. 1983: 17.

Fogarty, John. "Economic History and the Limits of Staple Theory." *Clio's Craft: A Primer of Historical Methods*. Ed. T.A. Crowley. Toronto: Copp Clark Pitman, 1988. 179–94.

Foster, Annie Harvie [Mrs W. Garland]. *The Mohawk Princess: Being Some Account of the Life of Tekahion-Wake*. Vancouver: Lions' Gate, 1931.

Fox, Luke. *North-West Fox, or, Fox from the North West Passage*. London: Alsp and Favvcet, 1635.

Francis, Daniel. *The Imaginary Indian: The Image of the Indian in Canadian Culture*. Vancouver: Arsenal Pulp, 1992.

Freiwald, Bina. "Tradition, Individual Talent, and 'A Young Woman/From Backwoods New Brunswick': Modernism and Elizabeth Brewster's (Auto) Poetics of the Subject." *Wider Boundaries of Daring: The Modernist Impulse in Canadian Women's Poetry*. Ed. Di Brandt and Barbara Godard. Waterloo: Wilfrid Laurier UP, 2009. 97–123.

French, Donald Graham, and John Daniel Logan. *Highways of Canadian Literature: A Synoptic Introduction to the Literary History of Canada (English) from 1760–1924*. Toronto: McClelland and Stewart, 1924.

Friedman, Susan Stanford. "Weavings: Intertextuality and the (Re)Birth of the Author." *Influence and Intertextuality in Literary History*. Ed. Jay Clayton and Eric Rothstein. Madison: U of Wisconsin P, 1991. 146–80.

Friesen, Gerald. *The Canadian Prairies: A History*. Toronto: U of Toronto P, 1984.

– "The Manitoba Historical Society: A Centennial History." *River Road: Essays on Manitoba and Prairie History*. Winnipeg: U of Manitoba P, 1996. 91–106.

Frisch, Michael. *A Shared Authority: Essays on the Craft and Meaning of Oral and Public History*. Albany: State University of New York, 1990.

Friskney, Janet B. *New Canadian Library: The Ross-McClelland Years, 1952–1978*. Toronto: U of Toronto P, 2007.

Frye, Northrop. "Conclusion to *A Literary History of Canada*." 1965. *The Bush Garden*. Toronto: Anansi, 1971: 213–52.

Fulford, Robert. "The Images of Atwood." *The Malahat Review* 41 (1977): 95–8.

Gaffield, Chad. "Theory and Method in Canadian Historical Demography." *Clio's Craft: A Primer of Historical Methods*. Ed. T.A. Crowley. Toronto: Copp Clark Pitman, 1988. 163–78.

Gagan, David. "The Historical Identity of the Denison Family of Toronto, 1792–1860." *Historical Papers* (1971): 124–37.

Gagan, David, and H.E. Turner. "Social History in Canada: A Report on the 'State of the Art.'" 1982. *Contemporary Approaches to Canadian History*. Ed. Carl Berger. Toronto: Copp Clark Pitman, 1987. 89–114.

Gage, John T. *In the Arresting Eye: The Rhetoric of Imagism*. Baton Rouge: Louisiana State UP, 1981.

Gallant, Mavis, and Geoff Hancock. "An Interview with Mavis Gallant." *Canadian Fiction Magazine* 28 (1978): 18–67.

Garvin, John W. *Canadian Poets*. Toronto: McClelland and Stewart, 1916.

Gasparini, Len. "Some Ghosts Are Clearer Than Others." *Books in Canada* 4.7 (1975): 18–19.

Gauld, Greg. "Multiculturalism: The Real Thing?" *Twenty Years of Multiculturalism: Successes and Failures*. Ed. Stella Hryniuk. Winnipeg: St John's College, 1992. 9–16.

Geddes, Gary. "Celebrating the Agonized Struggle for Art." *Globe and Mail*. 13 Dec. 1975: 38–9.

– "The Site of a Loss: or, the Pleasures of Rewriting the Text." *Literature of Region and Nation: Proceedings of the 6th International Literature of Region and Nation Conference, 2–7 August 1996*. Saint John: Social Sciences and Humanities Research Council of Canada with University of New Brunswick in Saint John, 1998. 58–72.

Gerson, Carole, and Gwendolyn Davies, eds. *Canadian Poetry from the Beginnings through the First World War*. Toronto: McClelland and Stewart, 1994.

Gerson, Carole, and Veronica Strong-Boag. *Paddling Her Own Canoe: The Times and Texts of E. Pauline Johnson (Tekahionwake)*. Toronto: U of Toronto P, 2000.

– "Championing the Native: E. Pauline Johnson Rejects the Squaw." *Contact Zones: Aboriginal and Settler Women in Canada's Colonial Past*. Ed. Katie Pickles and Myra Rutherford. Vancouver: U of British Columbia P, 2005. 47–66.

Gilbert, Gerry. *White Lunch: Poems*. Vancouver: Periwinkle, 1964.

Gillman, Laura. *Unassimilable Feminisms: Reappraising Feminist, Womanist, and Mestiza Identity Politics*. New York: Palgrave Macmillan, 2010.

Gingell, Susan [as Susan A. Beckman]. "Prairie Harvest: A Consideration of Two Anthologies of Prairie Poetry." *Essays on Canadian Writing* 18–19 (1980): 183–204.

– "The Ways of Speech Made Plains: Saskatchewan Poetry Finds Its Voices." *Writing Saskatchewan: 20 Critical Essays*. Ed. Kenneth G. Probert. Regina: Canadian Plains Research Center, 1989. 122–34.

– "Let Us Revise Mythologies: The Poetry of Lorna Crozier." *Essays on Canadian Writing* 43 (1991): 67–82.

Giroux, Henry. "Cultural Studies, Public Pedagogy, and the Responsibility of Intellectuals." *Communication and Critical/Cultural Studies* 1.1 (2004): 59–79. https://doi.org/10.1080/1479142042000180926

Glickman, Susan. "Afterword" to *Roughing It in the Bush*. 1852. Toronto: McClelland and Stewart, 1989. 535–43.

Goldie, Terry, and Daniel David Moses, eds. *An Anthology of Canadian Native Literature in English*. Toronto: Oxford UP, 1992.

Goldstein, Jan. "Introduction." *Foucault and the Writing of History*. Ed. Jan Goldstein. Oxford: Blackwell, 1994. 1–15.

Gom, Leona. *Land of Peace*. Saskatoon: Thistledown, 1980.

Grace, Sherrill. *Violent Duality: A Study of Margaret Atwood*. Montreal: Véhicule, 1980.

– "Calling Out the McLean Boys: George Bowering's *Shoot* and the Autobiography of British Columbia's History." *Canadian Literature* 184 (2005): 11–25.

Granatstein, J.L. *Who Killed Canadian History?* Toronto: Harper-Collins, 1998.

Gray, Charlotte. *Flint and Feather: The Life and Times of E. Pauline Johnson, Tekahionwake*. Toronto: HarperFlamingo, 2002.

Grekul, Lisa. *Leaving Shadows: Literature in English by Canada's Ukrainians*. Edmonton: U of Alberta P, 2005.

Groening, Laura. "*The Journals of Susanna Moodie*: A Twentieth-Century Look at a Nineteenth-Century Life." *Studies in Canadian Literature* 8.2 (1983): 166–80.

Gustafson. Ralph. *The Anthology of Canadian Poetry*. New York: Penguin, 1942.
– *The Penguin Book of Canadian Verse*. Harmondsworth: Penguin, 1958. Rpt 1967, 1975, 1977, 1980, 1984, 1989.
Gutteridge, Don. *Riel: A Poem for Voices*. Second edition. Toronto: Van Nostrand Reinhold, 1972.
Halfe, Louise. *Blue Marrow*. Toronto: McClelland and Stewart, 1998.
– *Blue Marrow*. 2nd ed. Regina: Coteau, 2004
– Email received by J.A. Weingarten. 21 Feb. 2016.
Hall, C.F. *Life with the Esquimaux*. London: Low, Son, and Marston, 1864.
Hammill, Faye. "Margaret Atwood, Carol Shields, and 'That Moodie Bitch.'" *American Review of Canadian Studies* 29.1 (1999): 67–92. https://doi.org/10.1080/02722019909481622
Hanham, H.J. "Canadian History in the 1970s." *Canadian Historical Review* 58.1 (1977): 2–22. https://doi.org/10.3138/CHR-058-01-02
Hanna, Anne. *The Canadian Centenary Council, 1959–1967*. Ottawa: The Council, 1968.
Hann, Russell G. "Oral History." *Clio's Craft: A Primer of Historical Methods*. Ed. T.A. Crowley. Toronto: Copp Clark Pitman, 1988. 42–64.
Harrison, Dick. *Unnamed Country: The Struggle for a Canadian Prairie Fiction*. Edmonton: U of Alberta P, 1977.
Harry, Margaret. "Literature in English by Native Canadians." *Studies in Canadian Literature* 10.1–2 (1985): 146–53.
Hart, Jonathan. "Afterword: Sense of Place: A Response to Regionalism." *A Sense of Place: Re-evaluating Regionalism in Canadian and American Writing*. Ed. Christian Riegal et al. Edmonton: U of Alberta P, 1997. 113–18.
Hawkins, William, and Harry Howith. *Two Longer Poems: The Seasons of Miss Nicky*. Toronto: Patrician, 1965.
Hawthorn, Harry Bertram et al. *A Survey of the Contemporary Indians of Canada: A Report on Economic, Political, Educational Needs, and Policies*. 2 vols. Ottawa: Indian Affairs, 1966–7.
Haywood, Ian. *The Making of History: A Study of the Literary Forgeries of James Macpherson and Thomas Chatterton in Relation to Eighteenth-Century Ideas of History and Fiction*. Rutherford: Farleigh Dickinson UP, 1986.
Hedges, Elaine, and Shelley Fisher Fishkin. "Introduction." *Listening to Silences: New Essays in Feminist Criticism*. Ed. Elaine Hedges and Shelley Fisher Fishkin. New York: Oxford UP, 1994. 3–14.
Heinemann, Michelle. "Saskatchewan Writers Guild: Its History and Impact on Writing in Saskatchewan." *Essays on Saskatchewan Writing*. Ed. E.F. Dyck. Regina: Saskatchewan Writers Guild, 1987. 3–21.
Henshaw, Peter. "John Buchan and the British Imperial Origins of Canadian Multiculturalism." *Canadas of the Mind: The Making and Unmaking of Canadian Nationalisms in the Twentieth Century*. Ed. Norman Hillmer and Adam Chapnick. Montreal: McGill-Queen's UP, 2007. 191–213.

Hesse, M.G. *Women in Canadian Literature*. Ottawa: Borealis, 1976.
High, Steven. "Sharing Authority in the Writing of Canadian History: The Case of Oral History." *Contesting Clio's Craft: New Directions and Debates in Canadian History*. Ed. Christopher Dummitt and Michael Dawson. London: Institute for the Study of the Americas, 2009. 21–46.
Hirsch, Marianne. *Family Frames: Photography, Narrative, and Postmemory*. Cambridge: Harvard UP, 1997.
Hoefnagels, Anna. "Native Activism and the Development of Powwows in the 1960s." *The Sixties in Canada: A Turbulent and Creative Decade*. Ed. M. Athena Palaeologu. Montreal: Black Rose, 2009. 233–45.
Holland, Patrick. "Louis Riel and Modern Canadian Poetry." *Images of Riel in Canadian Culture*. Ed. Ramon Hathorn and Patrick Holland. NY: Mellen, 1992. 211–33.
Holmes, Kristy A. "Negotiating Citizenship: Joyce Wieland's *Reason over Passion*." *The Sixties: Passion, Politics, and Style*. Ed. Dimitry Anastakis. Montreal: McGill-Queen's UP, 2008. 42–70.
Homer. *The Odyssey*. Trans. Samuel Butler. Maryland: Wildside Press, 2007.
Hood, Thomas. *The Poetical Works of Thomas Hood*. S.n., 1983.
Horace. *The Epistles of Horace*. Ed. David Ferry. New York: Farrar, Straus and Giroux, 2001.
Hopkins, Beth, and Anne Joyce. *Daughter by Adoption: A Play Based on the Writings of Susanna Moodie (1803–1885)*. Toronto: Playwrights Canada, 1981.
Howard, Joseph. *Strange Empire: A Narrative of the Northwest*. New York: Morrow, 1952.
Howells, Coral Ann. "Writing History, from *The Journals of Susanna Moodie* to *The Blind Assassin*." *Margaret Atwood: The Open Eye*. Ed. John Moss and Tobi Kozakewich. Ottawa: U of Ottawa P, 2006. 107–20.
Hulan, Renée. "Reading Historiography and Historical Fiction in Twentieth-Century Canada." *The Oxford Handbook of Canadian Literature*. Ed. Cynthia Sugars. New York: Oxford UP, 2016. 780–98.
Hume, David. *An Enquiry Concerning Human Understanding*. 1748. Ed. Peter Millican. Oxford: Oxford UP, 2007.
Hutcheon, Linda. *The Canadian Postmodern: A Study in Contemporary Canadian Fiction*.Toronto: Oxford University Press, 1988.
Hyde, G.E. *Red Cloud's Folk: A History of the Oglala Sioux Indians*. Norman: U of Oklahoma P, 1937.
Igartua, José Eduardo. *The Other Quiet Revolution: National Identities in English Canada, 1945–1971*. Vancouver: U of British Columbia P, 2006.
Ingstad, Helge. *Land under the Pole Star*. New York: St Martin's Press, 1966.
Innis, H.A. *The Fur Trade in Canada: An Introduction to Canadian Economic History*. New Haven: Yale UP, 1930.

Izenberg, Gerald. *Identity: The Necessity of a Modern Idea*. Philadelphia: U of Pennsylvania P, 2016.
Jackson, James A. *The Centennial History of Manitoba*. Toronto: McClelland and Stewart, 1970.
Jacobs, William Wymark. *Lady of the Barge and Others*. Whitefish: Kessinger, 2004.
Jewinski, Ed, and Andrew Stubbs. *The Politics of Art: Eli Mandel's Poetry and Criticism*. Amsterdam: Rodopi, 1992.
Johnson, E. Pauline (a.k.a. Tekahionwake). *Canadian Born*. Toronto: G.N. Morang, 1903.
– *Legends of Vancouver*. Vancouver: David Spencer, 1911.
– *E. Pauline Johnson, Tekahionwake: Collected Poems and Selected Prose*. Ed. Carole Gerson and Veronica Strong-Boag. Toronto: U of Toronto P, 2002.
– "The Stings of Civilization." *E. Pauline Johnson, Tekahionwake: Collected Poems and Selected Prose*. Ed. Carole Gerson and Veronica Strong-Boag. Toronto: U of Toronto P, 2002. 283–7.
– "A Strong Race Opinion: On the Indian Girl in Modern Fiction." *E. Pauline Johnson, Tekahionwake: Collected Poems and Selected Prose*. Ed. Carole Gerson and Veronica Strong-Boag. Toronto: U of Toronto P, 2002. 177–83.
Johnson, W.R. *The Idea of Lyric: Lyric Modes in Ancient and Modern Poetry*. Berkeley: U of California P, 1982.
Johnston, Jean. *Wilderness Women: Canada's Forgotten History*. Toronto: Peter Martin, 1973.
Johnston, Sheila. *Buckskin and Broadcloth: A Documentary Biography of E. Pauline Johnson-Tekahionwake*. Kingston: Quarry, 1994.
Jones, D.G. *Butterfly on Rock: A Study of Themes and Images in Canadian Literature*. Toronto: U of Toronto P, 1970.
Justice, Daniel Heath. "A Relevant Resonance: Considering the Study of Indigenous National Literatures." *Across Cultures / Across Borders: Canadian Aboriginal and Native American Literatures*. Ed. Paul Depasquale, Renate Eigenbrod, and Emma LaRocque. Toronto: Broadview, 2009. 61–76.
Kamboureli, Smaro. *On the Edge of Genre: The Contemporary Canadian Long Poem*. Toronto: U of Toronto P, 1991.
– "Introduction." *Making Difference: Canadian Multicultural Literature*. Ed. Smaro Kamboureli. Toronto: Oxford UP, 1996. 1–16.
Kaplan, Carla. "Reading Feminist Readings: Recuperative Reading and the Silent Heroine of Feminist Criticism." *Listening to Silences: New Essays in Feminist Criticism*. Ed. Elaine Hedges and Shelley Fisher Fishkin. New York: Oxford UP, 1994. 168–96.
Keats, John. *Complete Poems and Selected Letters of John Keats*. New York: Modern Library, 2001.

Keller, Betty. *Pauline: A Biography of Pauline Johnson*. Vancouver: Douglas & McIntyre, 1981.

– *Pauline Johnson: First Aboriginal Voice of Canada*. Montreal: XYZ, 1999.

Kelly, Peggy. "Politics, Gender, and *New Provinces*: Dorothy Livesay and F.R. Scott." *Canadian Poetry: Studies, Documents, Reviews* 53 (Fall/Winter 2003): 54–70.

Kerr, Don. "R.E. Rashley's Selected Poems." *Essays on Canadian Writing* 18–19 (1980): 169–78.

Kertzer, Jonathan. *Worrying the Nation: Imagining a National Literature in English Canada*. Toronto: U of Toronto P, 1998.

Kinnahan, Linda A. *Poetics of the Feminine: Authority and Literary Tradition in William Carlos Williams, Mina Loy, Denise Levertove, and Kathleen Fraser*. Cambridge: Cambridge UP, 1994.

Kiyooka, Roy. *Kyoto Airs*. Vancouver: Periwinkle, 1964.

Klinck, Carl F., and Reginald E. Watters. *Canadian Anthology*. Toronto: Gage, 1974.

Kostash, Myrna. *Long Way From Home: The Story of the Sixties Generation in Canada*. Toronto: Lorimer, 1980.

Kroetsch, Robert. *The Stone Hammer Poems*. Lantzville: Oolichan, 1976.

– *Seed Catalogue: Poems*. Winnipeg: Turnstone, 1977.

– "Beyond Nationalism: A Prologue." 1981. *The Lovely Treachery of Words: Essays Selected and New*. Toronto: Oxford UP, 1989. 64–72.

– "Disunity as Unity: A Canadian Strategy." 1985. *The Lovely Treachery of Words: Essays Selected and New*. Toronto: Oxford UP, 1989. 21–33.

– "For Play and Entrance: The Contemporary Canadian Long Poem." *The Lovely Treachery of Words: Essays Selected and New*. Toronto: Oxford UP, 1989. 117–34.

Kroetsch, Robert, Dennis Cooley, and Robert Enright. "Uncovering Our Dream World: An Interview with Robert Kroetsch." *Essays on Canadian Writing* 18–19 (1980): 21–32.

LaDuke, Winona. "The People Belong to the Land." *Paradigm Wars: Indigenous Peoples' Resistance to Globalization*. Ed. Jerry Mander and Victoria Tauli-Corpuz. San Francisco: Sierra Club, 2006. 23–5.

Lalonde, Jeremy. "Song and Silence in Al Purdy's Family Elegies." *The Ivory Thought*. Ed. Gerald Lynch et al. Ottawa: U of Ottawa P, 2008. 173–90.

Lane, Patrick. "The Poetry of Andrew Suknaski." *Essays on Canadian Writing* 18–19 (1980): 90–9.

– "The Unyielding Phrase." *Canadian Literature* 122–3 (1989): 57–64.

LaRocque, Emma. "Preface: Here Are Our Voices – Who Will Hear?" *Writing the Circle: Native Women of Western Canada*. Ed. Jeanne Martha Perreault and Sylvia Vance. Edmonton: NeWest, 1990. xv–xxx.

– *When the Other Is Me: Native Resistance Discourse, 1850–1990*. Winnipeg: U of Manitoba P, 2010.

Laurence, Margaret. "Books That Mattered to Me." 1981. *Margaret Laurence: An Appreciation*. Ed. Christl Verduyn. Peterborough: Broadview, 1988. 239–49.
Lawrence, Bonita. *"Real" Indians and Others: Mixed-Blood Urban Native Peoples and Indigenous Nationhood*. Lincoln: U of Nebraska P, 2004.
Lawrence, D.H. *The Complete Poems of D.H. Lawrence*. New York: Viking, 1971.
Lecker, Robert. *Keepers of the Code: English-Canadian Literary Anthologies and the Representation of the Nation*. Toronto: U of Toronto P, 2013.
Ledohowski, Lindy. "'A Vaguely Divided Guilt': The Aboriginal Ukrainian." *Re-imagining Ukrainian-Canadians: History, Politics, and Identity*. Ed. Rhonda L. Hinther and Jim Mochoruk. Toronto: U of Toronto P, 2011. 85–102.
Lee, Dennis. "Running and Dwelling: Homage to Al Purdy." *Saturday Night* 87 (1972): 14–16.
– "Introduction." *The New Canadian Poets, 1970–1985*. Toronto: McClelland and Stewart, 1985. xvii–liii.
Légaré, Evelyn. "Canadian Multiculturalism and Aboriginal People: Negotiating a Place in the Nation." *Identities*, 1.4 (1995): 347–66. https://doi.org/10.1080/1070289x.1995.9962515
Leggatt, Judith. "Native Writing, Academic Theory: Postcolonialism Across the Cultural Divide." *Is Canada Postcolonial?: Unsettling Canadian Literature*. Ed. Laura Moss. Waterloo: Wilfrid Laurier UP, 2003: 111–26.
Leighton, Mary Elizabeth. "Performing Pauline Johnson: Representations of 'the Indian Poetess' in the Periodical Press, 1892–95." *Essays on Canadian Writing* 65 (1998): 141–64.
"The Life and Voyages of Columbus." *Sea Stories: Tales of Discovery, Adventure, and Escape*. London: Thomas Harrild, 1855. 1–71.
Lischke, Ute, and David T. McNab. "We Are Still Here." *The Long Journey of a Forgotten People: Métis Identities and Family Histories*. Ed. Ute Lischke and David T. McNab. Waterloo: Wilfrid Laurier UP, 2007. 1–9.
Litt, Paul. *The Muses, the Masses, and the Massey Commission*. Toronto: U of Toronto P, 1992.
Livesay, Dorothy. *Collected Poems: The Two Seasons*. Toronto: McGraw-Hill, 1972.
Lochead, Richard. "Funding the Good Fight." *Oral History Forum* 25 (2005): 44–53.
Loehndorf, Esther. *The Master's Voices: Robert Browning, the Dramatic Monologue, and Modern Poetry*. Basel: Verlag, 1997.
Long, Tanya. Rev. of *Emily* by Florence McNeil. *Quill and Quire* 41.10 (1975): 18.
Lowell, Robert. *Life Studies*. New York: Vintage, 1956.
Lower, Arthur. "History as Pageant." *Dalhousie Review* 54.1 (1974): 5–15.
Luciuk, Lubomyr. *Without Just Cause: Canada's First National Internment Operations and the Ukrainian Canadians, 1914–1920*. Kingston: Kashtan, 2006.

Lynch, Gerald, ed., et al. *The Ivory Thought: Essays on Al Purdy*. Ottawa: U of Ottawa P, 2008.

Lyon, George. "Pauline Johnson: A Reconsideration." *Studies in Canadian Literature* 15.2 (1990): 136–59.

Lyotard, Jean-François. *The Postmodern Condition: A Report on Knowledge*. Minneapolis: U of Minnesota P, 1984.

MacDonald, Tanis. "'Exhibit Me Buckskinned': Indigenous Legacy and Rememory in Joan Crate's *Pale as Real Ladies: Poems for Pauline Johnson*." *Canadian Literature and Cultural Memory*. Ed. Cynthia Sugars and Eleanor Ty. Toronto: Oxford UP, 2014. 169–82.

MacEwen, Gwendolyn. *Terror and Erebus*. Toronto: G. MacEwen, 1965.

MacKendrick, Louis. "Al Purdy." *Canadian Writers and Their Works: Poetry Series Seven*. Ed. Jack David et al. Toronto: ECW, 1990. 135–90.

MacLaren, I.S. "Arctic Al: Purdy's Humanist Vision of the North." *The Ivory Thought*. Ed. Gerald Lynch et al. Ottawa: U of Ottawa P, 2008. 119–36.

Mandel, Eli. "Images of Prairie Man." *Another Time*. Erin: Press Porcepic, 1977. 45–53.

– *Out of Place: Poems*. Erin: Press Porcepic, 1977.

– "Writing West: On the Road to Wood Mountain." *The Canadian Forum* 57.672 (1977): 25–31.

– "Auschwitz and Poetry." 1984. *The Family Romance*. Turnstone: Winnipeg, 1986. 3–10.

– "The Death of the Long Poem." *Open Letter* 6.2/3 (1985): 11–23.

Mandel, Eli, et al. *Trio: First Poems*. Toronto: Contact, 1954.

Maracle, Lee. "Toward a National Literature." *Across Cultures / Across Borders: Canadian Aboriginal and Native American Literatures*. Ed. Paul Depasquale, Renate Eigenbrod, and Emma LaRocque. Toronto: Broadview, 2009. 77–96.

Marchessault, Jovette. *Saga of the Wet Hens*. Vancouver: Talonbooks, 1983.

Marlatt, Daphne. *How Hug a Stone*. Winnipeg: Turnstone, 1983.

Marriott, Anne. *The Wind Our Enemy*. Toronto: Ryerson, 1939.

Marshall, Tom. *Harsh and Lovely Land: The Major Canadian Poets and the Making of a Canadian Tradition*. Vancouver: U of British Columbia P, 1979.

– "Introduction." *Selected Poems of Elizabeth Brewster, 1944–1977*. Ottawa: Oberon, 1985. 5–7.

Marty, Sid. *The Tumbleweed Harvest*. Wood Mountain: Sundog, 1973.

Matthiessen, F.O. *The Achievement of T.S. Eliot: An Essay on the Nature of Poetry*. London: Oxford UP, 1935.

McCourt, Edward. *The Canadian West in Fiction*. 1949. Toronto: Ryerson, 1970.

McDaniel, Susan, and Wendy Mitchinson. "Canadian Family Fictions and Realities: Past and Present." *The New Quarterly* (May 1987): 11–25.

McInnis, Nadine. *Two Hemispheres*. London: Brick, 2007.

– Email received by J.A. Weingarten. 7–9 May 2016.

McKay, Ian. *Rebels, Reds, Radicals: Rethinking Canada's Left History*. Toronto: Between the Lines, 2005.
McKinnon, Barry. *I Wanted to Say Something*. Prince George: Caledonia, 1975.
– *Songs and Speeches*. Prince George: Caledonia, 1976.
– *Sex at Thirty One: A Poem*. Prince George: Caledonia, 1977.
– *The Caledonia Writing Series: A Chronicle*. Prince George: Gorse, 1989.
– *I Wanted to Say Something*. 1975. Red Deer: Red Deer College, 1990.
– Email received by J.A. Weingarten. 9 April 2012.
– Email received by J.A. Weingarten. 3 Feb. 2012.
– Email received by J.A. Weingarten. 30 Jan. 2012.
– Telephone interview. 12 March 2016.
McLay, Catherine M. *Canadian Literature: The Beginnings to the 20th Century*. Toronto: McClelland and Stewart, 1974.
McLeod, Neal. "Cree Poetic Discourse." *Across Cultures / Across Borders: Canadian Aboriginal and Native American Literatures*. Ed. Paul Depasquale, Renate Eigenbrod, and Emma LaRocque. Toronto: Broadview, 2009. 109–21.
McMullen, Lorraine. "Introduction." *Re(dis)covering Our Foremothers: Nineteenth-Century Canadian Women Writers*. Ottawa: U of Ottawa P, 1990. 1–4.
McNeil, Florence. *A Silent Green Sky*. Vancouver: Klanak, 1967.
– *Emily*. Toronto: Clarke & Irwin, 1975.
– *Ghost Towns*. Toronto: McClelland and Stewart, 1975.
– *A Balancing Act*. Toronto: McClelland and Stewart, 1979.
– *The Overlanders*. Saskatoon: Thistledown, 1982.
– *Barkerville*. Saskatoon: Thistledown, 1984.
– Letter received by J.A. Weingarten. 6 Dec. 2011.
McRoberts, Kenneth. *Misconceiving Canada: The Struggle for National Unity*. Toronto: Oxford UP, 1997.
Melnyk, George. *The Literary History of Alberta*. Edmonton: U of Alberta P, 1998–9.
Miedema, Gary R. *For Canada's Sake: Public Religion, Centennial Celebrations, and the Re-making of Canada in the 1960s*. Montreal: McGill-Queen's UP, 2005.
Miller, Jim, and Myra Rutherdale. "'It's Our Country': First Nations' Participation in the Indian Pavilion at Expo 67." *Journal of the Canadian Historical Association* 17.2 (2006): 148–73. https://doi.org/10.7202/016594ar
Miller, Nancy K. "Putting Ourselves in the Picture: Memoirs and Mourning." *The Familial Gaze*. Ed. Marianne Hirsch. Hanover: UP of New England, 1999. 51–66.
Mills, Sean. "Democracy, Dissent, and the City: Cross-Cultural Encounters in Sixties Montreal." *The Sixties in Canada: A Turbulent and Creative Decade*. Ed. M. Athena Palaeologu. Montreal: Black Rose, 2009. 150–64.
Montagnes, Anne. Rev. of *In the Name of Narid*. *Globe and Mail* 25 July 1981: E14.

Monture, Rick. "'Beneath the British Flag': Iroquois and Canadian Nationalism in the Work of Pauline Johnson and Duncan Campbell Scott." *Essays on Canadian Writing* 75 (2002): 118–41.

– *We Share Our Matters / Teionkwakhashion tsi niionkwariho:ten: Two Centuries of Writing and Resistance at Six Nations of the Grand River*. Winnipeg: U of Manitoba P, 2014.

Moodie, Susanna. *Roughing It in the Bush*. London: Bentley, 1852.

– *Life in the Clearings versus the Bush*. London: Bentley, 1853.

– *Life in the Clearings versus the Bush*. New York: DeWitt and Davenport, 1854.

– *Life in the Clearings*. 1853. Ed. Robert L. MacDougall. Toronto: Macmillan, 1959.

– *Roughing It in the Bush*. 1852. Ed. Carl F. Klinck. Toronto: McClelland and Stewart, 1962.

– *Life in the Clearings*. 1853. Toronto: McClelland and Stewart, 1989.

– *Roughing It in the Bush*. 1852. Toronto: McClelland and Stewart, 1989.

– *Roughing It in the Bush*. 1852. Ed. Michael A. Peterman. New York: Norton, 2007.

Moore, Christopher. "Lives of Men and Women." *The Beaver* 73.3 (1991): 50–3.

Morgan, Cara-Lyn. *What Became My Grieving Ceremony*. Saskatoon: Thistledown, 2014.

– Email received by J.A. Weingarten. 15 May 2016.

Morgan, Cecilia. "Performing for 'Imperial Eyes': Bernice Loft and Ethel Brant Monture, Ontario 1930s–1960s." *Contact Zones: Aboriginal and Settler Women in Canada's Colonial Past*. Ed. Katie Pickles and Myra Rutherdale. Vancouver: U of British Columbia P, 2005. 67–89.

Morgan, Dawn. *How Words Hook onto the World: A Literary Ethnography of Andrew Suknaski's Wood Mountain*. MA thesis. Carleton University, 1993.

Morgan, Robin, ed. *Sisterhood Is Powerful: An Anthology of Writing from the Women's Liberation Movement*. New York: Random House, 1970.

Morningside (CBC Radio). Transcript of broadcast. 1 April 1992. "The Public Face of the Cultural Appropriation Debate: Who Speaks for Whom?" *Textual Studies in Canada* 2 (1992): 30–48.

Morse, Garry Thomas. *Discovery Passages*. Vancouver: Talonbooks, 2011.

Moisan, Clément. *A Poetry of Frontiers: Comparative Studies in Quebec/Canadian Literature*. Victoria: Press Porcepic, 1983.

Morton, Desmond "History and Nationality in Canada: Variations on an Old Theme." *Historical Papers* (1979): 1–10.

Morton, W.L. "Clio in Canada: The Interpretation of Canadian History." 1946. *Contexts of Canada's Past: Selected Essays of W.L. Morton*. Ed. A.B. McKillop. Toronto: Macmillan, 1980: 103–12.

– *Manitoba: A History*. Toronto: U of Toronto P, 1957.

– "Foreword." Jackson, James A. *The Centennial History of Manitoba*. Toronto: McClelland and Stewart, 1970. n.p.

Moss, Laura. "Is Canada Postcolonial? Introducing the Question." *Is Canada Postcolonial? Unsettling Canadian Literature*. Ed. Laura Moss. Waterloo: Wilfrid Laurier UP, 2003. 1–23.

Munslow, Alun, and Robert A. Rosenstone. *Experiments in Rethinking History*. New York: Routledge, 2004.

Murray, Melanie. Rev. of *Emily* by Florence McNeil. *Atlantis* 2.2 (1977): 162–4.

Nadel, Ira B. *Various Positions: A Life of Leonard Cohen*. Austin: U of Texas P, 2007.

New, W.H. *A History of Canadian Literature*. Montreal: McGill-Queen's UP, 2003.

Newhouse, David. "Aboriginal Identities and the New Indian Problem." *Canadas of the Mind: The Making and Unmaking of Canadian Nationalisms in the Twentieth Century*. Ed Norman Hillmer and Adam Chapnick. Montreal: McGill-Queen's UP, 2007. 287–99.

Newlove, John. *Grave Sirs*. Vancouver: Reid and Tanabe, 1962.

– *Elephants, Mothers, & Others*. Vancouver: Periwinkle, 1963.

– *Moving in Alone*. Toronto: Contact, 1965.

– "The Pride." *The Tamarack Review* 36 (1965): 37–44.

– "Ride Off Any Horizon." *Prism International* 5.3–4 (1965–6): 20–4.

– *Black Night Window*. Toronto: McClelland and Stewart, 1968.

– *The Fat Man: Selected Poems, 1962–1972*. Toronto: McClelland and Stewart, 1977.

– *The Green Plain*. Lantzville: Oolichan, 1981.

– *Apology for Absence: Selected Poems 1962–1992*. Erin: Porcupine's Quill, 1993.

Newlove, John, and Jan Bartley. "An Interview with John Newlove." *Essays on Canadian Writing* 23 (1982): 135–56.

Newlove, John, and Jon Pearce. "The Dance of Words: John Newlove." *Twelve Voices: Interviews with Canadian Poets*. Ottawa: Borealis, 1980. 113–27.

Newlove, Susan. Telephone interview. 31 Aug. 2010.

Newlove, Thomas Vernon, and Albert J. Flint. *The Newlove Family Tree*. Salt Lake City: Genealogical Society of Utah, 1987.

Newman, Herta. *Virginia Woolf and Mrs Brown: Toward a Realism of Uncertainty*. New York: Garland, 1996.

Olsen, Tillie. *Silences*. New York: Delacorte, 1978.

Olson, Charles. *The Maximus Poems*. Ed. George F. Butterick. Berkeley: U of California P, 1983.

Ondaatje, Michael, ed. *The Long Poem Anthology*. Toronto: Coach House, 1979.

– *The Collected Works of Billy the Kid*. 1970. Toronto: Vintage, 2008.

Owram, Douglas. "The Myth of Louis Riel." *Canadian Historical Review* 63.3 (1982): 315–36. https://doi.org/10.3138/chr-063-03-01

Page, P.K. *The Hidden Room: Collected Poems*. Erin: Porcupine's Quill, 1997.

Palmater, Pamela D. *Beyond Blood: Rethinking Indigenous Identity*. Saskatoon: Purich, 2011.

Palmer, Bryan D. *Canada's 1960s: The Ironies of Identity in a Rebellious Era*. Toronto: U of Toronto P, 2009

Papp-Zubrits, Susan. "The Forgotten Generation: Canada's Hungarian Refugees of 1956." *Oral History Forum* 4.2 (1980): 29–34.

Park, Julian. "Preface." *The Contemporary Culture of Canada*. Ed. Julian Park. Toronto: Ryerson, 1957: v–xiii.

Percy, Owen D. "Melting History: Defrosting Moments in Novels by Wayne Johnston, Michael Winter, and Robert Kroetsch." *Studies in Canadian Literature* 32.1 (2007): 212–20.

Perl, Jeffrey M. *Skepticism and Modern Enmity: Before and After Eliot*. Baltimore: Johns Hopkins UP, 1989.

Perloff, Marjorie. "Lawrence's Lyric Theatre: Birds, Beasts, and Flowers." 1985. *Poetic License: Essays on Modernist and Postmodernist Lyric*. Evanston: Northwestern UP: 99–117.

Perrault, Jeanne, and Sylvia Vance. "Foreword." *Writing the Circle: Native Women of Western Canada*. Edmonton: NeWest, 1990. xi–xiv

Perry, Adele. "Nation, Empire, and the Writing of History in Canada in English." *Contesting Clio's Craft: New Directions and Debates in Canadian History*. Ed. Christopher Dummitt and Michael Dawson. London: Institute for the Study of the Americas, 2009. 123–40.

Pickles, Katie, and Myra Rutherdale. "Introduction." *Contact Zones: Aboriginal and Settler Women in Canada's Colonial Past*. Vancouver: U of British Columbia P, 2005. 1–14.

Pound, Ezra. *The Cantos of Ezra Pound*. New York: New Directions, 1970.

The Red Shoes. 1948. Dir. Michael Powell and Emeric Pressburger. Perf. Albert Basserman, Léonide Massine, Moira Shearer, Anton Walbrook, and Marius Goring. Criterion, 2010. DVD.

Prang, Margaret. "National Unity and the Uses of History." *Historical Papers* 12.1 (1977): 3–12. https://doi.org/10.7202/030817ar

Pratt, E.J. *The Collected Poems of E. J. Pratt*. Ed. Northrop Frye. Toronto: Macmillan, 1962.

Proctor, Jason. "CBC-Angus Reid Institute Poll: Canadians Want Minorities to Do More to 'Fit In.'" *CBC Online* 5 Oct. 2016. Retrieved 5 Oct. 2016 from www.cbc.ca/news/canada/british-columbia/poll-canadians-multiculturalism-immigrants-1.3784194.

Publications Supported by Multiculturalism Canada. Ottawa: Multiculturalism Directorate, 1984.

Purdy, Al. *The Enchanted Echo*. Vancouver: Clarke & Stuart, 1944.

– *Pressed on Sand*. Toronto: Ryerson, 1955.

– *Emu, Remember!* Fredericton: U of New Brunswick P, 1956.

– *The Crafte So Longe to Lerne*. Toronto: Ryerson, 1959.

– *Poems for All the Annettes*. Toronto: Contact, 1962.

– *The Cariboo Horses*. Toronto: McClelland and Stewart, 1965.
– "Landfall in Vinland." Rev. of Helge Ingstad's *Land under the Pole Star*. *Canadian Literature* 33 (1967): 63–7.
– *North of Summer: Poems from Baffin Island*. Toronto: McClelland and Stewart, 1967.
– "Introduction." *The New Romans: Candid Canadian Opinions of the US*. Ed. Al Purdy. Edmonton: M.G. Hurtig, 1968. i–iv.
– *Wild Grape Wine*. Toronto: McClelland and Stewart, 1968.
– [as A.W.]. "Atwood's Moodie." *Canadian Literature* 47 (1971): 80–4.
– , ed. *Storm Warning: The New Canadian Poets*. Toronto: McClelland and Stewart, 1971.
– "The Battle [*sic*] of Batoche." *Globe and Mail Weekend Magazine* 33.20 (May 1972): 23–5.
– *Hiroshima Poems*. Trumansburg: Crossing, 1972.
– *Selected Poems*. Toronto: McClelland and Stewart, 1972.
– *On the Bearpaw Sea*. Burnaby: Blackfish, 1973.
– *Sex and Death*. Toronto: McClelland and Stewart, 1973.
– *In Search of Owen Roblin*. Toronto: McClelland and Stewart, 1974.
– "Introduction." *Wood Mountain Poems*. By Andrew Suknaski. Toronto: Macmillan, 1976. 11–12.
– , ed. *Storm Warning 2*. Toronto: McClelland and Stewart, 1976.
– *A Handful of Earth*. Oakville: Mosaic, 1977.
– *Birdwatching at the Equator: The Galapagos Islands Poems*. Sutton West: Paget, 1982.
– *The Collected Poems of Al Purdy*. Toronto: McClelland and Stewart, 1986.
– "Disconnections." *Essays on Canadian Writing* 49 (1993): 180–221.
– *Reaching for the Beaufort Sea*. Ed. Alex Widen. Madeira Park: Harbour Publishing, 1993.
– *Naked with Summer in Your Mouth: Poems*. Toronto: McClelland and Stewart, 1994.
– "The Cartography of Myself." 1971. *Starting from Ameliasburgh: The Collected Prose of Al Purdy*. Ed. Sam Solecki. Madeira Park: Harbour Publishing, 1995. 15–18.
– "Her Gates Both East and West." 1972. *Starting from Ameliasburgh: The Collected Prose of Al Purdy*. Ed. Sam Solecki. Madeira Park: Harbour Publishing, 1998. 134–45.
– "Norma, Eunice, and Judy." 1974. *Starting from Ameliasburgh: The Collected Prose of Al Purdy*. Ed. Sam Solecki. Madeira Park: Harbour Publishing, 1998. 95–9.
– *Starting from Ameliasburgh: The Collected Prose of Al Purdy*. Ed. Sam Solecki. Madeira Park: Harbour Publishing, 1998.
– *Beyond Remembering: The Collected Poems of Al Purdy*. Ed. Sam Solecki. Madeira Park: Harbour Publishing, 2000.

– "Preface." *Beyond Remembering: The Collected Poems of Al Purdy*. Ed. Sam Solecki. Madeira Park: Harbour, 2000. 21–2.

Purdy, Al, and Doug Beardsley, eds. *No One Else Is Lawrence! A Dozen of D.H. Lawrence's Best Poems with Introduction and Commentary*. Madeira Park: Harbour, 1998.

Purdy, Al, and Peter O'Brien. "An Interview with Al Purdy." *Essays on Canadian Writing* 49 (1993): 147–62.

Purdy, Al, and Alan Twigg. "Al Purdy." *Strong Voices: Conversations with 50 Canadian Authors*. Ed. Alan Twigg. Madeira Park: Harbour, 1988. 225–30.

Quinones, Ricardo. *Mapping Literary Modernism: Time and Development*. Princeton: Princeton UP, 1985.

Raddeker, Hélène Bowen. *Sceptical History: Feminist and Postmodern Approaches in Practice*. New York: Routledge, 2007.

Raddysh, Gary. *Eye of a Stranger*. Moose Jaw: Coteau, 1978.

Rand, Theodore H. *A Treasury of Canadian Verse*. London: Dent & Co., 1900.

Rashley, R.E. *Paso Por Aqui*. Fredericton: Fiddlehead, 1973.

Reaney, James. *Twelve Letters to a Small Town*. Toronto: Ryerson, 1962.

Reder, Deanna. "Writing Autobiographically: A Neglected Indigenous Intellectual Tradition." *Across Cultures / Across Borders: Canadian Aboriginal and Native American Literatures*. Ed. Paul Depasquale, Renate Eigenbrod, and Emma LaRocque. Toronto: Broadview, 2009. 153–69.

Reid, Jennifer. *Louis Riel and the Creation of Modern Canada: Mythic Discourse and the Postcolonial State*. Albuquerque: U of New Mexico P, 2008.

Relke, Diana. "Double Voice, Single Vision: A Feminist Reading of Margaret Atwood's *The Journals of Susanna Moodie*." *Atlantis* 9.1 (1985): 35–48.

Report of the Royal Commission on Bilingualism and Biculturalism. Volume 4: The Cultural Contribution of the Other Ethnic Groups. Ottawa, 1969.

Report of the Royal Commission on the Status of Women in Canada. Ottawa, 1970. Retrieved 17 April 2011 from: http://epe.lac-bac.gc.ca/100/200/301/pco-bcp/commissions-ef/bird1970-eng/bird1970-eng.htm.

Ricou, Laurie. *Vertical Man/Horizontal World: Man and Landscape in Prairie Fiction*. Vancouver: U of British Columbia P, 1973.

– [a.k.a. Lawrence Ricou]. "Introduction." *Twelve Prairie Poets*. Ottawa: Oberon, 1976. 5–20.

– , ed. *Twelve Prairie Poets*. Ottawa: Oberon, 1976.

– "Poetry." *The Literary History of Canada: Volume IV*. Ed. W.H. New et al. Toronto: U of Toronto P, 1990. 3–45.

Riquelme, John Paul. *Harmony of Dissonances: T.S. Eliot, Romanticism, and Imagination*. Baltimore: Johns Hopkins UP, 1991.

Ristock, Janice L., and Jeri Dawn Wine. "Introduction: Feminist Activism in Canada." *Women and Social Change: Feminist Activism in Canada*. Ed. Janice L. Ristock and Jeri Dawn Wine. Toronto: Lorimer, 1988. 1–19.

Roberts, Charles G.D. *The Collected Poems of Sir Charles G.D. Roberts: A Critical Edition*. Ed. Desmond Pace and Graham Clevearne Adams. Wolfville: Wombat Press, 1985.

Robertson, Heather. *Grass Roots*. Toronto: James Lorimer and Company, 1973.

Rogers, Janet Marie. "Pauline Passed Here." *Indigenous Poetics in Canada*. Ed. Neal McLeod. Waterloo: Wilfrid Laurier UP, 2014. 39–41.

Rope, Lorna. "Lorna Rope." *Where Are the Children?* Retrieved 12 Sept. 2016 from http://wherearethechildren.ca/watc_story/lorna-rope/.

Rose, Marilyn. "'Bones Made of Light': Nature in the Poetry of Lorna Crozier." *Canadian Poetry: Studies, Documents, Reviews* 55 (2004): 53–64.

Ross, Sir John. *Narrative of a Second Voyage in Search of a North-West Passage*. London: Webster, 1835.

Ross, Malcolm, eds. *Poets of the Confederation*. Toronto: McClelland and Stewart, 1960.

– "Critical Theory: Some Trends." *The Impossible Sum of Our Traditions: Reflections on Canadian Literature*. Ed. David Staines. Toronto: McClelland and Stewart, 1986. 124–44.

Ross, Sinclair. *As for Me and My House*. 1941. Toronto: McClelland and Stewart, 1970.

– *"Collecting Stamps Would Have Been More Fun": Canadian Publishing and the Correspondence of Sinclair Ross, 1933–1986*. Ed. David Stouck and Jordan Stouck. Edmonton: U of Alberta P, 2010.

Roth, Lorna. "The Delicate Acts of "Colour Balancing": Multiculturalism and Canadian Television Broadcasting Policies and Practices." *Canadian Journal of Communication* 23.4 (1998): 487–506. https://doi.org/10.22230/cjc.1998v23n4a1061.

Roy, Gabrielle. *The Hidden Mountain*. Trans. Harry Lorin Binsse. Toronto: McClelland and Stewart, 1961.

Ruffo, Armand Garnet. *Grey Owl: The Mystery of Archie Belaney*. Regina: Coteau, 1996.

– "Out of the Silence – The Legacy of E. Pauline Johnson: An Inquiry into the Lost and Found Work of Dawendine, Bernice Loft Winslow." *Literary Pluralities*. Ed. Christl Verduyn. Peterborough: Broadview, 1998. 211–23.

– "Where the Voice Was Coming From." *Across Cultures / Across Borders: Canadian Aboriginal and Native American Literatures*. Ed. Paul Depasquale, Renate Eigenbrod, and Emma LaRocque. Toronto: Broadview, 2009. 171–93.

– "Introduction" *An Anthology of Canadian Native Literature in English*. 4th ed. Ed. Daniel David Moses, Terry Goldie, and Armand Garnet Ruffo. Oxford: Oxford UP, 2013. xxi–xxxv.

Ruffo, Armand Garnet, and Neal McLeod. "Interview with Armand Garnet Ruffo." *Indigenous Poetics in Canada*. Ed. Neal McLeod. Waterloo: Wilfrid Laurier UP, 2014. 23–30.

Ryan, Sean [a.k.a. Eugene McNamara]. "Florence McNeil and Pat Lowther." *Canadian Literature* 74 (1977): 21–9.

Said, Edward. *Orientalism*. London: Routledge, 1978.

Saklikar, Renée Sarojini. *Children of Air India: Un/authorized Exhibits and Interjections*. Gibsons: Nightwood, 2013.

Sample, Peggy. *Love and Work Enough*. Toronto: Playwrights Press, 1986.

Schüller, André. *A Life Composed: T.S. Eliot and the Morals of Modernism*. Piscataway: Transaction, 2002.

Schweickart, Patrocinio P. "Reading Ourselves: Toward a Feminist Theory of Reading." *Gender and Reading: Essays on Readers, Texts, and Contexts*. Ed. Elizabeth A. Flynn and Patrocinio P. Schweickart. Baltimore: Johns Hopkins UP, 1986. 31–62.

Scobie, Stephen. "Ghostly Voices." *NeWest Review* (Oct. 1978): 4.

Scofield, Gregory. *Singing Home the Bones*. Vancouver: Polestar, 2005.

– *Louis: The Heretic Poems*. Gibsons: Nightwood, 2011.

Scott, F.R. *The Collected Poems of F.R. Scott*. Toronto: McClelland and Stewart, 1981.

Scott, F.R., et al. *New Provinces: Poems of Several Authors*. Toronto: Macmillan, 1936.

Sethna, Christabelle. "'Chastity Outmoded!': The *Ubyssey*, Sex, and the Single Girl, 1960–70." *Creating Postwar Canada, 1945–75*. Ed. Magda Fahrni and Robert Rutherdale. Vancouver: U of British Columbia P, 2008: 289–314.

Seton, Ernest Thompson. "Tekahionwake (Pauline Johnson)." *The Shagganappi* by E. Pauline Johnson. Toronto: Briggs, 1913. 5–7.

Sheeran, Patrick. "The Narrative Creation of Place: Yeats and West-of-Ireland Landscapes." *Nature and Identity in Cross-Cultural Perspective*. Ed. Anne Buttimer and Luke Wallin. Norwell: Kluwer, 1999. 287–99.

Shelley, Percy B. *The Poems of Shelley: Volume Two*. Baltimore: Johns Hopkins UP, 2000–12.

Sherman, Kenneth, ed. *Relations: Family Portraits*. Oakville: Mosaic, 1986.

Shields, Carol. *Small Ceremonies*. Toronto: McGraw-Hill, 1976.

– *Susanna Moodie: Voice and Vision*. Ottawa: Borealis, 1977.

Shore, Marlene, ed. *The Contested Past: Reading Canada's History*. Toronto: U of Toronto P, 2002.

Showalter, Elaine. "Women and the Literary Curriculum." *College English* 32.8 (1971): 855–62. https://doi.org/10.2307/375623

Silverberg, Mark. "The Can(adi)onization of Al Purdy." *Essays on Canadian Writing* 70 (2000): 226–51.

Sinfield, Alan. *Dramatic Monologue*. London: Methuen, 1977.

Smith, A.J.M., ed. *The Book of Canadian Poetry: A Critical and Historical Anthology*. Chicago: U of Chicago P, 1943. Rpt 1948, 1957.

– , ed. *The Oxford Book of Canadian Verse in English and French*. Toronto: Oxford UP, 1960.

– , ed. *Modern Canadian Verse*. Toronto: Oxford UP, 1967.

Smith, Barbara Herrnstein. *Poetic Closure: A Study of How Poems End*. Chicago: U of Chicago P, 1968.

Smyth, Donna. *Susanna Moodie*. Toronto: Playwrights Press, 1976.

Solecki, Sam. *The Last Canadian Poet: An Essay on Al Purdy*. Toronto: U of Toronto P, 1999.

– , ed. *Yours, Al*. Madeira Park: Harbour, 2004.

Souster, Raymond. *A Local Pride*. Toronto: Contact, 1962.

– *Collected Poems of Raymond Souster: Volume 2, 1955–62*. Ottawa: Oberon, 1981.

– *Collected Poems of Raymond Souster: Volume 4, 1974–77*. Ottawa: Oberon, 1983.

– *Jubilee of Death: The Raid on Dieppe*. Ottawa: Oberon, 1984.

Spiegelman, Art. *Maus: A Survivor's Tale*. New York: Pantheon, 1986–1991.

Stacey, Robert. "Purdy's Ruins: *In Search of Owen Roblin*, Literary Power, and the Poetics of the Picturesque." *The Ivory Thought*. Ed. Gerald Lynch et al. Ottawa: U of Ottawa P, 2008. 103–18.

– "Introduction: Post-, Marked Canada." *RE: Reading the Postmodern: Canadian Literature and Criticism after Modernism*. Ed. Robert Stacey. Ottawa: U of Ottawa P, 2010. xi–xl.

Stanley, George F.G. *Louis Riel: Patriot or Rebel?* Ottawa: Canadian Historical Association, 1954.

– *Louis Riel*. Toronto: Ryerson, 1963.

Stanley, Timothy. "Why I Killed Canadian History: Towards an Anti-Racist History in Canada." *Histoire Sociale – Social History* 33.65 (2000): 79–103.

Statistics Canada. A125–163. "Origins of the Population, Census Dates, 1871 to 1971." Retrieved 8 Oct. 2010 from Statistics Canada: http://www.statcan.gc.ca/access_acces/archive.action?l=eng&loc=A125_163-eng.csv.

Steffler, Margaret. "'Living in a Land of Giants': Locating and Sustaining Boyhood." *The Ivory Thought*. Ed. Gerald Lynch et al. Ottawa: U of Ottawa P, 2008. 143–58.

Stein, Karen F. *Margaret Atwood Revisited*. New York: Twayne, 1999.

Stephen, Sid. Rev. of *The Journals of Susanna Moodie*. *White Pelican* 2.2 (1972): 32–6.

Stephens, Donald G., ed. *Writers of the Prairies*. Vancouver: U of British Columbia P, 1973.

Stephenson, Marylee. *Women in Canada*. Toronto: New Press, 1973.

Sterne, Jonathan. *The Audible Past: Cultural Origins of Sound Reproduction*. Durham: Duke UP, 2003.

Stevens, Peter. *Family Feelings & Other Poems*. Guelph: Alive, 1974.

Strong-Boag, Veronica. "Contested Space: The Politics of Canadian Memory." *Journal of the Canadian Historical Association* 5.1 (1994): 3–17. https://doi.org/10.7202/031070ar.

Struthers, James. "Multiculturalism: Retrospect and Prospect." *Journal of Canadian Studies* 17.1 (1982): 3–4. https://doi.org/10.3138/jcs.17.1.3.

Suknaski, Andrew. *Rose Way in the East* (a.k.a. *Rose Far in the East*). Banff: gr0nk, 1971.

– *These Fragments I Have Gathered for Ezra*. Edinburg, TX: Funch, 1973.

– *Wood Mountain Poems*. Wood Mountain: Anak, 1973.

– *Leaving Wood Mountain*. Wood Mountain: Sundog, 1975.

– *Wood Mountain Poems*. Toronto: Macmillan, 1976.

– *The Ghosts Call You Poor*. Toronto: Macmillan, 1978.

– *East of Myloona*. Saskatoon: Thistledown, 1979.

– "The Prairie Graveyard." *Essays on Canadian Writing* 18–19 (1980): 112–24.

– *In the Name of Narid: New Poems*. Erin: Porcupine's Quill, 1981.

– *Silk Trail*. Toronto: Nightwood, 1985.

– "Foreword." *I Wanted to Say Something*. Red Deer: Red Deer College, 1990. n.p.

Suknaski, Andrew, and Jack David. "An Elfin Plotting: An Interview with Andrew Suknaski." *Contemporary Verse II* 3.1 (1977): 10–12.

Suknaski, Andrew, and Doris Hillis. "Andrew Suknaski." *Plainspeaking: Interviews with Saskatchewan Writers*. Regina: Coteau, 1988. 105–26.

Suknaski, Andrew, and George Melnyk. "Interview: The Ghosts that Haunt the Poetic Lays of Andrew Suknaski, Westerner." *Books in Canada* 6.4 (1977): 31–2.

Suknaski, Andrew, et al. "Panel Discussion: 'Ethnicity and Identity': The Question of One's Literary Passport." *Identification: Ethnicity and the Writer in Canada*. Ed. Jars Balan. Edmonton: Canadian Institute of Ukrainian Studies, 1982. 67–87.

Sullivan, Rosemary. *The Red Shoes: Margaret Atwood Starting Out*. Toronto: HarperFlamingo, 1998.

Swan, Susan. *The Biggest Modern Woman of the World*. Toronto: Lester & Orpen Dennys, 1983.

Thammavongsa, Souvankham. *Found*. Toronto: Pedlar, 2007.

Thesen, Sharon. *The New Long Poem Anthology*. Toronto: Coach House, 1991.

Thistle, Jesse, and Paul Kennedy. "Return of the Michif Boy: Confronting Métis Trauma." *CBC Radio – Ideas*, 3 July 2017. http://www.cbc.ca/radio/ideas/return-of-the-michif-boy-confronting-m%C3%A9tis-trauma-1.4037672.

Thompson, David. *The Writings of David Thompson*. Ed. William Moreau. Montreal: McGill-Queen's UP, 2009.

Thompson, John Herd. "Integrating Regional Patterns into a National Canadian History." *Acadiensis* 20.1 (1990): 174–84.

Thompson, Lee Briscoe. "Real Ladies." *Canadian Literature* 145 (1995): 129–31.
Tippett, Maria. *Making Culture: English-Canadian Institutions and the Arts before the Massey Commission*. Toronto: U of Toronto P, 1990.
Trehearne, Brian. *The Montreal Forties: Modernist Poetry in Transition*. Toronto: U of Toronto P, 1999.
Trigger, Bruce G. "Ethnohistory: Problems and Prospects." *Clio's Craft: A Primer of Historical Methods*. Ed. T.A. Crowley. Toronto: Copp Clark Pitman, 1988. 132–53.
Underhill, Ian. *Family Portraits*. Toronto: McClelland and Stewart, 1978.
van Steen, Marcus. Rev. of *In Search of Owen Roblin by Al Purdy*. *Ottawa Citizen* 2 Nov. 1974: 68.
Vernon, Lorraine. "More Audible Than a Scream." *The Vancouver Sun* 1 Dec. 1972: 36a.
Verwaayen, Kim. "Appropriate Appropriations? Reading Responsibility in Joan Crate's *Pale as Real Ladies*." *Canadian Literature: A Quarterly* 215 (2012): 35–52.
Wah, Fred. "Contemporary Saskatchewan Poetry." *Essays on Saskatchewan Writing*. Ed. E.F. Dyck. Regina: Saskatchewan Writers Guild, 1987. 197–219.
Wainwright, Andy, ed. *Notes for a Native Land: A New Encounter with Canada*. Ottawa: Oberon, 1969.
Walker, Alice. *In Search of Our Mothers' Gardens*. San Diego: Harcourt, 1983.
Wardhaugh, Robert. "Introduction: Tandem and Tangent." *Toward Defining the Prairies: Region, Culture, and History*. Winnipeg: U of Manitoba P, 2001. 3–12.
Waubageshig. *The Only Good Indian: Essays by Canadian Indians*. Toronto: New Press 1970.
Weaver, Robert. "Three Canadian Books That Might Get Overlooked." *Toronto Star* 3 July 1965: 10.
– "John Newlove Is Today's Poet." *Toronto Star* 29 June 1968: 39.
Weaver, Sally. *Making Canadian Indian Policy: The Hidden Agenda 1968–70*. Toronto: U of Toronto P, 1981.
Webb, Phyllis. *Naked Poems*. Vancouver: Periwinkle, 1965.
Weidhorn, Manfred. *An Anatomy of Skepticism*. New York: iUniverse, 2006.
Weingarten, J.A. "'A Half-Understood Massiveness': Revisiting John Newlove's 'The Pride.'" *Studies in Canadian Literature* 28.1 (2013): 113–35.
– "'Stories in the Poems': Al Purdy and the Editing of Andrew Suknaski's *Wood Mountain Poems*." *Canadian Poetry: Studies, Documents, Reviews* 71 (2013): 68–87.
– "Modernist Poetry in Canada, 1920–1960." *The Oxford Handbook of Canadian Literature*. Ed. Cynthia Sugars. Toronto: Oxford UP, 2015. 314–36.
White, Hayden. *Metahistory*. Baltimore: Johns Hopkins UP, 1973.
Whitworth, Michael H. *Modernism*. Malden: Blackwell, 2007.

– *Reading Modernist Poetry*. Malden: Blackwell, 2010.
Williams, William Carlos. *Paterson*. 1946–58. New York: New Directions, 1992.
Wiseman, Christopher. "Reticence and Emergence: The Poetry of Florence McNeil." *Contemporary Verse II* 4.2 (1979): 36–40.
Wittke, Carl. *A History of Canada*. New York: Knopf, 1928.
Wollaeger, Mark A. *Joseph Conrad and the Fictions of Skepticism*. Stanford: Stanford UP, 1990.
Wood, Susan. "Participation in the Past: John Newlove and 'The Pride.'" *Essays on Canadian Writing* 20 (1980–1): 230–40.
Woodcock, George. "Swarming of Poets: An Editorial Reportage." *Canadian Literature* 50 (Autumn 1971): 3–16.
– "Poetry." *Literary History of Canada Volume III*. 2nd ed. Toronto: U of Toronto P, 1976. 284–317.
– "The Strong New Voices of the West." *Globe and Mail* 23 Nov. 1981: BL7.
– "The Meeting of Time and Space: Regionalism in Canadian Literature." *Northern Spring: The Flowering of Canadian Literature*. Vancouver: Douglas & McIntyre, 1987. 21–43.
– "Canadian Poetry: The Emergent Tradition." *Northern Spring: The Flowering of Canadian Literature*. Vancouver: Douglas & McIntyre, 1987. 181–95.
– *A Social History of Canada*. Markham: Viking, 1988.
Wordsworth, William. *Collected Works of William Wordsworth: Poems in Two Volumes*. Charleston: Bibliobazaar, 2007.
Wright, Donald. *The Professionalization of History in English Canada*. Toronto: U of Toronto P, 2005.
– *Donald Creighton: A Life in History*. Toronto: U of Toronto P, 2015.
Wyile, Herb. *Speculative Fictions: Contemporary Canadian Novelists and the Writing of History*. Montreal: McGill-Queen's UP, 2002.
– "Attack of the 'Latté-Drinking Relativists': Postmodernism, Historiography, and Historical Fiction." *RE: Reading the Postmodern: Canadian Literature and Criticism after Modernism*. Ed. Robert Stacey. Ottawa: U of Ottawa P, 2010. 183–202.
Yeats, W.B. "*Per Amica Silentia Lunae*." 1917. *The Collected Works of W.B. Yeats Volume V: Later Essays*. Ed. William H. O'Donnell. New York: Scribner's Sons, 1994: 1–33.
York, Lorraine. *The Other Side of Dailiness: Photography in the Works of Alice Munro, Timothy Findley, and Margaret Laurence*. Toronto: ECW, 1988.
– "The Ivory Thought: The North as Poetic Icon in Al Purdy and Patrick Lane." *Essays on Canadian Writing* 49 (1993): 45–56.
– *Literary Celebrity in Canada*. Toronto: U of Toronto P, 2007.
Zamora, Lois Parkinson. *The Usable Past: The Imagination of History in Recent Fiction of the Americas*. Cambridge: Cambridge UP, 1997.

Zieroth, David (a.k.a. Dale Zieroth). *Clearing: Poems from a Journey*. Toronto: Anansi, 1973.
– *Mid-River*. Toronto: Anansi, 1981.
– Email received by J.A. Weingarten. 14 Sept. 2011.
Zimmerman, Sarah M. *Romanticism, Lyric, and History*. Albany: State U of New York P, 1999.

Index

www.ingramcontent.com/pod-product-compliance
Lightning Source LLC
LaVergne TN
LVHW041112090826
844660LV00061B/745/J

* 9 7 8 1 4 8 7 5 0 1 0 4 4 *